WOMEN IN AMERICAN SOCIETY

ISSN 1557-6302

WOMEN IN AMERICAN SOCIETY

Melissa J. Doak

INFORMATION PLUS® REFERENCE SERIES
Formerly Published by Information Plus, Wylie, Texas

THOMSON

GALE

Detroit • New York • San Francisco • San Diego • New Haven, Conn. • Waterville, Maine • London • Munich

Women in American Society
Melissa J. Doak
Paula Kepos, Series Editor

Project Editor
John McCoy

Permissions
Margaret Abendroth, Edna Hedblad,
Emma Hull

Composition and Electronic Prepress
Evi Seoud

Manufacturing
Drew Kalasky

ISBN 0-7876-5103-6 (set)
ISBN 1-4144-0430-1
ISSN 1557-6302

This title is also available as an e-book.
ISBN 1-4144-1043-3 (set)
Contact your Thomson Gale sales representative for ordering information.

Printed in the United States of America
10 9 8 7 6 5 4 3 2 1

TABLE OF CONTENTS

PREFACE vii

CHAPTER 1
American Women—Who Are They? 1
This chapter introduces the contemporary American woman from a variety of demographic standpoints—age, race, life expectancy, country of birth, and marital status. Living arrangements, household types, and household sizes are also analyzed.

CHAPTER 2
Women's Education 15
Modern American women have more educational opportunities than previous generations of women did. School attendance and achievement (from test scores to college degrees earned) are discussed, along with the topics of single-sex versus co-ed schools and female participation in school-sponsored athletic programs.

CHAPTER 3
Women in the Labor Force 33
A history of women's participation in the American workforce begins this chapter, which then investigates contemporary female workers by occupation, age, race, marital status, education level, and the presence of children. Information on work-related issues of interest to women, such as part-time jobs, flextime schedules, and telecommuting, is included, along with rates of and reasons for unemployment among women. A discussion of future projections closes the chapter.

CHAPTER 4
Women's Occupations. 55
Though most women still work in traditionally "female" jobs, more are moving into fields historically reserved for men. This chapter contains information on women in construction, law, and finance; in the corporate world; in the fields of science, engineering, and technology; in academia; and in the military. Women-owned businesses and future prospects for female progress in previously male-dominated professions are also considered.

CHAPTER 5
Money, Income, and Poverty 69
Women's incomes have been rising in comparison with men's since the mid-twentieth century. Still, there is a substantial earnings gap between the sexes, which differs with race, marital status, motherhood, occupation, and education. Single-mother families, welfare reform, lack of child support, the elderly, and a shortage of pensions are explored to explain why more women than men live in poverty.

CHAPTER 6
Women and Their Children 93
A look at birth rates by mothers' age, race, ethnicity, education, income, employment, residence, family size, and marital status begins this chapter. Multiple births, unmarried childbearing, and births to teenagers are also examined, along with health issues related to pregnancy and motherhood. The focus then shifts to other reproductive issues, such as contraception, abortion, childlessness, and adoption. Lastly, the chapter addresses family and work arrangements for single and working mothers.

CHAPTER 7
Child Care and Elder Care 117
Although mothers who stay at home may also need assistance with child care, this need is particularly great for mothers who work outside the home. This chapter provides numbers of working mothers and details various kinds of child care available. Accounts of child care costs, employee benefits, and government laws that assist working parents follow. Shifting to elder care issues, the chapter then looks at the dilemmas of the "sandwich generation," in which women may have to care for children and elderly parents simultaneously. Business and governmental responses to these problems are also covered.

CHAPTER 8
Women in American Politics 131
Women are exerting growing influence in American politics. Women's patterns of voter registration and turnout and their positions on issues are described here, and detailed information about women serving in Congress and in state and municipal governments is also presented. The chapter ends with a discussion of women as presidential and vice-presidential candidates and as cabinet members.

CHAPTER 9
Women as Victims 143
Women are less likely than men to be victims of violent crime, but they outnumber men as victims of certain types of crimes, including rape and sexual assault. This chapter provides detailed statistics on the who, what, where, why, and when of female crime victims. Domestic violence and sexual harassment (in business, the military, and prisons, as well as on college campuses) are discussed in depth.

CHAPTER 10

Women as Criminals 163

Women commit only about 20% of crimes, but their arrest rates are rising, as compared with men's, in many categories. This chapter presents and interprets statistics on violent crimes committed by women, female prisoners, and the death sentence as applied to women.

CHAPTER 11

Women's Health 173

Women's health issues are the focus of this chapter, which begins by surveying access to health care. Cardiovascular disease, cancer, and other leading causes of death in women are discussed, along with HIV/AIDS, other sexually transmitted diseases, and osteoporosis. The chapter examines mental health, including depression and eating disorders, and also considers preventive measures like smoking cessation, substance abuse control, diet, nutrition, and exercise.

IMPORTANT NAMES AND ADDRESSES 201

RESOURCES 203

INDEX 207

PREFACE

Women in American Society is part of the *Information Plus Reference Series*. The purpose of each volume of the series is to present the latest facts on a topic of pressing concern in modern American life. These topics include today's most controversial and most studied social issues: abortion, capital punishment, care for the elderly, crime, the environment, health care, immigration, minorities, national security, social welfare, women, youth, and many more. Although written especially for the high school and undergraduate student, this series is an excellent resource for anyone in need of factual information on current affairs.

By presenting the facts, it is Thomson Gale's intention to provide its readers with everything they need to reach an informed opinion on current issues. To that end, there is a particular emphasis in this series on the presentation of scientific studies, surveys, and statistics. These data are generally presented in the form of tables, charts, and other graphics placed within the text of each book. Every graphic is directly referred to and carefully explained in the text. The source of each graphic is presented within the graphic itself. The data used in these graphics are drawn from the most reputable and reliable sources, in particular from the various branches of the U.S. government and from major independent polling organizations. Every effort has been made to secure the most recent information available. The reader should bear in mind that many major studies take years to conduct, and that additional years often pass before the data from these studies are made available to the public. Therefore, in many cases the most recent information available in 2006 dated from 2003 or 2004. Older statistics are sometimes presented as well if they are of particular interest and no more recent information exists.

Although statistics are a major focus of the *Information Plus Reference Series*, they are by no means its only content. Each book also presents the widely held positions and important ideas that shape how the book's subject is

discussed in the United States. These positions are explained in detail and, where possible, in the words of their proponents. Some of the other material to be found in these books includes: historical background; descriptions of major events related to the subject; relevant laws and court cases; and examples of how these issues play out in American life. Some books also feature primary documents or have pro and con debate sections giving the words and opinions of prominent Americans on both sides of a controversial topic. All material is presented in an evenhanded and unbiased manner; the reader will never be encouraged to accept one view of an issue over another.

HOW TO USE THIS BOOK

As they marry later in life, have fewer children, receive more education, and participate in the labor force in growing numbers, American women are playing changing roles. However, in terms of caregiving responsibility, earnings and assets, and gender-linked jobs, many women have experienced little change in their roles. These conflicting developments are illuminated by information on women's demographic trends, educational achievement, employment, financial status, parental responsibilities, political roles, victimization, and health issues, all presented and explained in this book.

Women in American Society consists of eleven chapters and three appendices. Each of the chapters is devoted to a particular aspect of American women. For a summary of the information covered in each chapter, please see the synopses provided in the Table of Contents at the front of the book. Chapters generally begin with an overview of the basic facts and background information on the chapter's topic, then proceed to examine subtopics of particular interest. For example, Chapter 7, Child Care and Elder Care, begins with a discussion of working mothers and the various kinds of child care available to them. Child care costs are explored, and the means through which business and government assist in providing child care are listed and explained. Problems specific to elder care and the responses of employers and the government to them are also included. Readers can find their way through a chapter by looking for the section and subsection headings, which are clearly set off from the text. They can also refer to the book's extensive index if they already know what they are looking for.

Statistical Information

The tables and figures featured throughout *Women in American Society* will be of particular use to the reader in learning about this issue. These tables and figures represent an extensive collection of the most recent and important statistics on women and related issues—for example, graphics in the book cover changes in the male–female ratio in the past century, the number of bachelor's degrees earned by both genders, the employment status of women, median weekly earnings of men and women, birth rates for women younger than age twenty, percentages of workers with access to employer assistance for child care, and the number of women holding elective office. Thomson Gale believes that making this information available to the reader is the most important way in which we fulfill the goal of this book: to help readers understand the issues and controversies surrounding women in American society in the United States and to reach their own conclusions.

Each table or figure has a unique identifier appearing above it for ease of identification and reference. Titles for the tables and figures explain their purpose. At the end of each table or figure, the original source of the data is provided.

In order to help readers understand these often complicated statistics, all tables and figures are explained in the text. References in the text direct the reader to the relevant statistics. Furthermore, the contents of all tables and figures are fully indexed. Please see the opening section of the Index at the back of this volume for a description of how to find tables and figures within it.

Appendices

In addition to the main body text and images, *Women in American Society* has three appendices. The first is the Important Names and Addresses directory. Here the reader will find contact information for a number of government and private organizations that can provide further information on women. The second appendix is the Resources section, which can also assist the reader in conducting his or her own research. In this section the author and editors of *Women in American Society* describe some of the sources that were most useful during the compilation of this book. The final appendix is the detailed Index, which facilitates reader access to specific topics in this book.

ADVISORY BOARD CONTRIBUTIONS

The staff of Information Plus would like to extend its heartfelt appreciation to the Information Plus Advisory Board. This dedicated group of media professionals provides feedback on the series on an ongoing basis. Their comments allow the editorial staff who work on the project to make the series better and more user-friendly. Our top priority is to produce the highest-quality and most useful books possible, and the Advisory Board's contributions to this process are invaluable.

The members of the Information Plus Advisory Board are:

- Kathleen R. Bonn, Librarian, Newbury Park High School, Newbury Park, California

- Madelyn Garner, Librarian, San Jacinto College—North Campus, Houston, Texas

- Anne Oxenrider, Media Specialist, Dundee High School, Dundee, Michigan

- Charles R. Rodgers, Director of Libraries, Pasco-Hernando Community College, Dade City, Florida

- James N. Zitzelsberger, Library Media Department Chairman, Oshkosh West High School, Oshkosh, Wisconsin

COMMENTS AND SUGGESTIONS

The editors of the *Information Plus Reference Series* welcome your feedback on *Women in American Society*. Please direct all correspondence to:

Editors
Information Plus Reference Series
27500 Drake Rd.
Farmington Hills, MI 48331-3535

CHAPTER 1
AMERICAN WOMEN—WHO ARE THEY?

POPULATION

The U.S. Census Bureau estimated that on July 1, 2004, the noninstitutionalized U.S. population was 293,655,404. More than half (50.8%), or 149,117,996, were female; 144,537,408 were male ("Table 1: Annual Estimates of the Population by Sex and Five-Year Age Groups for the United States, April 1, 2000 to July 1, 2004," NC-EST2004-01, Population Division, U.S. Census Bureau, June 9, 2005, http://www.census.gov/popest/national/asrh/NC-EST2004-sa.html). By 2050 the population of the United States is expected to reach almost 420 million, of which more than 213 million will be women ("Table 2a. Projected Population of the United States, by Age and Sex: 2000 to 2050," U.S. Census Bureau, March 18, 2004, http://www.census.gov/ipc/www/usinterimproj/natprojtab02a.pdf).

Age and Race

According to the Census Bureau, in 2003, 25.1% of the population was under age eighteen, 62.5% was between eighteen and sixty-four, and 12.4% was sixty-five or older. The largest proportion of females were between the ages of twenty-five and forty-four (28.3%), followed by those age eighteen and under (24.1%), and those aged forty-five to sixty-four (23.8%). (See Table 1.1.)

Of almost 148 million females, 68.1% were non-Hispanic whites; 12.6% were non-Hispanic African-Americans; and 13.1% were Hispanic. (Hispanics can be of any race.) Asian-Americans made up 4.6% of the female population, Native Hawaiian and other Pacific Islanders made up 0.3%, and Native Americans/Alaska Natives made up 1.2%. (See Table 1.2.)

Male–Female Ratios

From 1990 to 2003 the female population of the United States increased by 4.7%, whereas the male population increased by 5.6%. The difference is attributed to a decrease in male death rates and an increase in male immigration.

In 2003 there were 96.8 males for every one hundred females in the United States. Among African-Americans, the ratio is ninety-one males for every one hundred females. But among Hispanics or Latinos of any race, there are 106.7 males for every one hundred females.

In younger age groups, males outnumber females, but that ratio generally decreases as people age. (See Figure 1.1.) In 2002 the gender ratio (the number of males for every one hundred females) for children age five to seventeen was 105.1; the gender ratio for adults in the thirty-five to forty-four category, however, was 97.2. In the sixty-five and older population, women outnumbered men by 5.3 million.

Figure 1.2 documents the change in the male–female ratio between 1900 and 2000. Prior to the medical advances of the twentieth century, it was common for women to die from complications of childbearing, and men often outlived several wives. The 1950 census was the first to record more women than men living in the United States.

Life Expectancy

In 2002 the life expectancy at birth in the United States was 79.9 years for females and 74.5 years for males. (See Table 1.3.) Both white and African-American females had a longer life expectancy than males. However, white women had a longer life expectancy (80.3 years) than did African-American women (75.6 years), and white men had a longer life expectancy (75.1 years) than African-American men (68.8 years). The U.S. Census Bureau projects that by the year 2100 female life expectancy at birth will be between 89.3 and 95.2 years (Frederick W. Hollmann, Tammany J. Mulder, and Jeffrey E. Kallan, "Projected Life Expectancy at Birth by Race and Hispanic Origin, 1999 to 2100," *Methodology and Assumptions for the Population Projections of the*

TABLE 1.1

Population estimates, by sex and selected age groups, 2000–03

Sex and age	Population estimates				April 1, 2000	
	July 1, 2003	July 1, 2002	July 1, 2001	July 1, 2000	Estimates base	Census
Both sexes	**290,809,777**	**287,973,924**	**285,093,813**	**282,177,754**	**281,423,231**	**281,421,906**
Under 18 years	73,043,506	72,846,774	72,603,552	72,342,618	72,294,521	72,293,812
Under 5 years	19,769,279	19,575,536	19,363,867	19,212,312	19,175,997	19,175,798
5 to 13 years	36,752,056	36,951,809	37,058,591	37,037,950	37,025,715	37,025,346
14 to 17 years	16,522,171	16,319,429	16,181,094	16,092,356	16,092,809	16,092,668
18 to 64 years	181,847,097	179,519,609	177,152,543	174,753,991	174,136,592	174,136,341
18 to 24 years	28,899,571	28,460,518	27,918,979	27,311,145	27,141,017	27,143,454
25 to 44 years	84,243,194	84,461,957	84,733,191	84,963,775	85,042,219	85,040,251
45 to 64 years	68,704,332	66,597,134	64,500,373	62,479,071	61,953,356	61,952,636
65 years and over	35,919,174	35,607,541	35,337,718	35,081,145	34,992,118	34,991,753
85 years and over	4,713,465	4,570,403	4,429,621	4,294,969	4,239,670	4,239,587
16 years and over	225,953,387	223,267,035	220,557,315	217,860,760	217,149,804	217,149,127
18 years and over	217,766,271	215,127,150	212,490,261	209,835,136	209,128,710	209,128,094
15 to 44 years	125,448,356	125,139,524	124,772,225	124,330,402	124,223,776	124,224,142
Male	**143,037,260**	**141,533,390**	**140,008,546**	**138,456,499**	**138,055,457**	**138,053,563**
Under 18 years	37,389,865	37,300,720	37,192,964	37,080,268	37,059,555	37,059,196
Under 5 years	10,105,415	10,008,567	9,903,298	9,830,460	9,810,833	9,810,733
5 to 13 years	18,815,697	18,922,442	18,980,111	18,970,087	18,964,111	18,963,914
14 to 17 years	8,468,753	8,369,711	8,309,555	8,279,721	8,284,611	8,284,549
18 to 64 years	90,698,910	89,464,832	88,205,934	86,918,792	86,586,109	86,584,742
18 to 24 years	14,874,785	14,630,060	14,323,203	13,972,579	13,873,143	13,873,829
25 to 44 years	42,356,147	42,405,505	42,485,118	42,544,714	42,569,871	42,568,327
45 to 64 years	33,467,978	32,429,267	31,397,613	30,401,499	30,143,095	30,142,586
65 years and over	14,948,485	14,767,838	14,609,648	14,457,439	14,409,793	14,409,625
85 years and over	1,444,924	1,376,521	1,312,843	1,250,132	1,227,014	1,226,998
16 years and over	109,845,867	108,412,927	106,965,987	105,515,115	105,135,793	105,134,229
18 years and over	105,647,395	104,232,670	102,815,582	101,376,231	100,995,902	100,994,367
15 to 44 years	63,538,723	63,304,262	63,037,752	62,726,333	62,648,050	62,647,145
Female	**147,772,517**	**146,440,534**	**145,085,267**	**143,721,255**	**143,367,774**	**143,368,343**
Under 18 years	35,653,641	35,546,054	35,410,588	35,262,350	35,234,966	35,234,616
Under 5 years	9,663,864	9,566,969	9,460,569	9,381,852	9,365,164	9,365,065
5 to 13 years	17,936,359	18,029,367	18,078,480	18,067,863	18,061,604	18,061,432
14 to 17 years	8,053,418	7,949,718	7,871,539	7,812,635	7,808,198	7,808,119
18 to 64 years	91,148,187	90,054,777	88,946,609	87,835,199	87,550,483	87,551,599
18 to 24 years	14,024,786	13,830,458	13,595,776	13,338,566	13,267,874	13,269,625
25 to 44 years	41,887,047	42,056,452	42,248,073	42,419,061	42,472,348	42,471,924
45 to 64 years	35,236,354	34,167,867	33,102,760	32,077,572	31,810,261	31,810,050
65 years and over	20,970,689	20,839,703	20,728,070	20,623,706	20,582,325	20,582,128
85 years and over	3,268,541	3,193,882	3,116,778	3,044,837	3,012,656	3,012,589
16 years and over	116,107,520	114,854,108	113,591,328	112,345,645	112,014,011	112,014,898
18 years and over	112,118,876	110,894,480	109,674,679	108,458,905	108,132,808	108,133,727
15 to 44 years	61,909,633	61,835,262	61,734,473	61,604,069	61,575,726	61,576,997

SOURCE: "Table 2. Annual Estimates of the Population by Sex and Selected Age Groups for the United States: April 1, 2000 to July 1, 2003 (NC-EST2003-02)," U.S. Census Bureau, Population Division, June 14, 2004, http://www.census.gov/popest/national/asrh/NC-EST2003/NC-EST2003-02.pdf (accessed June 7, 2005)

United States: 1999 to 2100, Population Division Working Paper No. 38, U.S. Census Bureau, 2000).

Foreign-Born Women

In March 2003 the foreign-born population of the United States was 33.5 million, with roughly half of them women ("Table 1.1. Population by Sex, Age, and U.S. Citizenship Status: 2003, U.S. Census Bureau, Current Population Survey," Annual Economic Supplement, 2003, http://www.census.gov/population/socdemo/foreign/ppl-174/tab01-01.pdf). By comparison, in 1960 the foreign-born population was 9.7 million, and the gender ratio was 95.6. In 1960, 37% of the foreign-born population fell into the forty-five to sixty-four age bracket (Dianne Schmidley, "Figure 10–3. Age and Sex of the Foreign-Born Population: 1960 to 2000," in *Profile of the Foreign-Born Population in the United States: 2000*, Current Population Reports, P23–206, U.S. Census Bureau, December 2001). A major shift occurred in the subsequent four decades. In 2003, 45.1% of the foreign-born population fell into the twenty-five to forty-four age category, while 24.7% were forty-five to sixty-four. (See Figure 1.3.)

The United States also is home to millions of undocumented foreign-born women, who may or may not have been counted in Census 2000. According to a 2003 state legislative report published by the Center for Women Policy Studies, sometimes these women are brought into the United States by traffickers in the sex trade. Between twenty thousand and one hundred thousand women are illegally trafficked into the United States each year from

TABLE 1.2

Population estimates, by sex, race, and Hispanic origin, 2000–03

Sex, race and Hispanic or Latino origin	Population estimates				April 1, 2000	
	July 1, 2003	July 1, 2002	July 1, 2001	July 1, 2000	Estimates base	Census
Both sexes	**290,809,777**	**287,973,924**	**285,093,813**	**282,177,754**	**281,423,231**	**281,421,906**
One race	286,502,202	283,794,261	281,040,350	278,249,651	277,525,540	277,524,226
White	234,196,357	232,369,198	230,501,667	228,610,089	228,105,838	228,104,485
Black or African American	37,098,946	36,675,922	36,247,214	35,809,931	35,704,255	35,704,124
American Indian and Alaska Native	2,786,652	2,749,116	2,711,350	2,673,267	2,663,842	2,663,818
Asian	11,924,912	11,514,716	11,104,960	10,691,345	10,589,069	10,589,265
Native Hawaiian and other Pacific Islanders	495,335	485,309	475,159	465,019	462,536	462,534
Two or more races	4,307,575	4,179,663	4,053,463	3,928,103	3,897,691	3,897,680
Race alone or in combination:*						
White	237,899,403	235,955,628	233,973,250	231,967,665	231,435,748	231,434,388
Black or African American	38,749,034	38,247,616	37,741,866	37,228,240	37,104,378	37,104,248
American Indian and Alaska Native	4,366,174	4,323,118	4,279,844	4,236,065	4,225,100	4,225,058
Asian	13,502,956	13,042,929	12,583,816	12,121,020	12,006,689	12,006,894
Native Hawaiian and other Pacific Islanders	959,603	943,447	927,065	910,819	906,794	906,785
Not Hispanic or Latino	**250,910,888**	**249,485,606**	**248,032,151**	**246,527,651**	**246,116,931**	**246,116,088**
One race	247,163,862	245,845,125	244,496,436	243,096,293	242,710,676	242,709,840
White	197,326,272	196,832,773	196,314,423	195,756,664	195,576,402	195,575,485
Black or African American	35,593,148	35,204,916	34,811,287	34,409,779	34,313,108	34,313,007
American Indian and Alaska Native	2,180,318	2,154,961	2,129,524	2,103,706	2,097,455	2,097,440
Asian	11,673,494	11,269,014	10,865,026	10,457,278	10,356,608	10,356,804
Native Hawaiian and other Pacific Islanders	390,630	383,461	376,176	368,866	367,103	367,104
Two or more races	3,747,026	3,640,481	3,535,715	3,431,358	3,406,255	3,406,248
Race alone or in combination:*						
White	200,535,332	199,945,074	199,331,780	198,679,531	198,476,515	198,475,591
Black or African American	36,988,665	36,534,298	36,075,905	35,610,148	35,498,273	35,498,173
American Indian and Alaska Native	3,545,708	3,518,189	3,490,567	3,462,426	3,455,557	3,455,525
Asian	13,089,199	12,641,020	12,193,881	11,742,890	11,631,726	11,631,935
Native Hawaiian and other Pacific Islanders	790,640	778,811	766,795	754,800	751,846	751,844
Hispanic or Latino	**39,898,889**	**38,488,318**	**37,061,662**	**35,650,103**	**35,306,300**	**35,305,818**
One race	39,338,340	37,949,136	36,543,914	35,153,358	34,814,864	34,814,386
White	36,870,085	35,536,425	34,187,244	32,853,425	32,529,436	32,529,000
Black or African American	1,505,798	1,471,006	1,435,927	1,400,152	1,391,147	1,391,117
American Indian and Alaska Native	606,334	594,155	581,826	569,561	566,387	566,378
Asian	251,418	245,702	239,934	234,067	232,461	232,461
Native Hawaiian and other Pacific Islanders	104,705	101,848	98,983	96,153	95,433	95,430
Two or more races	560,549	539,182	517,748	496,745	491,436	491,432
Race alone or in combination:*						
White	37,364,071	36,010,554	34,641,470	33,288,134	32,959,233	32,958,797
Black or African American	1,760,369	1,713,318	1,665,961	1,618,092	1,606,105	1,606,075
American Indian and Alaska Native	820,466	804,929	789,277	773,639	769,543	769,533
Asian	413,757	401,909	389,935	378,130	374,963	374,959
Native Hawaiian and other Pacific Islanders	168,963	164,636	160,270	156,019	154,948	154,941
Male	**143,037,260**	**141,533,390**	**140,008,546**	**138,456,499**	**138,055,457**	**138,053,563**
One race	140,919,143	139,480,177	138,019,213	136,530,569	136,145,179	136,143,314
White	115,821,221	114,818,831	113,796,188	112,753,919	112,477,791	112,476,314
Black or African American	17,671,832	17,458,998	17,244,749	17,024,829	16,971,554	16,971,124
American Indian and Alaska Native	1,395,508	1,376,391	1,357,234	1,337,761	1,332,958	1,332,929
Asian	5,778,553	5,579,076	5,379,313	5,177,571	5,127,671	5,127,744
Native Hawaiian and other Pacific Islanders	252,029	246,881	241,729	236,489	235,205	235,203
Two or more races	2,118,117	2,053,213	1,989,333	1,925,930	1,910,278	1,910,249
Race alone or in combination:*						
White	117,648,081	116,586,438	115,505,591	114,405,641	114,115,315	114,113,814
Black or African American	18,471,062	18,218,231	17,964,794	17,706,148	17,643,512	17,643,072
American Indian and Alaska Native	2,160,036	2,138,128	2,116,222	2,093,841	2,088,190	2,088,142
Asian	6,565,930	6,341,358	6,116,783	5,890,232	5,834,187	5,834,258
Native Hawaiian and other Pacific Islanders	482,695	474,604	466,444	458,273	456,195	456,190

Asia, Africa, Latin America, and Eastern Europe (Fact Sheet from the National Institute on State Policy on Trafficking of Women and Girls, 2004, http://www.centerwomenpolicy .org/report.cfm?ReportID=91). These women are lured to the United States with promises of steady work and good pay, but they usually are forced into prostitution.

MARITAL STATUS

Married Women

The marriage rate declined steadily between 1980 and 2004, dropping to a low of 7.4 marriages per one thousand people in 2004 ("Births, Marriages, Divorces, and Death: Provisional Data for November

TABLE 1.2

Population estimates, by sex, race, and Hispanic origin, 2000–03 [CONTINUED]

Sex, race and Hispanic or Latino origin	Population estimates				April 1, 2000	
	July 1, 2003	July 1, 2002	July 1, 2001	July 1, 2000	Estimates base	Census
Not Hispanic or Latino	**122,438,159**	**121,681,587**	**120,911,853**	**120,108,888**	**119,893,372**	**119,891,768**
One race	120,597,631	119,894,999	119,178,187	118,427,888	118,225,207	118,223,631
White	96,736,003	96,440,528	96,132,410	95,798,311	95,696,973	95,695,752
Black or African American	16,934,267	16,739,441	16,543,232	16,341,877	16,293,454	16,293,049
American Indian and Alaska Native	1,076,391	1,064,078	1,051,855	1,039,263	1,036,263	1,036,240
Asian	5,653,898	5,457,374	5,260,612	5,061,945	5,012,898	5,012,971
Native Hawaiian and other Pacific Islanders	197,072	193,578	190,078	186,492	185,619	185,619
Two or more races	1,840,528	1,786,588	1,733,666	1,681,000	1,668,165	1,668,137
Race alone or in combination:*						
White	98,317,386	97,972,887	97,616,760	97,234,974	97,122,042	97,120,797
Black or African American	17,608,341	17,379,802	17,150,674	16,916,714	16,860,492	16,860,076
American Indian and Alaska Native	1,734,893	1,721,532	1,708,262	1,694,550	1,691,224	1,691,183
Asian	6,361,538	6,142,985	5,924,533	5,704,066	5,649,688	5,649,759
Native Hawaiian and other Pacific Islanders	395,945	390,269	384,560	378,773	377,305	377,303
Hispanic or Latino	**20,599,101**	**19,851,803**	**19,096,693**	**18,347,611**	**18,162,085**	**18,161,795**
One race	20,321,512	19,585,178	18,841,026	18,102,681	17,919,972	17,919,683
White	19,085,218	18,378,303	17,663,778	16,955,608	16,780,818	16,780,562
Black or African American	737,565	719,557	701,517	682,952	678,100	678,075
American Indian and Alaska Native	319,117	312,313	305,379	298,498	296,695	296,689
Asian	124,655	121,702	118,701	115,626	114,773	114,773
Native Hawaiian and other Pacific Islanders	54,957	53,303	51,651	49,997	49,586	49,584
Two or more races	277,589	266,625	255,667	244,930	242,113	242,112
Race alone or in combination:*						
White	19,330,695	18,613,551	17,888,831	17,170,667	16,993,273	16,993,017
Black or African American	862,721	838,429	814,120	789,434	783,020	782,996
American Indian and Alaska Native	425,143	416,596	407,960	399,291	396,966	396,959
Asian	204,392	198,373	192,250	186,166	184,499	184,499
Native Hawaiian and other Pacific Islanders	86,750	84,335	81,884	79,500	78,890	78,887
Female	**147,772,517**	**146,440,534**	**145,085,267**	**143,721,255**	**143,367,774**	**143,368,343**
One race	145,583,059	144,314,084	143,021,137	141,719,082	141,380,361	141,380,912
White	118,375,136	117,550,367	116,705,479	115,856,170	115,628,047	115,628,171
Black or African American	19,427,114	19,216,924	19,002,465	18,785,102	18,732,701	18,733,000
American Indian and Alaska Native	1,391,144	1,372,725	1,354,116	1,335,506	1,330,884	1,330,889
Asian	6,146,359	5,935,640	5,725,647	5,513,774	5,461,398	5,461,521
Native Hawaiian and other Pacific Islanders	243,306	238,428	233,430	228,530	227,331	227,331
Two or more races	2,189,458	2,126,450	2,064,130	2,002,173	1,987,413	1,987,431
Race alone or in combination:*						
White	120,251,322	119,369,190	118,467,659	117,562,024	117,320,433	117,320,574
Black or African American	20,277,972	20,029,385	19,777,072	19,522,092	19,460,866	19,461,176
American Indian and Alaska Native	2,206,138	2,184,990	2,163,622	2,142,224	2,136,910	2,136,916
Asian	6,937,026	6,701,571	6,467,033	6,230,788	6,172,502	6,172,636
Native Hawaiian and other Pacific Islanders	476,908	468,843	460,621	452,546	450,599	450,595
Not Hispanic or Latino	**128,472,729**	**127,804,019**	**127,120,298**	**126,418,763**	**126,223,559**	**126,224,320**
One race	126,566,231	125,950,126	125,318,249	124,668,405	124,485,469	124,486,209
White	100,590,269	100,392,245	100,182,013	99,958,353	99,879,429	99,879,733
Black or African American	18,658,881	18,465,475	18,268,055	18,067,902	18,019,654	18,019,958
American Indian and Alaska Native	1,103,927	1,090,883	1,077,669	1,064,443	1,061,192	1,061,200
Asian	6,019,596	5,811,640	5,604,414	5,395,333	5,343,710	5,343,833
Native Hawaiian and other Pacific Islanders	193,558	189,883	186,098	182,374	181,484	181,485
Two or more races	1,906,498	1,853,893	1,802,049	1,750,358	1,738,090	1,738,111
Race alone or in combination:*						
White	102,217,946	101,972,187	101,715,020	101,444,557	101,354,473	101,354,794
Black or African American	19,380,324	19,154,496	18,925,231	18,693,434	18,637,781	18,638,097
American Indian and Alaska Native	1,810,815	1,796,657	1,782,305	1,767,876	1,764,333	1,764,342
Asian	6,727,661	6,498,035	6,269,348	6,038,824	5,982,038	5,982,176
Native Hawaiian and other Pacific Islanders	394,695	388,542	382,235	376,027	374,541	374,541

2004," *National Vital Statistics Reports*, vol. 53, no. 19, May 3, 2005, http://www.cdc.gov/nchs/data/nvsr/nvsr53/nvsr53_19.pdf; for historical data, see "MS-1. Marital Status of the Population 15 Years Old and Over, by Sex and Race: 1950 to Present," U.S. Census Bureau, June 29, 2005, http://www.census.gov/population/socdemo/hh-fam/ms1.pdf). In March 2003 about 58.6 million American women age fifteen and over were married and living with their spouses. (See Table 1.4.) Additionally, almost 1.5 million married women were not living with their spouses, and approximately 2.8 million women were legally separated from their spouses.

A greater percentage of men (57.2%) than women (54%) were married; but men were also more likely than women to have never married (32.1% and 25.5%,

TABLE 1.2

Population estimates, by sex, race, and Hispanic origin, 2000–03 [CONTINUED]

Sex, race and Hispanic or Latino origin	Population estimates				April 1, 2000	
	July 1, 2003	July 1, 2002	July 1, 2001	July 1, 2000	Estimates base	Census
Hispanic or Latino	**19,299,788**	**18,636,515**	**17,964,969**	**17,302,492**	**17,144,215**	**17,144,023**
One race	19,016,828	18,363,958	17,702,888	17,050,677	16,894,892	16,894,703
White	17,784,867	17,158,122	16,523,466	15,897,817	15,748,618	15,748,438
Black or African American	768,233	751,449	734,410	717,200	713,047	713,042
American Indian and Alaska Native	287,217	281,842	276,447	271,063	269,692	269,689
Asian	126,763	124,000	121,233	118,441	117,688	117,688
Native Hawaiian and other Pacific Islanders	49,748	48,545	47,332	46,156	45,847	45,846
Two or more races	282,960	272,557	262,081	251,815	249,323	249,320
Race alone or in combination:*						
White	18,033,376	17,397,003	16,752,639	16,117,467	15,965,960	15,965,780
Black or African American	897,648	874,889	851,841	828,658	823,085	823,079
American Indian and Alaska Native	395,323	388,333	381,317	374,348	372,577	372,574
Asian	209,365	203,536	197,685	191,964	190,464	190,460
Native Hawaiian and other Pacific Islanders	82,213	80,301	78,386	76,519	76,058	76,054

*'In combination' means in combination with one or more other races. The sum of the five race groups adds to more than the total population because individuals may report more than one race.

SOURCE: "Table 3. Annual Estimates of the Population by Sex, Race and Hispanic or Latino Origin for the United States: April 1, 2000 to July 1, 2003 (NC-EST2003-03)," U.S. Census Bureau, Population Division, June 14, 2004, http://www.census.gov/popest/national/asrh/NC-EST2003/NC-EST2003-03.pdf (accessed June 7, 2005)

FIGURE 1.1

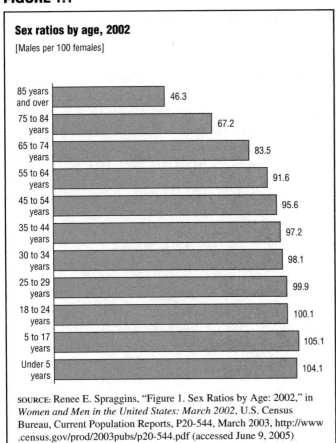

SOURCE: Renee E. Spraggins, "Figure 1. Sex Ratios by Age: 2002," in *Women and Men in the United States: March 2002*, U.S. Census Bureau, Current Population Reports, P20-544, March 2003, http://www.census.gov/prod/2003pubs/p20-544.pdf (accessed June 9, 2005)

FIGURE 1.2

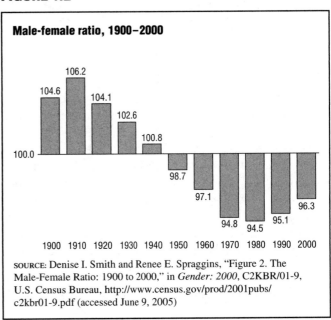

SOURCE: Denise I. Smith and Renee E. Spraggins, "Figure 2. The Male-Female Ratio: 1900 to 2000," in *Gender: 2000*, C2KBR/01-9, U.S. Census Bureau, http://www.census.gov/prod/2001pubs/c2kbr01-9.pdf (accessed June 9, 2005)

respectively). The percent never married rose for both men and women between 1970 and 2003, reflecting the decreasing marriage rate. (See Table 1.4.) The reduction in marriage rates has been particularly high among African-Americans. According to the Census Bureau, in 2003, 55.1% of white women, 57.7% of Asian-American women, and 51.5% of Hispanic women were married. By contrast, only 30.9% of African-American women were married in 2003, compared with 54% in 1970 ("Table A1. Marital Status of People 15 Years and Over, by Age, Sex, Personal Earnings, Race, and Hispanic Origin," *America's Families and Living Arrangements, 2003*, U.S. Census Bureau, September 15, 2004, http://www.census.gov/population/www/socdemo/hh-fam/cps2003.html).

TABLE 1.3

Expectation of life, by age, race, and sex, 2002

[In years]

Age	All races			White			Black		
	Total	Male	Female	Total	Male	Female	Total	Male	Female
0	77.3	74.5	79.9	77.7	75.1	80.3	72.3	68.8	75.6
1	76.8	74.1	79.4	77.2	74.6	79.7	72.4	68.8	75.6
5	72.9	70.2	75.4	73.3	70.7	75.8	68.5	65.0	71.7
10	67.9	65.3	70.5	68.3	65.7	70.8	63.6	60.1	66.8
15	63.0	60.3	65.5	63.4	60.8	65.9	58.7	55.2	61.8
20	58.2	55.6	60.7	58.6	56.1	61.0	53.9	50.5	57.0
25	53.5	51.0	55.8	53.8	51.4	56.1	49.3	46.0	52.1
30	48.7	46.3	51.0	49.0	46.7	51.2	44.7	41.6	47.4
35	44.0	41.6	46.1	44.3	42.0	46.4	40.1	37.1	42.7
40	39.3	37.0	41.4	39.6	37.4	41.6	35.6	32.8	38.1
45	34.8	32.6	36.7	35.0	32.9	36.9	31.3	28.5	33.7
50	30.3	28.3	32.2	30.5	28.5	32.4	27.3	24.6	29.5
55	26.1	24.1	27.7	26.2	24.3	27.9	23.4	21.0	25.4
60	22.0	20.2	23.5	22.1	20.3	23.6	19.9	17.6	21.6
65	18.2	16.6	19.5	18.2	16.6	19.5	16.6	14.6	18.0
70	14.7	13.2	15.8	14.7	13.3	15.8	13.5	11.8	14.7
75	11.5	10.3	12.4	11.5	10.3	12.3	10.9	9.5	11.7
80	8.8	7.8	9.4	8.7	7.7	9.3	8.6	7.5	9.2
85	6.5	5.7	6.9	6.4	5.7	6.8	6.6	5.8	7.0
90	4.8	4.2	5.0	4.7	4.1	4.9	5.1	4.5	5.3
95	3.6	3.2	3.7	3.4	3.0	3.5	3.9	3.6	4.0
100	2.7	2.5	2.8	2.4	2.3	2.5	3.0	2.9	3.0

SOURCE: "Table A. Expectation of Life by Age, Race, and Sex: United States, 2002," in *National Vital Statistics Reports*, vol. 53, no. 6, November 10, 2004, http://www.cdc.gov/nchs/data/nvsr/nvsr53/nvsr53_06.pdf (accessed May 22, 2005)

Single Women

The percentage of unmarried individuals continued to grow in the early 2000s. In 2003, 46% of females age fifteen and over were single (never married, divorced, or widowed), as were 42.9% of males ("Table A1. Marital Status of People 15 Years and Over, by Age, Sex, Personal Earnings, Race, and Hispanic Origin," *America's Families and Living Arrangements, 2003*, U.S. Census Bureau). Although more men than women never marry, women are more likely to be single because they are less likely than men to remarry following divorce or the death of a spouse.

POSTPONING MARRIAGE. The age at which women marry continues to rise. As Figure 1.4 shows, since 1970 women have consistently married at a younger median age than men, although the gap between men and women has narrowed over the years. The median age for a woman's first marriage rose from 20.8 years in 1970 to 25.3 years in 2003. In March 2003, 74.5% of women aged twenty to twenty-four had never been married, whereas in 1970 only 35.8% of women in that age group had not been married. (See Table 1.3.) Many women now postpone marriage to pursue their education and careers.

DIVORCED WOMEN. It is estimated that approximately half of all marriages in the United States end in divorce. According to the National Center for Health Statistics, the divorce rate for the twelve-month period ending November 2004 was 3.7 per one thousand people

("Births, Marriages, Divorces, and Death: Provisional Data for November 2004," *National Vital Statistics Reports*, vol. 53, no. 19, May 3, 2005, http://www.cdc.gov/nchs/data/nvsr/nvsr53/nvsr53_19.pdf). This rate is slightly lower than the rate for 2002 and 2001 (four per one thousand both years). The 2004 rate shows a significant decrease from the 1992 rate of 4.8 divorces per one thousand people.

In 2003 approximately 12.7 million American women age fifteen and over, or 10.9%, were divorced and had not remarried ("Table A1. Marital Status of People 15 Years and Over, by Age, Sex, Personal Earnings, Race, and Hispanic Origin," *America's Families and Living Arrangements, 2003*, U.S. Census Bureau). More women remain unmarried after divorce than men: 11.3% of white women and 8.9% of white men were divorced and had not remarried; 12.8% of black women and 8.7% of black men were divorced and had not remarried; and 8% of Hispanic women and 5.6% of Hispanic men had divorced and had not remarried.

WIDOWHOOD. A great number of single women sixty-five and older are widows. (See Table 1.4.) Of the 11.3 million American widows in 2003, 77.3% were sixty-five or over. Almost half (44.3%) of all women age sixty-five and older were widows who had not remarried. By contrast, only 2.7 million men were widowed, and only 14.3% of men sixty-five and over were

FIGURE 1.3

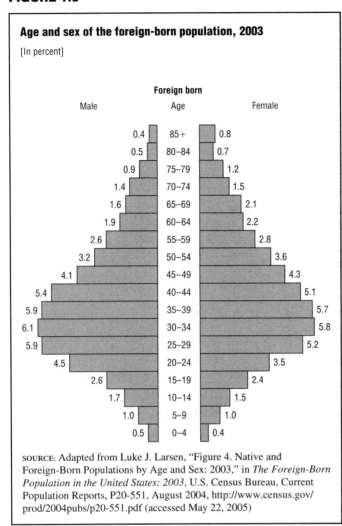

Age and sex of the foreign-born population, 2003

[In percent]

Foreign born

Male	Age	Female
0.4	85+	0.8
0.5	80–84	0.7
0.9	75–79	1.2
1.4	70–74	1.5
1.6	65–69	2.1
1.9	60–64	2.2
2.6	55–59	2.8
3.2	50–54	3.6
4.1	45–49	4.3
5.4	40–44	5.1
5.9	35–39	5.7
6.1	30–34	5.8
5.9	25–29	5.2
4.5	20–24	3.5
2.6	15–19	2.4
1.7	10–14	1.5
1.0	5–9	1.0
0.5	0–4	0.4

SOURCE: Adapted from Luke J. Larsen, "Figure 4. Native and Foreign-Born Populations by Age and Sex: 2003," in *The Foreign-Born Population in the United States: 2003*, U.S. Census Bureau, Current Population Reports, P20-551, August 2004, http://www.census.gov/prod/2004pubs/p20-551.pdf (accessed May 22, 2005)

widowers who had not remarried. Almost one in ten women age fifteen and older (9.7%) were widows in 2003.

NEVER-MARRIED WOMEN. Being unmarried used to be considered a temporary or transitional state for most people. But after 1970 there was a large increase in the number of individuals who had never been married. Between 1970 and 2003 the percentage of never-married women increased significantly in every age group between fifteen and fifty-four. (See Table 1.4.) The percentages of never-married males likewise increased significantly in these age groups. The percentage of never-married people in the oldest age groups, however, has declined. Among women age sixty-five and older, the percentage never married in 2003 was 3.7%, down from 7.7% in 1970.

Cohabitation

As attitudes change in the United States, marital status may no longer accurately reflect the personal relationships of individuals. Changes in attitudes toward cohabitation have contributed to the rise in the median age for first marriages, as well as to the increasing numbers of individuals who never marry or who do not remarry following divorce or death of a spouse. Among many Americans, marriage is no longer viewed as a prerequisite for living together and raising children.

The proportion of households headed by unmarried partners has increased from 2.9% of all households in 1996 to 4.2% of all households in 2003. The proportion of unmarried couples living together is probably even higher, as some couples maintain other households or are reluctant to describe themselves as cohabitating couples (Jason Fields, *America's Families and Living Arrangements: 2003*, Current Population Reports, P20–553, U.S. Census Bureau, November 2004). In 2003 the Census Bureau reported 4.6 million households headed by unmarried partners, compared with 58.6 million married couples. (See Table 1.5.) Almost as large a proportion of unmarried partner households contained children under the age of eighteen (41%) as did married-couple households (45%).

Table 1.5 highlights several interesting differences between married and unmarried couples. Women in unmarried partnerships tend to be younger than those in marriages. In 2003 only 3.8% of married women were between the ages of fifteen and twenty-four; however, 24.3% of women in unmarried partnerships were in that age group. By contrast, although 77.2% of married women were thirty-five and over, only 43.5% of women in unmarried couples were over thirty-four.

A higher percentage of unmarried couples are African-American or Hispanic as compared with married couples. Women in unmarried partnerships are more likely than married women to be in the labor force (72.4% and 59.5%, respectively). Almost 41% of cohabitating couples live with the children of one or both partners. This is only slightly less than the nearly 46% of married-partner families that include children under eighteen.

Lesbian Partners

Lesbians are estimated to comprise somewhere between 2% and 10% of the U.S. adult female population (David M. Smith and Gary J. Gates, *Gay and Lesbian Families in the United States: Same-Sex Unmarried Partner Households*, Human Rights Campaign, August 22, 2001). Many lesbian couples live together in long-term committed relationships. Many lesbian couples consider themselves to be married or have had a commitment or marriage ceremony.

In 2000 Vermont was the first state that legalized same-sex civil unions granting same-sex couples the benefits of marriage. On November 18, 2003, a 4–3

TABLE 1.4

Marital status of the population 15 years and over, by sex and age, March 1970 and 2003

[In thousands]

Sex and age	2003 Number							Percent never married	March 1970 percent never married*
	Total	Married spouse present	Married spouse absent	Separated	Divorced	Widowed	Never married		
Both sexes									
Total 15 years and over	225,057	117,172	3,139	4,723	21,649	13,995	64,380	28.6	24.9
15 to 19 years	20,176	257	43	70	39	16	19,751	97.9	93.9
20 to 24 years	19,856	3,181	177	213	243	16	16,026	80.7	44.5
25 to 29 years	18,696	8,158	308	476	832	50	8,872	47.5	14.7
30 to 34 years	20,505	12,268	317	515	1,606	80	5,720	27.9	7.8
35 to 44 years	44,025	28,633	759	1,461	5,567	407	7,197	16.3	5.9
45 to 54 years	40,196	27,299	606	1,056	6,478	842	3,914	9.7	6.1
55 to 64 years	27,387	18,949	393	550	4,157	1,779	1,558	5.7	7.2
65 years and over	34,217	18,427	535	382	2,725	10,806	1,341	3.9	7.6
Males									
Total 15 years and over	108,696	58,586	1,651	1,905	8,976	2,697	34,881	32.1	28.1
15 to 19 years	10,241	66	13	37	21	7	10,098	98.6	97.4
20 to 24 years	9,953	1,156	78	63	93	—	8,563	86.0	54.7
25 to 29 years	9,366	3,573	170	171	327	14	5,112	54.6	19.1
30 to 34 years	10,177	5,733	187	185	678	21	3,371	33.1	9.4
35 to 44 years	21,702	14,045	406	587	2,335	88	4,242	19.5	6.7
45 to 54 years	19,578	13,704	322	413	2,821	202	2,117	10.8	7.5
55 to 64 years	13,158	9,970	200	260	1,679	292	757	5.8	7.8
65 years and over	14,521	10,341	274	190	1,022	2,074	621	4.3	7.5
Females									
Total 15 years and over	116,361	58,586	1,488	2,817	12,673	11,297	29,499	25.4	22.1
15 to 19 years	9,935	193	30	32	18	9	9,652	97.2	90.3
20 to 24 years	9,903	2,025	99	150	150	16	7,463	75.4	35.8
25 to 29 years	9,330	4,585	138	305	505	36	3,760	40.3	10.5
30 to 34 years	10,329	6,535	130	330	928	58	2,349	22.7	6.2
35 to 44 years	22,322	14,588	353	875	3,233	319	2,955	13.2	5.2
45 to 54 years	20,617	13,595	283	643	3,658	640	1,797	8.7	4.9
55 to 64 years	14,229	8,980	193	290	2,478	1,487	801	5.6	6.8
65 years and over	19,696	8,086	261	192	1,704	8,732	720	3.7	7.7

*The 1970 percentages include 14-year-olds, and thus are for 14+ and 14–19.
— Represents zero or rounds to zero.

SOURCE: Jason Fields, "Table 6. Marital Status of the Population 15 Years and Over by Sex and Age: March 1970 and 2003," in *America's Families and Living Arrangements: 2003*, U.S. Census Bureau, Current Population Reports, P20-553, November 2004, http://www.census.gov/prod/2004pubs/p20-553.pdf (accessed May 23, 2005).

ruling by the Massachusetts Supreme Judicial Court found in favor of gay and lesbian marriages in the state of Massachusetts, and on May 17, 2004, Massachusetts began to legally marry gay and lesbian couples. A Connecticut civil union law was signed by Governor M. Jodi Rell on April 20, 2005, and was effective on October 1, 2005. Although couples in all three states receive state recognition and benefits from their unions, because President Bill Clinton signed the "Defense of Marriage Act" in 1996, which excluded same-gender couples from the definition of marriage and barred them from receiving the federal benefits and protections that are afforded to opposite-gender couples, more than one thousand federal rights and privileges are withheld from the couples. By April 2005, forty-two states had passed defense of marriage acts.

According to a 2001 report by the Urban Institute, a Washington, D.C.-based nonpartisan economic and social policy research organization, Census 2000 (the first census to count same-sex couples) counted 297,061 lesbian families. Although this was a 314% increase over statistics compiled by the Census Bureau in 1990, the Human Rights Campaign suggests that the number of gay and lesbian families may have been undercounted by as much as 62% in 2000 (David M. Smith and Gary J. Gates, *Gay and Lesbian Families in the United States: Same-Sex Unmarried Partner Households*, Human Rights Campaign).

Many employers now offer the same benefits to same-sex and opposite-sex domestic partners of employees that they offer to the spouses of employees. Some well-known companies that offer domestic-partner benefits (DPB) include Eastman Kodak, Nike, Capital One, Xerox Corporation, American Airlines, and many others. By 2005, 236 of all *Fortune* 500 companies were offering same-sex domestic-partner

FIGURE 1.4

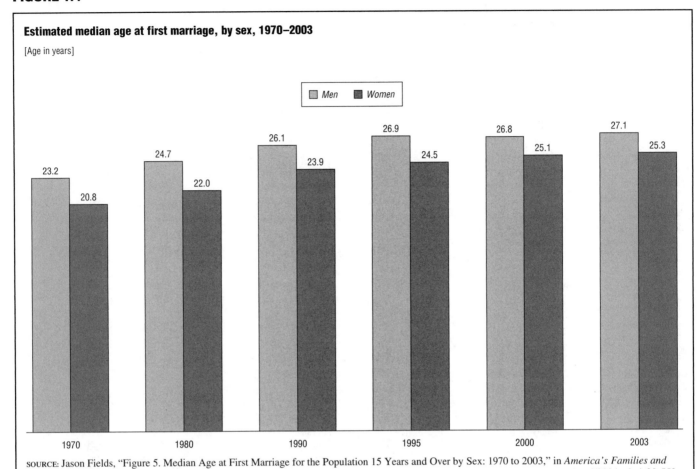

Estimated median age at first marriage, by sex, 1970–2003

[Age in years]

☐ Men ■ Women

	1970	1980	1990	1995	2000	2003
Men	23.2	24.7	26.1	26.9	26.8	27.1
Women	20.8	22.0	23.9	24.5	25.1	25.3

SOURCE: Jason Fields, "Figure 5. Median Age at First Marriage for the Population 15 Years and Over by Sex: 1970 to 2003," in *America's Families and Living Arrangements: 2003*, U.S. Census Bureau, Current Population Reports, P20-553, November 2004, http://www.census.gov/prod/2004pubs/p20-553 .pdf (accessed May 23, 2005)

benefits, as were eleven state governments, 129 city and county governments, and 295 colleges and universities. According to the Human Rights Campaign, in 2005 there were approximately 7,600 private-sector companies offering DPBs, many of them limited to same-sex couples only.

A major milestone in the legal recognition of same-sex unions resulted from the terrorist attacks on September 11, 2001, that razed the landmark Twin Towers in New York City and damaged the Pentagon in Washington, D.C. Civilian army management analyst Sheila Hein was killed in the attack on the Pentagon. Hein left behind her partner of eighteen years, Peggy Neff. The federal government awarded Neff more than $557,000 to help compensate for the loss of her partner. This event was widely celebrated by gay activists throughout the nation, as it was the first time a lesbian union was legally recognized by the federal government.

LIVING ARRANGEMENTS

More and more Americans are marrying later, choosing to remain single, divorcing, and cohabitating without marriage. Many people are choosing to raise children in homes other than a traditional married-couple household. As a result of these trends, the living arrangements of America's households have changed in significant ways. The average household size has decreased dramatically; between 1970 and 2003, the average household size decreased from 3.14 to 2.57. In 1970, 21% of all households had five or more people; in 2003 only 10% of households were that large. At the same time, the percent of households with only one or two people increased from 46% in 1970 to 60% in 2003 (Jason Fields, *America's Families and Living Arrangements: 2003*, Current Population Reports).

Types of Households

The Census Bureau defines a household as everyone who lives in a single housing unit. One of the people who owns, is buying, or rents the housing unit is designated the householder. Households are categorized by the Census Bureau as either family or nonfamily households. A family household comprises at least two people who are related by birth, adoption, or marriage but may include other individuals who are not

TABLE 1.5

Characteristics of unmarried partners and married spouses, by sex, 2003

[In thousands]

	Unmarried partners				Married spouses			
	Total		With children under 18*		Total		With children under 18*	
Characteristic	Men	Women	Men	Women	Men	Women	Men	Women
Total	**4,622**	**4,622**	**1,877**	**1,877**	**58,586**	**58,586**	**26,445**	**26,445**
Age								
15 to 24 years	751	1,121	292	452	1,221	2,217	702	1,355
25 to 34 years	1,577	1,490	770	758	9,306	11,120	6,603	8,338
35 to 44 years	1,141	983	588	528	14,045	14,588	11,239	11,506
45 to 54 years	689	641	175	131	13,704	13,595	6,668	4,864
55 to 64 years	288	280	42	9	9,970	8,980	1,104	318
65 years and over	174	106	9	—	10,341	8,086	128	63
Race and ethnicity								
White only	3,713	3,755	1,420	1,466	50,822	50,590	22,367	22,306
Non-Hispanic	3,103	3,146	1,051	1,083	44,628	44,313	18,423	18,299
Black only	661	558	343	287	4,360	4,167	1,295	2,058
Asian only	96	149	30	38	2,384	2,744	602	1,460
Hispanic (of any race)	679	678	402	421	6,599	6,701	4,227	4,295
Education								
Less than high school	843	736	452	411	8,435	7,105	3,475	2,992
High school graduate	1,799	1,627	858	770	17,293	19,425	7,344	7,440
Some college	1,178	1,395	420	531	14,289	15,652	6,787	7,493
Bachelor's degree or higher	801	863	147	164	18,570	16,403	8,838	8,519
Labor force status								
Employed	3,705	3,345	1,527	1,260	43,439	34,848	24,001	17,554
Unemployed	351	249	181	125	1,903	1,379	1,041	751
Not in labor force	566	1,028	169	492	13,244	22,359	1,403	8,140
Earnings in 2002								
Without earnings	510	904	177	401	12,145	20,942	1,263	7,424
With earnings	4,111	3,718	1,699	1,477	46,439	37,643	25,182	19,020
Under $5,000	207	370	104	210	1,629	3,791	579	2,236
$5,000 to $9,999	276	360	116	155	1,507	3,426	592	1,884
$10,000 to $14,999	345	491	163	214	2,227	4,137	1,104	2,125
$15,000 to $19,999	487	513	216	188	2,843	4,013	1,564	2,045
$20,000 to $24,999	488	497	241	209	3,370	4,110	1,937	2,109
$25,000 to $29,999	458	412	198	185	3,359	3,569	1,873	1,720
$30,000 to $39,999	766	472	285	158	7,440	5,665	3,977	2,771
$40,000 to $49,999	424	266	173	78	5,727	3,497	3,138	1,601
$50,000 to $74,999	421	269	130	65	9,530	3,695	5,340	1,658
$75,000 and over	239	68	73	15	8,807	1,740	5,078	871

*May be "own children" of either partner or both partners. Excludes ever married children under 18 years.
— Represents zero or rounds to zero.

SOURCE: Jason Fields, "Table 8. Characteristics of Unmarried Partners and Married Spouses by Sex: 2003," in *America's Families and Living Arrangements: 2003*, U.S. Census Bureau, Current Population Reports, P20-553, November 2004, http://www.census.gov/prod/2004pubs/p20-553.pdf (accessed May 23, 2005)

related. A nonfamily household consists of either a householder living alone or a householder who is not related to any of the other people who live in the same housing unit. These people may include roommates or unmarried partners. However, people other than the householder in a nonfamily household may be related to each other. The majority of households in the United States are family households, although the proportion of family households declined from 81.2% in 1970 to 67.9% in 2003. (See Figure 1.5.)

Family Households

Between 1970 and 2003, the proportion of households consisting of a married couple with children decreased from 40.3% to 23.3%. (See Figure 1.5.) The proportion of households consisting of married couples without children decreased as well, but not as drastically, from 30.3% in 1970 to 28.2% in 2003. This group includes couples who have not yet had children but intend to, couples who do not intend to have children, and older couples whose children have left home.

In 2003 most householders in married-couple households were non-Hispanic whites (76.9%), 10.8% were Hispanic, 8.3% were African-American, and 4% were Asian-American/Pacific Islander. The average household size for married couples was 3.22 people. (See Table 1.6.) Related children under eighteen lived

FIGURE 1.5

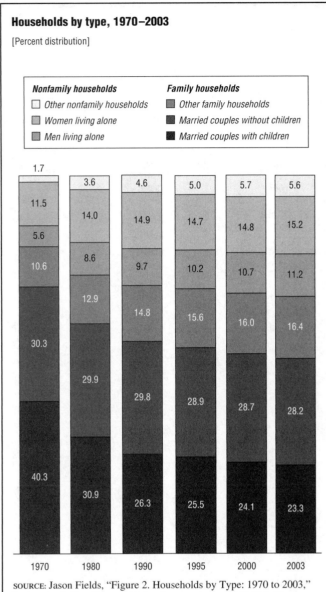

Households by type, 1970–2003

[Percent distribution]

Nonfamily households	Family households
☐ Other nonfamily households	▨ Other family households
▨ Women living alone	▦ Married couples without children
▨ Men living alone	■ Married couples with children

SOURCE: Jason Fields, "Figure 2. Households by Type: 1970 to 2003," in *America's Families and Living Arrangements: 2003*, U.S. Census Bureau, Current Population Reports, P20-553, November 2004, http://www.census.gov/prod/2004pubs/p20-553.pdf (accessed May 23, 2005)

in 47.2% of married-couple households. Most of these married-couple households had only one or two children; only 10.3% of married-couple households contained three or more related children.

In 2003 one quarter of households with children were headed by a single, female householder (26.1%). (See Figure 1.6.) Single-mother families increased from three million in 1970 to 10.1 million in 2003. Only 5.8% of families with children, or 2.3 million households, were headed by a single father, up from less than half a million in 1970. Single mothers in 2003 were disproportionately women of color. Almost half of single mothers (48%) were white, 30.8% were black, and 17.8% were Hispanic.

Women Living Alone

The majority of nonfamily households consist of women or men living alone. (See Figure 1.5.) Women made up 57.5% of all one-person households in 2003. The average age of women who lived alone in 2002 was 51.6 years, compared with 45.1 years for men. Almost four in ten women over age sixty-five (39.7%) lived alone in 2003, compared with only 18.8% of men, due in large part to the shorter life expectancy of men and the lower remarriage rates of women after divorce or death of a spouse.

TABLE 1.6

Households by type and selected characteristics, 2003

[In thousands, except average size]

Characteristic	All households Number	Family households Total	Married couple	Other families Male householder	Other families Female householder	Nonfamily households Total	Nonfamily households Male householder	Nonfamily households Female householder
All households	111,278	75,596	57,320	4,656	13,620	35,682	16,020	19,662
Age of householder								
15 to 24 years	6,611	3,551	1,379	789	1,383	3,060	1,507	1,552
25 to 34 years	19,056	13,438	9,536	1,011	2,892	5,617	3,343	2,274
35 to 44 years	24,069	18,741	14,001	1,087	3,652	5,328	3,278	2,051
45 to 54 years	22,623	16,863	13,297	922	2,644	5,760	2,971	2,789
55 to 64 years	16,260	11,261	9,543	413	1,305	4,999	2,023	2,976
65 years and over	22,659	11,741	9,565	434	1,743	10,918	2,898	8,020
Race and ethnicity of householder								
White only	91,645	62,297	49,915	3,500	8,881	29,349	13,070	16,278
Non-Hispanic	81,166	53,845	44,101	2,674	7,070	27,321	11,968	15,353
Black only	13,465	8,928	4,165	762	4,000	4,538	2,043	2,495
Asian only	3,917	2,845	2,286	223	337	1,073	526	547
Hispanic (of any race)	11,339	9,090	6,189	872	2,029	2,249	1,228	1,021
Size of households								
1 person	29,431	(X)	(X)	(X)	(X)	29,431	12,511	16,919
2 people	37,078	32,047	24,310	1,992	5,745	5,031	2,660	2,371
3 people	17,889	17,076	11,526	1,403	4,147	813	556	257
4 people	15,967	15,672	12,754	733	2,185	295	212	83
5 people	7,029	6,969	5,719	296	955	60	42	17
6 people	2,521	2,489	2,004	142	344	31	19	12
7 or more people	1,364	1,343	1,007	90	246	22	19	2
Average size	2.57	3.19	3.22	3.11	3.12	1.24	1.32	1.17
Number of related children under 18								
No related children	72,367	36,685	30,261	2,240	4,183	35,682	16,020	19,662
With related children	38,911	38,911	27,059	2,416	9,437	(X)	(X)	(X)
1 child	16,511	16,511	10,378	1,429	4,704	(X)	(X)	(X)
2 children	14,333	14,333	10,800	683	2,850	(X)	(X)	(X)
3 children	5,771	5,771	4,235	220	1,317	(X)	(X)	(X)
4 or more children	2,296	2,296	1,646	84	566	(X)	(X)	(X)
Presence of own children under 18								
No own children	75,310	39,628	31,406	2,741	5,481	35,682	16,020	19,662
With own children	35,968	35,968	25,914	1,915	8,139	(X)	(X)	(X)
With own children under 12	26,251	26,251	19,168	1,295	5,788	(X)	(X)	(X)
With own children under 6	15,584	15,584	11,743	729	3,111	(X)	(X)	(X)
With own children under 3	9,081	9,081	7,014	451	1,615	(X)	(X)	(X)
With own children under 1	2,917	2,917	2,255	181	481	(X)	(X)	(X)
Tenure								
Owner	75,909	57,092	47,676	2,721	6,695	18,817	7,742	11,075
Renter	33,799	17,604	9,007	1,873	6,724	16,195	7,951	8,244
Occupies without payment	1,570	900	637	62	201	670	327	343

X Not applicable.
Note: Data are not shown separately for the other race groups because of the small sample sizes in the Current Population Survey in the 2003 Annual Social and Economic Supplement.

SOURCE: Jason Fields, "Table 1. Households by Type and Selected Characteristics: 2003," in *America's Families and Living Arrangements: 2003*, U.S. Census Bureau, Current Population Reports, P20-553, November 2004, http://www.census.gov/prod/2004pubs/p20-553.pdf (accessed May 23, 2005)

FIGURE 1.6

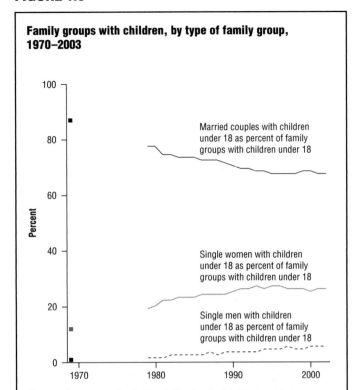

Family groups with children, by type of family group, 1970–2003

Note: *Family groups* are family households plus all related and unrelated subfamilies. These subfamilies may consist of either married couples or parent-child units, and the reference person of that family group may be either related or unrelated to the householder.

SOURCE: Jason Fields, "Figure 1. Family Groups with Children by Type of Family Group: 1970 to 2003," in *America's Families and Living Arrangements: 2003*, U.S. Census Bureau, Current Population Reports, P20-553, November 2004, http://www.census.gov/prod/2004pubs/ p20-553.pdf (accessed May 23, 2005)

CHAPTER 2
WOMEN'S EDUCATION

Prior to the nineteenth century, few American girls attended school. By the early nineteenth century, female seminaries were being established, primarily to teach domestic chores and social graces. Mount Holyoke in Massachusetts, founded in 1837, was one of the first female seminaries to stress academics, and in 1888 it became a women's college. Most of the graduates of the early female seminaries and normal schools became teachers. (Normal schools were those founded specifically to graduate teachers for public schools.) In the 1830s Oberlin College in Ohio became the first coeducational institute of higher learning. In the second half of the nineteenth century, American and European women undertook a major campaign to gain admission to medical schools, laying the groundwork for subsequent struggles for women's equity in education. Although by the twentieth century most public universities admitted at least a few women, it was not until the 1960s and 1970s that elite American universities such as Harvard, Yale, and Princeton began to accept women students. Many of the women's colleges also became coeducational during this period.

Despite this push for higher education for women, few young women in the early twentieth century even completed high school. Those who did go beyond high school usually trained to be teachers, nurses, or social workers. Business schools prepared young women for clerical duties, never for management. By the late twentieth century, increasing numbers of American women were undertaking higher levels of education and preparing for essentially all occupations.

EDUCATIONAL ATTAINMENT

According to the Department of Education's National Center for Education Statistics (NCES), in 1940, 12.4% of females and 15.1% of males over age twenty-four had attended fewer than five years of elementary school, and 26.3% of American females and 22.7% of males had completed high school ("Table 8. Percent of Persons Age 25 and Over and 25 to 29, by Years of School Completed, Race/Ethnicity, and Sex: Selected Years, 1910 to 2002," in *Digest of Education Statistics, 2003*, U.S. Department of Education, National Center for Education Statistics, NCES 2005–025, December 2004). Only 3.8% of women and 5.5% of men had completed four years of college. Most African-Americans had only an elementary school education in 1940; only 6.9% of men and 8.4% of women completed high school.

Table 2.1 shows that in 2004, 32.8% of all American females age twenty-five and older had graduated high school but had not attended college. Another 26.5% had attended some college or earned an associate's degree; 17.6% had earned a bachelor's degree; and 14.6% of women age twenty-five and older had not graduated from high school in 2004.

Nine out of ten (90.1%) non-Hispanic white females age twenty-five and over were high school graduates in 2004; 85% of Asian-American females, 80.8% of African-American females, and 59.5% of Hispanic females age twenty-five and over were high school graduates. In comparison, 85.3% of non-Hispanic white males age twenty-five and over, 88.7% of Asian-American males, 80.4% of African-American males, and 57.3% of Hispanic males age twenty-five and over were high school graduates. Although only 12.3% of Hispanic women age twenty-five and older had bachelor's degrees or higher, 18.5% of African-American women, 26.4% of non-Hispanic white women, and 45.6% of Asian-American women had bachelor's degrees or higher.

SCHOOL ATTENDANCE AND ACHIEVEMENT
The Educational Attainment Level of Women Surpasses That of Men

In 2003 a slightly greater proportion of male three- and four-year-olds were enrolled in nursery school or kindergarten than females (55.9% and 54.1%, respectively). (See Table 2.2.) Among seven- to nine-year-olds,

TABLE 2.1

Women's educational attainment, by age, 2004

[Numbers in thousands. Civilian noninstitutionalized population.]

All races and female	Total									Educational attainment						
		None	1st–4th grade	5th–6th grade	7th–8th grade	9th grade	10th grade	11th grade	High school graduate	Some college no degree	Associate degree, occupational	Associate degree, academic	Bachelor's degree	Master's degree	Professional degree	Doctorate degree
15 years and over	117,371	491	953	1,930	3,951	4,184	5,017	6,573	35,795	21,951	4,981	4,701	18,491	6,521	1,029	801
15 to 17 years	6,418	4	4	19	1,037	1,956	2,086	1,204	69	35	1	—	3	—	—	—
18 to 19 years	3,557	11	12	6	37	57	185	1,074	1,019	1,131	13	9	3	—	—	—
20 to 24 years	10,077	20	31	92	110	203	249	526	2,786	3,989	305	340	1,352	70	2	—
25 to 29 years	9,465	30	49	176	124	156	227	378	2,525	1,972	442	414	2,343	468	106	55
30 to 34 years	10,138	14	58	172	134	204	181	370	2,699	1,929	520	479	2,343	797	160	77
35 to 39 years	10,483	36	63	188	130	187	205	335	3,116	1,828	569	553	2,351	692	125	106
40 to 44 years	11,560	35	70	173	145	211	192	391	3,603	2,088	720	648	2,237	789	159	100
45 to 49 years	11,130	32	50	167	188	154	197	310	3,556	1,909	684	674	2,133	829	130	119
50 to 54 years	9,856	36	63	137	132	151	160	289	3,136	1,764	512	511	1,796	940	117	113
55 to 59 years	8,307	33	69	128	180	122	165	313	2,865	1,486	377	377	1,281	759	71	81
60 to 64 years	6,517	20	62	87	175	142	210	269	2,515	1,083	251	278	883	435	46	61
65 to 69 years	5,252	38	106	159	217	137	241	274	2,155	821	172	115	506	234	37	40
70 to 74 years	4,631	53	86	112	337	153	228	284	1,853	631	131	101	423	191	32	17
75 years and over	9,980	129	230	314	1,006	351	492	555	3,899	1,284	285	202	838	317	45	31
15 to 17 years	6,418	4	4	19	1,037	1,956	2,086	1,204	69	35	1	—	3	—	—	—
18 years and over	110,953	488	949	1,911	2,915	2,228	2,931	5,369	35,726	21,916	4,980	4,701	18,489	6,521	1,029	801
15 to 24 years	20,052	34	47	117	1,184	2,216	2,520	2,804	3,874	5,156	319	350	1,357	70	2	—
25 years and over	97,319	457	906	1,813	2,767	1,967	2,497	3,768	31,921	16,796	4,662	4,351	17,134	6,451	1,027	801
15 to 64 years	97,508	271	531	1,344	2,392	3,542	4,057	5,460	27,889	19,216	4,394	4,283	16,724	5,779	915	712
65 years and over	19,862	220	422	585	1,559	642	961	1,113	7,907	2,736	588	418	1,767	742	114	89

Note: A dash (—) represents zero or rounds to zero.

SOURCE: Adapted from "Table 1. Educational Attainment of the Population 15 Years and Over, by Age, Sex, Race, and Hispanic Origin: 2004," U.S. Census Bureau, Current Population Survey, March 2005, http://www.census.gov/population/socdemo/education/cps2004/tab01-01.pdf (accessed May 23, 2005)

TABLE 2.2

School enrollment of the population three years old and over, by age, sex, race, Hispanic origin, nativity, and selected educational characteristics, October 2003

[Numbers in thousands. Civilian noninstitutionalized population.]

All races	Population	Enrolled in school										Not enrolled in school					
		Total		Nursery or kindergarten		Elementary		High school		College		Total		High school graduate		Not high school graduate	
	Number	Number	Percent	Number	Percent	Number	Percent	Number	Percent	Number	Percent	Number	Percent	Number	Percent	Number	Percent
Both sexes																	
Total	275,323	74,911	27.2	8,647	3.1	32,565	11.8	17,062	6.2	16,638	6.0	200,412	72.8	164,478	59.7	35,934	13.1
3 and 4 years old	8,336	4,590	55.1	4,590	55.1	—	—	—	—	—	—	3,746	44.9	—	—	3,746	44.9
5 and 6 years old	7,730	7,309	94.5	4,004	51.8	3,305	42.8	—	—	—	—	421	5.5	—	—	421	5.5
7 to 9 years old	11,930	11,706	98.1	53	0.4	11,653	97.7	—	—	—	—	224	1.9	—	—	224	1.9
10 to 13 years old	16,744	16,478	98.4	—	—	16,218	96.9	260	1.6	—	—	266	1.6	—	—	266	1.6
14 and 15 years old	8,543	8,329	97.5	—	—	1,308	15.3	7,010	82.0	11	0.1	215	2.5	33	0.4	182	2.1
16 and 17 years old	8,613	8,177	94.9	—	—	44	0.5	7,993	92.8	140	1.6	436	5.1	113	1.3	323	3.8
18 and 19 years old	7,533	4,856	64.5	—	—	10	0.1	1,334	17.7	3,512	46.6	2,676	35.5	1,859	24.7	817	10.9
20 and 21 years old	7,635	3,684	48.3	—	—	14	0.2	138	1.8	3,533	46.3	3,950	51.7	3,032	39.7	918	12.0
22 to 24 years old	12,237	3,397	27.8	—	—	—	—	77	0.6	3,320	27.1	8,841	72.2	7,348	60.0	1,493	12.2
25 to 29 years old	18,741	2,212	11.8	—	—	—	—	48	0.3	2,164	11.5	16,530	88.2	14,053	75.0	2,477	13.2
30 to 34 years old	20,353	1,378	6.8	—	—	3	—	45	0.2	1,330	6.5	18,975	93.2	16,525	81.2	2,451	12.0
35 to 44 years old	43,670	1,635	3.7	—	—	8	—	100	0.2	1,526	3.5	42,036	96.3	37,072	84.9	4,964	11.4
45 to 54 years old	40,760	879	2.2	—	—	—	—	44	0.1	835	2.0	39,881	97.8	35,563	87.2	4,318	10.6
55 years old and over	62,497	283	0.5	—	—	3	—	11	—	269	0.4	62,214	99.5	48,882	78.2	13,332	21.3
Male																	
Total	134,239	37,323	27.8	4,525	3.4	16,845	12.5	8,635	6.4	7,318	5.5	96,916	72.2	79,017	58.9	17,899	13.3
3 and 4 years old	4,357	2,437	55.9	2,437	55.9	—	—	—	—	—	—	1,920	44.1	—	—	1,920	44.1
5 and 6 years old	3,897	3,689	94.7	2,059	52.8	1,630	41.8	—	—	—	—	208	5.3	—	—	208	5.3
7 to 9 years old	6,141	6,014	97.9	29	0.5	5,985	97.5	—	—	—	—	127	2.1	—	—	127	2.1
10 to 13 years old	8,704	8,553	98.3	—	—	8,439	97.0	114	1.3	—	—	151	1.7	—	—	151	1.7
14 and 15 years old	4,262	4,155	97.5	—	—	743	17.4	3,406	79.9	7	0.2	107	2.5	11	0.2	96	2.3
16 and 17 years old	4,419	4,199	95.0	—	—	28	0.6	4,116	93.2	55	1.2	220	5.0	49	1.1	170	3.9
18 and 19 years old	3,764	2,348	62.4	—	—	7	0.2	773	20.5	1,568	41.7	1,416	37.6	935	24.9	480	12.8
20 and 21 years old	3,741	1,625	43.4	—	—	9	0.2	65	1.8	1,551	41.5	2,116	56.6	1,584	42.3	532	14.2
22 to 24 years old	6,176	1,611	26.1	—	—	—	—	33	0.5	1,578	25.5	4,565	73.9	3,703	60.0	863	14.0
25 to 29 years old	9,325	1,009	10.8	—	—	—	—	27	0.3	982	10.5	8,315	89.2	6,995	75.0	1,321	14.2
30 to 34 years old	10,064	629	6.3	—	—	—	—	22	0.2	607	6.0	9,435	93.7	8,031	79.8	1,403	13.9
35 to 44 years old	21,431	611	2.9	—	—	5	—	59	0.3	547	2.6	20,820	97.1	18,147	84.7	2,673	12.5
45 to 54 years old	19,897	333	1.7	—	—	—	—	13	0.1	320	1.6	19,564	98.3	17,356	87.2	2,209	11.1
55 years old and over	28,063	111	0.4	—	—	—	—	7	—	104	0.4	27,952	99.6	22,206	79.1	5,745	20.5

TABLE 2.2

School enrollment of the population three years old and over, by age, sex, race, Hispanic origin, nativity, and selected educational characteristics, October 2003 [CONTINUED]

[Numbers in thousands. Civilian noninstitutionalized population.]

| | Population | Enrolled in school | | | | | | | | | | Not enrolled in school | | | | | |
| | | Total | | Nursery or kindergarten | | Elementary | | High school | | College | | Total | | High school graduate | | Not high school graduate | |
All races	Number	Number	Percent	Number	Percent	Number	Percent	Number	Percent	Number	Percent	Number	Percent	Number	Percent	Number	Percent
Female																	
Total	**141,085**	**37,588**	**26.6**	**4,123**	**2.9**	**15,719**	**11.1**	**8,427**	**6.0**	**9,319**	**6.6**	**103,497**	**73.4**	**85,461**	**60.6**	**18,036**	**12.8**
3 and 4 years old	3,979	2,154	54.1	2,154	54.1	—	—	—	—	—	—	1,826	45.9	—	—	1,826	45.9
5 and 6 years old	3,834	3,620	94.4	1,945	50.7	1,675	43.7	—	—	—	—	214	5.6	—	—	214	5.6
7 to 9 years old	5,789	5,692	98.3	24	0.4	5,668	97.9	—	—	—	—	97	1.7	—	—	97	1.7
10 to 13 years old	8,040	7,925	98.6	—	—	7,778	96.7	147	1.8	—	—	116	1.4	—	—	116	1.4
14 and 15 years old	4,282	4,173	97.5	—	—	565	13.2	3,604	84.2	4	0.1	108	2.5	22	0.5	86	2.0
16 and 17 years old	4,194	3,978	94.8	—	—	16	0.4	3,877	92.4	85	2.0	216	5.2	63	1.5	153	3.6
18 and 19 years old	3,769	2,508	66.6	—	—	3	0.1	561	14.9	1,944	51.6	1,260	33.4	923	24.5	337	8.9
20 and 21 years old	3,894	2,059	52.9	—	—	5	0.1	73	1.9	1,982	50.9	1,835	47.1	1,449	37.2	386	9.9
22 to 24 years old	6,061	1,786	29.5	—	—	—	—	44	0.7	1,742	28.7	4,275	70.5	3,645	60.1	630	10.4
25 to 29 years old	9,417	1,203	12.8	—	—	—	—	21	0.2	1,181	12.5	8,214	87.2	7,058	75.0	1,156	12.3
30 to 34 years old	10,289	749	7.3	—	—	3	—	23	0.2	723	7.0	9,541	92.7	8,493	82.5	1,048	10.2
35 to 44 years old	22,239	1,024	4.6	—	—	3	—	41	0.2	979	4.4	21,216	95.4	18,925	85.1	2,291	10.3
45 to 54 years old	20,863	547	2.6	—	—	—	—	31	0.1	515	2.5	20,316	97.4	18,207	87.3	2,110	10.1
55 years old and over	34,434	171	0.5	—	—	3	—	4	—	165	0.5	34,263	99.5	26,676	77.5	7,587	22.0

— Represents zero or rounds to zero.

SOURCE: "Table 1. Enrollment Status of the Population 3 Years Old and Over, by Sex, Age, Race, Hispanic Origin, Foreign Born, and Foreign-Born Parentage: October 2003," U.S. Census Bureau, Current Population Survey, May 2005, http://www.census.gov/population/www/socdemo/school/cps2003.html (accessed June 7, 2005)

TABLE 2.3

Percent of 16- to 24-year-olds who were status dropouts, by sex and race/ethnicity, 1972–2001

	Male				Female			
Year	Total[a]	White	Black	Hispanic	Total[a]	White	Black	Hispanic
1972	14.1	11.6	22.3	33.7	15.1	12.8	20.5	34.8
1974	14.2	12.0	20.1	33.8	14.3	11.8	22.1	22.1
1976	14.1	12.1	21.2	30.3	14.2	11.8	19.9	32.3
1978	14.6	12.2	22.5	33.6	13.9	11.6	18.3	33.1
1980	15.1	12.3	20.8	37.2	13.1	10.5	17.7	33.2
1982	14.5	12.0	21.2	30.5	13.3	10.8	15.9	32.8
1984	14.0	11.9	16.8	30.6	12.3	10.1	14.3	29.0
1986	13.1	10.3	15.0	32.8	11.4	9.1	13.5	27.2
1988	13.5	10.3	15.0	36.0	12.2	8.9	14.0	35.4
1990	12.3	9.3	11.9	34.3	11.8	8.7	14.4	30.3
1991	13.0	8.9	13.5	39.2	11.9	8.9	13.7	31.1
1992[b]	11.3	8.0	12.5	32.1	10.7	7.4	14.8	26.6
1993[b]	11.2	8.2	12.6	28.1	10.9	7.6	14.4	26.9
1994[b]	12.3	8.0	14.1	31.6	10.6	7.5	11.3	28.1
1995[b]	12.2	9.0	11.1	30.0	11.7	8.2	12.9	30.0
1996[b]	11.4	7.3	13.5	30.3	10.9	7.3	12.5	28.3
1997[b]	11.9	8.5	13.3	27.0	10.1	6.7	13.5	23.4
1998[b]	13.3	8.6	15.5	33.5	10.3	6.9	12.2	25.0
1999[b]	11.9	7.7	12.1	31.0	10.5	6.9	13.0	26.0
2000[b]	12.0	7.0	15.3	31.8	9.9	6.9	11.1	23.5
2001[b]	12.2	7.9	13.0	31.6	9.3	6.7	9.0	22.1

[a]Included in the total but not shown separately are dropouts from other racial/ethnic groups.
[b]Beginning in 1992, data reflect new wording of the educational attainment item in the Current Population Survey.
Note: Status dropouts are persons who are not enrolled in school and who are not high school completers. People who have received GED credentials are counted as completers.

SOURCE: "Table 19. Percent of 16- to 24-Year-Olds Who Were Status Dropouts, by Sex and Race/Ethnicity: Various Years 1972 to 2001," in *Trends in Educational Equity of Girls & Women: 2004*, National Center for Education Statistics, U.S. Department of Education, NCES 2005-016, November 2004, http://nces.ed.gov/pubs2005/2005016.pdf (accessed June 7, 2005)

elementary school enrollment of males (97.5%) and females (97.9%) was about equal. A slightly higher proportion of sixteen- to seventeen-year-old males (93.2%) than females (92.4%) were enrolled in high school. Women led enrollment at the college undergraduate level; among eighteen- to nineteen-year-olds, 41.7% of males and 51.6% of females were enrolled in college. Until 1979, the reverse was true.

In 2001 a smaller proportion of sixteen- to twenty-four-year-old females (9.3%) than males (12.2%) were high school dropouts. (See Table 2.3.) Female dropout rates fell below male rates in 1976. Although the dropout rate for both males and females had decreased between 1972 and 2001, the decrease was much larger for females (15.1% to 9.3%) than males (14.1% to 12.2%). In 2001 the gender difference was true for all race/ethnic groups. The dropout rate was 6.7% for white females and 7.9% for white males; 9% for African-American females and 13% for African-American males; and 22.1% for Hispanic females and 31.6% for Hispanic males.

According to the NCES, among high school seniors in 2001, 62.4% of girls and 51.1% of boys planned to graduate from a four-year college. This was up from 33.6% of girls and 35.6% of boys in 1980. Among girls in 2001, 19.9% planned to graduate from a two-year college program, as did 15.5% of boys, up from 13.6% of girls and 9.6% of boys in 1980. Only 7.9% of females

and 9.9% of males planned to attend a technical or vocational school after graduation. Among girls, 24.9% planned to attend graduate or professional schools, up drastically from 9.8% in 1980. Among senior boys, 16.1% planned to go on to graduate or professional school, up from 11.5% in 1980 ("Table 23. Percent of High School Seniors Reporting Plans for Postsecondary Education, by Sex and Program Type: 1980, 1990, and 2001," in *Trends in Educational Equity of Girls & Women: 2004*, National Center for Education Statistics, U.S. Department of Education, NCES 2005–016, November 2004).

Test Scores

From 1992 to 2003 girls consistently scored higher than boys in reading exams at every age level. (See Figure 2.1.) Although boys have tended to score better than girls in mathematics, by 2003 the difference among all ages was three or fewer points. (See Figure 2.2.) Girls score below boys in science at every age level. In fact, between 1996 and 2000 girls' science scores in grades four, eight, and twelve declined several points. (See Figure 2.3.)

SATs. Female college-bound high school seniors score below males on both the verbal and mathematics sections of the SAT (formerly called the Scholastic Assessment Test), although this gender gap began narrowing slowly after 1991. According to the College

FIGURE 2.1

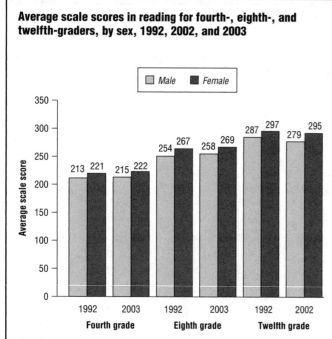

Average scale scores in reading for fourth-, eighth-, and twelfth-graders, by sex, 1992, 2002, and 2003

Note: These test scores are from the National Assessment of Educational Progress (NAEP). Accommodations were not permitted for the 1992 assessment. Scale ranges from 0 to 500.

SOURCE: "Figure 5-A. Average Scale Scores in Reading for Fourth-, Eighth- and Twelfth-Graders, by Sex: 1992, 2002, and 2003," in *Trends in Educational Equity of Girls & Women: 2004*, National Center for Education Statistics, U.S. Department of Education, NCES 2005-016, November 2004, http://nces.ed.gov/pubs2005/2005016.pdf (accessed June 7, 2005)

Board (http://www.collegeboard.com/prod_downloads/about/news_info/cbsenior/yr2004/CBS2004Report.pdf), women averaged eight points lower than men on the verbal exam (504 versus 512) and thirty-six points lower on math (537 versus 501) in 2004. This difference between male and female scores is a subject of much debate and controversy. The College Board argues that the larger number of female test takers contributes to girls' lower scores, since lower average scores are to be expected when more people from a self-selected population take the exam. Since the early 1970s more women than men have taken the SAT; in 2004, 1.4 million students took the SATs, 53.5% of them female. Critics question if this is enough to explain the difference considering that 61% of students who described themselves as having an A+ grade point average, 62% of those with an A average, and 58% of those with an A- average were females. In contrast, 58% of students who described themselves as having a C average and 59% of those with a D, E, or F were male.

FairTest: The National Center for Fair and Open Testing cites many studies that suggest that the gender disparity in SAT mathematics test scores is due to gender bias built into the tests ("Gender Bias in College Admissions Test," http://www.fairtest.org/facts/genderbias.htm). The organization questions the validity of the SAT's scores. They note that the SAT exam is designed to predict students' first-year college grades, yet while women consistently earn higher grades throughout high school and college, they earn lower scores on the SAT. FairTest believes several factors may contribute to this disparity: biased test questions, the multiple-choice format, and the timed nature of the test.

Others see the gender difference in SAT scores as confirmation of the stereotypical view of women as having less ability in math and science than men. For example, in 2005 the president of Harvard University, Lawrence H. Summers, began a firestorm of controversy by suggesting that the small number of women who held high-level positions in science and engineering is due in part to women's lesser innate mathematic and science ability ("Remarks at NBER Conference on Diversifying the Science & Engineering Workforce," January 14, 2005, http://www.president.harvard.edu/speeches/2005/nber.html). Many people find this view to be an offensive stereotype. Anne Tweed of the National Science Teachers Association (NSTA) responded to this controversy by arguing that the gender difference in math and science was due not to differences in innate ability, but to gender inequity in education, a position with which the College Board agrees. Tweed supports the NSTA position statement "Gender Equity in Science Education," which gives science teachers guidelines for equitable education.

Advanced Placement

Gender differences are also evident in the types of high-level classes and advanced placement exams that males and females pursue in high school. The Congressional Commission on the Advancement of Women and Minorities in Science, Engineering, and Technology Development (CAWMSET) reported in 2000 that high school girls were taking advanced mathematics and science courses at the same rate as boys. And in 2002 more females (54.4%) than males (45.6%) took advanced placement exams ("Table 22-B. Number and Percentage Distribution of Advanced Placement Examinations Taken, by Subject Area and Sex: 2002," in *Trends in Educational Equity of Girls and Women: 2004*, National Center for Education Statistics, U.S. Department of Education, NCES 2005–016, November 2004). Nevertheless, far more boys than girls took advanced placement exams in calculus (85.7% versus 14.3%), computer science (85.7% versus 14.3%), and science (57.3% versus 42.7%). Far more girls than boys took advanced placement exams in social studies (54.6% versus 45.4%), English (63.5% versus 36.5%), and foreign languages (64.9% versus 35.1%). Of the SAT-takers who were

FIGURE 2.2

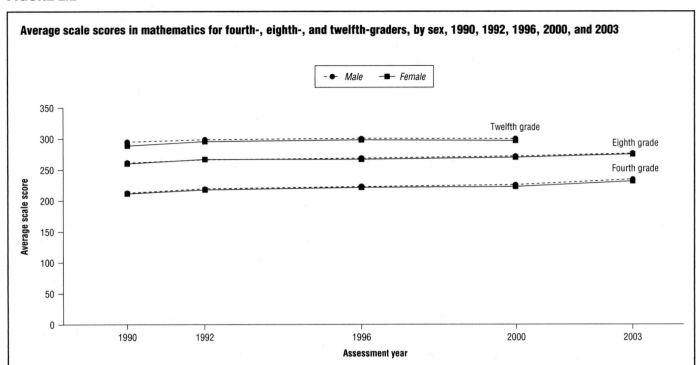

Average scale scores in mathematics for fourth-, eighth-, and twelfth-graders, by sex, 1990, 1992, 1996, 2000, and 2003

Note: These test scores are from the National Assessment of Educational Progress (NAEP) Main Assessment. Scale ranges from 0 to 500. Accommodations were not permitted for the 1990 and 1992 assessments.

SOURCE: "Figure 6-A. Average Scale Scores in Mathematics for Fourth-, Eighth-, and Twelfth-Graders, by Sex: 1990, 1992, 1996, 2000, and 2003," in *Trends in Educational Equity of Girls & Women: 2004*, National Center for Education Statistics, U.S. Department of Education, NCES 2005-016, November 2004, http://nces.ed.gov/pubs2005/2005016.pdf (accessed June 7, 2005)

FIGURE 2.3

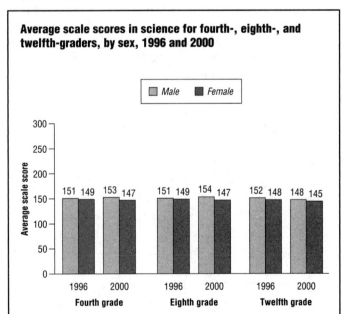

Average scale scores in science for fourth-, eighth-, and twelfth-graders, by sex, 1996 and 2000

Note: These test scores are from the National Assessment of Educational Progress (NAEP) Main Assessment. Scale ranges from 0 to 300.

SOURCE: "Figure 6-B. Average Scale Scores in Science for Fourth-, Eighth-, and Twelfth-Graders, by Sex: 1996 and 2000," in *Trends in Educational Equity of Girls & Women: 2004*, National Center for Education Statistics, U.S. Department of Education, NCES 2005-016, November 2004, http://nces.ed.gov/pubs2005/2005016.pdf (accessed June 7, 2005)

planning to major in engineering and computer science, three-quarters were male. By the eighth grade, twice as many boys as girls were interested in science and engineering careers. Although eighth-grade girls did as well as boys in math, their interest and self-confidence in math had diminished since their younger years. Fewer girls than boys enrolled in computer science classes or felt confident using computers. Biology was the only scientific field that attracted more high school girls than boys. These differences are attributed to the attitudes of parents, teachers, and peers who—consciously or not—steer girls away from math and science. Furthermore, female role models in science and technology remain rare, and women scientists and engineers are underrepresented in media coverage.

HIGHER EDUCATION

College Enrollment

In the 1930s approximately equal numbers of men and women attended college, but the overall numbers were quite small. Between 1940 and 1970 the number of men who attended college increased dramatically as a result of the G.I. Bill, which offered tuition assistance to servicemen returning from World War II, the Korean conflict, and the Vietnam War. However, since the

1980s tremendous growth has occurred in the number of women attending colleges and universities.

In 1960 only 37.9% of females who had recently completed high school entered college, compared to 54% of males. (See Table 2.4.) Every year from 1974 to 2002, more women than men enrolled in college. By 2002, 68.4% of females who had recently completed high school entered college, while only 62.1% of males did. The total college enrollment of women who had completed high school in the past twelve months increased from 740,000 in 1990 to 947,000 in 2002, a 21.9% increase. The NCES projects, in *The Condition of Education 2005*, that college enrollment by women will continue to increase at a faster rate than male enrollment, reaching a new high each year through 2014.

Associate and Bachelor's Degrees

Women earned 15% of the bachelor's degrees awarded in 1969–70. Since 1977 they have earned more associate degrees then men, and since 1981 they have earned more bachelor's degrees than men. Between 1987–88 and 2000–01, the number of degrees awarded to women rose at all levels. In the academic year 2000–01, women were awarded 347,000 associate degrees; men were awarded 232,000 associate degrees. (See Figure 2.4.) By 2012–13, the number of associate degrees awarded to women is projected to increase to 451,000. About half of associate degrees awarded to women are academic and the other half are occupational.

Since 1987–88, women have earned an increasing percentage of bachelor's degrees. In 2000–01 women earned 712,000 bachelor's degrees and men earned 532,000. (See Figure 2.4.) The number of bachelor's degrees awarded yearly to women is projected to increase by 25.4% to 893,000 in 2012–13. In the same period the number of bachelor's degrees awarded to men is projected to increase by 15.8%, to 616,000.

FIELDS OF STUDY. The proportion of degrees earned by women in most major fields steadily increased after 1971 at all degree levels. In 2001–02 women earned high percentages of bachelor's degrees granted in such "traditional" female subjects as home economics (88%), health professions (85.5%), library science (75.7%), education (77.4%), psychology (77.5%), and English (68.6%). They earned much lower proportions of the degrees in traditionally male fields such as mechanics (4.3%), construction trades (9.9%), and engineering (20.7%). The number of bachelor's degrees in other fields, like business, parks and recreation, and social sciences and history, were equally earned by men and women. (See Table 2.5.)

Master's Degrees

Since 1985–86, women have earned more master's degrees every year than have men, and women's share of these degrees continues to increase. In 2000–01 women earned 58.5% of all master's degrees. (See Figure 2.5.) Fields of study for master's degrees were similar to those for bachelor's degrees in 2001–02. Women earned most of the master's degrees in home economics (85.1%), library science (81.8%), health professions and sciences (77.6%), education (76.4%), and psychology (76.4%). They earned 57.6% of the master's degrees in visual and performing arts and 57.8% of the degrees in biological sciences but only 33.3% of the degrees in computer science, 21.2% of the engineering degrees, and 37.6% of the degrees in physical sciences. (See Table 2.6.)

In 2001–02 women were awarded 41.1% of master's of business administration (MBA) degrees. (See Table 2.6.) An MBA degree is often a prerequisite for a successful business career. But the enrollment of women in MBA programs has not kept pace with their enrollment increases in other graduate programs. The admissions offices at several business schools explained some reasons for this. Women were less willing than men to meet the common requirement of working for several years before beginning their MBA studies. They worried that by postponing their education, they would be starting careers just when they hoped to start families. Women also worried that after spending as much as $130,000 to earn an MBA, they could not command salaries comparable to those of their male counterparts. In addition, women were worried about sexual harassment in the workplace and hitting the "glass ceiling" that prevents women from advancing in their careers beyond a certain level. Finally, they feared that if they chose to have children, they would be forced into the slower-moving career path called the "mommy track."

Doctoral Degrees

Both the number of female doctorates and the percentage of doctoral degrees going to women have increased steadily over the years. In 1960–61, women earned 1,112 doctoral degrees, 11% of the total. By 1987–88, women earned 12,000 doctoral degrees, 34.2% of the total degrees awarded. In 2000–01, women earned 20,000 doctoral degrees, 44.4% of the total. And by 2012–13, women are projected to earn almost 50% of all doctoral degrees awarded. (See Figure 2.5.)

In 2000–01 women earned the majority of doctoral degrees in education, health professions and related sciences, and psychology. (See Table 2.7.) Women earned only 16.5% of the doctoral degrees in engineering, 17.7% of doctoral degrees in computer and infor-

TABLE 2.4

College enrollment rates of recent high school completers, by sex, 1960–2002

[Numbers in thousands]

Year	High school completers[a]			Enrolled in college[b]					
	Total	Males	Females	Total		Males		Females	
				Number	Percent	Number	Percent	Number	Percent
1	2	3	4	5	6	7	8	9	10
1960	1,679	756	923	758	45.1	408	54.0	350	37.9
1961	1,763	790	973	847	48.0	445	56.3	402	41.3
1962	1,838	872	966	900	49.0	480	55.0	420	43.5
1963	1,741	794	947	784	45.0	415	52.3	369	39.0
1964	2,145	997	1,148	1,037	48.3	570	57.2	467	40.7
1965	2,659	1,254	1,405	1,354	50.9	718	57.3	636	45.3
1966	2,612	1,207	1,405	1,309	50.1	709	58.7	600	42.7
1967	2,525	1,142	1,383	1,311	51.9	658	57.6	653	47.2
1968	2,606	1,184	1,422	1,444	55.4	748	63.2	696	48.9
1969	2,842	1,352	1,490	1,516	53.3	812	60.1	704	47.2
1970	2,758	1,343	1,415	1,427	51.7	741	55.2	686	48.5
1971	2,875	1,371	1,504	1,538	53.5	790	57.6	749	49.8
1972	2,964	1,423	1,542	1,459	49.2	750	52.7	709	46.0
1973	3,058	1,460	1,599	1,424	46.6	730	50.0	694	43.4
1974	3,101	1,491	1,611	1,475	47.6	736	49.4	740	45.9
1975	3,185	1,513	1,672	1,615	50.7	796	52.6	818	49.0
1976	2,986	1,451	1,535	1,458	48.8	685	47.2	773	50.3
1977	3,141	1,483	1,659	1,590	50.6	773	52.1	817	49.3
1978	3,163	1,485	1,677	1,585	50.1	759	51.1	827	49.3
1979	3,160	1,475	1,685	1,559	49.3	744	50.4	815	48.4
1980	3,088	1,498	1,589	1,523	49.3	700	46.7	823	51.8
1981	3,056	1,491	1,565	1,648	53.9	817	54.8	831	53.1
1982	3,100	1,509	1,592	1,569	50.6	741	49.1	828	52.0
1983	2,963	1,389	1,573	1,562	52.7	721	51.9	841	53.4
1984	3,012	1,429	1,584	1,663	55.2	801	56.0	862	54.5
1985	2,668	1,287	1,381	1,540	57.7	755	58.6	785	56.8
1986	2,786	1,332	1,454	1,498	53.8	743	55.8	755	51.9
1987	2,647	1,278	1,369	1,503	56.8	746	58.3	757	55.3
1988	2,673	1,334	1,339	1,575	58.9	761	57.1	814	60.7
1989	2,450	1,204	1,246	1,460	59.6	693	57.6	767	61.6
1990	2,362	1,173	1,189	1,420	60.1	680	58.0	740	62.2
1991	2,276	1,140	1,136	1,423	62.5	660	57.9	763	67.1
1992	2,397	1,216	1,180	1,483	61.9	729	60.0	754	63.8
1993	2,342	1,120	1,223	1,467	62.6	670	59.9	797	65.2
1994	2,517	1,244	1,273	1,559	61.9	754	60.6	805	63.2
1995	2,599	1,238	1,361	1,610	61.9	775	62.6	835	61.3
1996	2,660	1,297	1,363	1,729	65.0	779	60.1	950	69.7
1997	2,769	1,354	1,415	1,856	67.0	860	63.6	995	70.3
1998	2,810	1,452	1,358	1,844	65.6	906	62.4	938	69.1
1999	2,897	1,474	1,423	1,822	62.9	905	61.4	917	64.4
2000	2,756	1,251	1,505	1,745	63.3	749	59.9	996	66.2
2001	2,545	1,275	1,270	1,569	61.7	762	59.7	808	63.6
2002	2,796	1,412	1,384	1,824	65.2	877	62.1	947	68.4

[a]Individuals age 16 to 24 who graduated from high school or completed a GED during the preceding 12 months.
[b]Enrollment in college as of October of each year for individuals age 16 to 24 who completed high school during the preceding 12 months.
Note: Data are based upon sample surveys of the civilian population. High school graduate data in this table differ from figures appearing in other tables because of varying survey procedures and coverage. High school graduates include GED recipients. Some data revised from previously published figures. Detail may not sum to totals due to rounding.

SOURCE: Thomas D. Snyder, Alexandra G. Tan, and Charlene M. Hoffman, "Table 186. College Enrollment and Enrollment Rates of Recent High School Completers, by Sex: 1960 to 2002," in *Digest of Education Statistics 2003*, National Center for Education Statistics, U.S. Department of Education, NCES 2005-025, December 2004, http://nces.ed.gov/programs/digest/d03/tables/pdf/table186.pdf (accessed May 25, 2005)

mation sciences, 26.8% of doctoral degrees in physical sciences, and 33.5% of doctoral degrees in business management.

In 1976–77 non-Hispanic white women earned 84.3% of all doctorate degrees; by 2001–2002 that percentage had dropped to 66.4%%. African-American women earned 6% of all doctorate degrees in 1976–77 and 7.2% in 2001–2002. Hispanic women earned 1.7% of all doc-

torate degrees in 1976–77 and 3.8% in 2001–2002. Asian-American women earned 1.5% of all doctorate degrees in 1976–77 and 5.3% in 2001–2002 (*Digest of Education Statistics, 2003*, National Center for Education Statistics).

First-Professional Degrees

A first-professional degree signifies completion of the academic requirements for beginning practice in a given profession and a level of professional skill beyond

FIGURE 2.4

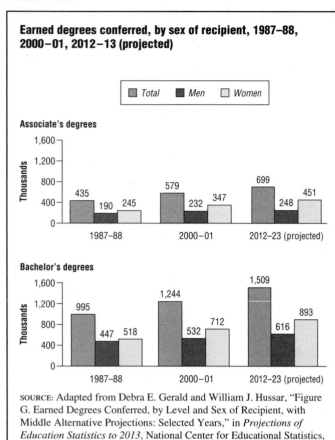

Earned degrees conferred, by sex of recipient, 1987–88, 2000–01, 2012–13 (projected)

Total ■ Men □ Women

Associate's degrees

Bachelor's degrees

SOURCE: Adapted from Debra E. Gerald and William J. Hussar, "Figure G. Earned Degrees Conferred, by Level and Sex of Recipient, with Middle Alternative Projections: Selected Years," in *Projections of Education Statistics to 2013*, National Center for Educational Statistics, U.S. Department of Education, NCES 2004-013, October 2003, http://nces.ed.gov/pubs2004/2004013.pdf (accessed May 25, 2005)

that normally required for a bachelor's degree. It is based on a program that requires at least two academic years of work before entrance and a total of at least six years of work to complete the program. These degrees include fields such as dentistry, medicine, and law, among others.

In 2000–01 women earned 36,845 first-professional degrees (46.2% of total) in fields including medicine, dentistry, pharmacy, veterinary medicine, theology, and law, compared to 42,862 such degrees awarded to men. (See Figure 2.5.) By 2012–13 women are expected to earn 47.9% of all first-professional degrees. As recently as 1987–88, women earned only 35.2% of all first-professional degrees.

Almost half (49%) of women's first-professional degrees were in law in 2001–02. (See Table 2.8.) In fact, women earned almost half (48%) of all law degrees that year, up from just 7% in 1970–71. Medical doctor (MD) degrees accounted for 17.7% of professional degrees to women, and 44.4% of all MD degrees went to women, up from 9% in 1970–71. Women earned 65.7% of the degrees in pharmacy, 71.5% of those in veterinary medicine, 38.5% of dentistry degrees, and 32.9% of theology degrees.

In 1976–77 non-Hispanic white women earned 88.9% of all first-professional degrees granted to women; by 2001–2002 that percentage had dropped to 69.8%. African-American women earned 6.5% of all first-professional degrees in 1976–77 and 9.4% in 2001–2002. Hispanic women earned 1.5% of all first professional degrees in 1976–77 and 5% in 2001–2002. Asian-American women earned 2% of all first-professional degrees in 1976–77 and 13% in 2001–2002 (*Digest of Education Statistics, 2003*, National Center for Education Statistics).

Distance Education

For a number of reasons, including the increase in the number of single mothers who must work to support a family, distance education for women has become a more popular option for learning in recent years. According to the NCES, in the 2000–01 academic year there were an estimated three million enrollments in all distance education courses offered by two- and four-year institutions. (See Figure 2.6.) The majority of these enrollments (more than 2.8 million) were in college-level courses, with 82% at the undergraduate level. Nearly half (48%) of all distance education enrollments were in public two-year institutions. At the graduate level, public four-year institutions had a larger number of enrollments than did private four-year institutions (60% versus 40%).

ACHIEVING EDUCATIONAL EQUITY

Single-Sex or Coeducational Schools?

Prior to the late 1960s many private high schools and colleges were single-sex schools. By the end of the twentieth century, most schools were coeducational. But in the 1990s there was renewed interest and an increase in the number of single-sex schools, particularly for girls.

In 1992 the American Association of University Women (AAUW) published a study, *How Schools Shortchange Girls*, which reported that teachers paid more attention to boys and that girls received less encouragement in math and science. A second AAUW study, *Gaining a Foothold: Women's Transitions through Work and College* (1999), found that high school boys were more likely than girls to take all three core science courses (biology, chemistry, and physics) and that far fewer girls than boys took physics. Girls made up only a small percentage of students in computer science and computer design classes.

Another AAUW study, *Separated by Sex: A Critical Look at Single-Sex Education for Girls* (1998), found that girls could succeed in co-ed classrooms if they were treated fairly and that all children excelled in small classes with a strong curriculum. AAUW Educational Foundation president Maggie Ford concluded that

TABLE 2.5

Bachelor's degrees conferred by degree-granting institutions, by sex, racial/ethnic group, and major field of study, 2001–02

Major field of study	Total							Men							Women						
	Total	White, non-Hispanic	Black, non-Hispanic	Hispanic	Asian/Pacific Islander	American Indian/Alaska Native	Non-resident alien	Total	White, non-Hispanic	Black, non-Hispanic	Hispanic	Asian/Pacific Islander	American Indian/Alaska Native	Non-resident alien	Total	White, non-Hispanic	Black, non-Hispanic	Hispanic	Asian/Pacific Islander	American Indian/Alaska Native	Non-resident alien
1	2	3	4	5	6	7	8	9	10	11	12	13	14	15	16	17	18	19	20	21	22
All fields, total	1,291,900	958,585	116,624	82,969	83,101	9,165	41,456	549,816	414,885	39,194	32,953	37,666	3,625	21,493	742,084	543,700	77,430	50,016	45,435	5,540	19,963
Agriculture and natural resources	23,353	20,659	653	744	760	191	346	12,643	11,365	281	378	334	107	178	10,710	9,294	372	366	426	84	168
Architecture and related programs	8,808	6,518	348	640	729	58	515	5,224	3,932	203	395	360	39	295	3,584	2,586	145	245	369	19	220
Area, ethnic, and cultural studies	6,557	3,841	881	775	758	132	170	2,042	1,193	290	239	223	46	51	4,515	2,648	591	536	535	86	119
Biological sciences, life sciences	60,256	42,831	4,807	3,256	7,485	426	1,451	23,612	17,263	1,329	1,307	3,008	169	536	36,644	25,568	3,478	1,949	4,477	257	915
Business	281,330	199,906	28,153	17,557	20,083	1,810	13,821	140,566	105,165	10,088	8,140	8,961	858	7,354	140,764	94,741	18,065	9,417	11,122	952	6,467
Communications	62,791	49,483	5,540	3,510	2,368	344	1,546	22,914	18,474	1,873	1,127	765	122	553	39,877	31,009	3,667	2,383	1,603	222	993
Communications technologies	1,110	781	149	94	62	5	19	699	478	76	78	53	4	10	411	303	73	16	9	1	9
Computer and information sciences	47,299	28,311	5,030	2,442	7,408	239	3,869	34,248	22,111	2,670	1,689	4,988	152	2,638	13,051	6,200	2,360	753	2,420	87	1,231
Construction trades	202	182	6	10	1	0	3	182	166	4	10	1	0	1	20	16	2	0	0	0	2
Education	106,383	90,475	6,976	4,893	1,916	1,018	1,105	24,051	20,102	1,822	1,096	474	239	318	82,332	70,373	5,154	3,797	1,442	779	787
Engineering	59,481	41,192	3,099	3,208	7,400	320	4,262	47,171	33,492	1,966	2,484	5,475	243	3,511	12,310	7,700	1,133	724	1,925	77	751
Engineering-related technologies*	14,117	10,567	1,387	875	739	102	447	12,480	9,536	1,077	746	652	87	382	1,637	1,031	310	129	87	15	65
English language and literature/letters	53,162	43,129	4,049	2,908	2,233	308	535	16,704	13,892	1,029	913	634	88	148	36,458	29,237	3,020	1,995	1,599	220	387
Foreign languages and literatures	15,318	10,885	622	2,558	726	73	454	4,413	3,276	153	641	211	26	106	10,905	7,609	469	1,917	515	47	348
Health professions and related sciences	70,517	53,533	8,011	3,700	3,961	528	784	10,257	7,418	1,041	721	819	86	172	60,260	46,115	6,970	2,979	3,142	442	612
Home economics and vocational home economics	18,153	14,722	1,659	724	653	123	272	2,182	1,715	235	101	74	12	45	15,971	13,007	1,424	623	579	111	227
Law and legal studies	1,971	1,359	303	146	136	15	12	588	414	58	46	62	4	4	1,383	945	245	100	74	11	8
Liberal arts and sciences, general studies, and humanities	39,333	27,786	4,688	4,106	1,572	442	739	12,902	9,630	1,399	989	460	138	286	26,431	18,156	3,289	3,117	1,112	304	453
Library science	74	67	0	1	4	0	2	18	15	0	0	2	0	1	56	52	0	1	2	0	1
Mathematics	12,395	9,190	935	695	1,057	59	459	6,608	4,970	417	356	550	31	284	5,787	4,220	518	339	507	28	175
Mechanics and repairers	164	104	18	21	13	0	8	157	100	17	20	13	0	7	7	4	1	1	0	0	1
Multi/interdisciplinary studies	27,629	19,866	2,739	2,793	1,474	194	563	8,948	6,616	824	623	579	65	241	18,681	13,250	1,915	2,170	895	129	322
Parks, recreation, leisure and fitness studies	20,554	16,795	1,751	1,068	447	157	336	9,919	7,902	951	591	222	69	184	10,635	8,893	800	477	225	88	152
Philosophy and religion	9,306	7,661	481	472	474	56	162	5,688	4,684	273	325	280	31	95	3,618	2,977	208	147	194	25	67
Physical sciences and science technologies	17,851	13,900	1,142	709	1,379	114	607	10,314	8,316	463	424	695	63	353	7,537	5,584	679	285	684	51	254
Precision production trades	468	391	25	24	16	1	11	324	268	21	18	9	1	7	144	123	4	6	7	0	4
Protective services	25,536	17,262	4,484	2,659	715	306	110	13,727	9,980	1,812	1,284	441	156	54	11,809	7,282	2,672	1,375	274	150	56
Psychology	76,671	55,824	8,107	6,381	4,426	567	1,366	17,275	12,525	1,614	1,524	1,171	131	310	59,396	43,299	6,493	4,857	3,255	436	1,056
Public administration and services	19,392	12,529	4,036	1,847	595	178	207	3,706	2,316	757	378	173	40	42	15,686	10,213	3,279	1,469	422	138	165
R.O.T.C. and military sciences	3	3	0	0	0	0	0	3	3	0	0	0	0	0	0	0	0	0	0	0	0
Social sciences and history	132,874	96,346	12,530	9,917	9,258	886	3,937	64,170	48,921	4,493	4,269	4,198	385	1,904	68,704	47,425	8,037	5,648	5,060	501	2,033
Theological studies and religious vocations	7,785	6,699	411	258	161	28	228	5,293	4,596	247	164	109	15	162	2,492	2,103	164	94	52	13	66
Transportation and material moving workers	4,020	3,339	220	181	101	29	150	3,555	2,949	197	153	96	22	138	465	390	23	28	5	7	12
Visual and performing arts	66,773	52,224	3,373	3,787	3,983	456	2,950	27,130	21,020	1,506	1,718	1,571	196	1,119	39,643	31,204	1,867	2,069	2,412	260	1,831
Not classified by field of study	264	225	11	10	8	0	10	103	82	8	6	3	0	4	161	143	3	4	5	0	6

*Excludes "construction trades" and "mechanics and repairers," which are listed separately.

Note: Reported racial/ethnic distributions of students by level of degree, field of degree, and sex were used to estimate race/ethnicity for students whose race/ethnicity was not reported. "Agriculture and natural resources" includes agricultural business and production, agricultural sciences, and conservation and renewable natural resources; and "business" includes business management and administrative services, marketing operations/marketing and distribution, and consumer and personal services.

SOURCE: Thomas D. Snyder, Alexandra G. Tan, and Charlene M. Hoffman. "Table 265. Bachelor's Degrees Conferred by Degree-Granting Institutions, by Sex, Racial/Ethnic Group, and Major Field of Study: 2001–02," in *Digest of Education Statistics, 2003*, National Center for Education Statistics, U.S. Department of Education, NCES 2005-025, December 2004, http://nces.ed.gov/programs/digest/d03/tables/pdf/table265.pdf (accessed May 26, 2005)

FIGURE 2.5

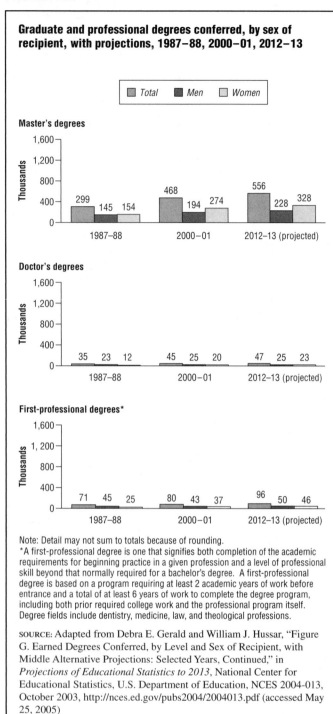

Graduate and professional degrees conferred, by sex of recipient, with projections, 1987–88, 2000–01, 2012–13

Note: Detail may not sum to totals because of rounding.

*A first-professional degree is one that signifies both completion of the academic requirements for beginning practice in a given profession and a level of professional skill beyond that normally required for a bachelor's degree. A first-professional degree is based on a program requiring at least 2 academic years of work before entrance and a total of at least 6 years of work to complete the degree program, including both prior required college work and the professional program itself. Degree fields include dentistry, medicine, law, and theological professions.

SOURCE: Adapted from Debra E. Gerald and William J. Hussar, "Figure G. Earned Degrees Conferred, by Level and Sex of Recipient, with Middle Alternative Projections: Selected Years, Continued," in *Projections of Educational Statistics to 2013*, National Center for Educational Statistics, U.S. Department of Education, NCES 2004-013, October 2003, http://nces.ed.gov/pubs2004/2004013.pdf (accessed May 25, 2005)

"separating by sex is not the answer to inequities in the schools."

In January 2000 the Goodman Research Group conducted a survey for the National Coalition of Girls' Schools (NCGS). They surveyed 4,274 alumnae from the graduating classes of 1983, 1987, 1991, and 1995, from sixty-four NCGS schools. The report, *Achievement, Leadership and Success: A Report on Educational, Professional, and Life Outcomes at Girls' Schools in the United States*, found that a large majority of the alumnae believed that girls' schools were more relevant to the academic, personal, and social development of females, as compared with coeducational schools. A large majority of the alumnae (91%) rated their schools as very good or excellent at challenging students academically and preparing them for college. Most respondents believed that they were better prepared for college, both academically and socially, than were their peers from coeducational high schools. In particular, they felt that their schools had provided them with more leadership opportunities and had encouraged them in math, science, and technology. The NCGS alumnae had higher-than-average SAT scores, and almost all attended college, where 13% of them majored in math and science, as compared to 2% of females nationwide. Most alumnae (78%) rated their schools as very good or excellent at instilling self-confidence in students. Most (88%) said they would choose a girls' school again, and 84% said they would encourage their daughters to attend a girls' school.

Educators have found that girls in single-sex classrooms participate much more than they do in coeducational classes. At the Bronx High School of Science, girls in a single-sex physics class worked together cooperatively, learned concepts better, and asked more questions. The co-ed physics class was dominated by boys and was very competitive, with little interaction among the students.

Increasingly, public school systems are experimenting with single-sex education. In 1996 the Young Women's Leadership School opened in East Harlem with fifty-six seventh-grade girls. In 1999–2000 the school served 275 middle and high school girls. In 1999 their reading and math scores far exceeded the averages for students across New York City. According to the National Association for Single Sex Public Education, in 2004–05, 161 public schools across the nation offered gender-separate educational opportunities.

The NCGS reported a 23% increase in enrollment at girls' schools from 1991 to 2005. During that period thirty-five new girls' schools opened in the United States. Although only 2.5% of college women attend a single-sex college, enrollment has been increasing there as well. The Women's College Coalition reports that graduates of women's colleges are more likely to continue on for doctorates in traditionally male fields like math, science, and engineering, are more likely to hold leadership positions and top jobs, have higher self-esteem, and are more likely to graduate than women enrolled in coeducational schools.

Military Schools

As increasing numbers of women sought out all-female institutions, other women were trying to break

TABLE 2.6

Master's degrees conferred by degree-granting institutions, by racial/ethnic group, major field of study, and sex of student, 2001–02

Major field of study	Total							Men							Women						
	Total	White, non-His-panic	Black, non-His-panic	His-panic	Asian/ Pacific Islander	American Indian/ Alaska Native	Non-resident alien	Total	White, non-His-panic	Black, non-His-panic	His-panic	Asian/ Pacific Islander	American Indian/ Alaska Native	Non-resident alien	Total	White, non-His-panic	Black, non-His-panic	His-panic	Asian/ Pacific Islander	American Indian/ Alaska Native	Non-resident alien
1	2	3	4	5	6	7	8	9	10	11	12	13	14	15	16	17	18	19	20	21	22
All fields, total	**482,118**	**327,635**	**40,373**	**22,387**	**25,414**	**2,626**	**63,683**	**199,120**	**128,770**	**11,796**	**8,431**	**11,749**	**994**	**37,380**	**282,998**	**198,865**	**28,577**	**13,956**	**13,665**	**1,632**	**26,303**
Agriculture and natural resources	4,519	3,454	122	117	139	27	660	2,345	1,806	61	71	50	19	338	2,174	1,648	61	46	89	8	322
Architecture and related programs	4,566	2,797	164	220	267	14	1,104	2,606	1,660	76	122	117	11	620	1,960	1,137	88	98	150	3	484
Area, ethnic, and cultural studies	1,578	959	130	125	106	23	235	610	391	36	62	40	6	75	968	568	94	63	66	17	160
Biological sciences/life sciences	6,205	4,265	303	261	552	35	789	2,616	1,846	92	123	239	14	302	3,589	2,419	211	138	313	21	487
Business	120,785	76,435	10,434	5,024	8,352	510	20,030	71,157	46,963	3,962	2,862	4,745	315	12,310	49,628	29,472	6,472	2,162	3,607	195	7,720
Communications	5,510	3,512	532	189	251	19	1,007	1,906	1,294	116	59	79	5	353	3,604	2,218	416	130	172	14	654
Communications technologies	549	312	36	11	22	2	166	295	181	14	6	9	1	84	254	131	22	5	13	1	82
Computer and information sciences	16,113	5,144	745	307	2,264	36	7,617	10,753	3,774	403	212	1,329	22	5,013	5,360	1,370	342	95	935	14	2,604
Construction trades	9	2	1	2	0	0	4	8	2	1	2	0	0	3	1	0	0	0	0	0	1
Education	136,579	107,793	13,069	7,751	3,095	955	3,916	32,172	25,471	2,829	1,819	694	237	1,122	104,407	82,322	10,240	5,932	2,401	718	2,794
Engineering	26,015	11,215	794	775	2,378	61	10,792	20,512	8,974	512	560	1,758	44	8,664	5,503	2,241	282	215	620	17	2,128
Engineering-related technologies*	896	583	75	21	36	4	177	647	430	49	17	24	3	124	249	153	26	4	12	1	53
English language and literature/letters	7,268	5,897	349	243	250	43	486	2,326	1,931	74	85	80	17	139	4,942	3,966	275	158	170	26	347
Foreign languages and literatures	2,861	1,598	55	351	115	7	735	881	529	17	89	33	4	209	1,980	1,069	38	262	82	3	526
Health professions and related sciences	43,644	33,012	3,249	1,740	3,304	227	2,112	9,797	6,883	568	456	998	74	818	33,847	26,129	2,681	1,284	2,306	153	1,294
Home economics and vocational home economics	2,616	1,911	270	130	104	22	179	390	276	36	21	10	6	41	2,226	1,635	234	109	94	16	138
Law and legal studies	4,053	1,304	176	167	211	11	2,184	2,360	799	82	86	114	6	1,273	1,693	505	94	81	97	5	911
Liberal arts and sciences, general studies, and humanities	2,754	2,156	214	119	72	20	173	1,030	813	66	47	32	7	65	1,724	1,343	148	72	40	13	108
Library science	5,113	4,280	259	212	152	31	179	932	767	35	41	30	3	56	4,181	3,513	224	171	122	28	123
Mathematics	3,487	1,727	126	85	239	10	1,300	2,009	986	55	54	131	9	774	1,478	741	71	31	108	1	526
Multi/interdisciplinary studies	3,211	2,236	250	156	150	24	395	1,237	852	63	61	56	7	198	1,974	1,384	187	95	94	17	197
Parks, recreation, leisure and fitness studies	2,754	2,231	210	71	56	9	177	1,358	1,083	102	42	25	3	103	1,396	1,148	108	29	31	6	74
Philosophy and religion	1,334	1,063	60	36	64	4	107	830	647	37	22	42	3	79	504	416	23	14	22	1	28
Physical sciences and science technologies	5,034	3,056	149	148	267	21	1,393	3,142	1,916	74	91	146	11	904	1,892	1,140	75	57	121	10	489
Precision production trades	2	0	0	1	1	0	0	1	0	0	0	1	0	0	1	0	0	1	0	0	0
Protective services	2,935	2,119	482	159	59	25	91	1,613	1,222	205	88	29	12	57	1,322	897	277	71	30	13	34
Psychology	14,888	10,931	1,837	921	592	111	496	3,517	2,610	381	231	129	31	135	11,371	8,321	1,456	690	463	80	361
Public administration and services	25,448	16,889	4,386	1,743	882	228	1,320	6,505	4,145	1,010	446	215	53	636	18,943	12,744	3,376	1,297	667	175	684
Social sciences and history	14,112	8,660	1,022	670	570	80	3,110	6,941	4,328	403	295	227	38	1,650	7,171	4,332	619	375	343	42	1,460
Theological studies and religious vocations	4,952	3,570	334	164	276	10	598	3,064	2,178	178	105	165	6	432	1,888	1,392	156	59	111	4	166
Transportation and material moving workers	709	604	32	31	11	3	28	633	541	29	28	8	3	24	76	63	3	3	8	0	4
Visual and performing arts	11,595	7,906	508	437	577	54	2,113	4,912	3,464	230	228	194	24	772	6,683	4,442	278	209	383	30	1,341
Not classified by field of study	24	14	0	0	0	0	10	15	8	0	0	0	0	7	9	6	0	0	0	0	3

*Excludes "construction trades" which is listed separately.

SOURCE: Thomas D. Snyder, Alexandra G. Tan, and Charlene M. Hoffman, "Table 268. Master's Degrees Conferred by Degree-Granting Institutions, by Sex, Racial/Ethnic Group, and Major Field of Study: 2001–02," in *Digest of Education Statistics 2003*, National Center for Education Statistics, U.S. Department of Education, NCES 2005-025, December 2004, http://nces.ed.gov/programs/digest/d03/tables/pdf/table268.pdf (accessed May 25, 2005)

TABLE 2.7

Percent of female doctorate recipients by broad field,1969–70 to 2000

Degree and selected field of study	1969–70	1974–75	1979–80	1984–85	1989–90	1994–95	1999–2000	2000–01
Doctor's degrees	13.3	21.3	29.7	34.1	36.4	39.4	44.1	44.9
Business management	1.6	4.2	14.7	17.2	25.2	27.3	31.9	33.5
Biological sciences/life sciences	14.3	22.0	26.0	32.8	37.7	40.3	44.1	44.1
Computer and information sciences	1.9	6.6	11.3	10.1	14.8	18.2	16.9	17.7
Education	19.8	30.4	43.9	52.0	57.3	62.0	64.6	64.9
Engineering	0.7	2.1	3.8	6.4	8.9	11.9	15.5	16.5
Health professions and related sciences	16.2	28.6	44.7	52.9	54.2	58.1	61.2	60.9
Physical sciences and science technologies	5.4	8.3	12.4	16.2	19.4	23.5	25.5	26.8
Psychology	23.3	32.1	43.4	49.6	58.9	62.6	67.4	68.3
Social sciences and history	12.8	20.8	27.0	32.2	32.9	37.7	41.2	41.4

*First-professional degrees are degrees awarded in the fields of dentistry (D.D.S. or D.M.D.), medicine (M.D.), optometry, (O.D.) osteopathic medicine (D.O.), pharmacy (D.Phar.), podiatric medicine (D.P.M.), veterinary medicine (D.V.M), chiropractic medicine (D.C. or D.C.M.), law (J.D.), and the theological professions (M.Div. or M.H.L.).

SOURCE: Adapted from "Table 31. Percent of Master's, First-Professional, and Doctor's Degrees Conferred to Females, by Selected Fields of Study: Various Years, 1969–70 to 2000–01," in *Trends in Educational Equity of Girls & Women: 2004*, National Center for Education Statistics, U.S. Department of Education, NCES 2005-016, November 2004, http://nces.ed.gov/pubs2005/2005016.pdf (accessed June 7, 2005)

into all-male schools. Following the July 22, 1994, ruling of a federal district court judge that a publicly financed school could not bar women, the Citadel, a college that trains future military officers, was forced to admit women. In 1994 Shannon Faulkner became the first full-time female student at the Citadel, although she withdrew before completing introductory training. During her studies at the school she was confronted with discrimination from other students because of her gender and the controversy surrounding a woman being admitted to a formerly all-male school. The stress of the treatment she received contributed to her decision to leave.

Hoping to retain their male-only status, both the Citadel and the Virginia Military Institute (VMI) set up separate "leadership programs" for women. In 1996 the U.S. Supreme Court, in *United States v. Virginia* (508 U.S. 946), ruled that the all-male admissions policies violated the Constitution and that the alternative leadership programs were inadequate. The Court further ruled that women could not be kept out of state-supported military colleges.

In 2004, 1,333 cadets were enrolled at VMI; 6% were female. The Citadel graduated its first woman in 1999. Women made up 15% of the 1999 graduating class of the Naval Academy in Annapolis, Maryland. Five of its top ten graduates were women. Of the class of 2006, women comprised 16% (192 enrollees).

HIGH SCHOOL AND COLLEGE ATHLETICS

Title IX of the Education Amendments of 1972 prohibits sex discrimination in any education program or activity that receives federal funding, including athletics. According to the report *Youth Risk Behavior Surveillance*, published by the Centers for Disease Control and Prevention (CDC), 55.7% of high school students were enrolled in a physical education (PE) class in 2003; 28.4% of those attended PE class daily. (See Table 2.9.) More than half (52.8%) of high school girls were enrolled, but only 26.4% attended daily. Overall, 75.3% of girls exercised more than twenty minutes during an average PE class; 84.5% of boys did. More boys than girls did strengthening exercises (60.1% versus 43.4%) and played on a sports team (64% versus 51%). (See Table 2.10.)

Title IX has increased the opportunities for college scholarships for female athletes. Between 1981 and 1999 there was an 81% increase in the participation of women athletes at National Collegiate Athletic Association (NCAA) and National Association of Intercollegiate Athletics (NAIA) schools. During that period the number of women's teams increased from 5,695 to 9,479, resulting in more women's teams than men's teams. Some women's sports grew dramatically between 1981–82 and 2002–03. Women's basketball grew from 9,624 athletes to 14,674, an increase of 52.5%; women's golf grew from 1,060 athletes to 3,482, an increase of 228.5%; women's rowing grew from 1,187 athletes to 6,690, an increase of 463.6%; and women's soccer grew from 1,855 to 19,871 athletes, an increase of 971.1%.

In March 2005 the Department of Education announced a new policy that would weaken the requirements of Title IX. The policy states that schools may now be considered in compliance with Title IX if they sent an e-mail survey to female students asking them if they felt that the sports opportunities at their schools were sufficient. Using the results of the surveys, schools would then be able to shape their sports programs based on female students' interests. The National Women's Law Center stated that this policy is discriminatory against women and girls, because they "may not express interest and ability in particular sports if they have not had the chance to play them"

TABLE 2.8

First professional degrees conferred by degree-granting institutions, by racial/ethnic group, major field of study, and sex of student, 2001–02

	Total							Men							Women						
Major field of study	Total	White, non-His-panic	Black, non-His-panic	His-panic	Asian/ Pacific Islander	American Indian/ Alaska Native	Non-resident alien	Total	White, non-His-panic	Black, non-His-panic	His-panic	Asian/ Pacific Islander	American Indian/ Alaska Native	Non-resident alien	Total	White, non-His-panic	Black, non-His-panic	His-panic	Asian/ Pacific Islander	American Indian/ Alaska Native	Non-resident alien
1	2	3	4	5	6	7	8	9	10	11	12	13	14	15	16	17	18	19	20	21	22
All fields	80,698	58,874	5,811	3,965	9,584	581	1,883	42,507	32,224	2,223	2,045	4,613	292	1,110	38,191	26,650	3,588	1,920	4,971	289	773
Dentistry (D.D.S. or D.M.D.)	4,239	2,630	155	173	974	26	281	2,608	1,730	63	98	540	20	157	1,631	900	92	75	434	6	124
Medicine (M.D.)	15,237	10,148	1,104	757	2,959	123	146	8,469	5,834	407	408	1,661	63	96	6,768	4,314	697	349	1,298	60	50
Optometry (O.D.)	1,280	800	22	40	344	8	66	565	399	10	10	109	4	33	715	401	12	30	235	4	33
Osteopathic medicine (D.O.)	2,416	1,825	97	67	414	10	3	1,415	1,112	39	37	221	4	2	1,001	713	58	30	193	6	1
Pharmacy (Pharm.D.)	7,076	4,551	570	229	1,501	57	168	2,428	1,613	190	97	440	27	61	4,648	2,938	380	132	1,061	30	107
Podiatry (Pod.D. or D.P.) or podiatric medicine (D.P.M.)	474	332	38	15	71	7	11	315	229	16	12	43	5	10	159	103	22	3	28	2	1
Veterinary medicine (D.V.M.)	2,289	2,055	67	61	65	22	19	652	586	17	19	14	11	5	1,637	1,469	50	42	51	11	14
Chiropractic medicine (D.C. or D.C.M.)	3,284	2,426	116	121	354	20	247	2,248	1,672	63	86	251	11	165	1,036	754	53	35	103	9	82
Naturopathic medicine	227	200	4	2	11	1	9	69	64	2	0	3	0	9	158	136	2	2	8	1	9
Law (LL.B. or J.D.)	38,981	30,125	3,002	2,368	2,621	299	566	20,254	16,445	1,092	1,169	1,121	145	282	18,727	13,680	1,910	1,199	1,500	154	284
Theology (M.Div., M.H.L., B.D., or Ord.)	5,195	3,782	636	132	270	8	367	3,484	2,540	324	109	210	2	299	1,711	1,242	312	23	60	6	68

source: Thomas D. Snyder, Alexandra G. Tan, and Charlene M. Hoffman, "Table 274. First-Professional Degrees Conferred by Degree-Granting Institutions, by Sex, Racial/Ethnic Group, and Major Field of Study: 2001–02," in *Digest of Education Statistics 2003*, National Center for Education Statistics, U.S. Department of Education, NCES 2005-025, December 2004, http://nces.ed.gov/programs/digest/d03/tables/pdf/table274 .pdf (accessed May 25, 2005)

FIGURE 2.6

Percentage distribution of enrollment in college-level, credit-granting distance education courses in two-year and four-year Title IV degree-granting institutions, by level of course offerings, 2000–01

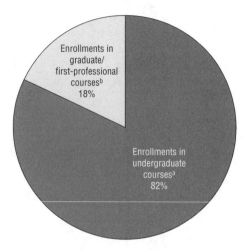

Enrollments in graduate/first-professional courses[b] 18%

Enrollments in undergraduate courses[a] 82%

[a]Percent based on the 2,350,000 enrollments in undergraduate distance education courses out of 2,876,000 total enrollments in college-level, credit-granting distance education courses.
[b]Percent based on the 510,000 enrollments in graduate/first-professional distance education courses out of 2,876,000 total enrollments in college-level, credit-granting distance education courses.
Note: Enrollments may include duplicated counts of students, since institutions were instructed to count a student enrolled in multiple courses for each course in which he or she was enrolled. Enrollments in undergraduate and graduate/first-professional distance education courses do not sum to the total enrollment because of rounding and missing data.

SOURCE: Tiffany Waits and Laurie Lewis, "Figure 2. Percentage Distribution of Enrollment in College-Level, Credit-Granting Distance Education Courses in 2-Year and 4-Year Title IV Degree-Granting Institutions, by Level of Course Offerings: 2000–2001," in *Distance Education at Degree-Granting Postsecondary Institutions: 2000–2001*, U.S. Department of Education, National Center for Education Statistics, July 2003, http://nces.ed.gov/pubs2003/2003017.pdf (accessed May 26, 2005)

("Dept. of Education Weakens Title IX Compliance Standards for College Athletics," *Feminist Daily News Wire*, March 23, 2005, http://www.feminist.org/news/newsbyte/uswirestory.asp?id=8964). Other critics note that response levels to all surveys in general are historically low and that forming women's sports programs based on the results would be misguided, adding that men's athletics programs do not operate based on the responses of surveys. NCAA President Myles Brand expressed his disappointment publicly: "The e-mail survey suggested in the clarification will not provide an adequate indicator of interest among young women to participate in college sports, nor does it encourage young women to participate—a failure that will likely stymie the growth of women's athletics and could reverse the progress made over the last three decades" ("Statement from NCAA President Myles Brand Regarding Department of Education Title IX Clarification," March 22, 2005, http://www.ibcsports.com/ncaa/2005/education-title-IX.htm).

TABLE 2.9

Physical fitness and education activities of high school students, by sex, race/ethnicity, and grade, 2003

Category	Enrolled in PE class[a]			Attended PE class daily[b]			Exercised or played sports > 20 minutes during an average PE class[c]		
	Female %	Male %	Total %	Female %	Male %	Total %	Female %	Male %	Total %
Race/ethnicity									
White[d]	51.5	55.9	53.7	23.1	26.8	24.9	76.6	85.8	81.5
Black[d]	49.3	63.1	56.0	29.0	37.1	33.0	66.7	80.0	74.0
Hispanic	56.1	61.4	58.8	34.0	39.5	36.7	73.5	82.5	78.2
Grade									
9	71.2	70.8	71.0	38.0	37.7	37.9	75.7	84.8	80.3
10	58.3	63.0	60.7	29.1	33.5	31.3	77.0	83.2	80.3
11	40.8	50.5	45.7	19.2	26.0	22.6	71.6	83.7	78.4
12	34.6	44.5	39.5	15.2	21.4	18.2	74.9	87.2	81.8
Total	**52.8**	**58.5**	**55.7**	**26.4**	**30.5**	**28.4**	**75.3**	**84.5**	**80.3**

[a]On one or more days in an average week when they were in school.
[b]5 days in an average week when they were in school.
[c]Among the 55.7% of students enrolled in PE (physical education) class.
[d]Non-Hispanic.

SOURCE: Jo Anne Grunbaum, et al., "Table 54. Percentage of High School Students Who Were Enrolled in Physical Education (PE) Class, Attended PE Class Daily, and Spent >20 Minutes Exercising or Playing Sports During an Average PE Class, by Sex, Race/Ethnicity, and Grade—United States, Youth Risk Behavior Survey, 2003," in *Morbidity and Mortality Weekly Report*, vol. 53, no. SS-2, Department of Health and Human Services, Centers for Disease Control and Prevention, May 21, 2004, http://www.cdc.gov/mmwr/PDF/SS/SS5302.pdf (accessed May 26, 2005)

TABLE 2.10

Percentage of high school students who did strengthening exercises, played on one or more sports teams, and who watched three or more hours per day of television, by sex, race/ethnicity, and grade, 2003

Category	Did strengthening exercises			Played on ≥ 1 sports teams			Watched ≥ 3 hours/day of TV		
	Female %	Male %	Total %	Female %	Male %	Total %	Female %	Male %	Total %
Race/ethnicity									
White*	46.1	60.6	53.6	55.9	65.4	60.8	26.8	31.7	29.3
Black*	31.3	59.6	45.4	39.6	67.5	53.2	70.0	64.3	67.2
Hispanic	43.6	59.4	51.5	42.8	56.2	49.5	45.1	46.8	45.9
Grade									
9	47.9	63.1	55.8	55.2	65.0	60.3	41.2	46.5	44.0
10	49.2	60.1	54.7	53.9	62.0	58.0	39.0	42.9	41.0
11	39.8	62.3	51.2	47.8	66.3	57.2	34.7	34.1	34.4
12	34.4	54.6	44.6	45.9	62.3	54.0	31.3	29.9	30.6
Total	**43.4**	**60.1**	**51.9**	**51.0**	**64.0**	**57.6**	**37.0**	**39.3**	**38.2**

*Non-Hispanic

SOURCE: Jo Anne Grunbaum et al., "Table 56. Percentage of High School Students Who Did Strengthening Exercises, Played on One or More Sports Teams, and Who Watched 3 or More Hours/Day of Television, by Sex, Race/Ethnicity, and Grade—United States, Youth Risk Behavior Survey, 2003," in *Morbidity and Mortality Weekly Report*, vol. 53, no. SS-2, Department of Health and Human Services, Centers for Disease Control and Prevention, May 21, 2004, http://www.cdc.gov/mmwr/PDF/SS/SS5302.pdf (accessed May 26, 2005)

CHAPTER 3
WOMEN IN THE LABOR FORCE

A LEGACY OF WORK

Women have always labored hard. Early American women worked long hours, primarily in their own homes and on their farms and ranches. In 1800 only 5% of white women worked outside the home. Over the next fifty years that percentage doubled as more white women became domestic servants, seamstresses, tavern keepers, and storeowners. African-American women slaves labored in the fields and homes of their owners and tended their own small gardens. By the end of the American Civil War (1861–65), 14% of both African-American and white women were in the paid labor force.

By the turn of the twentieth century, one in five women were working for pay outside of the home. For the most part, these were young, single women or widows; many of them were nonwhite. Most women had low-paying, low-skilled jobs that were considered to be temporary arrangements prior to marriage. Although most women were denied educations that would prepare them for prestigious professions, increasing numbers of women did move into newer fields, such as nursing, teaching, and social work. Other women worked for volunteer causes and became political activists. As a result, by the early twentieth century there existed a large population of women with impressive organizational and administrative skills.

With the onset of the Great Depression in 1929, many women lost their jobs. Some state and local governments limited or banned the employment of married women. Even employed women who were the sole support of their families were seen as taking jobs away from men.

By 1940, 28% of American women worked outside the home, and nearly half of all single women and those age twenty to twenty-four were in the labor force, according to the U.S. Department of Labor's Bureau of Labor Statistics (BLS). With U.S. entry into World War II in late 1942, a huge number of American men either were drafted or volunteered to serve in the military, leaving behind their jobs, and American factories went into overdrive to keep pace with the needs of combat-related products. The need for workers at home became so great that even married women were encouraged to take jobs outside the home. In some cases child care was made available to working mothers. An estimated six million women who had never worked outside the home took jobs during the war years. By 1944, 36% of American women were in the labor force, 5.2 million more than in 1940.

With the end of World War II in 1945 women were expected to return to their homes, making jobs available for discharged servicemen. But the postwar economy was strong enough to support working women, and more educated, middle-class married women began entering the labor force. In 1946, 31% of American women were still working outside the home, according to the BLS.

LABOR FORCE PARTICIPATION AND EMPLOYMENT

1950 to the Present

The BLS carefully tracks labor force participation, employment, and unemployment. Since the labor force includes the unemployed who are actively looking for work, a distinction is made between labor force participation and employment.

In 1950, 33.9% of women sixteen and over were in the civilian labor force. More women began joining the labor force in the 1960s, and their participation continued to grow steadily. In 1971, 43.4% of women were in the labor force; by 2004, 59.2% of women were in the labor force. This participation rate was still much lower than that of men; in 2004, 73.3% of men were in the labor force. (See Table 3.1.) The primary reason for the higher labor force participation rates of men was that many more women than men were over age sixty-five and therefore retired.

TABLE 3.1

Employment status of the civilian noninstitutional population 16 years and over, by sex, 1971–2004

[Numbers in thousands]

Year	Civilian noninstitutional population	Civilian labor force		Employed				Unemployed		Not in labor force
		Total	Percent of population	Total	Percent of population	Agriculture	Nonagricultural industries	Number	Percent of labor force	
Men										
1971	65,942	52,180	79.1	49,390	74.9	2,795	46,595	2,789	5.3	13,762
1972*	67,835	53,555	78.9	50,896	75.0	2,849	48,047	2,659	5.0	14,280
1973*	69,292	54,624	78.8	52,349	75.5	2,847	49,502	2,275	4.2	14,667
1974	70,808	55,739	78.7	53,024	74.9	2,919	50,105	2,714	4.9	15,069
1975	72,291	56,299	77.9	51,857	71.7	2,824	49,032	4,442	7.9	15,993
1976	73,759	57,174	77.5	53,138	72.0	2,744	50,394	4,036	7.1	16,585
1977	75,193	58,396	77.7	54,728	72.8	2,671	52,057	3,667	6.3	16,797
1978*	76,576	59,620	77.9	56,479	73.8	2,718	53,761	3,142	5.3	16,956
1979	78,020	60,726	77.8	57,607	73.8	2,686	54,921	3,120	5.1	17,293
1980	79,398	61,453	77.4	57,186	72.0	2,709	54,477	4,267	6.9	17,945
1981	80,511	61,974	77.0	57,397	71.3	2,700	54,697	4,577	7.4	18,537
1982	81,523	62,450	76.6	56,271	69.0	2,736	53,534	6,179	9.9	19,073
1983	82,531	63,047	76.4	56,787	68.8	2,704	54,083	6,260	9.9	19,484
1984	83,605	63,835	76.4	59,091	70.7	2,668	56,423	4,744	7.4	19,771
1985	84,469	64,411	76.3	59,891	70.9	2,535	57,356	4,521	7.0	20,058
1986*	85,798	65,422	76.3	60,892	71.0	2,511	58,381	4,530	6.9	20,376
1987	86,899	66,207	76.2	62,107	71.5	2,543	59,564	4,101	6.2	20,692
1988	87,857	66,927	76.2	63,273	72.0	2,493	60,780	3,655	5.5	20,930
1989	88,762	67,840	76.4	64,315	72.5	2,513	61,802	3,525	5.2	20,923
1990*	90,377	69,011	76.4	65,104	72.0	2,546	62,559	3,906	5.7	21,367
1991	91,278	69,168	75.8	64,223	70.4	2,589	61,634	4,946	7.2	22,110
1992	92,270	69,964	75.8	64,440	69.8	2,575	61,866	5,523	7.9	22,306
1993	93,332	70,404	75.4	65,349	70.0	2,478	62,871	5,055	7.2	22,927
1994*	94,354	70,817	75.1	66,450	70.4	2,554	63,896	4,367	6.2	23,538
1995	95,178	71,360	75.0	67,377	70.8	2,559	64,818	3,983	5.6	23,818
1996	96,206	72,086	74.9	68,207	70.9	2,573	65,634	3,880	5.4	24,119
1997*	97,715	73,261	75.0	69,685	71.3	2,552	67,133	3,577	4.9	24,454
1998*	98,758	73,959	74.9	70,693	71.6	2,553	68,140	3,266	4.4	24,799
1999*	99,722	74,512	74.7	71,446	71.6	2,432	69,014	3,066	4.1	25,210
2000*	101,964	76,280	74.8	73,305	71.9	1,861	71,444	2,975	3.9	25,684
2001	103,282	76,886	74.4	73,196	70.9	1,708	71,488	3,690	4.8	26,396
2002	104,585	77,500	74.1	72,903	69.7	1,724	71,179	4,597	5.9	27,085
2003*	106,435	78,238	73.5	73,332	68.9	1,695	71,636	4,906	6.3	28,197
2004*	107,710	78,980	73.3	74,524	69.2	1,687	72,838	4,456	5.6	28,730

NEW JOBS FOR WOMEN. According to the Department of Labor Women's Bureau, of the more than seventy million new jobs created in the United States between 1964 and 1999, forty-three million went to women. Service industries accounted for 43% of all new jobs, retail trade for 20%, and government for 15%. Each of these sectors provided more new jobs for women than for men. The number of women's jobs doubled in every industry except manufacturing. Within the service sector 6.6 million new jobs for women were created in health services alone. Within the government sector four million new jobs for women were created in state and local education.

AGE. Since 1950 the biggest increase in labor force participation has been among women between the ages of twenty-five and fifty-four. In the early post–World War II era, the highest rates of labor force participation were among women under age twenty-five, the age by which women had left the labor force to raise their children. As more women enroll in higher education and marry and have children at later ages, the pattern of women's labor force participation has come to resemble that of men. As women complete their education, their presence in the labor force increases steadily, peaking between the ages of thirty-five and fifty-four. Among women in 2004, 75.6% of thirty-five- to forty-four-year-olds and 76.5% of forty-five- to fifty-four-year-olds were in the labor force. After age fifty-five, labor force participation begins a slow decline, as workers start to retire or are downsized ("Table 3. Employment Status of the Civilian Noninstitutional Population by Age, Sex, and Race," Current Population Survey, Bureau of Labor Statistics, 2004).

Among women over age sixty-four, only 11.1% were in the labor force in 2004, up only slightly from 1950, when 10% of women over sixty-four were still working. The labor force participation of men over sixty-four dropped from 46% in 1950 to 19% in 2004. The decline usually is attributed to the increased availability of pensions and disability payments.

TABLE 3.1

Employment status of the civilian noninstitutional population 16 years and over, by sex, 1971–2004 [CONTINUED]

[Numbers in thousands]

Year	Civilian noninstitutional population	Civilian labor force									Not in labor force
		Total	Percent of population	Employed				Unemployed			
				Total	Percent of population	Agriculture	Nonagricultural industries	Number	Percent of labor force		
Women											
1971	74,274	32,202	43.4	29,976	40.4	599	29,377	2,227	6.9		42,072
1972*	76,290	33,479	43.9	31,257	41.0	635	30,622	2,222	6.6		42,811
1973*	77,804	34,804	44.7	32,715	42.0	622	32,093	2,089	6.0		43,000
1974	79,312	36,211	45.7	33,769	42.6	596	33,173	2,441	6.7		43,101
1975	80,860	37,475	46.3	33,989	42.0	584	33,404	3,486	9.3		43,386
1976	82,390	38,983	47.3	35,615	43.2	588	35,027	3,369	8.6		43,406
1977	83,840	40,613	48.4	37,289	44.5	612	36,677	3,324	8.2		43,227
1978*	85,334	42,631	50.0	39,569	46.4	669	38,900	3,061	7.2		42,703
1979	86,843	44,235	50.9	41,217	47.5	661	40,556	3,018	6.8		42,608
1980	88,348	45,487	51.5	42,117	47.7	656	41,461	3,370	7.4		42,861
1981	89,618	46,696	52.1	43,000	48.0	667	42,333	3,696	7.9		42,922
1982	90,748	47,755	52.6	43,256	47.7	665	42,591	4,499	9.4		42,993
1983	91,684	48,503	52.9	44,047	48.0	680	43,367	4,457	9.2		43,181
1984	92,778	49,709	53.6	45,915	49.5	653	45,262	3,794	7.6		43,068
1985	93,736	51,050	54.5	47,259	50.4	644	46,615	3,791	7.4		42,686
1986*	94,789	52,413	55.3	48,706	51.4	652	48,054	3,707	7.1		42,376
1987	95,853	53,658	56.0	50,334	52.5	666	49,668	3,324	6.2		42,195
1988	96,756	54,742	56.6	51,696	53.4	676	51,020	3,046	5.6		42,014
1989	97,630	56,030	57.4	53,027	54.3	687	52,341	3,003	5.4		41,601
1990*	98,787	56,829	57.5	53,689	54.3	678	53,011	3,140	5.5		41,957
1991	99,646	57,178	57.4	53,496	53.7	680	52,815	3,683	6.4		42,468
1992	100,535	58,141	57.8	54,052	53.8	672	53,380	4,090	7.0		42,394
1993	101,506	58,795	57.9	54,910	54.1	637	54,273	3,885	6.6		42,711
1994*	102,460	60,239	58.8	56,610	55.3	855	55,755	3,629	6.0		42,221
1995	103,406	60,944	58.9	57,523	55.6	881	56,642	3,421	5.6		42,462
1996	104,385	61,857	59.3	58,501	56.0	871	57,630	3,356	5.4		42,528
1997*	105,418	63,036	59.8	59,873	56.8	847	59,026	3,162	5.0		42,382
1998	106,462	63,714	59.8	60,771	57.1	825	59,945	2,944	4.6		42,748
1999*	108,031	64,855	60.0	62,042	57.4	849	61,193	2,814	4.3		43,175
2000*	110,613	66,303	59.9	63,586	57.5	602	62,983	2,717	4.1		44,310
2001	111,811	66,848	59.8	63,737	57.0	591	63,147	3,111	4.7		44,962
2002	112,985	67,363	59.6	63,582	56.3	587	62,995	3,781	5.6		45,621
2003*	114,733	68,272	59.5	64,404	56.1	580	63,824	3,868	5.7		46,461
2004*	115,647	68,421	59.2	64,728	56.0	546	64,182	3,694	5.4		47,225

*Not strictly comparable with data for prior years.

SOURCE: "Employment Status of the Civilian Noninstitutional Population 16 Years and Over by Sex, 1971 to Date," U.S. Department of Labor, Bureau of Labor Statistics, 2004, http://www.bls.gov/cps/cpsaat2.pdf (accessed May 31, 2005)

RACE AND ETHNICITY. Among women, African-Americans have the highest labor force participation rates and Hispanics the lowest. Among men, Hispanics have the highest labor force participation rates, while African-Americans have the lowest.

In 1890 nearly two out of five nonwhite women between the ages of twenty and sixty-four were in the labor force. Often these women were supplementing their husbands' meager earnings. By the turn of the century many African-Americans were leaving rural areas and seeking employment in northern cities. Most African-American women found work in private households or laundries. In 1947 only 31% of white women were in the labor force, compared with 44% of women of other races. During the 1960s and 1970s many white and African-American women entered the labor force, but the increase was higher for white women. In 2004, 61.5% of African-American women

age sixteen and older were in the labor force, as were 58.9% of white women. Among Hispanic women, 56.1% of those over sixteen were in the labor force in 2004, up from about 50% in 1986; 57.6% of Asian-American women of the same age were in the labor force ("Table 3. Employment Status of the Civilian Noninstitutional Population by Age, Sex, and Race," and "Table 4. Employment Status of the Hispanic or Latino Population by Age and Sex," Current Population Survey, Bureau of Labor Statistics, 2004).

MARITAL STATUS. As in the past, single women are more likely to be in the labor force than married women. Furthermore, the population of single women has increased, as more people postpone marriage, get divorced, or choose not to marry. Among women who maintained families with no spouse present, 64% were employed in 2004. (See Table 3.2.) In almost one in four families maintained exclusively by women (23.9%), no

TABLE 3.2

Families, by presence and relationship of employed members and family type, 2003–04

[Numbers in thousands]

Characteristic	Number		Percent distribution	
	2003	2004	2003	2004
Married-couple families				
Total	57,074	57,188	100.0	100.0
Member(s) employed, total	47,535	47,767	83.3	83.5
Husband only	11,403	11,712	20.0	20.5
Wife only	3,863	3,843	6.8	6.7
Husband and wife	29,077	28,991	50.9	50.7
Other employment combinations	3,193	3,222	5.6	5.6
No member(s) employed	9,539	9,420	16.7	16.5
Families maintained by women*				
Total	13,450	13,614	100.0	100.0
Member(s) employed, total	10,187	10,358	75.7	76.1
Householder only	5,987	6,021	44.5	44.2
Householder and other member(s)	2,539	2,701	18.9	19.8
Other member(s), not householder	1,660	1,636	12.3	12.0
No member(s) employed	3,263	3,255	24.3	23.9
Families maintained by men*				
Total	4,777	5,071	100.0	100.0
Member(s) employed, total	4,039	4,299	84.6	84.8
Householder only	1,954	2,060	40.9	40.6
Householder and other member(s)	1,427	1,557	29.9	30.7
Other member(s), not householder	658	682	13.8	13.5
No member(s) employed	739	772	15.5	15.2

*No spouse present.
Note: Detail may not sum to totals due to rounding. Data for 2004 reflect revised population controls used in the Current Population Survey.

SOURCE: "Table 2. Families by Presence and Relationship of Employed Members and Family Type, 2003–04 Annual Averages," in "Employment Characteristics of Families in 2004," Press Release, U.S. Department of Labor, Bureau of Labor Statistics, June 9, 2005, http://www.bls.gov/news.release/pdf/famee.pdf (accessed June 9, 2005)

members were employed, an indicator of the greater likelihood of poverty in these households. (See Chapter 5.)

As more families require two incomes and as more women choose to pursue careers after marriage, the proportion of married women in the labor force has increased. In about half of married-couple families in 2004 (50.7%), both the husband and wife were employed; in 6.7% of married-couple families, only the wife was employed. In one out of five married couples (20.5%) the husband was employed while the wife stayed home. (See Table 3.2.)

CHILDREN. According to the BLS, only a slight increase occurred in the percentage of women without children under the age of eighteen who participated in the labor force between 1980 (48.1%) and 2004 (54%). However, the increase in the percentage of women in the labor force with children under eighteen increased significantly for that same time period (56.6% in 1980 and 70.4% in 2004). (See Table 3.3.) In 2004, 77.3% of women with children age six to seventeen were in the labor force, and 61.8% of women with children under the age of six were in the labor force.

In married-couple families with their own children under eighteen—a group in which the parents were unlikely to be retired—66.3% of the mothers were employed in 2003, down slightly from 67.3% in 1995. (See Table 3.4.) In 60.7% of married-couple families with children under eighteen, both parents worked. Only the father was employed in 30.5% of married-couple families with children under age eighteen, up from 28.5% in 1995. The percentage of married-couple families with children under age six in which only the father worked also increased, from 35.3% in 1995 to 39% in 2003, while the labor force participation rate of mothers in married-couple families with children under age six decreased from 60.9% in 1995 to 57.6% in 2003.

The labor force participation rate for mothers with no spouse present was 76.9% in 2003, up from 72.1% in 1995. The participation rate was 63.8% for mothers with no spouse present with children under six, up from 52.5%. (See Table 3.4.) The increase in single mothers in the workforce was due mainly to the provisions of the Personal Responsibility and Work Opportunity Reconciliation Act (PRWORA) of 1996, which was designed to move people, primarily single mothers, off welfare and into the workforce. (See Chapter 5.)

Employment Sectors

As seen in Table 3.5, only 546,000 women age sixteen and older were employed in agriculture in 2004, compared to more than 1.6 million men. Of the more than 60.5 million female wage and salary workers, 81.2% were employed in private industry. Only 1.5% of those women worked in private households; 98.5% worked in other private industries. The remaining wage and salary workers were government employees. Men were more likely than women to be employed by private industry, but only a very small fraction of men were employed in private households. Of the 9.5 million self-employed Americans in 2004, 38.1% were women, most of whom were thirty-five years or older.

Far more women than men in all age groups work in service industries. In May 2005 women held 57.2% of all service jobs. (See Table 3.6.) Women accounted for 89.2% of all workers in healthcare support occupations, 56.2% of all workers in food preparation and service occupations, and 80.1% of all workers in personal care and service occupations. They also accounted for 62.7% of all workers in sales and office occupations. Women were underrepresented in production, transportation, and material moving occupations, making up less than a quarter of the workforce there (22.9%).

In 2004, 12.5% of employed female wage and salary workers were represented by unions, and 11.1% were union members; 15% of males were represented by unions, and 13.8% were union members. Union representation and membership has dropped steadily since 1983

TABLE 3.3

Employment status of the population, by sex, marital status, and presence and age of own children under 18, 2003–04

[Numbers in thousands]

Characteristic	2003			2004		
	Total	Men	Women	Total	Men	Women
With own children under 18 years						
Civilian noninstitutional population	64,932	28,402	36,530	64,758	28,272	36,486
Civilian labor force	52,727	26,739	25,988	52,288	26,607	25,681
Participation rate	81.2	94.1	71.1	80.7	94.1	70.4
Employed	50,103	25,638	24,466	49,957	25,696	24,261
Employment-population ratio	77.2	90.3	67.0	77.1	90.9	66.5
Full-time workers[a]	42,880	24,762	18,118	42,758	24,794	17,964
Part-time workers[b]	7,223	876	6,347	7,200	902	6,298
Unemployed	2,624	1,101	1,523	2,331	911	1,420
Unemployment rate	5.0	4.1	5.9	4.5	3.4	5.5
Married, spouse present						
Civilian noninstitutional population	52,476	26,049	26,427	52,109	25,852	26,258
Civilian labor force	42,776	24,638	18,138	42,247	24,449	17,798
Participation rate	81.5	94.6	68.6	81.1	94.6	67.8
Employed	41,128	23,712	17,416	40,847	23,703	17,144
Employment-population ratio	78.4	91.0	65.9	78.4	91.7	65.3
Full-time workers[a]	35,315	22,954	12,360	35,141	22,935	12,206
Part-time workers[b]	5,813	757	5,056	5,706	768	4,938
Unemployed	1,648	926	722	1,400	747	653
Unemployment rate	3.9	3.8	4.0	3.3	3.1	3.7
Other marital status[c]						
Civilian noninstitutional population	12,455	2,354	10,102	12,649	2,420	10,229
Civilian labor force	9,950	2,100	7,850	10,042	2,158	7,883
Participation rate	79.9	89.2	77.7	79.4	89.2	77.1
Employed	8,975	1,926	7,050	9,110	1,993	7,117
Employment-population ratio	72.1	81.8	69.8	72.0	82.4	69.6
Full-time workers[a]	7,566	1,807	5,759	7,617	1,859	5,757
Part-time workers[b]	1,411	118	1,291	1,494	134	1,360
Unemployed	976	175	800	931	165	766
Unemployment rate	9.8	8.3	10.2	9.3	7.6	9.7
With own children 6 to 17 years, none younger						
Civilian noninstitutional population	35,943	15,653	20,290	35,874	15,597	20,277
Civilian labor force	30,362	14,572	15,790	30,182	14,516	15,666
Participation rate	84.5	93.1	77.8	84.1	93.1	77.3
Employed	29,040	14,008	15,032	29,013	14,056	14,957
Employment-population ratio	80.8	89.5	74.1	80.9	90.1	73.8
Full-time workers[a]	25,116	13,558	11,557	25,069	13,597	11,473
Part-time workers[b]	3,925	450	3,475	3,944	459	3,485
Unemployed	1,322	564	758	1,170	460	709
Unemployment rate	4.4	3.9	4.8	3.9	3.2	4.5
With own children under 6 years						
Civilian noninstitutional population	28,988	12,749	16,240	28,884	12,675	16,210
Civilian labor force	22,365	12,167	10,198	22,106	12,091	10,014
Participation rate	77.2	95.4	62.8	76.5	95.4	61.8
Employed	21,063	11,630	9,433	20,944	11,640	9,304
Employment-population ratio	72.7	91.2	58.1	72.5	91.8	57.4
Full-time workers[a]	17,764	11,203	6,561	17,689	11,197	6,491
Part-time workers[b]	3,299	426	2,872	3,256	443	2,813
Unemployed	1,302	538	765	1,162	451	710
Unemployment rate	5.8	4.4	7.5	5.3	3.7	7.1

for both men and women ("Table 38. Union Affiliation of Employed Wage and Salary Workers by Sex, Annual Averages, 1983–2004," *Women in the Labor Force: A Databook*, Bureau of Labor Statistics, U.S. Department of Labor, May 2005). The median weekly earnings of women not represented by unions was $523, compared with $691 for women represented by unions and $696 for women members of unions. More than four in ten government workers (40.7%) were represented by unions, but fewer than one in ten private-sector workers (8.6%)

were unionized ("Union Members Summary," Press Release, Bureau of Labor Statistics, U.S. Department of Labor, January 27, 2005). Since 1983 the rate of unionization for government employees has remained steady; it has fallen by nearly half over the same time period for private-sector employees.

Job Tenure

In general, men have worked at their current jobs for longer than women, although that gap narrowed after

TABLE 3.3

Employment status of the population, by sex, marital status, and presence and age of own children under 18, 2003–04 [CONTINUED]

[Numbers in thousands]

Characteristic	2003			2004		
	Total	Men	Women	Total	Men	Women
With no own children under 18 years						
Civilian noninstitutional population	154,714	76,510	78,204	156,900	77,739	79,160
Civilian labor force	92,319	50,036	42,284	93,511	50,771	42,740
Participation rate	59.7	65.4	54.1	59.6	65.3	54.0
Employed	86,233	46,294	39,939	87,748	47,282	40,467
Employment-population ratio	55.7	60.5	51.1	55.9	60.8	51.1
Full-time workers[a]	69,073	39,245	29,827	70,244	40,134	30,110
Part-time workers[b]	17,160	7,049	10,111	17,505	7,148	10,357
Unemployed	6,087	3,741	2,345	5,763	3,489	2,274
Unemployment rate	6.6	7.5	5.5	6.2	6.9	5.3

[a]Usually work 35 hours or more a week at all jobs.
[b]Usually work less than 35 hours a week at all jobs.
[c]Includes never-married, divorced, separated, and widowed persons.

SOURCE: "Table 5. Employment Status of the Population by Sex, Marital Status, and Presence and Age of Own Children Under 18, 2003–04 Annual Averages," in "Employment Characteristics of Families in 2004," Press Release, U.S. Department of Labor, Bureau of Labor Statistics, June 9, 2005, http://www.bls.gov/news.release/pdf/famee.pdf (accessed June 9, 2005)

1996 ("Employee Tenure Summary," Press Release, Bureau of Labor Statistics, U.S. Department of Labor, September 21, 2004). In 2004 the median years of tenure with current employer for female wage and salary workers was 3.8, compared with 4.1 for males. Among workers twenty-five years and older, 32.4% of males and 28.6% of females had been with their current employer for ten or more years.

In a June 2001 report the BLS announced that the younger adults of the baby boom generation, those born between the years 1957 and 1964, have held nearly ten jobs by the age of thirty-six. On average, men held 9.9 jobs and women 9.3. Whites held 4.6 jobs from ages eighteen to twenty-two while African-Americans held 3.6 and Hispanics 4.

ALTERNATIVE WORK ARRANGEMENTS
Part-Time Work

In 2004 nearly one-third of employed women (32.9%) worked part-time, while only 17.2% of employed men worked part-time. Among white employed women, 33.6% worked part-time, compared with 24.6% of African-American employed women. Never-married women were more likely to work part-time (37.6%), compared with married women with a spouse present (31.7%) and widowed, divorced, or separated women (26.2%).

In 2004 most people who worked part-time did so for noneconomic reasons, such as caring for a child or other family member. Many of those working part-time in 2004, including 21.1% of white female part-time workers and 28% of African-American female part-time workers, usually worked full-time. Almost one out of every five male part-time workers (18.8%) but only one in ten female part-time workers (11.1%) worked part-time for economic reasons such as job cutbacks or the inability to find full-time work. However, 19.9% of African-American women worked part-time for such economic reasons.

Nearly nine out of ten companies offer some benefits to part-time workers, most of whom are in clerical and sales positions. The federal government is the largest employer of part-time workers as a result of the Federal Employees Part-Time Career Employment Act of 1978 (PL 95–437). This Act gave part-time federal employees benefits and permanent status. The federal Office of Personnel Management reported that the number of part-time managers and executives has risen more than 150% since the enactment of the legislation. Both companies and the federal government now use part-time status as a way to recruit talented women who do not want to work full-time or are unable to do so because of other commitments.

Some women manage to work part-time by sharing what would otherwise be full-time jobs. In particular, some teachers, librarians, receptionists, and health-care professionals have been able to job-share successfully.

Flextime

Changes in the structure of the American family have led many businesses to offer alternatives to the traditional forty-hour work week. Flextime enables employees to vary their work hours to accommodate family needs, education, or other personal situations. In its 2003 annual survey of the one hundred best companies for working mothers, *Working Mother* magazine focused on flextime, advancement, and

TABLE 3.4

Employment status of parents for families with own children, 1995 and 2003

[In thousands, except percent distribution. Annual average of monthly figures (33,544 represents 33,544,000). For families with own children.]

Characteristic	Number		Percent	
	1995	2003	1995	2003
With own children under 18 years old				
Total families	**33,544**	**35,428**	**100.0**	**100.0**
Parent(s) employed	29,659	32,002	88.4	90.3
No parent employed	3,886	3,426	11.6	9.7
Married-couple families	24,604	25,383	100.0	100.0
Parent(s) employed	23,643	24,553	96.1	96.7
Mother employed	16,629	16,820	67.6	66.3
Both parents employed	15,491	15,420	63.0	60.7
Mother employed, not father	1,137	1,400	4.6	5.5
Father employed, not mother	7,014	7,733	28.5	30.5
Neither parent employed	962	830	3.9	3.3
Families maintained by women*	7,433	8,069	100.0	100.0
Mother employed	4,755	5,804	64.0	71.9
Mother not employed	2,678	2,265	36.0	28.1
Families maintained by men*	1,507	1,975	100.0	100.0
Father employed	1,261	1,645	83.7	83.3
Father not employed	245	331	16.3	16.8
With own children 6 to 17 years old				
Total families	**18,270**	**20,125**	**100.0**	**100.0**
Parent(s) employed	16,391	18,309	89.7	91.0
No parent employed	1,878	1,814	10.3	9.0
Married-couple families	13,001	13,917	100.0	100.0
Parent(s) employed	12,484	13,473	96.0	96.8
Mother employed	9,562	10,214	73.6	73.4
Both parents employed	8,846	9,323	68.0	67.0
Mother employed, not father	717	890	5.5	6.4
Father employed, not mother	2,921	3,261	22.5	23.4
Neither parent employed	517	443	4.0	3.2
Families maintained by women*	4,360	5,009	100.0	100.0
Mother employed	3,142	3,851	72.1	76.9
Mother not employed	1,219	1,157	27.9	23.1
Families maintained by men*	908	1,199	100.0	100.0
Father employed	766	985	84.3	82.2
Father not employed	143	214	15.7	17.8
With own children under 6 years old				
Total families	**15,275**	**15,302**	**100.0**	**100.0**
Parent(s) employed	13,267	13,692	86.9	89.5
No parent employed	2,007	1,608	13.1	10.5
Married-couple families	11,604	11,466	100.0	100.0
Parent(s) employed	11,159	11,080	96.2	96.6
Mother employed	7,066	6,607	60.9	57.6
Both parents employed	6,646	6,097	57.3	53.2
Mother employed, not father	421	510	3.6	4.4
Father employed, not mother	4,092	4,474	35.3	39.0
Neither parent employed	445	385	3.8	3.4
Families maintained by women*	3,073	3,061	100.0	100.0
Mother employed	1,613	1,953	52.5	63.8
Mother not employed	1,460	1,107	47.5	36.2
Families maintained by men*	598	776	100.0	100.0
Father employed	496	659	82.8	84.9
Father not employed	102	116	17.1	14.9

*No spouse present

SOURCE: "Table 581. Families with Own Children—Employment Status of Parents: 1995 and 2003," in *Statistical Abstract of the United States: 2004–2005*, U.S. Census Bureau, 2005, http://www.census.gov/prod/2004pubs/04statab/labor.pdf (accessed May 31, 2005)

equitable distribution of benefits. The magazine viewed flextime as essential for working moms. Workers agree. Bizjournals.com published the findings of a 2003 survey sponsored by OfficeTeam, a California-based temporary staffing agency. Workers ranked schedule flexibility higher in importance than the ability to have autonomy in making decisions, project variety, and collaboration of others. One-third of participants said greater flexibility would result in increased job satisfaction.

However, Table 3.7 shows that in 2001, the latest year for which flextime data was available, men were somewhat more likely than women to have flexible work schedules (30% and 27.4%, respectively). Only women under age twenty-four had more access to flextime than men, although an increasing number of women have flexible schedules during their peak childbearing years. White women (28.6%) use flextime more than Hispanic (21.9%) or African-American (21.5%) women.

Flextime is most available to professionals, such as scientists, lawyers, and teachers, and people in sales occupations. Managers, executives, and administrators also enjoy high percentages of flextime. Others, such as computer equipment operators, farm and forestry workers, and transportation and construction workers, as well as many part-time workers, often work variable hours out of choice or at the convenience of their employers. Women and nonwhites are more likely to have unpredictable work schedules, in part because of the types of jobs they hold.

Nontraditional Work Arrangements

Table 3.8 shows that more women than men had nontraditional or alternative work arrangements in February 2001. However, women made up 46.9% of on-call workers and 58.9% of people who worked through temporary help agencies—both nontraditional arrangements that are not necessarily able to accommodate family obligations—whereas 64.5% of independent contractors and 70.6% of people who work through contract firms were men. Thus, women with nontraditional arrangements tended to work in lower-skilled, lower-paying jobs. Although there are numerous types of contract workers, many women contract workers are poorly paid immigrants performing tasks such as garment work at home. In recent years there has been a resurgence in this type of arrangement, which was very common in the nineteenth century, when it was called "outworking."

Telecommuting

Personal and laptop computers, cellular phones, and other technologies are enabling a growing number of Americans to work from home. The Bureau of Labor Statistics reported that in 2001, 19.8 million persons did some work at home as part of their job each week ("Work at Home in 2001," Press Release, Bureau of Labor Statistics, U.S. Department of Labor, March 1, 2002). Half of those workers took work home from the

TABLE 3.5

Employed persons in agriculture and nonagricultural industries, by age, sex, and class of worker, 2004

[In thousands]

	2004											
	Agriculture and related industries				Nonagricultural industries							
						Wage and salary workers						
							Private industries					
Age and sex	Total	Wage and salary workers	Self-employed workers	Unpaid family workers	Total	Total	Total	Private house-hold workers	Other private industries	Government	Self-employed workers	Unpaid family workers
Total, 16 years and over	**2,232**	**1,242**	**964**	**27**	**137,020**	**127,463**	**107,480**	**779**	**106,701**	**19,983**	**9,467**	**90**
16 to 19 years	121	102	6	13	5,786	5,699	5,423	101	5,322	276	78	8
16 to 17 years	57	46	3	8	2,136	2,095	2,011	58	1,953	84	36	5
18 to 19 years	64	56	3	5	3,650	3,604	3,412	43	3,369	192	42	3
20 to 24 years	143	123	15	5	13,580	13,261	12,155	92	12,062	1,106	310	10
25 to 34 years	352	267	83	2	30,071	28,526	24,831	122	24,709	3,695	1,530	15
35 to 44 years	442	287	153	3	34,137	31,650	26,642	160	26,483	5,008	2,468	18
45 to 54 years	494	257	234	3	31,976	29,386	23,355	147	23,208	6,031	2,565	25
55 to 64 years	376	141	235	—	16,955	15,161	11,887	117	11,770	3,274	1,786	8
65 years and over	304	65	237	1	4,515	3,780	3,186	40	3,147	593	730	6
Men, 16 years and over	**1,687**	**970**	**702**	**15**	**72,838**	**66,951**	**58,335**	**60**	**58,275**	**8,616**	**5,860**	**27**
16 to 19 years	90	79	4	7	2,861	2,800	2,664	11	2,654	136	56	5
16 to 17 years	39	33	2	4	998	970	931	6	925	39	25	3
18 to 19 years	52	46	3	3	1,863	1,830	1,733	4	1,729	97	32	2
20 to 24 years	113	98	10	4	7,133	6,921	6,442	15	6,427	479	207	6
25 to 34 years	284	229	54	1	16,533	15,593	13,987	8	13,979	1,606	937	3
35 to 44 years	333	219	113	2	18,366	16,887	14,744	11	14,734	2,143	1,475	4
45 to 54 years	374	197	177	—	16,577	14,993	12,497	8	12,489	2,496	1,578	6
55 to 64 years	270	103	167	—	8,904	7,792	6,338	7	6,331	1,454	1,112	1
65 years and over	222	46	176	—	2,462	1,965	1,663	2	1,661	302	495	2
Women, 16 years and over	**546**	**271**	**262**	**12**	**64,182**	**60,512**	**49,145**	**719**	**48,426**	**11,367**	**3,607**	**63**
16 to 19 years	31	23	2	6	2,924	2,899	2,759	90	2,669	140	22	3
16 to 17 years	18	13	1	4	1,138	1,125	1,080	51	1,028	45	11	2
18 to 19 years	12	10	1	2	1,786	1,774	1,679	39	1,641	95	10	2
20 to 24 years	30	24	5	1	6,447	6,340	5,713	78	5,635	627	104	4
25 to 34 years	68	38	29	1	13,538	12,933	10,845	115	10,730	2,088	593	12
35 to 44 years	109	68	40	1	15,771	14,763	11,898	149	11,749	2,865	993	15
45 to 54 years	120	60	57	3	15,398	14,393	10,858	139	10,719	3,535	987	19
55 to 64 years	106	37	69	—	8,051	7,369	5,549	110	5,439	1,820	674	7
65 years and over	82	20	61	1	2,053	1,815	1,523	38	1,485	292	235	3

Note: Beginning in January 2004, data reflect revised population controls used in the household survey. Dash indicates no data or data that do not meet publication criteria.

SOURCE: "Table 15. Employed Persons in Agriculture and Related and in Nonagricultural Industries by Age, Sex, and Class of Worker," U.S. Department of Labor, Bureau of Labor Statistics, 2004, http://www.bls.gov/cps/cpsaat15.pdf (accessed May 31, 2005)

TABLE 3.6

Employed persons, by occupation, sex, and age, 2004–05

[In thousands]

Occupation	Total 16 years and over		Men 16 years and over		Men 20 years and over		Women 16 years and over		Women 20 years and over	
	May 2004	May 2005	May 2004	May 2005	May 2004	May 2005	May 2004	May 2005	May 2004	May 2005
Total	**138,867**	**141,591**	**74,089**	**75,997**	**71,306**	**73,242**	**64,778**	**65,594**	**61,872**	**62,642**
Management, professional, and related occupations	48,610	49,249	23,992	24,253	23,870	24,088	24,617	24,996	24,434	24,822
Management, business, and financial operations occupations	20,219	20,082	11,696	11,627	11,680	11,599	8,523	8,455	8,507	8,424
Management occupations	14,589	14,396	9,140	9,050	9,126	9,025	5,449	5,347	5,437	5,328
Business and financial operations occupations	5,630	5,686	2,556	2,577	2,554	2,574	3,073	3,109	3,070	3,096
Professional and related occupations	28,391	29,167	12,296	12,626	12,190	12,489	16,095	16,541	15,927	16,397
Computer and mathematical occupations	2,912	3,232	2,165	2,352	2,154	2,343	747	880	744	880
Architecture and engineering occupations	2,773	2,886	2,379	2,486	2,374	2,476	394	400	394	400
Life, physical, and social science occupations	1,269	1,385	756	801	747	798	513	584	513	584
Community and social services occupations	2,249	2,139	875	851	866	850	1,374	1,288	1,360	1,278
Legal occupations	1,571	1,596	813	819	813	819	758	777	758	777
Education, training, and library occupations	8,356	8,437	2,175	2,146	2,162	2,106	6,181	6,291	6,096	6,218
Arts, design, entertainment, sports, and media occupations	2,605	2,748	1,417	1,443	1,376	1,375	1,189	1,305	1,161	1,261
Healthcare practitioner and technical occupations	6,656	6,745	1,716	1,728	1,698	1,723	4,941	5,018	4,902	5,001
Service occupations	22,840	23,056	9,662	9,783	8,670	8,815	13,178	13,274	11,959	12,029
Healthcare support occupations	2,911	3,015	289	324	270	305	2,622	2,690	2,536	2,620
Protective service occupations	2,542	2,822	2,010	2,196	1,977	2,156	532	626	488	585
Food preparation and serving related occupations	7,658	7,638	3,373	3,343	2,721	2,695	4,286	4,295	3,455	3,435
Building and grounds cleaning and maintenance occupations	5,207	5,080	3,097	3,026	2,930	2,865	2,110	2,054	2,057	1,999
Personal care and service occupations	4,522	4,502	893	894	772	795	3,629	3,608	3,422	3,390
Sales and office occupations	35,162	35,875	12,949	13,396	12,195	12,619	22,213	22,479	20,882	21,103
Sales and related occupations	15,742	16,612	8,160	8,534	7,696	8,103	7,582	8,078	6,680	7,202
Office and administrative support occupations	19,420	19,263	4,789	4,862	4,499	4,516	14,631	14,401	14,202	13,901
Natural resources, construction, and maintenance occupations	14,336	15,339	13,677	14,634	13,266	14,247	659	704	621	672
Farming, fishing, and forestry occupations	1,012	959	789	712	733	660	223	247	189	222
Construction and extraction occupations	8,285	9,161	8,108	8,923	7,844	8,682	176	239	174	233
Installation, maintenance, and repair occupations	5,039	5,218	4,780	5,000	4,689	4,905	260	218	259	217
Production, transportation, and material moving occupations	17,919	18,071	13,809	13,931	13,305	13,473	4,110	4,141	3,975	4,016
Production occupations	9,351	9,545	6,564	6,714	6,414	6,554	2,787	2,831	2,724	2,757
Transportation and material moving occupations	8,568	8,527	7,245	7,217	6,891	6,918	1,323	1,310	1,252	1,259

SOURCE: "Table A-19. Employed Persons by Occupation, Sex, and Age," U.S. Department of Labor, Bureau of Labor Statistics, 2004, http://www.bls.gov/web/cpseea19.pdf (accessed June 13, 2005)

TABLE 3.7

Persons on flexible schedules, 2001

[In thousands (99,631 represents 99,631,000) except percent. As of May. For employed full-time wage and salary workers 16 years old and over. Excludes the self-employed. Data relate to the primary job.]

Item	Total	Total[a]	With flexible schedules Number	With flexible schedules Percent	Male Total[a]	Male Number	Male Percent	Female Total[a]	Female Number	Female Percent
Total	**99,631**	**28,724**	**28.8**		**56,066**	**16,792**	**30.0**	**43,566**	**11,931**	**27.4**
Age										
16 to 19 years old	1,761	339	19.2		988	167	16.9	773	171	22.2
20 to 24 years old	9,343	2,327	24.9		5,219	1,203	23.0	4,124	1,124	27.2
25 to 34 years old	24,552	7,434	30.3		14,058	4,370	31.1	10,494	3,064	29.2
35 to 44 years old	28,702	8,578	29.9		16,522	5,120	31.0	12,180	3,458	28.4
45 to 54 years old	23,946	6,990	29.2		12,902	4,032	31.2	11,044	2,958	26.8
55 to 64 years old	9,971	2,633	26.4		5,531	1,590	28.8	4,440	1,043	23.5
65 years old and over	1,357	423	31.2		847	311	36.7	510	112	22.0
Race and Hispanic origin										
White	82,205	24,647	30.0		47,498	14,734	31.0	34,707	9,913	28.6
Black	12,390	2,629	21.2		5,776	1,209	20.9	6,614	1,420	21.5
Hispanic origin[b]	11,919	2,356	19.8		7,305	1,344	18.4	4,614	1,011	21.9
Occupation										
Executive, administrative, and managerial	16,279	7,404	45.5		8,748	4,277	48.9	7,531	3,128	41.5
Professional specialty	16,681	5,922	35.5		8,037	3,678	45.8	8,644	2,244	26.0
Technical and related support	3,757	1,181	31.4		1,863	683	36.7	1,894	498	26.3
Sales	9,852	4,011	40.7		5,424	2,404	44.3	4,428	1,607	36.3
Administrative support, including clerical	13,997	3,426	24.5		3,206	753	23.5	10,791	2,672	24.8
Private household	377	132	35.0		5	3	*	371	129	34.8
Protective service	2,144	343	16.0		1,773	291	16.4	371	52	14.0
Service, exc. private household and protective	8,207	1,755	21.4		3,324	698	21.0	4,883	1,057	21.6
Precision production, craft and repair	12,061	2,209	18.3		11,000	2,026	18.4	1,061	183	17.3
Operators, fabricators, and laborers	14,621	1,999	13.7		11,324	1,689	14.9	3,297	310	9.4

*Percent not shown where base is less than 75,000.
[a]Includes persons who did not provide information on flexible schedules.
[b]Persons of Hispanic origin may be of any race.

SOURCE: "Table 588. Persons on Flexible Schedules: 2001," in *Statistical Abstract of the United States: 2004–2005*, U.S. Census Bureau, 2005, http://www.census.gov/prod/2004pubs/04statab/labor.pdf (accessed May 31, 2005)

---

office and were unpaid for the extra work; 17% had a formal, paid arrangement with their employers; and 30% were self-employed. A slightly greater proportion of female workers (15.2%) than male workers (14.8%) worked from home; 18.9% of women who worked from home were paid for that work, while only 16% of men were.

Telecommuting allows workers to be available for children and other family members while generating income. It eliminates commuting time and costs. In 2001 women with children under eighteen were more likely to work from home than were women without children (16.6% and 14.9%, respectively). Women with children were more likely than women without children to be paid by their employers for the work they did at home (21.6% and 16.9%, respectively).

Telecommuting also saves money for businesses. According to the 2003 American Interactive Consumer Survey conducted by the Dieringer Research Group, telecommuting is on the rise because a number of major corporations are recognizing the benefits of telework programs, including AT&T, Morgan Stanley, Schering-Plough, and Merrill Lynch. Such firms have found telework is a way to reduce costs and increase productivity. According to a 2003 NetworkWorldFusion (www.nwfusion.com) article, Cigna employs 38,000 people and saves $3,000 per teleworker per year in office space. In addition, the company reports a 30% decrease in turnover and a 15% increase in productivity since implementing its telework program.

Multiple Jobholders

In 2003, 5.6% of employed women (3.6 million) held more than one job, as did 5.1% (3.7 million) of employed men. (See Table 3.9.) Women between the ages of twenty and twenty-four were most likely to hold more than one job (6.7%) in 2003. A larger proportion of white women (5.9%) than African-American (4%) or Hispanic (3.3%) women held multiple jobs. Married women living with their spouses were less likely to be multiple jobholders, as compared with women who had never been married or who were widowed, divorced, or separated. Almost half of women with multiple jobs (46.2%) had one full-time and one part-time job. Another 31.7% had two part-time jobs.

TABLE 3.8

Employed workers with alternative and traditional work arrangements, by selected characteristics, February 2001

[Percent distribution]

Characteristic	Workers with alternative arrangements				Workers with traditional arrangements
	Independent contractors	On-call workers	Temporary help agency workers	Workers provided by contract firms	
Age and sex					
Total, 16 years and over	100.0	100.0	100.0	100.0	100.0
16 to 19 years	1.2	9.7	3.5	1.1	5.1
20 to 24 years	2.7	14.8	18.8	10.9	10.1
25 to 34 years	15.3	17.0	26.5	23.3	22.9
35 to 44 years	29.0	25.7	24.9	28.9	27.2
45 to 54 years	28.1	17.9	14.1	23.9	22.0
55 to 64 years	15.8	9.1	10.6	7.6	10.0
65 years and over	7.9	5.7	1.5	4.4	2.6
Men, 16 years and over	64.5	53.1	41.1	70.6	52.2
16 to 19 years	.7	3.9	1.3	1.1	2.6
20 to 24 years	1.4	8.5	7.0	8.9	5.2
25 to 34 years	9.0	11.7	11.1	18.2	12.2
35 to 44 years	19.0	12.0	13.2	21.8	14.3
45 to 54 years	18.0	8.6	4.4	12.0	11.2
55 to 64 years	10.6	4.7	3.6	6.1	5.2
65 years and over	5.7	3.6	.6	2.4	1.5
Women, 16 years and over	35.5	46.9	58.9	29.4	47.8
16 to 19 years	.5	5.8	2.2	—	2.5
20 to 24 years	1.3	6.3	11.8	1.9	5.0
25 to 34 years	6.3	5.3	15.4	5.1	10.6
35 to 44 years	9.9	13.7	11.8	7.1	12.9
45 to 54 years	10.1	9.3	9.7	11.9	10.8
55 to 64 years	5.2	4.5	7.0	1.4	4.8
65 years and over	2.2	2.1	.9	2.0	1.2
Race and Hispanic origin					
White	88.3	83.6	68.4	76.8	83.8
Black	7.0	13.3	25.4	14.9	11.4
Hispanic origin	7.2	11.1	17.6	10.4	11.0
Full- or part-time status					
Full-time workers	75.2	52.6	79.2	89.7	83.2
Part-time workers	24.8	47.4	20.8	10.3	16.8

Note: Workers with traditional arrangements are those who do not fall into any of the "alternative arrangements" categories. Detail for the above race and Hispanic-origin groups will not sum to totals because data for the "other races" group are not presented and Hispanics are included in both the white and black population groups. Detail for other characteristics may not sum to totals due to rounding.

SOURCE: "Table 29. Percent Distribution of Employed Persons by Age, Sex, and Alternative Work Arrangements, February 2001," in *Women in the Labor Force: A Databook*, U.S. Department of Labor, Bureau of Labor Statistics, May 2005, http://www.bls.gov/cps/wlf-table29-2005.pdf (accessed June 9, 2005)

The BLS conducted a study titled *Twenty-first Century Moonlighters* (2002) to determine why more than one in twenty Americans held more than one job. Results indicated that one in three "moonlighters" worked multiple jobs to earn extra money. Another 27.8% moonlighted to meet expenses or pay off debt. Another reason cited by 17.4% of moonlighters was that they enjoyed the second job. Still another 4.6% wanted to build a business. Younger people tended to work more so that they could make extra money. Hispanic workers were almost equally split between holding multiple jobs to pay off debt or meet expenses (40.9%) and wanting to earn extra cash (38.3%). Nearly half of African-American moonlighters held more than one job to earn extra money. About one in five white moonlighters held more than one job because they liked the nature of the second job. Women were more likely than men to hold a second job to meet expenses or pay off debt (29% and 26.6%, respectively). Overall, the number of multiple jobholders has declined since 1997.

According to the Census Bureau, most women hold multiple jobs to meet household expenses. About one in ten women has a second job in order to pay off debts, and another 10% are working because they enjoy their second job. Smaller numbers of women are working multiple jobs to save for the future or to save up to buy something special.

UNEMPLOYMENT

Unemployment Rates

The labor force includes both people who are employed and people who are looking for work. In May 2005 the unemployment rate of adult women was 4.6%

TABLE 3.9

Multiple jobholders, 2003

[Annual average of monthly figures (7,315 represents 7,315,000). For the civilian noninstitutional population 16 years old and over. Multiple jobholders are employed persons who either 1) had jobs as wage or salary workers with two employers or more; 2) were self-employed and also held a wage and salary job; or 3) were unpaid family workers on their primary jobs but also held a wage and salary job.]

Characteristic	Total		Male		Female	
	Number (1,000)	Percent of employed	Number (1,000)	Percent of employed	Number (1,000)	Percent of employed
Total[a]	7,315	5.3	3,716	5.1	3,599	5.6
Age						
16 to 19 years old	280	4.7	107	3.7	173	5.7
20 to 24 years old	778	5.8	350	5.0	428	6.7
25 to 54 years old	5,266	5.4	2,742	5.3	2,525	5.6
55 to 64 years old	837	5.0	430	4.9	407	5.2
65 years old and over	154	3.3	87	3.4	67	3.3
Race and Hispanic origin						
White[b]	6,273	5.5	3,190	5.2	3,083	5.9
Black[b]	645	4.4	328	4.8	317	4.0
Asian[b]	196	3.4	96	3.1	100	3.7
Hispanic[c]	554	3.2	325	3.1	229	3.3
Marital status						
Married, spouse present	4,067	5.1	2,398	5.4	1,669	4.8
Widowed, divorced, or separated	1,270	5.8	410	4.6	860	6.6
Single, never married	1,978	5.4	907	4.6	1,070	6.4
Full- or part-time status						
Primary job full time, secondary job part time	3,825	(X)	2,164	(X)	1,661	(X)
Both jobs part time	1,651	(X)	510	(X)	1,141	(X)
Both jobs full time	273	(X)	187	(X)	86	(X)
Hours vary on primary or secondary job	1,523	(X)	831	(X)	692	(X)

X Not applicable.
[a]Includes a small number of persons who work part time on their primary job and full time on their secondary job(s), not shown separately. Includes other races, not shown separately.
[b]For persons who selected only one race. Excludes persons who selected more than one race.
[c]Persons of Hispanic or Latino origin may be of any race.

SOURCE: "Table 590. Multiple Jobholders: 2003," in *Statistical Abstract of the United States: 2004–2005*, U.S. Census Bureau, 2005, http://www.census.gov/prod/2004pubs/04statab/labor.pdf (accessed May 31, 2005)

and the rate for adult men was 4.4%. Young people were most likely to be unemployed. In 2004 the unemployment rate was 15.5% for young women age sixteen to nineteen years, 8.7% for twenty- to twenty-four-year-olds, 4.6% for women age twenty-five to fifty-four years, and 3.6% for women age fifty-five to sixty-four years. (See Table 3.10.) African-American women were also more likely to be unemployed than white women (9.8% versus 4.7%).

In May 2005 almost 3.6 million women workers sixteen and over were unemployed. The unemployment rate for women in 2000 was the lowest since before 1971, but the rate in 2003 was the highest it had been since 1994. (See Table 3.1.) The unemployment rate for men in 1971 was 5.3%, but it was 6.9% for women in that year. During the early 1990s the unemployment rate for women went through a rare period when it was lower than the unemployment rate for men.

Unemployed Mothers

In 2004, 77.2% of single women with children under eighteen years old were in the civilian labor force; fully 9.6% of these single mothers were unemployed, almost twice the unemployment rate of all women in

that year (5.6%) ("Table 6. Employment Status of Women by Presence and Age of Youngest Child, Marital Status, Race, and Hispanic or Latino Ethnicity, 2004," *Women in the Labor Force: A Databook*, Bureau of Labor Statistics, U.S. Department of Labor, May 2005). Many unmarried mothers have a lower socioeconomic status, lack job skills, and have limited access to child care. More financially well-off mothers often choose to remain at home until their children reach school age, either because of inadequate child care or from a desire to spend more time with their children during the formative years. Many of these women return to work when their children are older.

Duration of Unemployment

In 2004 the majority of unemployed people, including 31.1% of unemployed women age twenty and over, had been out of work for less than five weeks. (See Table 3.11.) Among unemployed women over nineteen, 29.6% had been out of work between five and fourteen weeks, and 39.3% had been unemployed for at least fifteen weeks. On average, men age sixteen and over stayed unemployed for 20.3 weeks, while women of the same age stayed unemployed for an average of 18.8 weeks ("Table 31.

TABLE 3.10

Employment status by age, sex, and race, 2004

[Numbers in thousands]

Age, sex, and race	Civilian noninstitutional population	Civilian labor force							Not in labor force
					Employed		Unemployed		
		Total	Percent of population	Total	Percent of population	Number	Percent of labor force		
Total									
16 years and over	223,357	147,401	66.0	139,252	62.3	8,149	5.5		75,956
16 to 19 years	16,222	7,114	43.9	5,907	36.4	1,208	17.0		9,108
16 to 17 years	8,574	2,747	32.0	2,193	25.6	554	20.2		5,827
18 to 19 years	7,648	4,367	57.1	3,714	48.6	653	15.0		3,281
20 to 24 years	20,197	15,154	75.0	13,723	67.9	1,431	9.4		5,043
25 to 54 years	123,410	102,122	82.8	97,472	79.0	4,650	4.6		21,288
25 to 34 years	38,939	32,207	82.7	30,423	78.1	1,784	5.5		6,732
25 to 29 years	18,985	15,569	82.0	14,615	77.0	955	6.1		3,415
30 to 34 years	19,954	16,638	83.4	15,808	79.2	829	5.0		3,317
35 to 44 years	43,226	36,158	83.6	34,580	80.0	1,578	4.4		7,068
35 to 39 years	20,573	17,169	83.5	16,370	79.6	799	4.7		3,404
40 to 44 years	22,653	18,989	83.8	18,210	80.4	779	4.1		3,664
45 to 54 years	41,245	33,758	81.8	32,469	78.7	1,288	3.8		7,488
45 to 49 years	21,886	18,310	83.7	17,586	80.4	724	4.0		3,577
50 to 54 years	19,359	15,448	79.8	14,883	76.9	565	3.7		3,911
55 to 64 years	28,919	18,013	62.3	17,331	59.9	682	3.8		10,906
55 to 59 years	16,327	11,603	71.1	11,166	68.4	437	3.8		4,724
60 to 64 years	12,592	6,410	50.9	6,166	49.0	245	3.8		6,182
65 years and over	34,609	4,998	14.4	4,819	13.9	179	3.6		29,611
65 to 69 years	9,800	2,710	27.7	2,614	26.7	96	3.5		7,090
70 to 74 years	8,381	1,280	15.3	1,234	14.7	46	3.6		7,100
75 years and over	16,429	1,007	6.1	971	5.9	36	3.6		15,421
Men									
16 years and over	107,710	78,980	73.3	74,524	69.2	4,456	5.6		28,730
16 to 19 years	8,234	3,616	43.9	2,952	35.9	664	18.4		4,617
16 to 17 years	4,318	1,329	30.8	1,037	24.0	292	22.0		2,989
18 to 19 years	3,916	2,288	58.4	1,915	48.9	372	16.3		1,628
20 to 24 years	10,125	8,057	79.6	7,246	71.6	811	10.1		2,068
25 to 54 years	60,773	54,972	90.5	52,468	86.3	2,504	4.6		5,801
25 to 34 years	19,358	17,798	91.9	16,818	86.9	980	5.5		1,560
25 to 29 years	9,478	8,618	90.9	8,083	85.3	535	6.2		861
30 to 34 years	9,879	9,180	92.9	8,735	88.4	446	4.9		699
35 to 44 years	21,255	19,539	91.9	18,700	88.0	839	4.3		1,716
35 to 39 years	10,135	9,397	92.7	8,967	88.5	430	4.6		738
40 to 44 years	11,121	10,142	91.2	9,733	87.5	409	4.0		979
45 to 54 years	20,160	17,635	87.5	16,951	84.1	684	3.9		2,525
45 to 49 years	10,729	9,581	89.3	9,193	85.7	388	4.1		1,148
50 to 54 years	9,432	8,054	85.4	7,758	82.3	296	3.7		1,378
55 to 64 years	13,894	9,547	68.7	9,174	66.0	373	3.9		4,347
55 to 59 years	7,916	6,139	77.6	5,899	74.5	240	3.9		1,776
60 to 64 years	5,978	3,408	57.0	3,275	54.8	133	3.9		2,570
65 years and over	14,684	2,787	19.0	2,683	18.3	104	3.7		11,897
65 to 69 years	4,573	1,490	32.6	1,436	31.4	54	3.6		3,082
70 to 74 years	3,721	721	19.4	693	18.6	28	3.8		3,000
75 years and over	6,391	576	9.0	554	8.7	22	3.8		5,814

Unemployed Persons by Age, Sex, Race, Hispanic or Latino Ethnicity, Marital Status, and Duration of Unemployment," U.S. Department of Labor, Bureau of Labor Statistics, 2004).

In 2004 people of Hispanic origin had the shortest average unemployment rates (17.3 weeks), although women had a higher average (18.7 weeks) than men (16.3 weeks). African-Americans and whites remained unemployed longer on average (23 weeks and 18.5 weeks, respectively), but both black and white females remain unemployed on average fewer weeks than males of either race. Never-married men and women remain unemployed for a shorter average period than married individuals living with their spouses. Widowed, divorced, or separated individuals remain unemployed for longer periods ("Table 31. Unemployed Persons by Age, Sex, Race, Hispanic or Latino Ethnicity, Marital Status, and Duration of Unemployment," Bureau of Labor Statistics).

Reasons for Unemployment

Among unemployed women age twenty and over in 2004, 48.5% had lost their jobs or had completed temporary jobs. (See Table 3.11.) Of these women, 21.3% were on temporary layoff. Another 35.1% of

TABLE 3.10

Employment status by age, sex, and race, 2004 [CONTINUED]

[Numbers in thousands]

Age, sex, and race	Civilian noninstitutional population	2004						
		Civilian labor force						Not in labor force
				Employed		Unemployed		
		Total	Percent of population	Total	Percent of population	Number	Percent of labor force	
Women								
16 years and over	115,647	68,421	59.2	64,728	56.0	3,694	5.4	47,225
16 to 19 years	7,989	3,498	43.8	2,955	37.0	543	15.5	4,491
16 to 17 years	4,257	1,418	33.3	1,156	27.2	262	18.5	2,838
18 to 19 years	3,732	2,080	55.7	1,799	48.2	281	13.5	1,652
20 to 24 years	10,072	7,097	70.5	6,477	64.3	619	8.7	2,975
25 to 54 years	62,636	47,150	75.3	45,003	71.8	2,147	4.6	15,486
25 to 34 years	19,581	14,409	73.6	13,605	69.5	804	5.6	5,172
25 to 29 years	9,506	6,952	73.1	6,532	68.7	420	6.0	2,555
30 to 34 years	10,075	7,457	74.0	7,073	70.2	384	5.1	2,618
35 to 44 years	21,970	16,619	75.6	15,880	72.3	739	4.4	5,352
35 to 39 years	10,438	7,772	74.5	7,403	70.9	369	4.7	2,666
40 to 44 years	11,532	8,847	76.7	8,477	73.5	370	4.2	2,686
45 to 54 years	21,085	16,123	76.5	15,518	73.6	605	3.7	4,962
45 to 49 years	11,158	8,729	78.2	8,393	75.2	335	3.8	2,429
50 to 54 years	9,927	7,394	74.5	7,125	71.8	269	3.6	2,533
55 to 64 years	15,025	8,466	56.3	8,157	54.3	309	3.6	6,559
55 to 59 years	8,411	5,463	65.0	5,266	62.6	197	3.6	2,948
60 to 64 years	6,614	3,002	45.4	2,890	43.7	112	3.7	3,612
65 years and over	19,925	2,211	11.1	2,135	10.7	75	3.4	17,714
65 to 69 years	5,227	1,220	23.3	1,178	22.5	42	3.5	4,007
70 to 74 years	4,660	560	12.0	541	11.6	19	3.3	4,100
75 years and over	10,038	431	4.3	416	4.1	14	3.4	9,607
White								
16 years and over	182,643	121,086	66.3	115,239	63.1	5,847	4.8	61,558
16 to 19 years	12,599	5,929	47.1	5,039	40.0	890	15.0	6,669
16 to 17 years	6,561	2,309	35.2	1,895	28.9	414	17.9	4,252
18 to 19 years	6,038	3,620	60.0	3,145	52.1	476	13.1	2,417
20 to 24 years	15,817	12,192	77.1	11,233	71.0	959	7.9	3,626
25 to 54 years	99,434	83,034	83.5	79,741	80.2	3,293	4.0	16,400
25 to 34 years	30,585	25,548	83.5	24,337	79.6	1,211	4.7	5,037
25 to 29 years	14,885	12,401	83.3	11,762	79.0	639	5.2	2,485
30 to 34 years	15,699	13,147	83.7	12,575	80.1	572	4.3	2,552
35 to 44 years	34,845	29,305	84.1	28,176	80.9	1,130	3.9	5,539
35 to 39 years	16,448	13,783	83.8	13,224	80.4	559	4.1	2,664
40 to 44 years	18,397	15,522	84.4	14,951	81.3	571	3.7	2,875
45 to 54 years	34,005	28,181	82.9	27,228	80.1	953	3.4	5,823
45 to 49 years	17,952	15,186	84.6	14,647	81.6	539	3.6	2,766
50 to 54 years	16,052	12,995	81.0	12,581	78.4	414	3.2	3,057
55 to 64 years	24,549	15,522	63.2	14,965	61.0	557	3.6	9,026
55 to 59 years	13,867	9,977	71.9	9,625	69.4	352	3.5	3,890
60 to 64 years	10,682	5,546	51.9	5,340	50.0	206	3.7	5,136
65 years and over	30,245	4,408	14.6	4,260	14.1	148	3.3	25,837
65 to 69 years	8,386	2,370	28.3	2,295	27.4	75	3.2	6,016
70 to 74 years	7,251	1,135	15.7	1,094	15.1	41	3.7	6,116
75 years and over	14,607	903	6.2	872	6.0	31	3.4	13,705

unemployed women over nineteen were trying to reenter the labor force after having left for a time. Women who had left their jobs accounted for 12.2% of unemployed women. The remaining 4.2% of unemployed women were trying to enter the labor force for the first time.

Displaced workers are people age twenty years and older who have lost jobs because their plants or companies have closed or moved, because there is insufficient work for them to do, or because their positions or shifts have been abolished. According to the Census Bureau, women are more likely than men to be unemployed or out of the labor force after being displaced.

Out of the Labor Force

Discouraged workers are job seekers who have stopped looking or people who want to work but who are unable to because they lack child care or transportation. Discouraged workers are not considered to be part of the labor force. According to the Bureau of Labor Statistics, of 47.2 million women who were not in the labor force in 2004, 5.7% wanted to be working. Of these women who wanted work, 28.5%

TABLE 3.10

Employment status by age, sex, and race, 2004 [CONTINUED]

[Numbers in thousands]

Age, sex, and race	Civilian noninstitutional population	2004						
		Civilian labor force						Not in labor force
				Employed		Unemployed		
		Total	Percent of population	Total	Percent of population	Number	Percent of labor force	
Men								
16 years and over	89,044	65,994	74.1	62,712	70.4	3,282	5.0	23,050
16 to 19 years	6,429	3,050	47.4	2,553	39.7	497	16.3	3,379
16 to 17 years	3,301	1,127	34.1	903	27.4	224	19.8	2,174
18 to 19 years	3,129	1,923	61.5	1,650	52.7	274	14.2	1,205
20 to 24 years	8,024	6,586	82.1	6,026	75.1	560	8.5	1,438
25 to 54 years	49,724	45,555	91.6	43,724	87.9	1,830	4.0	4,169
25 to 34 years	15,486	14,429	93.2	13,735	88.7	694	4.8	1,057
25 to 29 years	7,570	7,009	92.6	6,635	87.6	375	5.3	561
30 to 34 years	7,916	7,420	93.7	7,100	89.7	319	4.3	496
35 to 44 years	17,404	16,192	93.0	15,572	89.5	620	3.8	1,212
35 to 39 years	8,240	7,718	93.7	7,410	89.9	308	4.0	522
40 to 44 years	9,163	8,474	92.5	8,162	89.1	312	3.7	690
45 to 54 years	16,834	14,934	88.7	14,418	85.6	516	3.5	1,900
45 to 49 years	8,915	8,075	90.6	7,781	87.3	293	3.6	840
50 to 54 years	7,919	6,860	86.6	6,637	83.8	223	3.2	1,059
55 to 64 years	11,922	8,326	69.8	8,018	67.3	307	3.7	3,596
55 to 59 years	6,788	5,335	78.6	5,140	75.7	194	3.6	1,453
60 to 64 years	5,134	2,991	58.3	2,878	56.1	113	3.8	2,143
65 years and over	12,946	2,478	19.1	2,390	18.5	88	3.5	10,468
65 to 69 years	3,934	1,308	33.3	1,265	32.1	43	3.3	2,626
70 to 74 years	3,274	645	19.7	621	19.0	25	3.8	2,629
75 years and over	5,737	524	9.1	505	8.8	19	3.7	5,213
Women								
16 years and over	93,599	55,092	58.9	52,527	56.1	2,565	4.7	38,508
16 to 19 years	6,169	2,879	46.7	2,486	40.3	393	13.6	3,290
16 to 17 years	3,260	1,182	36.3	991	30.4	191	16.1	2,078
18 to 19 years	2,909	1,697	58.3	1,495	51.4	202	11.9	1,212
20 to 24 years	7,794	5,606	71.9	5,207	66.8	399	7.1	2,188
25 to 54 years	49,710	37,480	75.4	36,016	72.5	1,463	3.9	12,231
25 to 34 years	15,099	11,119	73.6	10,602	70.2	516	4.6	3,980
25 to 29 years	7,315	5,391	73.7	5,127	70.1	264	4.9	1,924
30 to 34 years	7,784	5,727	73.6	5,475	70.3	252	4.4	2,056
35 to 44 years	17,441	13,114	75.2	12,604	72.3	510	3.9	4,327
35 to 39 years	8,207	6,065	73.9	5,815	70.9	251	4.1	2,142
40 to 44 years	9,234	7,048	76.3	6,789	73.5	259	3.7	2,186
45 to 54 years	17,170	13,247	77.1	12,810	74.6	437	3.3	3,924
45 to 49 years	9,037	7,111	78.7	6,865	76.0	246	3.5	1,926
50 to 54 years	8,133	6,135	75.4	5,945	73.1	191	3.1	1,998
55 to 64 years	12,627	7,197	57.0	6,947	55.0	250	3.5	5,430
55 to 59 years	7,079	4,642	65.6	4,485	63.4	157	3.4	2,437
60 to 64 years	5,548	2,555	46.0	2,462	44.4	92	3.6	2,993
65 years and over	17,299	1,930	11.2	1,870	10.8	60	3.1	15,369
65 to 69 years	4,452	1,062	23.9	1,030	23.1	32	3.0	3,390
70 to 74 years	3,977	490	12.3	473	11.9	17	3.4	3,487
75 years and over	8,871	378	4.3	367	4.1	11	3.0	8,492

were both available to work and had looked for work in the past twelve months, but they were not currently looking for work and were therefore not considered to be part of the labor force. Of the 765,000 women in this category, 23.3% had become discouraged with their job prospects. They may have been unable to find a job or they may lack training or education. This also includes women who may have been discriminated against, perhaps for being a single mother or for being a member of the "wrong" age or race ("Table 35. Persons Not in the Labor Force by Desire and Availability for Work, Age, and Sex," Current Population Survey, Bureau of Labor Statistics, U.S. Department of Labor, 2004).

EDUCATION AND THE LABOR FORCE

There is a strong correlation between a woman's education and her labor force status. (See Table 3.12.) Overall, 59.6% of the civilian female population age twenty-five and over was in the labor force in 2003. Only 32.7% of women without a high school diploma were participating in the labor force; 55% of women who had graduated high school (but not attended

TABLE 3.10

[Numbers in thousands]

Age, sex, and race	Civilian noninstitutional population	2004						
		Civilian labor force						Not in labor force
				Employed		Unemployed		
		Total	Percent of population	Total	Percent of population	Number	Percent of labor force	
Black or African American								
16 years and over	26,065	16,638	63.8	14,909	57.2	1,729	10.4	9,428
16 to 19 years	2,423	762	31.4	520	21.5	241	31.7	1,661
16 to 17 years	1,350	272	20.2	169	12.5	103	37.8	1,078
18 to 19 years	1,072	489	45.6	351	32.7	138	28.3	583
20 to 24 years	2,821	1,926	68.3	1,572	55.7	353	18.4	896
25 to 54 years	15,095	12,033	79.7	11,006	72.9	1,027	8.5	3,062
25 to 34 years	5,020	4,076	81.2	3,635	72.4	441	10.8	945
25 to 29 years	2,492	1,968	79.0	1,726	69.2	242	12.3	525
30 to 34 years	2,528	2,108	83.4	1,909	75.5	199	9.5	420
35 to 44 years	5,335	4,380	82.1	4,039	75.7	341	7.8	956
35 to 39 years	2,571	2,142	83.3	1,961	76.3	182	8.5	429
40 to 44 years	2,764	2,237	80.9	2,078	75.2	159	7.1	527
45 to 54 years	4,739	3,578	75.5	3,332	70.3	245	6.9	1,162
45 to 49 years	2,583	2,014	78.0	1,881	72.8	133	6.6	569
50 to 54 years	2,156	1,564	72.5	1,451	67.3	112	7.2	592
55 to 64 years	2,827	1,538	54.4	1,452	51.4	86	5.6	1,290
55 to 59 years	1,564	987	63.1	932	59.6	55	5.6	577
60 to 64 years	1,263	551	43.6	520	41.2	31	5.6	712
65 years and over	2,899	380	13.1	359	12.4	21	5.5	2,519
65 to 69 years	944	213	22.5	199	21.1	13	6.2	732
70 to 74 years	724	97	13.4	94	13.0	3	3.3	627
75 years and over	1,231	70	5.7	66	5.3	5	6.8	1,161
Men								
16 years and over	11,656	7,773	66.7	6,912	59.3	860	11.1	3,884
16 to 19 years	1,195	359	30.0	231	19.3	128	35.6	837
16 to 17 years	680	128	18.8	76	11.1	52	40.8	552
18 to 19 years	516	231	44.7	155	30.1	75	32.7	285
20 to 24 years	1,326	927	69.9	739	55.7	188	20.3	399
25 to 54 years	6,774	5,585	82.5	5,094	75.2	491	8.8	1,189
25 to 34 years	2,242	1,931	86.1	1,720	76.7	211	10.9	311
25 to 29 years	1,121	937	83.6	818	73.0	119	12.7	184
30 to 34 years	1,121	995	88.7	902	80.4	92	9.3	127
35 to 44 years	2,382	2,000	84.0	1,840	77.2	160	8.0	382
35 to 39 years	1,141	987	86.5	898	78.7	89	9.0	154
40 to 44 years	1,241	1,013	81.7	942	75.9	72	7.1	228
45 to 54 years	2,150	1,654	76.9	1,534	71.4	120	7.2	496
45 to 49 years	1,175	929	79.1	863	73.5	66	7.1	246
50 to 54 years	975	724	74.3	671	68.8	54	7.4	250
55 to 64 years	1,250	714	57.1	668	53.4	46	6.4	537
55 to 59 years	706	471	66.7	441	62.5	30	6.3	235
60 to 64 years	544	243	44.6	226	41.6	16	6.7	302
65 years and over	1,111	188	17.0	180	16.2	8	4.2	922
65 to 69 years	413	104	25.1	99	24.0	5	4.5	309
70 to 74 years	276	50	18.0	48	17.4	2	3.1	227
75 years and over	422	35	8.3	33	7.8	2	5.1	387

college), 67.2% of women with some college, and 73.1% of female college graduates participated in the labor force. Regardless of race or ethnicity, more educated women had higher labor force participation rates.

These trends are expected to continue. As Table 3.13 shows, the Bureau of Labor Statistics projects a total employment growth of 15.2% between 2000 and 2010. The Bureau projects that jobs requiring an associate degree will grow by 32%, those requiring bachelor's degrees will grow by 22.5%, and those requiring doctoral degrees will grow by 23.7%. Jobs that require nothing but

short-term on-the-job training are projected to grow by only 14.4%. Over the same period, there are projected to be 57.9 million job openings because of replacements and new jobs. Of these, 57.8% will require only short- or medium-term on-the-job training. However, 20.9% are expected to require a bachelor's or higher degree.

LABOR FORCE PROJECTIONS

The Bureau of Labor Statistics expects the labor force to grow steadily through 2012 (Mitra Toossi, "Labor Force Projections to 2012: The Graying of the U.S. Workforce," *Monthly Labor Review*, February

TABLE 3.10

Employment status by age, sex, and race, 2004 [CONTINUED]

[Numbers in thousands]

Age, sex, and race	Civilian noninstitutional population	2004						
		Civilian labor force						Not in labor force
				Employed		Unemployed		
		Total	Percent of population	Total	Percent of population	Number	Percent of labor force	
Women								
16 years and over	14,409	8,865	61.5	7,997	55.5	868	9.8	5,544
16 to 19 years	1,227	403	32.8	289	23.6	114	28.2	824
16 to 17 years	670	144	21.5	93	13.9	51	35.2	526
18 to 19 years	557	259	46.5	196	35.2	63	24.3	298
20 to 24 years	1,495	999	66.8	833	55.7	166	16.6	497
25 to 54 years	8,321	6,448	77.5	5,912	71.0	536	8.3	1,873
25 to 34 years	2,778	2,144	77.2	1,914	68.9	230	10.7	634
25 to 29 years	1,371	1,031	75.2	907	66.2	123	12.0	341
30 to 34 years	1,407	1,113	79.1	1,007	71.6	107	9.6	293
35 to 44 years	2,954	2,380	80.6	2,199	74.5	180	7.6	574
35 to 39 years	1,430	1,156	80.8	1,063	74.3	93	8.0	275
40 to 44 years	1,523	1,224	80.3	1,137	74.6	87	7.1	299
45 to 54 years	2,590	1,924	74.3	1,798	69.4	126	6.5	665
45 to 49 years	1,408	1,085	77.0	1,018	72.3	67	6.2	323
50 to 54 years	1,181	839	71.0	780	66.1	59	7.0	342
55 to 64 years	1,577	824	52.3	784	49.7	40	4.8	753
55 to 59 years	858	516	60.1	490	57.2	25	4.9	342
60 to 64 years	719	308	42.9	294	40.8	15	4.8	411
65 years and over	1,789	192	10.7	179	10.0	13	6.8	1,597
65 to 69 years	532	109	20.5	100	18.9	8	7.8	423
70 to 74 years	447	47	10.6	46	10.2	2	3.4	400
75 years and over	810	36	4.4	33	4.0	3	8.5	774
Asian								
16 years and over	9,519	6,271	65.9	5,994	63.0	277	4.4	3,248
16 to 19 years	606	172	28.4	152	25.1	20	11.5	434
16 to 17 years	337	63	18.6	54	16.1	8	13.6	274
18 to 19 years	269	109	40.5	98	36.3	11	10.4	160
20 to 24 years	876	539	61.5	493	56.3	46	8.6	337
25 to 54 years	5,944	4,748	79.9	4,570	76.9	178	3.7	1,196
25 to 34 years	2,234	1,714	76.7	1,646	73.7	68	4.0	520
25 to 29 years	1,034	754	72.9	719	69.5	35	4.7	280
30 to 34 years	1,200	960	80.0	927	77.3	33	3.4	240
35 to 44 years	2,044	1,671	81.7	1,613	78.9	58	3.5	374
35 to 39 years	1,061	849	80.1	818	77.1	31	3.6	212
40 to 44 years	984	821	83.5	794	80.7	27	3.3	162
45 to 54 years	1,665	1,363	81.8	1,312	78.8	51	3.8	302
45 to 49 years	900	758	84.2	731	81.2	27	3.6	142
50 to 54 years	765	605	79.1	581	75.9	24	4.0	160
55 to 64 years	1,052	676	64.2	649	61.7	27	4.0	376
55 to 59 years	613	459	74.9	437	71.3	22	4.7	154
60 to 64 years	440	217	49.4	212	48.3	5	2.4	222
65 years and over	1,041	137	13.1	130	12.5	6	4.7	904
65 to 69 years	321	86	26.9	81	25.4	5	5.7	234
70 to 74 years	295	28	9.6	27	9.1	1	*	267
75 years and over	425	22	5.2	22	5.2	—	*	403

2004). The rate of women's labor force participation is expected to stay higher than the overall labor force participation rate. Women are expected to increase their share of the labor force from 46.5% in 2002 o 47.5% in 2012, while men's share will decline.

Labor force growth was incredibly rapid in the 1970s because of the baby boom generation as well as a more general acceptance of women working outside the home. As the baby boomers age, the labor force will become older. The BLS projects an annual increase of 4.1% in the labor force population age fifty-five and older from 2002 to 2012, four times the annual growth rate of the overall labor force. This age group is expected to comprise 19.1% of the labor force by 2012, according to Toossi.

Due mostly to immigration, a younger population, and higher fertility rates, Hispanics and Asian-Americans will continue to have the highest percentage growth in the labor force. According to Toossi, the annual growth rate in labor force participation during the 2002–12 period for people of Hispanic origin is expected to be 2.9%, twice the annual growth rate of the overall labor force, and for Asian-Americans the rate is expected to be 4.2%, four times the annual growth rate of the overall labor force.

TABLE 3.10

Employment status by age, sex, and race, 2004 [CONTINUED]

[Numbers in thousands]

Age, sex, and race	Civilian noninstitutional population	2004 Civilian labor force						Not in labor force
		Total	Percent of population	Employed		Unemployed		
				Total	Percent of population	Number	Percent of labor force	
Men								
16 years and over	4,529	3,396	75.0	3,243	71.6	153	4.5	1,133
16 to 19 years	313	91	29.0	78	24.9	13	14.0	222
16 to 17 years	171	30	17.4	24	14.4	5	(*)	141
18 to 19 years	143	61	42.8	54	37.5	8	12.4	82
20 to 24 years	434	277	63.8	255	58.6	23	8.2	157
25 to 54 years	2,846	2,582	90.7	2,484	87.3	98	3.8	264
25 to 34 years	1,089	957	87.8	918	84.2	39	4.1	133
25 to 29 years	506	425	83.9	406	80.3	19	4.4	81
30 to 34 years	583	532	91.2	512	87.7	20	3.8	51
35 to 44 years	986	917	93.0	883	89.5	34	3.7	69
35 to 39 years	504	468	92.9	449	89.1	19	4.1	36
40 to 44 years	482	448	93.0	434	90.0	14	3.2	34
45 to 54 years	770	709	92.0	683	88.7	26	3.6	61
45 to 49 years	418	395	94.4	380	90.7	15	3.9	24
50 to 54 years	352	314	89.2	304	86.2	11	3.4	38
55 to 64 years	490	361	73.8	347	70.9	14	3.9	129
55 to 59 years	288	239	83.0	227	78.9	12	4.9	49
60 to 64 years	202	123	60.6	120	59.5	2	1.9	80
65 years and over	445	84	18.9	79	17.8	5	5.9	361
65 to 69 years	151	58	38.7	54	36.2	4	6.4	92
70 to 74 years	123	15	12.4	14	11.4	1	*	108
75 years and over	171	11	6.3	11	6.3	—	*	161
Women								
16 years and over	4,990	2,876	57.6	2,751	55.1	124	4.3	2,114
16 to 19 years	293	81	27.7	74	25.3	7	8.7	212
16 to 17 years	166	33	19.8	30	17.8	3	*	133
18 to 19 years	127	48	38.0	44	35.0	4	7.8	79
20 to 24 years	442	262	59.3	238	54.0	24	9.0	180
25 to 54 years	3,098	2,165	69.9	2,086	67.3	79	3.7	932
25 to 34 years	1,144	757	66.2	728	63.6	29	3.9	387
25 to 29 years	527	329	62.4	312	59.2	17	5.1	198
30 to 34 years	617	428	69.4	416	67.4	13	2.9	189
35 to 44 years	1,058	754	71.2	730	68.9	24	3.2	304
35 to 39 years	557	381	68.4	369	66.3	12	3.0	176
40 to 44 years	502	373	74.4	360	71.8	13	3.5	128
45 to 54 years	895	654	73.1	629	70.2	25	3.9	241
45 to 49 years	482	364	75.4	352	72.9	12	3.3	119
50 to 54 years	413	291	70.4	277	67.1	13	4.6	122
55 to 64 years	562	315	55.9	302	53.7	13	4.1	248
55 to 59 years	325	220	67.7	210	64.6	10	4.6	105
60 to 64 years	237	95	39.9	92	38.7	3	2.9	143
65 years and over	596	53	8.8	51	8.6	1	2.7	543
65 to 69 years	170	28	16.5	27	15.8	1	*	142
70 to 74 years	172	13	7.5	13	7.4	—	*	159
75 years and over	254	11	4.5	11	4.5	—	*	243

*Data not shown where base is less than 35,000.
Note: Estimates for the above race groups (white, black or African American, and Asian) do not sum to totals because data are not presented for all races. Beginning in January 2004, data reflect revised population controls used in the household survey. Dash indicates no data or data that do not meet publication criteria.

SOURCE: "Table 3. Employment Status of the Civilian Noninstitutional Population by Age, Sex, and Race," U.S. Department of Labor, Bureau of Labor Statistics, 2004, http://www.bls.gov/cps/cpsaat3.pdf (accessed June 9, 2005)

TABLE 3.11

Unemployed persons, by reason of unemployment, sex, age, and duration of unemployment, 2004

[Percent distribution]

| | Total unemployed | | Duration of unemployment | | 15 weeks and over | | |
| | | | | | | | |
Reason, sex, and age	Thousands of persons	Percent	Less than 5 weeks	5 to 14 weeks	Total	15 to 26 weeks	27 weeks and over
Total, 16 years and over	**8,149**	**100.0**	**33.1**	**29.2**	**37.7**	**15.9**	**21.8**
Job losers and persons who completed temporary jobs	4,197	100.0	32.8	28.5	38.7	16.6	22.1
On temporary layoff	998	100.0	53.3	30.6	16.1	10.3	5.8
Not on temporary layoff	3,199	100.0	26.5	27.8	45.8	18.6	27.2
Permanent job losers	2,386	100.0	23.6	26.8	49.6	19.3	30.3
Persons who completed temporary jobs	813	100.0	34.9	30.6	34.6	16.6	18.0
Job leavers	858	100.0	38.5	29.9	31.7	15.3	16.4
Reentrants	2,408	100.0	31.6	29.1	39.3	15.3	23.9
New entrants	686	100.0	32.9	33.7	33.4	13.7	19.7
Men, 20 years and over	**3,791**	**100.0**	**31.1**	**28.0**	**40.9**	**16.2**	**24.7**
Job losers and persons who completed temporary jobs	2,503	100.0	31.9	28.1	39.9	16.6	23.3
On temporary layoff	613	100.0	49.5	31.7	18.8	12.1	6.7
Not on temporary layoff	1,890	100.0	26.3	27.0	46.7	18.1	28.6
Permanent job losers	1,366	100.0	23.2	25.7	51.1	18.5	32.6
Persons who completed temporary jobs	524	100.0	34.3	30.4	35.4	17.0	18.4
Job leavers	398	100.0	35.6	29.6	34.8	14.8	20.0
Reentrants	791	100.0	27.4	26.5	46.1	15.7	30.4
New entrants	99	100.0	21.3	30.5	48.2	13.3	34.9
Women, 20 years and over	**3,150**	**100.0**	**31.1**	**29.6**	**39.3**	**17.1**	**22.2**
Job losers and persons who completed temporary jobs	1,529	100.0	31.0	29.2	39.8	17.7	22.0
On temporary layoff	326	100.0	55.4	32.0	12.6	7.7	4.8
Not on temporary layoff	1,202	100.0	24.4	28.4	47.1	20.4	26.7
Permanent job losers	949	100.0	22.1	27.8	50.0	21.2	28.8
Persons who completed temporary jobs	253	100.0	33.0	30.7	36.3	17.5	18.7
Job leavers	384	100.0	38.0	30.8	31.3	16.8	14.4
Reentrants	1,107	100.0	29.5	29.3	41.2	16.6	24.6
New entrants	131	100.0	24.4	33.1	42.5	16.0	26.5
Both sexes, 16 to 19 years	**1,208**	**100.0**	**44.6**	**32.1**	**23.4**	**11.6**	**11.8**
Job losers and persons who completed temporary jobs	165	100.0	62.9	26.2	10.9	6.1	4.9
On temporary layoff	59	100.0	80.6	12.0	7.4	5.0	2.4
Not on temporary layoff	107	100.0	53.2	33.9	12.9	6.7	6.2
Permanent job losers	71	100.0	51.6	34.6	13.8	7.7	6.1
Persons who completed temporary jobs	36	100.0	56.1	32.7	11.2	4.6	6.6
Job leavers	76	100.0	55.9	26.9	17.2	10.3	7.0
Reentrants	510	100.0	42.9	32.6	24.5	12.2	12.3
New entrants	456	100.0	37.8	34.5	27.6	13.2	14.4

Note: Beginning in January 2004, data reflect revised population controls used in the household survey.

SOURCE: "Table 29. Unemployed Persons by Reason for Unemployment, Sex, Age, and Duration of Unemployment," U.S. Department of Labor, Bureau of Labor Statistics, 2004, http://www.bls.gov/cps/cpsaat29.pdf (accessed May 31, 2005).

TABLE 3.12

Civilian labor force and participation rates, by educational attainment, sex, race, and Hispanic origin, 1992–2003

[106,490 represents 106,490,000. Annual averages of monthly figures. For the civilian noninstitutional population 25 years of age and older.]

Year, sex, and race	Total (1,000)	Civilian labor force — Percent distribution				Participation rate				
		Less than high school diploma	High school graduate, no degree	Less than a bachelor's degree	College graduate	Total	Less than high school diploma	High school graduates, no degree	Less than a bachelor's degree	College graduate
Total:[a]										
1992	106,490	12.6	35.6	25.4	26.4	66.5	41.2	66.4	75.3	81.3
1995	110,851	10.8	33.1	27.9	28.1	66.7	39.9	65.4	74.5	81.0
2000	120,061	10.4	31.4	27.7	30.5	67.3	43.5	64.4	73.9	79.4
2002	122,497	10.3	30.8	27.4	31.4	67.2	44.4	64.2	73.1	78.6
2003	124,412	10.2	30.5	27.4	32.0	67.2	44.9	63.8	72.8	78.2
Male:										
1992	58,439	14.1	34.0	24.0	27.9	77.0	54.7	78.3	83.9	86.9
1995	59,986	12.2	32.3	26.1	29.4	76.0	52.1	76.5	82.1	85.8
2000	64,490	11.8	31.1	25.9	31.2	76.1	56.0	75.1	80.9	84.4
2002	65,861	11.9	30.7	25.5	31.9	75.9	57.2	74.5	80.2	84.0
2003	66,717	11.9	30.5	25.4	32.2	75.5	57.7	74.0	79.5	83.2
Female:										
1992	48,051	10.7	37.5	27.1	24.7	57.1	29.5	56.8	67.8	74.8
1995	50,865	9.2	34.2	30.0	26.6	58.3	29.2	56.4	68.1	75.4
2000	55,572	8.8	31.8	29.7	29.7	59.4	32.3	55.5	68.0	74.0
2002	56,636	8.4	30.9	29.7	31.0	59.4	32.5	55.3	67.2	73.0
2003	57,695	8.2	30.4	29.6	31.8	59.6	32.7	55.0	67.2	73.1
White:[b]										
1992	90,627	11.8	35.5	25.5	27.2	66.3	41.1	65.4	74.6	81.0
1995	94,139	10.1	33.0	27.8	29.1	66.7	40.0	64.8	73.8	80.6
2000	99,964	10.1	31.4	27.5	31.0	67.0	44.1	63.6	73.1	79.0
2002	101,711	10.0	30.8	27.3	31.9	67.0	44.9	63.4	72.5	78.2
2003	102,509	10.0	30.4	27.2	32.5	66.9	45.7	62.9	72.2	77.8
Black:[b]										
1992	11,583	18.2	39.5	26.4	15.9	66.7	40.6	72.9	80.9	86.2
1995	12,152	13.9	37.1	30.7	18.3	66.0	36.2	69.7	79.8	85.6
2000	13,582	12.4	36.0	31.2	20.5	68.2	39.3	69.9	79.3	84.4
2002	13,787	12.5	35.4	31.5	20.5	67.6	40.8	68.4	77.8	82.8
2003	13,863	11.5	35.5	31.2	21.8	67.5	39.8	68.1	77.0	82.3
Asian:[b,c]										
2000	5,402	9.1	20.7	20.2	50.1	70.9	46.0	65.6	76.4	79.1
2003	5,420	8.7	19.4	17.3	54.5	69.8	46.3	65.0	71.9	77.4
Hispanic:[d]										
1992	8,728	38.9	29.6	20.0	11.5	68.3	56.3	75.5	82.2	83.2
1995	9,599	37.2	29.3	21.7	11.7	67.5	55.3	74.3	79.7	83.1
2000	12,975	36.7	29.3	20.6	13.4	71.5	61.9	75.0	80.8	83.5
2002	14,162	36.3	29.4	20.3	13.9	71.0	61.3	74.1	80.7	83.2
2003	15,181	36.4	29.2	20.4	14.0	70.7	61.6	73.9	79.2	81.8

[a]Includes other races, not shown separately.
[b]Beginning 2003, for persons in this race group only.
[c]Prior to 2003, includes Pacific Islanders.
[d]Persons of Hispanic or Latino origin may be of any race.

SOURCE: "Table 573. Civilian Labor Force and Participation Rates by Educational Attainment, Sex, Race, and Hispanic Origin: 1992–2003," in *Statistical Abstract of the United States: 2004–2005*, U.S. Census Bureau, 2005, http://www.census.gov/prod/2004pubs/04statab/labor.pdf (accessed May 31, 2005)

TABLE 3.13

Employment and total job openings by education or training category, 2000–10

Most significant source of education or training	Employment				Change, 2000–2010			Total job openings due to growth and net replacements, 2000–2010*	
	Number		Percent distribution			Percent distribution	Percent	Number	Percent distribution
	2000	2010	2000	2010	Number				
Total, all occupations	145,594	167,754	100.0	100.0	22,160	100.0	15.2	57,932	100.0
Bachelor's or higher degree	30,072	36,556	20.7	21.8	6,484	29.3	21.6	12,130	20.9
First professional degree	2,034	2,404	1.4	1.4	370	1.7	18.2	691	1.2
Doctoral degree	1,492	1,845	1.0	1.1	353	1.6	23.7	760	1.3
Master's degree	1,426	1,759	1.0	1.0	333	1.5	23.4	634	1.1
Bachelor's or higher degree, plus work experience	7,319	8,741	5.0	5.2	1,422	6.4	19.4	2,741	4.7
Bachelor's degree	17,801	21,807	12.2	13.0	4,006	18.1	22.5	7,304	12.6
Associate degree or postsecondary vocational award	11,761	14,600	8.1	8.7	2,839	12.8	24.1	5,383	9.3
Associate degree	5,083	6,710	3.5	4.0	1,626	7.3	32.0	2,608	4.5
Postsecondary vocational award	6,678	7,891	4.6	4.7	1,213	5.5	18.2	2,775	4.8
Work-related training	103,760	116,597	71.3	69.5	12,837	57.9	12.4	40,419	69.8
Work experience in a related occupation	10,456	11,559	7.2	6.9	1,102	5.0	10.5	3,180	5.5
Long-term on-the-job training	12,435	13,373	8.5	8.0	938	4.2	7.5	3,737	6.5
Moderate-term on-the-job training	27,671	30,794	19.0	18.4	3,123	14.1	11.3	8,767	15.1
Short-term on-the-job training	53,198	60,871	36.5	36.3	7,673	34.6	14.4	24,735	42.7

*Total job openings represent the sum of employment increases and net replacements. If employment change is negative, job openings due to growth are zero and total job openings equal net replacements.
Note: Detail may not equal total or 100 percent due to rounding.

SOURCE: "Table 4. Employment and Total Job Openings by Education or Training Category, 2000–2010," U.S. Department of Labor, Bureau of Labor Statistics, http://www2a.cdc.gov/niosh-Chartbook/appendix/ap-c/Bibliography/CPS/ecopro.txt (accessed May 31, 2005)

CHAPTER 4
WOMEN'S OCCUPATIONS

Until the second half of the twentieth century, women's occupations outside of the home were restricted primarily to a very few selected fields in which women would be unlikely to compete with men. Thus, women were household servants and nannies, farm workers, shop girls, seamstresses, laundresses, barmaids, and waitresses. Early businesswomen were mainly shopkeepers and innkeepers. With the Industrial Revolution, lower-class women went to work in factories, particularly in the garment industry. As women's educational opportunities improved, women became teachers of young children, nurses, and social workers. Other women began replacing men as clerical workers and secretaries.

LEGAL RESTRICTIONS

Tradition was codified into law in the latter part of the nineteenth century when the appalling conditions of factory sweatshops brought together diverse groups, including labor leaders and feminists, in support of labor laws for the protection of women and children. *U.S. v. Martin* (18 Stat 737, 1868) and other court rulings and laws that followed limited the hours that women could work and banned them from certain occupations that required exertion or that might be "morally corrupting." In some states women were banned from bartending and setting pins in bowling alleys as well as from freight handling and mining.

For the most part, barring women from secondary or higher education was enough to keep them out of professions in which they could compete with men. If that failed, the law was called upon. In *Bradwell v. Illinois* (83 U.S., 16 Wall, 1872), the U.S. Supreme Court upheld an Illinois law prohibiting women from practicing law. The high court held that:

> The natural proper timidity and delicacy which belongs to the female sex unfits it for many occupations of civil life. The constitution of the family organization, which

is founded in the divine ordinance, as well as in the nature of things, indicates the domestic sphere as that which properly belongs to the domain and functions of womanhood.

Well into the twentieth century employers were able to use labor laws and court rulings to justify not hiring women for certain jobs or for restricting their hours and paying them less than men. When the Civil Rights Act of 1964 (PL 88–352) and the case law built on it freed women to enter nearly any occupation, some employers resorted to old arguments about the reproductive functions of women in order to bar them from jobs.

Johnson Controls, for example, adopted a policy barring all women, regardless of age, from jobs involving contact with lead in its car battery manufacturing plant, unless the women had medical proof of sterility. As a result, women were kept out of some of the highest-paying jobs at the plant. In 1991 in *United Automobile Workers v. Johnson Controls* (499 U.S. 187), the Supreme Court ruled that the Civil Rights Act of 1964 prohibited companies from barring women from jobs that might jeopardize a developing fetus. The Court noted that "decisions about the welfare of future children must be left to the parents who conceive, bear, support and raise them rather than to the employers who hire those parents."

TRADITIONAL FEMALE OCCUPATIONS

While formal restrictions barring women from many occupations have for the most part disappeared, most women in the American labor force still work in what may be considered traditionally female occupations. In 2004 more than nine out of ten nurses, secretaries, preschool, kindergarten, and elementary school teachers, bookkeeping and accounting clerks, receptionists, and teacher assistants were women. (See Table 4.1.) There were more women working as secretaries and administrative assistants than in any other occupation, but while

TABLE 4.1

Twenty leading occupations of employed women full-time wage and salary workers, 2004

[Employment in thousands]

Occupation	Total employed women	Total employed (men and women)	Percent women	Women's median weekly earnings
Total, 16 years and older (all employed women, full-time wage and salary workers)	44,223	101,224	43.7	$573
Secretaries and administrative assistants	2,570	2,657	96.7	550
Elementary and middle school teachers	1,772	2,206	96.7	550
Registered nurses	1,651	1,800	91.8	895
Nursing, psychiatric, and home health aides	1,113	1,261	88.3	383
Cashiers	1,016	1,355	75	313
First-line supervisors/managers of office and administrative support	1,001	1,441	69.5	636
First-line supervisors/managers of retail sales workers	985	2,246	43.9	505
Customer service representatives	967	1,379	70.1	504
Bookkeeping, accounting, and auditing clerks	916	1,004	91.2	542
Accountants and auditors	842	1,385	60.8	757
Receptionists and information clerks	795	847	93.9	463
Retail salespersons	766	1,865	41.1	386
Maid and housekeeping cleaners	723	818	89.7	324
Office clerks, general	559	667	83.8	499
Secondary school teachers	555	1,013	54.8	824
Waiters and waitresses	538	799	67.3	327
Financial managers	535	961	55.7	839
Teacher assistants	500	545	91.7	373
Preschool and kindergarten teachers	473	484	97.7	515
Social workers	472	620	76.1	689

SOURCE: "Twenty Leading Occupations of Employed Women Full-Time Wage and Salary Workers 2004 Annual Averages," U.S. Department of Labor, Women's Bureau, 2005, http://www.dol.gov/wb/factsheets/20lead2004.htm (accessed June 1, 2005)

96.7% of secretaries and administrative assistants were women, 69.5% of the immediate supervisors of secretaries were female. Among teachers, women were concentrated in the lower-paying preschool and elementary school positions; 97.7% of preschool and kindergarten teachers and 96.7% of elementary school teachers were women, but only 54.8% of better-paid secondary school teachers were women.

In 2004 more than one-third of employed women over the age of sixteen (37.7%) were in management, professional, and related occupations; another third (35%) were in sales and office occupations; one in five (19.9%) were in service occupations; and the rest were in production, transportation, and material moving occupations or natural resources, construction, and maintenance occupations. (See Table 4.2.) In contrast, 32.4% of male workers were in management, professional, and related occupations, 12.3% in service occupations, and 17.2% in

sales and office occupations. Almost one-fifth of male workers (18.7%) were in natural resources, construction, and maintenance occupations, and nearly as many (18.6%) were in production, transportation, and material moving occupations. In general, male workers were more spread out among the five major occupational groups than were female workers, who were concentrated in management/professional occupations, sales/office occupations, and to a lesser extent in service occupations.

Of all employed white women in 2004, 38.6% were in management, professional, and related occupations, compared with 43.8% of Asian-American women, 30.6% of African-American women, and 22.4% of Hispanic women. (See Table 4.3.) A greater proportion of women than men were professionals (24.5% and 16.7%, respectively), and more men than women were in management, business, or financial operations (15.7% and 13.2%, respectively).

Almost 12.9 million American women age sixteen and older were in service occupations in 2004, compared with about 9.8 million men. Among employed white and Asian-American women, 18.8% were in service occupations, compared with 27% of employed black women and 30.3% of Hispanic women. (See Table 4.3.) A far greater proportion of men than women were in protective service occupations, while most workers in personal care and service were women. (See Table 4.2.)

Minority women were more likely than white women to be employed in the traditionally male occupation of production, transportation, and material moving occupations. Only 6% of white women were employed in these fields, compared with 8.2% of African-American women, 8.6% of Asian-American women, and 12.2% of Hispanic women. Only about 1% of all women worked in natural resources, construction, and maintenance occupations. (See Table 4.3.)

In all occupations, women earn less than men ("Table 18. Median Usual Weekly Earnings of Full-time Wage and Salary Workers by Detailed Occupation and Sex, 2004 Annual Averages," *Women in the Labor Force: A Database*, Bureau of Labor Statistics, U.S. Department of Labor, May 2005). In 2004 women earned 87.4% what men earned. In traditionally female occupations, the wage differential is particularly stark. In all education, training, and library occupations, for example, women earn 76.3% what men earn. In personal care and service occupations, women earn 76% of what men earn. (See Chapter 5 for more information on women's earnings.)

NEW OCCUPATIONS FOR WOMEN

Although the majority of women continue to work in occupations that traditionally have been considered female, the proportions of women in some traditional

TABLE 4.2

Employed persons, by occupation, sex, and age, 2003–04

[In thousands]

Occupation	Total 16 years and over		Men 16 years and over		Men 20 years and over		Women 16 years and over		Women 20 years and over	
	2003	2004	2003	2004	2003	2004	2003	2004	2003	2004
Total	**137,736**	**139,252**	**73,332**	**74,524**	**70,415**	**71,572**	**64,404**	**64,728**	**61,402**	**61,773**
Management, professional, and related occupations	47,929	48,532	23,735	24,136	23,597	23,989	24,194	24,396	23,978	24,198
Management, business, and financial operations occupations	19,934	20,235	11,534	11,718	11,508	11,685	8,400	8,517	8,372	8,493
Management occupations	14,468	14,555	9,094	9,210	9,075	9,183	5,374	5,344	5,356	5,326
Business and financial operations occupations	5,465	5,680	2,440	2,508	2,433	2,502	3,026	3,172	3,016	3,168
Professional and related occupations	27,995	28,297	12,201	12,418	12,089	12,304	15,794	15,879	15,606	15,705
Computer and mathematical occupations	3,122	3,140	2,223	2,292	2,209	2,277	900	848	895	843
Architecture and engineering occupations	2,727	2,760	2,343	2,380	2,334	2,375	384	380	382	377
Life, physical, and social science occupations	1,375	1,365	783	777	778	771	592	588	585	585
Community and social services occupations	2,184	2,170	862	845	857	838	1,323	1,325	1,313	1,314
Legal occupations	1,508	1,554	811	795	811	793	697	759	691	757
Education, training, and library occupations	7,768	7,900	2,038	2,104	2,004	2,078	5,730	5,796	5,642	5,717
Arts, design, entertainment, sports, and media occupations	2,663	2,687	1,395	1,425	1,357	1,382	1,267	1,262	1,223	1,219
Healthcare practitioner and technical occupations	6,648	6,721	1,746	1,799	1,739	1,789	4,902	4,922	4,876	4,894
Service occupations	22,086	22,720	9,460	9,826	8,408	8,776	12,626	12,894	11,393	11,677
Healthcare support occupations	2,926	2,921	311	311	286	296	2,616	2,609	2,528	2,519
Protective service occupations	2,727	2,847	2,164	2,230	2,109	2,178	563	616	515	566
Food preparation and serving related occupations	7,254	7,279	3,151	3,196	2,483	2,506	4,104	4,084	3,336	3,323
Building and grounds cleaning and maintenance occupations	4,947	5,185	2,920	3,085	2,722	2,907	2,027	2,100	1,956	2,030
Personal care and service occupations	4,232	4,488	915	1,004	807	889	3,316	3,484	3,059	3,238
Sales and office occupations	35,496	35,464	12,851	12,805	12,056	12,027	22,645	22,660	21,265	21,270
Sales and related occupations	15,960	15,983	8,137	8,105	7,662	7,645	7,823	7,878	6,936	6,968
Office and administrative support occupations	19,536	19,481	4,714	4,700	4,394	4,382	14,823	14,781	14,329	14,302
Natural resources, construction, and maintenance occupations	14,205	14,582	13,541	13,930	13,106	13,474	665	652	623	619
Farming, fishing, and forestry occupations	1,050	991	819	786	739	704	231	204	206	181
Construction and extraction occupations	8,114	8,522	7,891	8,306	7,636	8,030	223	216	214	208
Installation, maintenance, and repair occupations	5,041	5,069	4,830	4,838	4,730	4,740	211	231	204	230
Production, transportation, and material moving occupations	18,020	17,954	13,745	13,827	13,248	13,306	4,274	4,126	4,143	4,008
Production occupations	9,700	9,462	6,696	6,587	6,566	6,437	3,004	2,875	2,938	2,818
Transportation and material moving occupations	8,320	8,491	7,049	7,240	6,682	6,869	1,270	1,251	1,205	1,191

Note: Beginning in January 2004, data reflect revised population controls used in the household survey.

SOURCE: "Table 9. Employed Persons by Occupation, Sex, and Age," in *Average Annual Tables*, U.S. Department of Labor, Bureau of Labor Statistics, 2004, http://www.bls.gov/cps/cpsaat9.pdf (accessed June 1, 2005)

---

fields, such as waiting tables and cashiering, have fallen since the last quarter of the twentieth century. Over the same period, women have made impressive inroads into other occupations, even if the numbers remain small. According to the Bureau of Labor Statistics, women comprised 1% of engineers in 1975 but 10% in 2000. In 2002 women held 22.2% of all positions in architecture, engineering, and surveying services. In 1975, 3% of police and detectives were women, compared with 14% in 2000. In 2002 women occupied 33.9% of all jobs in justice, public order, and safety. The proportion of female physicians increased from 13% in 1975 to 30% in 2002. It is often easier for women to enter new or rapidly growing occupations. For example, the proportion of female financial managers has increased from 24% to 50.5% since 1975. As the number of women enrolling in higher education increases, the proportions of women in skilled and professional occupations will continue to rise.

Construction

The construction industry boomed during the 1990s, resulting in a serious labor shortage. Department of Labor projections indicate that job opportunities are excellent in construction, due to the continued growth in nonresidential construction and the lack of many good training programs in construction, which has led to a shortage in qualified workers.

According to the National Association of Women in Construction, women account for only 10% of construction jobs, a percentage that remained fairly steady in the early 2000s after rising steadily in the 1990s. In 2003,

TABLE 4.3

Employed persons by occupation, race, Hispanic or Latino ethnicity, and sex, 2003–04

[Percent distribution]

Occupation, race, and Hispanic or Latino ethnicity	Total		Men		Women	
	2003	2004	2003	2004	2003	2004
Total						
Total, 16 years and over (thousands)	137,736	139,252	73,332	74,524	64,404	64,728
Percent	100.0	100.0	100.0	100.0	100.0	100.0
Management, professional, and related occupations	34.8	34.9	32.4	32.4	37.6	37.7
Management, business, and financial operations occupations	14.5	14.5	15.7	15.7	13.0	13.2
Professional and related occupations	20.3	20.3	16.6	16.7	24.5	24.5
Service occupations	16.0	16.3	12.9	13.2	19.6	19.9
Sales and office occupations	25.8	25.5	17.5	17.2	35.2	35.0
Sales and related occupations	11.6	11.5	11.1	10.9	12.1	12.2
Office and administrative support occupations	14.2	14.0	6.4	6.3	23.0	22.8
Natural resources, construction, and maintenance occupations	10.3	10.5	18.5	18.7	1.0	1.0
Farming, fishing, and forestry occupations	.8	.7	1.1	1.1	.4	.3
Construction and extraction occupations	5.9	6.1	10.8	11.1	.3	.3
Installation, maintenance, and repair occupations	3.7	3.6	6.6	6.5	.3	.4
Production, transportation, and material moving occupations	13.1	12.9	18.7	18.6	6.6	6.4
Production occupations	7.0	6.8	9.1	8.8	4.7	4.4
Transportation and material moving occupations	6.0	6.1	9.6	9.7	2.0	1.9
White						
Total, 16 years and over (thousands)	114,235	115,239	61,866	62,712	52,369	52,527
Percent	100.0	100.0	100.0	100.0	100.0	100.0
Management, professional, and related occupations	35.5	35.6	33.0	33.1	38.4	38.6
Management, business, and financial operations occupations	15.2	15.3	16.6	16.6	13.5	13.6
Professional and related occupations	20.3	20.3	16.4	16.5	24.9	25.0
Service occupations	15.0	15.2	12.0	12.3	18.6	18.8
Sales and office occupations	25.9	25.5	17.4	17.1	35.9	35.6
Sales and related occupations	11.9	11.8	11.5	11.2	12.4	12.4
Office and administrative support occupations	14.0	13.7	5.9	5.8	23.5	23.2
Natural resources, construction, and maintenance occupations	11.0	11.2	19.5	19.7	1.1	1.0
Farming, fishing, and forestry occupations	.8	.8	1.2	1.1	.4	.3
Construction and extraction occupations	6.3	6.6	11.4	11.9	.4	.4
Installation, maintenance, and repair occupations	3.9	3.8	6.9	6.7	.3	.3
Production, transportation, and material moving occupations	12.6	12.4	18.1	17.9	6.1	6.0
Production occupations	6.8	6.6	9.0	8.7	4.2	4.1
Transportation and material moving occupations	5.8	5.9	9.1	9.2	1.9	1.9
Black or African American						
Total, 16 years and over (thousands)	14,739	14,909	6,820	6,912	7,919	7,997
Percent	100.0	100.0	100.0	100.0	100.0	100.0
Management, professional, and related occupations	26.6	26.5	21.6	21.7	30.9	30.6
Management, business, and financial operations occupations	9.3	9.4	8.5	8.9	10.0	9.9
Professional and related occupations	17.3	17.0	13.2	12.8	20.9	20.7
Service occupations	23.1	23.8	19.6	20.0	26.2	27.0
Sales and office occupations	26.3	26.3	18.4	18.2	33.2	33.3
Sales and related occupations	9.6	9.6	8.4	8.4	10.7	10.6
Office and administrative support occupations	16.7	16.7	10.0	9.8	22.5	22.7
Natural resources, construction, and maintenance occupations	6.9	6.8	14.1	13.6	.8	.9
Farming, fishing, and forestry occupations	.3	.4	.6	.6	.1	.1
Construction and extraction occupations	3.9	3.8	8.2	7.9	.2	.3
Installation, maintenance, and repair occupations	2.7	2.6	5.3	5.1	.4	.5
Production, transportation, and material moving occupations	17.0	16.7	26.3	26.5	9.0	8.2
Production occupations	8.2	7.5	10.4	10.0	6.2	5.4
Transportation and material moving occupations	8.8	9.2	15.9	16.5	2.7	2.8

975,000 women were employed in the construction industry. More than half (56.3%) of those women were employed in sales and construction offices, but almost a quarter (23.2%) were management/professional. The labor shortage is particularly severe in skilled construction trades, such as building and carpentry. In 2000 women filled only 2.6% of these positions.

Law

According to the Bureau of Labor Statistics, only 7% of lawyers were women in 1975, compared with 29.4% in 2004. This increase in women lawyers has had a profound effect on American society. Women lawyers have championed the legal rights of women, and record numbers of women have entered government and politics at every level. And that proportion is likely to increase; in 2003 women made up 49% of all law students (American Bar Association, "A Current Glance of Women in the Law," 2003).

Still, most women lawyers have difficulty achieving prestigious positions. According to the American Bar

TABLE 4.3

Employed persons by occupation, race, Hispanic or Latino ethnicity, and sex, 2003–04 [CONTINUED]

[Percent distribution]

Occupation, race, and Hispanic or Latino ethnicity	Total		Men		Women	
	2003	2004	2003	2004	2003	2004
Asian						
Total, 16 years and over (thousands)	5,756	5,994	3,073	3,243	2,683	2,751
Percent	100.0	100.0	100.0	100.0	100.0	100.0
Management, professional, and related occupations	45.2	45.2	47.2	46.3	42.9	43.8
Management, business, and financial operations occupations	14.7	15.1	15.6	15.5	13.7	14.6
Professional and related occupations	30.5	30.0	31.7	30.8	29.2	29.2
Service occupations	16.0	16.2	13.4	14.0	19.1	18.8
Sales and office occupations	22.5	23.0	18.7	18.7	27.0	28.2
Sales and related occupations	11.3	11.3	11.3	11.1	11.4	11.5
Office and administrative support occupations	11.2	11.8	7.4	7.6	15.6	16.7
Natural resources, construction, and maintenance occupations	4.0	4.4	6.9	7.5	.7	.6
Farming, fishing, and forestry occupations	.3	.4	.3	.4	.4	.3
Construction and extraction occupations	1.5	1.4	2.6	2.6	.1	.1
Installation, maintenance, and repair occupations	2.2	2.6	3.9	4.5	.2	.3
Production, transportation, and material moving occupations	12.3	11.2	13.9	13.4	10.4	8.6
Production occupations	8.9	8.4	8.7	9.0	9.1	7.6
Transportation and material moving occupations	3.4	2.9	5.2	4.4	1.3	1.1
Hispanic or Latino ethnicity						
Total, 16 years and over (thousands)	17,372	17,930	10,479	10,832	6,894	7,098
Percent	100.0	100.0	100.0	100.0	100.0	100.0
Management, professional, and related occupations	16.8	17.3	14.0	14.0	21.1	22.4
Management, business, and financial operations occupations	6.8	7.2	6.6	6.8	7.1	7.8
Professional and related occupations	10.1	10.1	7.5	7.2	14.0	14.6
Service occupations	24.0	24.2	20.1	20.2	30.0	30.3
Sales and office occupations	22.0	21.3	14.1	13.5	34.0	33.2
Sales and related occupations	9.5	9.2	7.7	7.2	12.2	12.3
Office and administrative support occupations	12.5	12.1	6.4	6.3	21.7	20.9
Natural resources, construction, and maintenance occupations	17.4	18.0	27.3	28.5	2.4	2.0
Farming, fishing, and forestry occupations	2.4	2.2	3.1	2.8	1.4	1.2
Construction and extraction occupations	11.1	11.9	18.1	19.4	.5	.4
Installation, maintenance, and repair occupations	3.9	4.0	6.1	6.3	.5	.5
Production, transportation, and material moving occupations	19.7	19.2	24.5	23.8	12.6	12.2
Production occupations	11.2	10.6	12.5	11.8	9.1	8.6
Transportation and material moving occupations	8.6	8.7	11.9	12.0	3.4	3.6

Note: Estimates for the above race groups (white, black or African American, and Asian) do not sum to totals because data are not presented for all races. In addition, persons whose ethnicity is identified as Hispanic or Latino may be of any race and, therefore, are classified by ethnicity as well as by race. Beginning in January 2004, data reflect revised population controls used in the household survey.

SOURCE: "Table 10. Employed Persons by Occupation, Race, Hispanic or Latino Ethnicity, and Sex," in *Average Annual Tables*, U.S. Department of Labor, Bureau of Labor Statistics, 2004, http://www.bls.gov/cps/cpsaat10.pdf (accessed June 1, 2005)

Association, women make up 42.4% of law firm associates, but only 16.3% of partners. Women make up only 14.9% of general counsels for *Fortune* 500 companies (the five hundred largest U.S.-based corporations). Only 17.4% of federal Court of Appeals judges were female, and 16.2% of U.S. District Court judges were female. In 1981 Sandra Day O'Connor became the first woman ever appointed as one of the nine justices of the U.S. Supreme Court. She was joined on the court in 1993 by Justice Ruth Bader Ginsberg. But in July 2005 O'Connor announced plans to retire, leaving a single female Supreme Court justice.

Wall Street

Just as large numbers of young women went into law in the 1970s, the 1980s saw a huge increase in the number of young people studying business and finance and earning MBAs. The proportion of female financial managers doubled after 1975. With the booming economy of the 1990s, record numbers of women became stockbrokers, stock analysts, and administrators, and many women began managing major stock portfolios. However, these gains have not come without legal battles.

MERRILL LYNCH. In 1997 eight female financial consultants filed a sexual discrimination lawsuit against their employer, the Merrill Lynch investment firm. Merrill Lynch settled in January 1998, agreeing to permit employees to bring future discrimination complaints to mediation, and then to federal court, rather than to binding arbitration panels, which were controlled by older, white male industry leaders. Under the terms of the settlement, financial consultants who worked at the firm between January 1994 and June 1998 could file discrimination claims. Most of the complaints filed were based on unfair economic practices: male employees were given most of the accounts, and female employees' earnings were below those of less-qualified male employees.

SMITH BARNEY. In November 1997 Smith Barney Inc. (now Salomon Smith Barney), a large Wall Street securities firm, faced a class-action suit brought by twenty-five former and current female brokers. The firm agreed to a multimillion-dollar settlement after the women demonstrated that they had been routinely subjected to discrimination and sexual harassment by male coworkers. The settlement included an uncapped (no maximum amount) compensation fund to cover approximately twenty thousand female brokers who had worked for the firm since May 1993. As part of the settlement, Smith Barney set up a diversity office to investigate discrimination complaints. The company also established hiring and promotion quotas for women and minorities and will pay a $100,000 penalty to anyone who is improperly denied a promotion.

As part of the settlement, Smith Barney funded Catalyst to undertake an independent survey of 838 men and women employed at seven leading securities firms (*Women in Financial Services: The Word on the Street*, 2001). More than half (65%) of the women reported that they had to work harder than men for the same rewards. Only 13% of the male respondents believed that women had to work harder. A majority of the women (51%) but only 8% of the men believed that women were paid less for the same work at their firms. Overall, the survey results indicate that many more men than women believe that women are treated fairly and have ample opportunities for advancement.

Women in the Corporate World

In 1978 women made up only 26% of executives, managers, and administrators. In 2004 about half (50.3%) were women. (See Table 4.2.) Women are more likely to be managers and executives in industries with more female employees at lower levels, such as insurance, banking, and retail trade. Women also appear to advance more rapidly in fast-growing industries such as business services and direct marketing, and in industries that are undergoing changes such as deregulation and restructuring. Women managers and executives are much less common in the communications, transportation, and utilities industries.

Working Mother's 100 Best Companies

Each year, *Working Mother* magazine publishes a list of the one hundred best companies for working mothers. In addition to rating companies on issues such as the percentage of women employees, distribution of benefits, flexible hours, child care, parental leave, and other work/life issues, the companies are rated on their records for advancing women up the corporate ladder. In 2004 the magazine named Discovery Communications the "family champion," for creating a work culture that helps people manage their family/personal lives and providing support for parents, as well as maintaining a workforce of 61% women and an executive committee that is 50% women. The magazine also lauded Bristol-Myers Squibb Company, JPMorgan Chase, PricewaterhouseCoopers LLP, and Prudential Financial for high levels of advancement and leadership training for women. Other top ten companies, chosen for family-friendly policies, were IBM, Johnson & Johnson, S. C. Johnson, and Wachovia Corporation.

THE *FORTUNE* 500. The *2002 Catalyst Census of Women Corporate Officers and Top Earners of the* Fortune *500* found that although women comprised about half of the managerial and professional positions in *Fortune* 500 companies, they made up only 15.7% (2,140 of 13,673) of corporate officers. However, this was up from 12.5% in 2000, 11.9% in 1999, and 8.7% in 1995. Of these corporate officers, only 1.6% were women of color. Industries with the highest percentage of women corporate officers included temporary help (34.9%), insurance (31%), and tobacco (29.7%). Corporate line officers were up 2.6% from 2000, to 9.9%. These are individuals with profit-or-loss or direct client responsibilities. Seventy-one (a decrease from ninety in 2000) of the *Fortune* 500 companies had no women corporate officers. However, Catalyst projects that the proportion of female corporate officers in *Fortune* 500 companies will continue to increase; by the year 2020 Catalyst expects 27.4% of the corporate officers to be female.

Women represented 5.2% (118 out of 2,259) of the top earners in *Fortune* 500 companies in 2002, up from 4.1% in 2000. One in five companies listed a woman as one of its highest-paid executives, up from one in twenty in 1995. Catalyst reports that in 2002 there were six women CEOs of *Fortune* 500 companies.

The increases experienced by women across the board are especially intriguing given that the economy was slow in the early years of the twenty-first century. Historically, women executives see increases in earnings and positions only when the economy is stable.

THE "GLASS CEILING." Although more women and minorities have professional occupations than ever before, they are usually confined to the lower levels of management. In 1984 the term "glass ceiling" first began appearing in the media to describe the invisible barrier women encounter in their attempts to achieve high management positions. The Department of Labor, in *A Report on the Glass Ceiling Initiative* (Washington, DC, 1991), defined the glass ceiling as "artificial barriers based on attitudinal or organizational bias that prevent qualified individuals from advancing upward in their organization into management level positions."

As a result of the report, the Civil Rights Act of 1991 established the Glass Ceiling Commission. In *Good for Business: Making Full Use of the Nation's Human Capital* (Washington, DC, 1995), the commission found three types of artificial barriers to the advancement of women and minorities in the private sector:

- Societal barriers that may be outside the direct control of business. These include what the commission calls the supply barrier, related to educational opportunity and attainment, and the difference barrier, characterized by conscious and unconscious stereotyping, prejudice, and bias related to gender, race, and/or ethnicity.

- Internal structure barriers that are within the direct control of business. Some of these include corporate climates that alienate and isolate women and minorities; lack of mentoring, management training, and opportunities for career development; and biased rating and testing systems.

- Government barriers. These include a lack of adequate, consistent monitoring and law enforcement and inadequate reporting and dissemination of information about the glass ceiling.

The commission found that corporate executives and women have very different perceptions of the glass ceiling and how much progress has been made. The majority of CEOs in the survey believed that the glass ceiling was no longer a problem for women, regardless of race. Without exception they expressed strong support for women's advancement to senior management. Most believed that white and minority women had reached pay equity, although they recognized that the disparity between men's and women's earnings had not been resolved.

In *A Solid Investment: Making Full Use of the Nation's Human Capital* (Washington, DC, 1995), the Glass Ceiling Commission offered several recommendations for business:

- Demonstrate commitment to change from the highest level (CEOs)

- Include diversity in strategic business plans

- Use affirmative action as a tool

- Select, promote, and train qualified workers

- Prepare minorities and women for senior positions in the corporate ranks

- Initiate family-friendly policies

The report stated that the government should lead by example and make equal opportunity a reality, strengthen enforcement of antidiscrimination laws, improve data collection, and increase disclosure of diversity data.

A 2002 report by the U.S. Government Accountability Office, *A New Look through the Glass Ceiling: Where Are the Women?*, found that little progress had been made since the 1995 Glass Ceiling Commission activities. The report emphasized that despite the general sense of gender equity in the workplace, "The majority of women managers were worse off, relative to men, in 2000 than they were in 1995." In seven to ten industries surveyed, the wage gap between men and women in management actually widened in those five years. In only half of the industries surveyed were women represented in management proportionate to their share of the workforce. The study also found that the glass ceiling was even harsher for mothers; 60% of women managers across the industries studied did not have children.

In 2004 Catalyst reported the results of a study that highlighted the continued existence of the glass ceiling ("Women and Men in U.S. Corporate Leadership: Same Workplace, Different Realities?" Press Release, June 24, 2004). While women and men in top management positions had equal aspirations for advancement, and both women and men used similar strategies to advance their careers, women faced cultural barriers to their advancement that men did not. Those barriers included gender-based stereotypes, exclusion from informal networks, a lack of role models, and an inhospitable corporate culture.

Science, Engineering, and Technology

Although the glass ceiling concept was originally applied to women in the corporate world, in recent years the metaphor has been used to describe the situation of women in science and engineering professions and in academia in general. The proportion of women earning degrees in science and engineering increased significantly in the late twentieth and early twenty-first centuries. But in 2002 women accounted for only 22.5% of the science and engineering labor force, approximately the same percentage as in 1993.

THE NATIONAL SCIENCE FOUNDATION REPORT. Every two years the National Science Foundation (NSF) publishes a congressionally mandated report on the status of women and minorities in science and engineering. The report published in 2002, *Women, Minorities, and Persons with Disabilities in Science and Engineering: 2002*, found that 80% of women in the science and engineering labor force were white and 11% were Asian-American/Pacific Islander, but only 5.6% were African-American, 4% were Hispanic, and 0.3% were Native American/Alaskan Native. In 2002, 30.8% of computer scientists were women, down from 33.6% in 1994; 65.7% of psychologists were women, up from 58.6% in 1994; 11.6% of engineers were women, up from 9.7% in 1994; and 35.2% of natural scientists were women, most in biological/life sciences and medical sciences, up from 31% in 1994

("Table H-5. Employed Persons 16 Years and Older, by Detailed Occupation, Sex, and Race/Ethnicity: 1994–2002 Annual Averages," in National Science Foundation, Division of Science Resources Statistics, *Women, Minorities, and Persons with Disabilities in Science and Engineering: 2004*, NSF 04–317, 2004).

About 13% of both men and women in the science and engineering labor force hold doctorates. Table 4.4 illustrates the positions of female doctoral scientists and engineers employed by universities and four-year colleges and universities in 2001. In every field a high proportion of women were adjunct (all other) faculty, the lowest-paid and lowest-status faculty position. In engineering women accounted for only 2.7% of the full professors who had earned their doctorates more than ten years before. Women scientists and engineers were less likely to be tenured than their male counterparts. Minority women were less likely than white women to be full professors or tenured. Furthermore, many women scientists were employed by small four-year and two-year colleges, where pay scales and opportunities for professional advancement are lower than at large research universities.

Doctoral scientists and engineers often choose jobs outside the academic sector. Of the 30,420 self-employed scientists and engineers in 2001, 39.2% were women. Women comprised 21.6% of all federal employees in their field and 27.5% of all state and local government employees in science and engineering ("Table H-19. Employed S&E Doctorate Holders, by Sector of Employment, Broad Occupation, Sex, Race/Ethnicity, and Disability Status, 2001," in National Science Foundation, Division of Science Resources Statistics, *Women, Minorities, and Persons with Disabilities in Science and Engineering: 2004*, NSF 04–317, 2004).

HARVARD CONTROVERSY. In 2005 the president of Harvard University, Lawrence H. Summers, set off a firestorm of controversy by suggesting females have less innate math and science ability than males. In a speech at a session on the progress of women in academia at a conference organized by the National Bureau of Economic Research, Summers remarked that the small number of women who held high-level positions in science and engineering was the result of both the decision of women with children to work fewer hours than men and women's lesser innate mathematic and scientific ability, reinforced by socialization and discrimination ("Remarks at NBER Conference on Diversifying the Science & Engineering Workforce," January 14, 2005, http://www.president.harvard.edu/speeches/2005/nber.html).

Summers's speech received widespread attention, outraging both women and men, and ultimately forcing Summers to apologize for his comments. Critics of Summers's speech argued that he downplayed the roles of socialization and of discrimination as significant factors that prevent women from reaching the top of their fields, and that he put too much emphasis on research that suggested females have less genetic aptitude for math and science. Anne Tweed of the National Science Teachers Association argued that innate ability was not the real issue; instead, she insisted, the lack of gender equity in science classrooms impeded women's advancement ("Achieving Gender Equality in the Science Classroom," *National Science Teachers Association*, February 18, 2005).

Summers's comments fueled faculty discontent at Harvard. A university committee on women's issues immediately sent Summers a letter, arguing that his remarks "impede our current efforts to recruit top women scholars." President Summers issued a letter one month later, admitting that he "substantially understated the impact of socialization and discrimination" ("Letter to the Faculty Regarding NBER Remarks," February 17, 2005, http://www.president.harvard.edu/speeches/2005/facletter.html). Nevertheless, the faculty of Arts and Sciences at the university took a vote of no confidence in him in March. Summers announced in May 2005 that Harvard would spend $50 million in ten years to recruit and promote more women and minority faculty.

REPORT OF THE CONGRESSIONAL COMMISSION ON THE ADVANCEMENT OF WOMEN AND MINORITIES IN SCIENCE, ENGINEERING, AND TECHNOLOGY DEVELOPMENT. The low number of women scientists and engineers, and the dearth of women in top positions in those fields, has received Congressional attention. The Report of the Congressional Commission on the Advancement of Women and Minorities in Science, Engineering, and Technology Development (CAWMSET), *Land of Plenty: Diversity as America's Competitive Edge in Science, Engineering, and Technology* (September 2000), made a number of recommendations for the advancement of women in the Science, Engineering, and Technology (SET) workforce:

- Implement high standards in math and science curricula, teacher qualifications, and technology in schools

- Intervene to promote SET careers among women, underrepresented minorities, and disabled students in high schools, community colleges, and universities

- Significantly increase federal and state expenditures to support underrepresented groups in SET higher education

- Make public and private SET employers accountable for the career development and advancement of women and underrepresented minorities

- Establish a representative body to transform the image of SET professionals into one that is positive and

TABLE 4.4

Employed doctoral scientists and engineers in universities and four-year colleges, by broad field of doctorate, sex, faculty rank, and years since doctorate, 2001

Field of doctorate/sex	Total		Full professor		Associate professor		Assistant professor		Instructor/lecturer		All other faculty*		Rank not applicable	
	Less than 10 years	10 or more years	Less than 10 years	10 or more years	Less than 10 years	10 or more years	Less than 10 years	10 or more years	Less than 10 years	10 or more years	Less than 10 years	10 or more years	Less than 10 years	10 or more years
All fields	86,010	159,040	1,640	84,760	12,320	40,590	37,370	10,420	4,640	2,850	2,840	4,270	27,190	16,140
Male	(60.3)	(77.8)	(56.9)	(85.0)	(65.8)	(71.8)	(61.5)	(59.8)	(53.8)	(52.7)	(48.2)	(71.6)	(58.7)	(72.2)
Female	(39.7)	(22.2)	(43.1)	(15.0)	(34.2)	(28.2)	(38.5)	(40.2)	(46.2)	(47.3)	(51.8)	(28.4)	(41.3)	(27.8)
Sciences	77,220	140,730	1,500	73,630	10,550	36,230	33,050	9,840	4,350	2,610	2,700	3,760	25,060	14,660
Male	(57.7)	(75.5)	(54.0)	(83.2)	(61.9)	(69.5)	(58.5)	(58.1)	(54.1)	(48.2)	(47.9)	(68.1)	(56.7)	(69.8)
Female	(42.3)	(24.5)	(46.0)	(16.8)	(38.1)	(30.5)	(41.5)	(41.9)	(45.9)	(51.8)	(52.1)	(31.9)	(43.3)	(30.2)
Computer and information sciences	2,160	1,600	70	700	930	780	890	S	S	S	S	S	180	S
Male	(76.7)	(80.1)	(70.8)	(84.7)	(80.5)	(79.3)	(75.4)	S	S	S	S	S	(70.0)	S
Female	(23.3)	(19.9)	S	(15.3)	(19.5)	(20.7)	(24.6)	S	S	S	S	S	(30.0)	S
Mathematical sciences	4,160	10,820	100	6,620	870	2,870	2,170	320	480	170	180	270	350	590
Male	(75.3)	(89.4)	(59.2)	(91.8)	(72.1)	(87.8)	(74.0)	(75.6)	(80.7)	(50.6)	(67.4)	(87.5)	(92.0)	(90.2)
Female	(24.7)	(10.6)	S	(8.2)	(27.9)	(12.2)	(26.0)	(24.4)	(19.3)	(49.4)	(32.6)	S	S	(9.8)
Biological and agricultural sciences	27,770	45,080	390	21,930	1,930	11,810	9,310	4,840	1,740	840	690	920	13,710	4,740
Male	(60.7)	(75.3)	(71.0)	(83.9)	(67.3)	(71.6)	(65.1)	(62.1)	(49.4)	(30.0)	(64.0)	(77.7)	(57.8)	(65.5)
Female	(39.3)	(24.7)	(29.0)	(16.1)	(32.7)	(28.4)	(34.9)	(37.9)	(50.6)	(70.0)	(36.0)	(22.3)	(42.2)	(34.5)
Health sciences	5,770	6,020	190	2,680	1,100	2,250	3,040	590	270	130	140	S	1,020	340
Male	(31.9)	(44.7)	S	(56.7)	(29.4)	(37.8)	(35.8)	(28.9)	(28.7)	(40.3)	S	S	(27.1)	(29.5)
Female	(68.1)	(55.3)	(86.4)	(43.3)	(70.6)	(62.2)	(64.2)	(71.1)	(71.3)	(59.7)	(66.5)	S	(72.9)	(70.5)
Physical and related sciences	11,720	25,420	210	13,550	1,210	5,390	4,560	1,160	410	480	350	670	4,990	4,170
Male	(77.2)	(89.3)	(88.3)	(93.6)	(77.5)	(84.9)	(77.7)	(64.8)	(76.4)	(80.2)	(61.3)	(86.7)	(77.3)	(89.3)
Female	(22.8)	(10.7)	S	(6.4)	(22.5)	(15.1)	(22.3)	(35.2)	(23.6)	(19.8)	(38.7)	(13.3)	(22.7)	(10.7)
Social sciences	14,700	32,530	420	18,550	3,180	8,500	8,050	1,420	680	610	730	1,100	1,640	2,350
Male	(56.0)	(73.8)	(46.0)	(81.2)	(65.7)	(64.8)	(56.7)	(58.8)	(59.9)	(58.3)	(41.0)	(63.7)	(41.8)	(66.0)
Female	(44.0)	(26.2)	(54.0)	(18.8)	(34.3)	(35.2)	(43.3)	(41.2)	(40.1)	(41.7)	(59.0)	(36.3)	(58.2)	(34.0)
Psychology	10,940	19,250	120	9,590	1,320	4,640	5,040	1,490	710	330	570	760	3,180	2,450
Male	(34.2)	(61.7)	S	(72.1)	(38.0)	(56.9)	(35.7)	(47.3)	(40.0)	(29.5)	(21.8)	(42.7)	(31.8)	(49.3)
Female	(65.8)	(38.3)	(81.5)	(27.9)	(62.0)	(43.1)	(64.3)	(52.7)	(60.0)	(70.5)	(78.2)	(57.3)	(68.2)	(50.7)
Engineering	8,790	18,320	140	11,130	1,780	4,360	4,310	590	290	240	140	520	2,130	1,480
Male	(83.4)	(95.5)	(88.7)	(97.3)	(88.7)	(91.3)	(84.7)	(87.4)	(50.4)	(100.0)	(54.7)	(97.2)	(82.3)	(95.8)
Female	(16.6)	(4.5)	S	(2.7)	(11.3)	(8.7)	(15.3)	(12.6)	(49.6)	S	(45.3)	S	(17.7)	(4.2)

*All other faculty includes adjunct or other faculty.

Note: S=Supressed due to too few cases (fewer than 50 weighted cases).

Percentage distribution is shown in parentheses. Numbers are rounded to nearest ten. Details may not add to total because of rounding.

SOURCE: "Employed Doctoral Scientists and Engineers in Universities and 4-Year Colleges, by Broad Field Doctorate, Sex, Faculty Rank, and Years since Doctorate: 2001," in *Women, Minorities, and Persons with Disabilities in Science and Engineering: 2004*, National Science Foundation, Division of Science Resources Statistics, NSF 04-317, 2004, http://www.nsf.gov/sbe/srs/wmpd/pdf/nsf04317.pdf (accessed June 1, 2005)

inclusive of women, minorities, and those with disabilities

- Establish a collaborative body to continue the work of the commission

AAAS SURVEY OF LIFE SCIENTISTS. In the summer of 2001 the American Association for the Advancement of Science (AAAS) surveyed nineteen thousand members who worked in the life sciences. Of the respondents, 93% had Ph.D.'s, MDs, or both. Women made up 27% of the respondents. On average they were younger than the male respondents. The National Science Foundation argues that the younger average age of women scientists and engineers accounts for some of the disparities between men and women in wages and other achievements.

The survey found other differences between men and women. Only 72% of the female scientists were married, compared with 88% of the male scientists, and many of the women were married to scientists. The survey found that although industry paid better than academia, men made one-third more money than women across the board. According to the report, "Women are paid less for similar work even when type of employer is held constant." The women in the survey felt that they had less job security than the men and that they got less recognition than men as exemplified by prestige, promotion, and salaries. Most of the married women scientists said that their careers had been constrained by the career needs of their husbands. In contrast, only 7% of the men said that their careers had been affected by their wives' career decisions.

The term for CAWMSET has expired, and the office no longer exists. Because its report is the most comprehensive of its kind, it is still referred to as the authority on statistics in the SET field.

Women in Academia

In 2004 almost half (46%) of college and university teachers were women ("Table 11. Employed Persons by Detailed Occupation and Sex, 2004 Annual Averages," *Women in the Labor Force: A Databook*, Bureau of Labor Statistics, U.S. Department of Labor, May 2005). Many of the issues confronting women scientists and engineers apply to women in academia in general.

In 1994 Nancy H. Hopkins, a professor of biology at the Massachusetts Institute of Technology (MIT), had her request for more laboratory space turned down. She took out her tape measure and discovered that, on average, the male faculty in her department had 50% more lab space than the women. That summer Hopkins joined with two other tenured women in the MIT School of Science to conduct an informal poll of female faculty. This led in the following year to the establishment of a committee to analyze the status of women in the School of Science.

The committee report, which was printed in 1999 and distributed over the World Wide Web, engendered a great deal of publicity, including front-page stories in major newspapers, as well as controversy. The report found that although junior women faculty worried that work–family conflicts would negatively affect their careers, it was the older, tenured women faculty who were extremely dissatisfied. They felt marginalized in their departments and discriminated against in salaries, laboratory space, resources, and awards, despite career accomplishments that were equal to those of the men. In an almost unprecedented step, MIT admitted discrimination against women and developed a five-year plan for improving the situation. More female faculty were hired and promoted, and the number of tenured women faculty in the School of Science increased by 40%.

Following the landmark MIT report, a number of other universities began analyzing the status of their female faculty, with findings similar to those at MIT. Early in 2001 a class-action suit representing as many as two thousand women was filed against the University of Washington in Seattle. The suit charged broad gender inequalities in pay, promotion, teaching loads, and access to grants and research funds. Although the grievance was awarded class-action suit status, the trial judge refused to hear it as such. The appeals court also denied class-action status. As of 2004, the Supreme Court refused to allow an appeal, so the five original petitioners began to move forward with the suit without the class-action status.

Dana E. Christmas, in "Women Faculty in Higher Education: Impeded by Academe" (Advancing Women in Leadership, Advancing Women Web site, http://www.advancingwomen.com, 2003), argued that statistics suggesting women are nearing half of college teachers mask the fact that many women are concentrated in part-time or temporary positions, and men continue to predominate in tenured positions. In addition, even when hired into tenure-track positions, women are tenured at a lower rate than are men. Women's salaries also continue to lag behind men's.

Women in the Military

In 1973, when the male military draft was replaced by an all-volunteer force, the number of women joining the military began increasing. According to the Women in Military Service for America Memorial Foundation (WIMSA), in April 2005, 206,308 women were on active duty in the armed services, 14.5% of the total military. (See Table 4.5.) Another 143,010 women were in the Reserve and Guard. The largest number of women were serving in the Army, but the Air Force had the highest percentage of women in its population (19.6%). The Marine Corps had the lowest percentage of women (6.1%).

TABLE 4.5

Number of women serving in the military, 2005

[Department of Defense (DoD) active duty, reserve and guard as of 4/30/05. Coast Guard as of 7/19/05.]

	Active duty		
	Women	Total	% women
Army	69,713	85,734	14.4%
Marine Corps	10,801	177,251	6.1%
Navy	51,397	359,530	14.3%
Air Force	69,848	356,683	19.6%
Total DoD	201,759	1,379,198	14.6%
Coast Guard	4,549	39,597	11.5%
Total	**206,308**	**1,418,795**	**14.5%**
Reserve & guard			
Army Guard	42,158	331,017	12.7%
Army Reserve	45,430	194,434	23.4%
Marine Corps Reserve	1,909	39,985	4.8%
Navy Reserve	16,003	77,563	20.6%
Air Guard	18,843	106,063	17.8%
Air Force Reserve	17,579	75,435	23.3%
Total DoD	141,922	824,497	17.2%
Coast Guard Reserve	1,088	7,668	14.2%
Total	**143,010**	**832,165**	**17.2%**

Note: More than 90% of all career fields in the armed forces are now open to women.

SOURCE: Women Serving Today, in *Statistics on Women in the Military*, Women in Military Service for America Memorial Foundation, Inc., July 19, 2005, http://www.womensmemorial.org/PDFs/StatsonWIM.pdf (accessed July 28, 2005)

According to WIMSA, forty-one thousand female soldiers (about 7% of all troops deployed) served in Operation Desert Storm, also known as the Persian Gulf War, in 1991. Of those soldiers, thirteen died and two were captured as prisoners of war. More than one thousand women participated in U.S. military operations in Somalia from 1992 to 1994, according to the Women's Research and Education Institute. As of March 2001, more than twenty thousand women had served in the peacekeeping operations in Bosnia and Kosovo. The Department of Defense does not track exactly how many women have been deployed as part of the war in Iraq that began in 2003. However, organizations such as the Women in Military Service for America Memorial Foundation Inc. estimate that more than thirty-seven thousand of the more than two hundred and fifty thousand soldiers deployed in Operation Iraqi Freedom in March 2003 were female—about 15%. A total of forty-six soldiers and civilian employees of the Department of Defense have died in the fighting in Iraq between March 20, 2003, and October 7, 2005 (Department of Defense press releases, as cited on Iraqi Coalition Casualty Count, http://icasualties.org/oif/female.aspx). Thirty-three of these deaths were attributed to hostile action; the other thirteen were related to nonhostile causes such as illness and accidents.

In operations in Iraq in both 1991 and 2003 onward, American women soldiers have had to contend with discrimination. In Iraq and in other Mideast countries where American troops are stationed, female soldiers have been harassed by foreign citizens and soldiers alike. In some of these countries women do not have the same rights as men. As such, they are not allowed to do some of the basic activities that American women do on a daily basis—drive a vehicle, appear in public without male accompaniment, or leave the house without covering their heads and/or faces. As American women soldiers do not observe these restrictions, this caused some concern in such countries and, in some cases, led to harassment.

MILITARY OCCUPATIONS. According to the American Forces Press Service (Rudi Williams, "Women Rising to Higher Positions in the Military," April 3, 2005), percentages of women at all levels increased between 1995 and 2004. The percentage of enlisted women on active duty increased from 13% to 15%. The number of active-duty women officers and enlisted women in nontraditional occupations like engineering, maintenance, and tactical operations also increased, from 42% to 45% during that period. The percentage of women officers at the rank of major and above, while still below their representation in the military in general, increased from 11.2% in 1995 to 12.7% in 2004.

The top five occupations for active-duty women officers were nurses, physicians, biomedical sciences and allied health officers, health services administration, and personnel. The top five occupations for active-duty enlisted women were general administration, supply administration, personnel, medical care and treatment, and operators and analysts. The top five civil occupations for women in the Department of Defense were management and program analysts, contract specialists, computer specialists, administration and program managers, jobs in human resources, and attorneys. Almost half of active-duty women and a third of civilian women with jobs in the Department of Defense were minority women, compared with a quarter of women in the labor force.

The number of female Army colonels, Navy captains, and Air Force colonels is rising as women who joined the military since the 1980s gain seniority. In addition, growing proportions of junior women officers are entering mainstream combat occupations. These include pilots, navigators, and aircrews in all of the services, and surface warfare in the Navy. Successful careers in these positions can lead to top leadership positions in the armed forces.

WOMEN-OWNED BUSINESSES

Women entrepreneurs are significantly affecting the American economy. According to the National Foundation for Women Business Owners (NFWBO), between 1997 and 2004 the number of women-owned firms increased by 28.1%, three times the growth rate of all U.S. privately held firms. By 2004 there were an estimated

10.6 million privately held 50%-or-more women-owned businesses, 47.7% of the total.

In 2004 nearly half (45%) of the 50%-or-more women-owned firms were in service industries; 16.4% were in retail; 8.9% were in finance, insurance, or real estate; and 6% were in construction. Women-owned firms were diversifying into industries traditionally dominated by men-owned firms. The greatest growth between 1997 and 2004 in these nontraditional firms were in construction (30% growth); transportation, communications, and public utilities (28.1% growth); and agricultural services (24.3% growth).

According to NFWBO, the most important reason that women start businesses is to improve the situation for themselves and their families. Other important reasons include working for oneself rather than an employer and fulfilling a long-standing dream.

Businesses Owned by Women of Color

According to the Center for Women's Business Research, in the United States in 2004 more than one in five (21.4%) privately held companies owned by women were owned by minority women. Such firms number 1.4 million, have sales of $147 billion, and staff nearly 1.3 million people. Between 1997 and 2004, the number of firms owned by women of color increased by 54.6% ("Businesses Owned by Women of Color in the United States, 2004: A Fact Sheet," Center for Women's Business Research, 2004).

The majority of these firms (61%) are in the service industries, with 12.4% in retail trade and 4% in goods-producing trades. (See Figure 4.1.) The Center for Women's Business Research lists the following states as home to the greatest number of minority women-owned firms in 2002: California, Texas, Illinois, New York, Florida, Maryland and New Jersey (tied), Michigan, Virginia, and Ohio.

Hispanics owned most of the minority women-owned businesses (37.4%). African-Americans owned 28%, Asian/Pacific Islanders owned 28.4%, and Native Americans/Alaska Natives owned 6.1%. (See Figure 4.2.)

Financing

Female business owners are applying for more bank credit and using more credit for business expansion than ever before. A 2005 study by the Center for Women's Business Research, "Access to Capital: Where We've Been, Where We're Going," found that in 1996 20% of female business owners used commercial credit, but by 2003 34% of female business owners did. The report notes, though, that women still lag behind men in their ability to raise capital. And, while women controlled about half of the privately owned businesses in the coun-

FIGURE 4.1

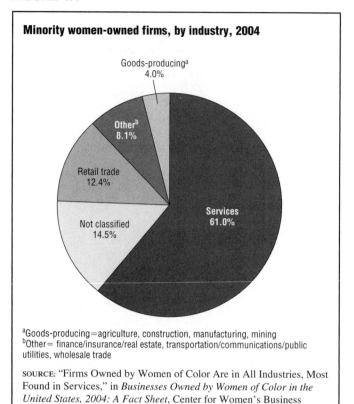

Minority women-owned firms, by industry, 2004

aGoods-producing=agriculture, construction, manufacturing, mining
bOther= finance/insurance/real estate, transportation/communications/public utilities, wholesale trade

SOURCE: "Firms Owned by Women of Color Are in All Industries, Most Found in Services," in *Businesses Owned by Women of Color in the United States, 2004: A Fact Sheet*, Center for Women's Business Research, 2004, http://www.nfwbo.org/minority/BusinessesOwnedby WomenofColorintheUS.pdf (accessed June 10, 2005)

try, only 22% of Small Business Administration loans went to female-owned businesses.

Home-Based Businesses

According to Lodinews.com's *Women in Business 2003*, 5.7% of all adult females in the United States are entrepreneurs. Collecting accurate data on home-based businesses is difficult to do because not all businesses obtain licenses, and the name of the person who runs a business from home does not necessarily identify it as such. In 2001 it was estimated that of the 3.5 million home-based, women-owned businesses in the United States, 63% have employees other than the owner. These provide full- or part-time employment for approximately fourteen million people, about 60% of whom are employed part-time or are contract employees. Home-based businesses are generally newer and smaller than other women-owned businesses. Women-owned, home-based businesses are more likely to finance growth using private sources and personal credit rather than business earnings. They also take out fewer business loans, lease less equipment, and use less vendor credit.

WOMEN'S OCCUPATIONS IN THE FUTURE

Until the 1970s most women had occupations that were very different from those of most men. A number of

FIGURE 4.2

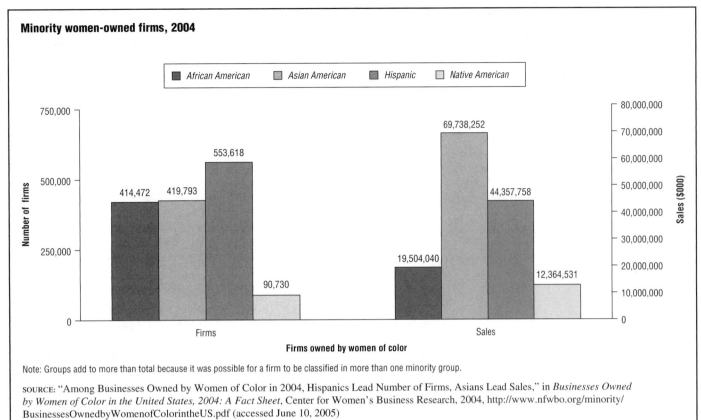

Minority women-owned firms, 2004

■ African American   ■ Asian American   ■ Hispanic   □ Native American

Note: Groups add to more than total because it was possible for a firm to be classified in more than one minority group.

SOURCE: "Among Businesses Owned by Women of Color in 2004, Hispanics Lead Number of Firms, Asians Lead Sales," in *Businesses Owned by Women of Color in the United States, 2004: A Fact Sheet,* Center for Women's Business Research, 2004, http://www.nfwbo.org/minority/BusinessesOwnedbyWomenofColorintheUS.pdf (accessed June 10, 2005)

factors have been responsible for the movement of women into previously male-dominated occupations:

- The influence of the feminist movement beginning in the 1960s

- Civil rights laws prohibiting discrimination based on gender

- Increased female enrollment in higher education

- Increased women's labor force participation

- Decreased gender stereotyping in education and employment

Since the 1970s women have been moving out of blue-collar, service, and administrative support jobs and into professional and managerial positions. However, traditional ideas of "women's work" and "men's work" are still prevalent in American society. For example, men tend to be truck drivers and women child-care givers. Although the stereotypes of women's occupations are beginning to fade, men in traditional female roles, such as kindergarten teachers, secretaries, or manicurists, are still considered unusual.

Obstacles Remain

Despite equal-opportunity laws and regulations and affirmative action policies, various personnel practices, including the wording of job descriptions and the struc-

ture of the corporate hierarchy, can keep women from entering male-dominated occupations. Women starting out in new fields in recent years lack the seniority necessary for advancing in their careers. Women entering male-dominated occupations may face suspicion, distrust, or outright hostility. Off-color comments or jokes, gossip, sexual harassment, or the refusal of help by co-workers may make the workplace intolerable for women.

Women consistently identify mentoring as a crucial factor for success. Since the majority of senior positions are occupied by men, it may be difficult for a female to find a mentor. As more women achieve higher-echelon jobs, more mentors will be available for younger women. Isolation and exclusion from an "old-boys network" are also cited as important obstacles for women moving into new occupations. As more women make their way up to more influential positions, this too may begin to change.

Other obstacles may be more difficult to eradicate. Many careers, particularly in science, technology, and the corporate world, may require relocating numerous times. This can be very difficult for married women, particularly if they have children and if their husbands are also pursuing careers.

The five fastest-growing occupations in the early twenty-first century were in the computer science and information technology fields. A critical labor shortage in these fields might be avoided if more women enter these occupations. It remains to be seen whether more women will move into these male-dominated fields, since the next five fastest-growing occupations are more traditionally female service jobs (Congressional Commission on the Advancement of Women and Minorities in Science, Engineering, and Technology Development, "Figure 1. Fastest Growing Occupations: 1998–2008," in *Land of Plenty: Diversity as America's Competitive Edge in Science, Engineering, and Technology*, National Science Foundation, September 2000).

CHAPTER 5
MONEY, INCOME, AND POVERTY

MONEY INCOME

Women earn less money than men, have fewer assets, and are far more likely to live in poverty. According to the Center on Budget and Policy Priorities (CBPP), a Washington, D.C.-based nonpartisan research organization and policy institute, income disparities between high-, middle-, and low-income families are the highest they have been since before World War II. In 2004 the median weekly earnings for women (one-half made more money and one-half made less money) were $573, compared to $713 for men. In addition to earnings from employment, money income may include such sources as child support payments, alimony, interest, dividends, capital gains, and other investment income. (See Table 5.1.)

THE EARNINGS GAP

A wage survey taken in 1833 in Philadelphia found that the majority of women workers in local textile factories received less for working seventy-eight hours per week than men were getting for one ten-hour day (W. Chafe, *The American Woman: Her Changing Social, Economic and Political Roles, 1920–1970,* London, 1972). Women entered the labor market by filling the lowest-paying jobs and mirroring the work they customarily did at home—cleaning, cooking, sewing, and child care. Despite women's increased education opportunities and participation in the workforce, women's generally lower status and salaries continue in the twenty-first century. The AFL-CIO labor organization has noted that as more women enter a new occupation, the wages for that occupation begin to fall.

Men continue to earn substantially more money than women. Figure 5.1 illustrates the median annual earnings of men and women from 1960 to 2003 in 2003 dollars. The median earnings of men remained unchanged between 2002 and 2003, at $40,668. But the real earnings of women declined over that period by 0.6%, to $30,724.

The "earnings gap" is quantified as women's earnings as a percentage of men's earnings. (See Table 5.2.) The gap between women's and men's earnings has narrowed significantly as women's earnings have increased and men's have declined in real terms. In 1973 women earned only 56.6% as much as men. The earnings gap was smallest in 2001, when women's earnings were 76.3% of men's. While the gap between men's and women's earnings had narrowed overall since the mid-1970s, it widened in the 2002–03 period, when the female-to-male earnings ratio declined from 76.6 to 75.5%.

Economists Heidi I. Hartmann and Stephen J. Rose argue that the traditional way to measure the earnings gap—comparing the annual wages of men and women who work full-time, year-round—grossly underestimates the actual gap. According to Dr. Hartmann, "This measure is misleading because it ignores the labor market experiences of over half of working women, who either work part-time or take time out of the labor force for family care. The long-term gender earnings gap measures not only women's earnings losses in a given year, but also the cumulative effect on women's earnings of balancing family and work responsibilities" ("Still A Man's Labor Market: The Long Term Earnings Gap," Institute for Women's Policy Research, Press Release, June 4, 2004). According to the report, women earn 62% less than men earn over a given fifteen-year period, a gap that is almost three times the gap based on the annual figures given in the U.S. Census Bureau's Current Population Reports.

Women's median pay is lower than men's for several reasons. Many women leave the workforce to stay at home while their children are young. Women are more likely to be in low-paying, entry-level jobs, and they often work fewer hours and have fewer job skills than men. In part the earnings gap between full-time workers is closing because women are accumulating job experience. Women's educational attainment has

TABLE 5.1

Median and weekly earnings of full-time wage and salary workers, by sex, age, and race/ethnicity, 2003–04

Characteristic	Number of workers (in thousands)		Median weekly earnings	
	2003	2004	2003	2004
Sex and age				
Total, 16 years and over	100,302	101,224	$620	$638
Men, 16 years and over	56,227	57,001	695	713
16 to 24 years	6,158	6,243	398	400
25 years and over	50,069	50,758	744	762
Women, 16 years and over	44,076	44,223	552	573
16 to 24 years	4,632	4,633	371	375
25 years and over	39,444	39,590	584	599
Race, sex, and Hispanic or Latino ethnicity				
White	81,916	82,468	636	657
Men	47,001	47,495	715	732
Women	34,916	34,972	567	584
Black	11,887	12,032	514	525
Men	5,585	5,706	555	569
Women	6,301	6,326	491	505
Asian	4,314	4,457	693	708
Men	2,442	2,504	772	802
Women	1,872	1,953	598	613
Hispanic or Latino	13,634	14,061	440	456
Men	8,677	8,996	464	480
Women	4,957	5,065	410	419

Note: Estimates for the race groups (white, black or African American, and Asian) do not sum to totals because data are not presented for all races. In addition, persons whose ethnicity is identified as Hispanic or Latino may be of any race and, therefore, are classified by ethnicity as well as race. Beginning in January 2004, data reflect revised population controls used in the household survey.

SOURCE: "Table 37. Median Weekly Earnings of Full-Time Wage and Salary Workers by Selected Characteristics," U.S. Department of Labor, Bureau of Labor Statistics, 2004, http://www.bls.gov/cps/cpsaat37.pdf (accessed June 6, 2005)

increased dramatically in recent years, and fewer women are leaving their jobs. Women with degrees tend to work for more years than women without degrees.

Weekly earnings may be a more accurate measure of the earnings gap than annual earnings, since many women do not work year-round. About half of all women leave the workforce at some point to care for children, and many women do not work when their children are out of school during the summer months. According to the Bureau of Labor Statistics, in 2004 the average median weekly earnings for all female full-time wage and salary workers ages sixteen and over was 80.4% of men's earnings. (See Table 5.3.) In 1979 the median usual weekly earnings of full-time working women was 63% of men's earnings.

Education

Between 1979 and 2002 men earned more than women at all levels of educational attainment. (See Figure 5.2.) In 2002 the median weekly earnings of female high school graduates was $459, compared with $616 for male graduates. The median of female college graduates' weekly earnings was $809, compared with $1,089 for men.

But between 1979 and 2002 women's earnings grew more than men's at all educational levels. (See Figure 5.3.) Men without a high school diploma lost more than 27% in constant (inflation-adjusted) dollar earnings over the period, whereas women lost only about 7%. Women with some college or an associate degree saw their earnings rise more than 11%, whereas men with a comparable amount of education lost about 4% in real earnings. Women college graduates saw their earnings rise about 33.7%, whereas the men's earnings rose only 19.9%.

Occupation

Pharmacists ($1,432), chief executives ($1,310), and lawyers ($1,255) had the highest median weekly earnings among women in 2004. Counter attendants ($282) and food preparation and serving workers ($308) had the lowest median weekly earnings. (See Table 5.3.)

Part-Time Workers

Women who worked fewer than thirty-five hours a week comprised 25.4% of all female wage and salary earners in 2004, according to the Bureau of Labor Statistics. Women working part-time had median weekly earnings of $201, compared with $183 for male part-time workers. Men's earnings are lower largely because most male part-time workers are young (51.1% are under twenty-five); younger workers tend to earn less than older workers.

Marital Status and Children

In 2003 married women living with their spouses and working full-time had higher median usual weekly earnings ($588) than did women who had never married, were divorced or separated, or were widowed. (See Table 5.4.) Women with children under age six earned less than childless women and women with children ages six to seventeen. Single women with children earned even less. On average, men with children had higher weekly median earnings than men without children, probably because men with children tended to be older than men without children, and children at home did not adversely affect their earnings. Thus, the earnings gap was largest for parents, with mothers earning only 70.3% of what fathers earned. Married women with no children under eighteen and living with a husband had the highest median weekly earnings, at $594.

The median usual hourly earnings for unmarried women in 2003 were closer to those of unmarried men than they were for married women compared to married men. Never-married women made, on average, 88.9% of what never-married men earned, whereas married women living with their spouses made only 79.4% as much as married men. (See Table 5.5.)

FIGURE 5.1

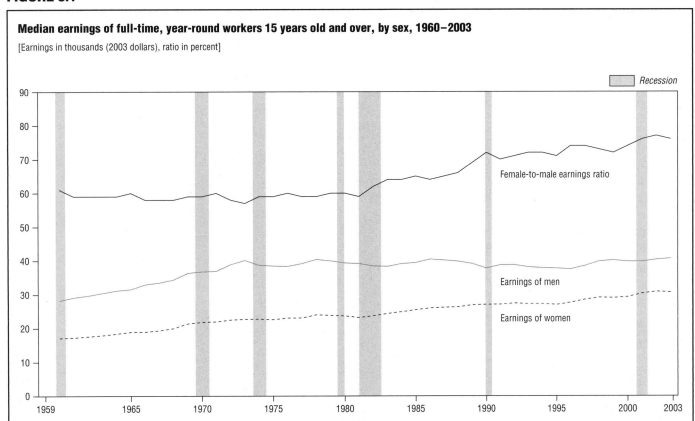

Median earnings of full-time, year-round workers 15 years old and over, by sex, 1960–2003

[Earnings in thousands (2003 dollars), ratio in percent]

Note: The data points are placed at the midpoints of the respective years. Data on earnings of full-time year-round workers are not readily available before 1960.

SOURCE: Carmen DeNavas-Walt, Bernadette D. Proctor, and Robert J. Mills, "Figure 2. Female-to-Male Earnings Ratio and Median Earnings of Full-Time, Year-Round Workers 15 Years Old and Over by Sex: 1960–2003," in *Income, Poverty, and Health Insurance Coverage in the United States: 2003*, U.S. Census Bureau, Current Population Reports, P60-226, August 2004, http://www.census.gov/prod/2004pubs/p60-226.pdf (accessed June 6, 2005)

Age and Racial Differences

The earnings gap varies with age. The female–male earnings ratio for twenty- to twenty-four-year-olds was 98.1 in the first quarter of 2005 ("Table 2. Median Usual Weekly Earnings of Full-Time Wage and Salary Workers by Age, Race, Hispanic or Latino Ethnicity, and Sex, First Quarter 2005," in "Usual Weekly Earnings of Wage and Salary Workers: First Quarter 2005," Press Release, Bureau of Labor Statistics, U.S. Department of Labor, April 21, 2005). The ratio for fifty-five- to sixty-four-year-olds was 70.9. Women between thirty-five and forty-four and women sixty-five and over earned only 74.5% and 73.4% of what men earned, respectively. Young women earned almost as much as young men earned; but men's earnings rose more rapidly than women's, and as women age the ratio of their earnings to men's shrinks.

The earnings gap also varies by race and ethnic group. Hispanic women made 87.3% of Hispanic men's weekly earnings in 2004, and African-American women made 88.8% of what African-American men made. (See Table 5.1.) But white women made only 79.8% of what white men made. This is because of the relatively low earnings of Hispanic and African-American men compared to white men. The median weekly earnings of white women were slightly higher than those of African-American men and substantially higher than those of Hispanic men.

In general, African-American women have less money income than non-Hispanic white women, and Hispanic women have even less. In 2004 Asian-American women had the highest weekly median income of $613. Non-Hispanic white women had a median weekly income of $584, African-American women had an income of $505, and Hispanic women had an income of $419. Hispanic women, therefore, made seventy-two cents for every dollar a non-Hispanic white woman made.

Hourly Wages

Gender comparisons of hourly earnings also are useful, since many more women than men work part-time, and since minimum wage laws are based on hourly wages. In 2003 slightly more women than men worked for hourly wages. (See Table 5.5.) Overall, women's median wage was $10.08 per hour, 84.8% of men's median of $11.89 per hour. The rate for women increased

TABLE 5.2

Women's earnings as a percentage of men's earnings, by race and Hispanic origin, 1960–2003

[Based on median earnings of full-time, year-round workers 15 years old and over as of March of the following year. Before 1989 earnings are for civilian workers only.]

Year	All races	White alone	White	White alone, not Hispanic	White, not Hispanic	Black
2003	75.5	75.6	(NA)	71.6	(NA)	83.7
2002	76.6	75.4	(NA)	73.9	(NA)	85.6
2001	76.3	(NA)	75.1	(NA)	73.9	(NA)
2000[a]	73.7	(NA)	73.1	(NA)	72.3	(NA)
1999[b]	72.3	(NA)	71.6	(NA)	67.8	(NA)
1998	73.2	(NA)	72.6	(NA)	71.2	(NA)
1997	74.2	(NA)	72.0	(NA)	70.8	(NA)
1996	73.8	(NA)	73.3	(NA)	70.2	(NA)
1995	71.4	(NA)	71.2	(NA)	68.8	(NA)
1994[c]	72.0	(NA)	71.6	(NA)	71.1	(NA)
1993[d]	71.5	(NA)	70.8	(NA)	70.0	(NA)
1992[e]	70.8	(NA)	70.0	(NA)	69.0	(NA)
1991	69.9	(NA)	68.7	(NA)	67.9	(NA)
1990	71.6	(NA)	69.4	(NA)	67.6	(NA)
1989	68.7	(NA)	66.3	(NA)	64.2	(NA)
1988	66.0	(NA)	65.4	(NA)	64.1	(NA)
1987[f]	65.2	(NA)	64.4	(NA)	63.5	(NA)
1986	64.3	(NA)	63.3	(NA)	(NA)	(NA)
1985	64.6	(NA)	63.0	(NA)	(NA)	(NA)
1984[g]	63.7	(NA)	62.2	(NA)	(NA)	(NA)
1983	63.6	(NA)	62.7	(NA)	(NA)	(NA)
1982	61.7	(NA)	60.9	(NA)	(NA)	(NA)
1981	59.2	(NA)	58.5	(NA)	(NA)	(NA)
1980	60.2	(NA)	58.9	(NA)	(NA)	(NA)
1979[h]	59.7	(NA)	58.8	(NA)	(NA)	(NA)
1978	59.4	(NA)	58.9	(NA)	(NA)	(NA)
1977	58.9	(NA)	57.6	(NA)	(NA)	(NA)
1976[i]	60.2	(NA)	59.0	(NA)	(NA)	(NA)
1975	58.8	(NA)	57.6	(NA)	(NA)	(NA)
1974	58.8	(NA)	57.9	(NA)	(NA)	(NA)
1973[j]	56.6	(NA)	55.9	(NA)	(NA)	(NA)
1972[k]	57.9	(NA)	56.6	(NA)	(NA)	(NA)
1971	59.5	(NA)	58.5	(NA)	(NA)	(NA)
1970	59.4	(NA)	58.7	(NA)	(NA)	(NA)
1969	58.9	(NA)	58.1	(NA)	(NA)	(NA)
1968[l]	58.2	(NA)	58.2	(NA)	(NA)	(NA)
1967	57.8	(NA)	57.9	(NA)	(NA)	(NA)
1966[m]	57.6	(NA)	(NA)	(NA)	(NA)	(NA)
1965	59.9	(NA)	(NA)	(NA)	(NA)	(NA)
1964	59.1	(NA)	(NA)	(NA)	(NA)	(NA)
1963[n]	58.9	(NA)	(NA)	(NA)	(NA)	(NA)
1962[o]	59.3	(NA)	(NA)	(NA)	(NA)	(NA)
1961	59.2	(NA)	(NA)	(NA)	(NA)	(NA)
1960	60.7	(NA)	(NA)	(NA)	(NA)	(NA)

by $1.05 from 2000 (from $9.03), while that for men increased just thirty-nine cents (from $11.50). In the low-paying jobs held by sixteen- to nineteen-year-olds, women made 97.6% as much as men. Women with college degrees who worked for hourly rates earned 98.5% of what male graduates earned, whereas women high school graduates with no college made only 75.9% as much as male high school graduates earned.

In 2004, 3.6% of women age sixteen and over who were paid hourly wages earned at or below the prevailing federal minimum wage of $5.15 per hour, compared with 1.8% of men. (See Table 5.6.) Most minimum wage workers were under twenty-five years old. Women have made great strides since 1979, when more than one in five (20.2%) hourly paid workers earned only the minimum wage or less, compared to 7.7% of men.

Unions

In 2003 women represented by unions earned $13.45 an hour, only 79.2% of men's hourly wages. (See Table 5.5.) Women not represented by unions earned only $9.89 per hour, 90.3% of what men not represented by unions earned. The average female union member earned 25.3% more per hour than a nonunion woman.

Equal Pay Laws

The Equal Pay Act of 1963 (PL 88–38) made it illegal to pay women less than men working at the same job. But equal pay for equal work laws have little effect when the workplace is gender-segregated. Hartmann and Rose reported that when ranking jobs into a three-tier schema of elite, good, and less-skilled jobs, most workers

TABLE 5.2

Women's earnings as a percentage of men's earnings, by race and Hispanic origin, 1960–2003 [CONTINUED]

[Based on median earnings of full-time, year-round workers 15 years old and over as of March of the following year. Before 1989 earnings are for civilian workers only.]

Year	Black alone	Black	Asian	Asian alone	Asian Pacific Islander	Hispanic (of any race)
2003	83.6	(NA)	71.9	71.5	(NA)	85.7
2002	85.6	(NA)	75.4	75.1	(NA)	84.4
2001	(NA)	84.8	(NA)	(NA)	73.3	85.7
2000[a]	(NA)	83.3	(NA)	(NA)	75.1	86.9
1999[b]	(NA)	81.5	(NA)	(NA)	77.4	86.5
1998	(NA)	83.7	(NA)	(NA)	77.7	86.3
1997	(NA)	83.4	(NA)	(NA)	80.1	87.8
1996	(NA)	81.3	(NA)	(NA)	74.2	88.6
1995[c]	(NA)	84.6	(NA)	(NA)	78.8	84.3
1994[d]	(NA)	83.9	(NA)	(NA)	76.3	86.5
1993[e]	(NA)	86.1	(NA)	(NA)	78.8	83.2
1992[f]	(NA)	88.2	(NA)	(NA)	74.7	87.4
1991	(NA)	84.8	(NA)	(NA)	70.2	82.2
1990	(NA)	85.4	(NA)	(NA)	79.7	81.9
1989	(NA)	85.1	(NA)	(NA)	75.9	85.3
1988	(NA)	81.2	(NA)	(NA)	71.3	83.2
1987	(NA)	82.4	(NA)	(NA)	(NA)	83.3
1986	(NA)	80.3	(NA)	(NA)	(NA)	82.3
1985[g]	(NA)	81.9	(NA)	(NA)	(NA)	76.6
1984[h]	(NA)	82.5	(NA)	(NA)	(NA)	74.1
1983	(NA)	78.6	(NA)	(NA)	(NA)	72.1
1982	(NA)	78.3	(NA)	(NA)	(NA)	72.2
1981	(NA)	76.0	(NA)	(NA)	(NA)	72.9
1980	(NA)	78.8	(NA)	(NA)	(NA)	71.4
1979[i]	(NA)	74.6	(NA)	(NA)	(NA)	68.2
1978	(NA)	71.5	(NA)	(NA)	(NA)	68.8
1977	(NA)	77.5	(NA)	(NA)	(NA)	69.7
1976	(NA)	75.7	(NA)	(NA)	(NA)	68.0
1975	(NA)	74.6	(NA)	(NA)	(NA)	68.3
1974[j]	(NA)	75.3	(NA)	(NA)	(NA)	66.7
1973	(NA)	69.6	(NA)	(NA)	(NA)	(NA)
1972[k]	(NA)	70.5	(NA)	(NA)	(NA)	(NA)
1971[l]	(NA)	75.2	(NA)	(NA)	(NA)	(NA)
1970	(NA)	69.8	(NA)	(NA)	(NA)	(NA)
1969	(NA)	68.2	(NA)	(NA)	(NA)	(NA)
1968	(NA)	65.6	(NA)	(NA)	(NA)	(NA)
1967	(NA)	66.9	(NA)	(NA)	(NA)	(NA)

[a]Implementation of a 28,000 household sample expansion.
[b]Implementation of Census 2000-based population controls.
[c]Data reflect full implementation of the 1990 census-based sample design and metropolitan definitions, 7,000 household sample reduction, and revised race edits.
[d]Data reflect introduction of 1990 census-based sample design.
[e]Data collection method changed from paper and pencil to computer-assisted interviewing. In addition, the March 1994 income supplement was revised to allow for the coding of different income amounts on selected questionnaire items. Child support and alimony limits decreased to $49,999. Limits increased in the following categories: earnings to $999,999; social security to $49,999; supplemental security income and public assistance income to $24,999; and veterans; benefits to $99,999.
[f]Data reflect implementation of 1990 census population controls.
[g]Recording of amounts for earnings from longest job were increased to $299,999. Data reflect full implementation of 1980 census-based sample design.
[h]Data reflect implementation of Hispanic population weighting controls and introduction of 1980 census-based sample design.
[i]Data reflect implementation of 1980 census population controls. Questionnaire expanded to show 27 possible values from 51 possible sources of income.
[j]Questionnaire expanded to ask 11 income questions.
[k]Data reflect full implementation of 1970 census-based sample design.
[l]Data reflect full introduction of 1970 census-based sample design and population controls.
[m]Questionnaire expanded to ask 8 income questions.
[n]Data reflect implementation of new procedures to impute missing data only.
[o]Data reflect full implementation of 1960 census-based sample design and population controls.

SOURCE: "Table P-40. Woman's Earnings as a Percentage of Men's Earnings by Race and Hispanic Origin: 1960 to 2003," in *Historical Income Tables—People*, U.S. Census Bureau, February 17, 2005, http://www.census.gov/hhes/income/histinc/p40.html (accessed June 6, 2005)

---

fall into an occupation where at least 75% are of one gender, and "women's jobs" pay less than "men's jobs" ("Still a Man's Labor Market: The Long-Term Earnings Gap"). In fact, women in the elite tier consistently earn less than men in the good tier.

Furthermore, even within identical occupations, equal pay laws may be poorly enforced. A 1999 study, *Equal Pay for Working Families: National and State* *Data on the Pay Gap and Its Costs* (Washington, DC), conducted by the AFL-CIO and the Institute for Women's Policy Research (IWPR), asserts that if equal pay were enforced by the states, the poverty rate for all working women would be cut by as much as 12%. In the AFL-CIO's 2002 "Ask a Working Woman" survey, equal pay was the number one policy issue among the respondents, with 92% saying that stronger equal pay laws were important.

TABLE 5.3

Median usual weekly earnings of full-time wage and salary workers, by occupation and sex, 2004

[Numbers in thousands]

Occupation	Both sexes		Women		Men		Women's earnings as percent of men's
	Total employed	Median weekly earnings	Total employed	Median weekly earnings	Total employed	Median weekly earnings	
Total, 16 years and over	101,224	$638	44,223	$573	57,001	$713	80.4
Management, professional, and related occupations	36,149	918	18,168	780	17,981	1,098	71.0
Management, business, and financial operations occupations	14,778	965	6,609	812	8,170	1,158	70.1
Management occupations	10,221	1,052	3,995	871	6,226	1,215	71.7
Chief executives	1,050	1,663	248	1,310	802	1,875	69.9
General and operations managers	727	1,129	175	872	552	1,166	74.8
Advertising and promotions managers	57	924	34	*	23	*	*
Marketing and sales managers	770	1,213	298	898	472	1,441	62.3
Administrative services managers	80	937	27	*	53	958	*
Computer and information systems managers	325	1,439	96	1,228	228	1,547	79.4
Financial managers	961	986	535	839	427	1,397	60.1
Human resources managers	261	1,051	171	958	90	1,259	76.1
Industrial production managers	269	1,107	49	*	220	1,172	*
Purchasing managers	163	1,092	59	46	104	1,153	82.0
Transportation, storage, and distribution managers	220	741	34	*	187	753	*
Farm, ranch, and other agricultural managers	103	621	16	*	86	612	*
Construction managers	425	1,027	23	*	402	1,036	*
Education administrators	651	1,019	405	905	246	1,172	77.2
Engineering managers	99	1,807	6	*	94	1,783	*
Food service managers	568	657	232	598	336	713	83.9
Lodging managers	102	733	50	659	52	778	84.7
Medical and health services managers	451	973	328	943	123	1,135	83.1
Property, real estate, and community association managers	304	681	186	623	118	767	81.2
Social and community service managers	241	819	156	768	85	1,014	75.7
Business and financial operations occupations	4,558	847	2,613	746	1,944	1,007	74.1
Wholesale and retail buyers, except farm products	146	808	71	609	75	935	65.1
Purchasing agents, except wholesale, retail, and farm products	267	782	141	694	125	883	78.6
Claims adjusters, appraisers, examiners, and investigators	257	762	171	677	85	952	71.1
Compliance officers, except agriculture, construction, health, safety, and transportation	116	922	62	835	54	1,070	78.0
Cost estimators	88	888	14	*	73	915	*
Human resources, training, and labor relations specialist	612	803	415	755	198	952	79.3
Management analysts	317	1,017	146	922	170	1,215	75.9
Accountants and auditors	1,385	851	842	757	543	1,016	74.5
Appraisers and assessors of real estate	78	863	29	*	50	1,021	*
Personal financial advisors	229	1,062	61	73	167	1,170	66.1
Insurance underwriters	89	859	65	772	24	*	*
Loan counselors and officers	381	799	216	695	165	1,001	69.4
Tax examiners, collectors, and revenue agents	77	818	49	*	28	*	*
Professional and related occupations	21,371	883	11,560	767	9,811	1,049	73.1
Computer and mathematical occupations	2,793	1,114	757	972	2,037	1,155	84.2
Computer scientists and systems analysts	604	1,027	186	902	418	1,092	82.6
Computer programmers	516	1,118	145	1,006	371	1,151	87.4
Computer software engineers	757	1,350	184	1,149	572	1,429	80.4
Computer support specialists	297	840	88	813	209	850	95.6
Database administrators	76	1,105	22	*	53	1,121	*
Network and computer systems administrators	178	1,038	33	*	145	1,064	*
Network systems and data communications analysts	233	1,027	44	*	189	1,097	*
Operations research analysts	84	1,083	41	*	43	*	*

There is a growing movement toward replacing equal pay laws with laws providing for pay equity or comparable worth for men and women. Comparable worth recognizes that some occupations traditionally done by women are underpaid simply because they are done by women. Comparable worth laws would provide for equal pay if men's and women's jobs are merely comparable rather than identical. Workers of both sexes in occupations that have traditionally been filled by women would gain from the implementation of comparable worth. Most

TABLE 5.3

Median usual weekly earnings of full-time wage and salary workers, by occupation and sex, 2004 [CONTINUED]

[Numbers in thousands]

Occupation	Both sexes		Women		Men		Women's earnings as percent of men's
	Total employed	Median weekly earnings	Total employed	Median weekly earnings	Total employed	Median weekly earnings	
Architecture and engineering occupations	2,500	$1,098	331	$880	2,170	$1,139	77.3
Architects, except naval	142	1,141	38	*	105	1,242	*
Aerospace engineers	105	1,347	10	*	94	1,369	*
Chemical engineers	65	1,221	10	*	55	1,242	*
Civil engineers	264	1,135	32	*	232	1,159	*
Computer hardware engineers	86	1,328	13	*	73	1,487	*
Electrical and electronics engineers	311	1,277	24	*	287	1,336	*
Industrial engineers, including health and safety	178	1,152	32	*	146	1,195	*
Mechanical engineers	292	1,187	16	*	276	1,201	*
Drafters	178	768	38	*	140	797	*
Engineering technicians, except drafters	394	829	73	696	320	867	80.3
Surveying and mapping technicians	66	672	9	*	57	711	*
Life, physical, and social science occupations	1,073	957	426	884	647	1,012	87.4
Biological scientists	109	929	49	*	60	946	*
Medical scientists	83	1,025	45	*	38	*	*
Chemists and materials scientists	133	1,048	42	*	91	1,146	*
Environmental scientists and geoscientists	75	1,008	20	*	55	1,144	*
Market and survey researchers	90	937	43	*	47	*	*
Psychologists	75	1,012	47	*	28	*	*
Chemical technicians	89	827	27	*	62	869	*
Community and social services occupations	1,846	707	1,082	661	764	766	86.3
Counselors	513	735	338	689	175	832	82.8
Social workers	620	698	472	689	148	720	95.7
Miscellaneous community and social service specialists	261	639	166	596	95	747	79.8
Clergy	351	771	47	*	304	795	*
Legal occupations	1,111	1,070	603	845	508	1,561	54.1
Lawyers	621	1,561	208	1,255	412	1,710	73.4
Judges, magistrates, and other judicial workers	58	1,333	33	*	25	*	*
Paralegals and legal assistants	280	731	244	713	36	*	*
Miscellaneous legal support workers	152	707	117	695	34	*	*
Education, training, and library occupations	5,941	781	4,273	729	1,668	956	76.3
Postsecondary teachers	813	1,034	337	886	476	1,162	76.2
Preschool and kindergarten teachers	484	521	473	515	11	*	*
Elementary and middle school teachers	2,206	806	1,772	776	435	917	84.6
Secondary school teachers	1,013	885	555	824	458	955	86.3
Special education teachers	325	804	271	795	54	841	94.5
Other teachers and instructors	297	776	158	654	139	873	74.9
Librarians	159	834	136	823	23	*	*
Teacher assistants	545	377	500	373	45	*	*
Arts, design, entertainment, sports, and media occupations	1,426	768	618	688	808	862	79.8
Artists and related workers	65	865	24	*	41	*	*
Designers	480	714	230	646	250	818	79.0
Producers and directors	98	1,030	35	*	63	1,211	*
Athletes, coaches, umpires, and related workers	99	745	17	*	82	792	*
News analysts, reporters and correspondents	64	835	33	*	31	*	*
Public relations specialists	102	823	61	739	40	*	*
Editors	110	856	54	759	56	946	80.2
Writers and authors	86	760	44	*	42	*	*
Broadcast and sound engineering technicians and radio operators	75	857	8	*	67	871	*
Photographers	53	650	17	*	36	*	*

comparable worth implementations have been the result of labor union negotiations, rather than legislation, and these agreements tend to be in the public rather than the private sector. The American Federation of State, County, and Municipal Employees has been particularly active in bargaining for comparable worth.

Families and Households

Of the 112 million American households in 2003, 9% had incomes under $10,000. The median income of American households was $43,318, almost $10,000 higher than in 1967. (See Table 5.7.) Asian-American households had the highest median income, at $55,699; Hispanics had the lowest, at $32,997. For married-couple families, the median income was $57,704. For female-headed families with no husband present, the median income in 2002 was $29,001, up 1.4% from 2001.

POVERTY

The federal government defines poverty as having an income below the poverty threshold as shown in

TABLE 5.3

Median usual weekly earnings of full-time wage and salary workers, by occupation and sex, 2004 [CONTINUED]

[Numbers in thousands]

Occupation	Both sexes		Women		Men		Women's earnings as percent of men's
	Total employed	Median weekly earnings	Total employed	Median weekly earnings	Total employed	Median weekly earnings	
Healthcare practitioner and technical occupations	4,680	$852	3,470	$808	1,210	$1,062	76.1
Dietitians and nutritionists	57	669	49	*	8	*	*
Pharmacists	162	1,578	72	1,432	90	1,684	85.0
Physicians and surgeons	555	1,660	173	978	382	1,874	52.2
Physician assistants	57	901	38	*	19	*	*
Registered nurses	1,800	904	1,651	895	148	1,031	86.8
Occupational therapists	56	923	51	906	5	*	*
Physical therapists	121	925	70	900	50	955	94.2
Respiratory therapists	79	782	38	*	41	*	*
Speech-language pathologists	65	879	62	869	3	*	*
Clinical laboratory technologists and technicians	267	727	188	710	79	763	3.1
Diagnostic related technologists and technicians	225	884	150	836	75	961	87.0
Emergency medical technicians and paramedics	121	690	37	*	84	717	1
Health diagnosing and treating practitioner support technicians	280	516	236	508	44	*	*
Licensed practical and licensed vocational nurses	385	637	362	629	23	*	*
Medical records and health information technicians	81	501	71	513	10	*	*
Service occupations	13,763	411	6,773	374	6,989	476	78.6
Healthcare support occupations	1,985	407	1,755	402	230	453	88.7
Nursing, psychiatric, and home health aides	1,261	388	1,113	383	148	420	91.2
Dental assistants	144	474	139	469	5	*	*
Protective service occupations	2,509	700	471	557	2,038	733	76.0
First-line supervisors/managers of police and detectives	134	1,015	27	*	107	1,055	*
Fire fighters	263	933	13	*	250	942	*
Bailiffs, correctional officers, and jailers	370	622	107	558	263	654	85.3
Detectives and criminal investigators	114	995	26	*	88	1,048	*
Police and sheriff's patrol officers	654	844	83	841	571	845	99.5
Private detectives and investigators	63	812	21	*	41	*	*
Security guards and gaming surveillance officers	641	457	138	418	502	471	88.7
Food preparation and serving related occupations	3,863	360	1,908	339	1,955	384	88.3
Chefs and head cooks	266	508	51	416	215	524	79.4
First-line supervisors/managers of food preparation and serving workers	504	435	282	418	222	464	90.1
Cooks	1,167	341	443	319	723	356	89.6
Food preparation workers	278	321	158	323	120	319	101.3
Bartenders	197	426	102	392	95	482	81.3
Combined food preparation and serving workers, including fast food	123	311	85	308	39	*	*
Counter attendants, cafeteria, food concession, and coffee shop	91	292	56	282	35	*	*
Waiters and waitresses	799	348	538	327	261	399	82.0
Food servers, nonrestaurant	94	363	60	333	34	*	*
Dining room and cafeteria attendants and bartender helpers	152	340	61	356	91	326	109.2
Dishwashers	141	306	30	*	111	311	*
Building and grounds cleaning and maintenance occupations	3,436	385	1,208	335	2,228	412	81.3
First-line supervisors/managers of housekeeping and janitorial work	139	479	50	410	89	531	77.2
First-line supervisors/managers of landscaping, lawn service, and groundskeeping workers	106	641	6	*	99	661	*
Janitors and building cleaners	1,460	405	379	343	1,081	425	80.7
Maids and housekeeping cleaners	818	331	723	324	95	402	80.6
Pest control workers	65	478	4	*	61	489	*
Grounds maintenance workers	848	372	46	*	803	371	*

Table 5.8. The poverty threshold depends on family size and the age of the householder. But calculations of poverty levels are controversial. Social scientists have for years debated about the best and most accurate means of establishing a poverty threshold. The central question that arises in debates about measuring poverty is whether to use an absolute or a relative means of updating the poverty rate on an annual or periodic basis. Once established, an absolute poverty measure is updated to account for price changes (inflation) only. A relative poverty measure is one that is updated based on changes in the median or mean income or compensation of the general population. The relative poverty measure adjusts for changing

TABLE 5.3

Median usual weekly earnings of full-time wage and salary workers, by occupation and sex, 2004 [CONTINUED]

[Numbers in thousands]

Occupation	Both sexes		Women		Men		Women's earnings as percent of men's
	Total employed	Median weekly earnings	Total employed	Median weekly earnings	Total employed	Median weekly earnings	
Personal care and service occupations	1,969	$402	1,431	$380	538	$500	76.0
First-line supervisors/managers of gaming workers	88	600	33	*	55	673	*
First-line supervisors/managers of personal service workers	64	597	36	*	28	*	*
Gaming services workers	75	558	41	*	34	*	*
Hairdressers, hairstylists, and cosmetologists	291	398	267	394	24	*	*
Baggage porters, bellhops, and concierges	60	498	11	*	50	491	*
Transportation attendants	76	575	54	473	22	*	*
Child care workers	413	334	387	334	26	*	*
Personal and home care aides	360	358	308	350	52	434	80.6
Recreation and fitness workers	153	498	89	473	65	585	80.9
Sales and office occupations	24,950	558	15,540	512	9,410	669	76.5
Sales and related occupations	9,984	604	4,422	464	5,562	747	62.1
First-line supervisors/managers of retail sales workers	2,246	613	985	505	1,260	737	68.5
First-line supervisors/managers of non-retail sales workers	936	860	284	678	652	927	73.1
Cashiers	1,355	322	1,016	313	339	380	82.4
Counter and rental clerks	97	429	46	*	51	514	*
Parts salespersons	120	530	13	*	107	554	*
Retail salespersons	1,865	496	766	386	1,100	597	64.7
Advertising sales agents	180	772	84	643	97	942	68.3
Insurance sales agents	360	726	190	615	170	970	63.4
Securities, commodities, and financial services sales agents	305	973	95	651	210	1,168	55.7
Travel agents	69	576	59	544	10	*	*
Sales representatives, services, all other	412	800	157	740	255	875	84.6
Sales representatives, wholesale and manufacturing	1,233	867	296	754	937	895	84.2
Real estate brokers and sales agents	431	744	233	663	197	834	79.5
Telemarketers	93	380	61	355	32	*	*
Door-to-door sales workers, news and street vendors, and related workers	61	442	23	*	38	*	*
Office and administrative support occupations	14,966	535	11,118	522	3,848	587	88.9
First-line supervisors/managers of office and administrative support	1,441	670	1,001	636	440	792	80.3
Switchboard operators, including answering service	55	450	50	459	4	*	*
Bill and account collectors	200	536	139	539	61	529	101.9
Billing and posting clerks and machine operators	363	518	330	510	32	*	*
Bookkeeping, accounting, and auditing clerks	1,004	543	916	542	88	563	96.3
Payroll and timekeeping clerks	136	554	123	541	13	*	*
Tellers	301	405	265	401	35	*	*
Court, municipal, and license clerks	82	526	76	518	6		*
Credit authorizers, checkers, and clerks	51	600	38	*	13	*	*
Customer service representatives	1,379	516	967	504	412	571	88.3
Eligibility interviewers, government programs	63	622	48	*	15	*	*
File clerks	264	528	205	525	58	543	96.7
Hotel, motel, and resort desk clerks	67	349	41	*	27	*	*
Interviewers, except eligibility and loan	102	497	89	498	12	*	*
Library assistants, clerical	51	468	47	*	4	*	*
Loan interviewers and clerks	170	536	143	522	28	*	*
Order clerks	90	529	67	512	23	*	*
Human resources assistants, except payroll and timekeeping	53	635	42	*	11	*	*
Receptionists and information clerks	847	462	795	463	52	454	102.0
Reservation and transportation ticket agents and travel clerks	125	502	85	489	40	*	*
Couriers and messengers	200	648	24	*	176	663	*
Dispatchers	232	586	122	516	109	701	73.6
Postal service clerks	162	768	73	778	89	761	102.2
Postal service mail carriers	314	791	112	743	203	834	89.1
Postal service mail sorters, processors, and processing machine operators	103	741	41	*	62	749	*

TABLE 5.3

Median usual weekly earnings of full-time wage and salary workers, by occupation and sex, 2004 [CONTINUED]

[Numbers in thousands]

Occupation	Both sexes		Women		Men		Women's earnings as percent of men's
	Total employed	Median weekly earnings	Total employed	Median weekly earnings	Total employed	Median weekly earnings	
Production, planning, and expediting clerks	266	$686	143	$613	123	$767	79.9
Shipping, receiving, and traffic clerks	537	501	144	469	393	512	91.6
Stock clerks and order fillers	946	429	349	420	597	438	95.9
Weighers, measurers, checkers, and samplers, recordkeeping	55	543	23	*	31	*	*
Secretaries and administrative assistants	2,657	552	2,570	550	87	598	92.0
Computer operators	170	579	91	580	79	575	100.9
Data entry keyers	394	495	315	486	78	556	87.4
Word processors and typists	239	527	223	525	16	*	*
Insurance claims and policy processing clerks	252	536	216	534	36	*	*
Mail clerks and mail machine operators except postal service	127	457	59	479	68	433	110.6
Office clerks, general	667	503	559	499	109	523	95.4
Office machine operators, except computer	51	433	31	*	20	*	*
Natural resources, construction, and maintenance occupations	11,280	621	445	453	10,835	626	72.4
Farming, fishing, and forestry occupations	718	356	133	322	585	367	87.7
Graders and sorters, agricultural products	61	355	46	*	15	*	*
Logging workers	61	465	2	*	59	470	*
Construction and extraction occupations	6,232	604	123	504	6,109	606	83.2
First-line supervisors/managers of construction trades and extraction workers	579	812	11	*	568	822	*
Brickmasons, blockmasons, and stonemasons	164	577	—	—	164	577	—
Carpenters	1,170	576	21	*	1,149	576	*
Carpet, floor, and tile installers and finishers	147	517	—	—	146	518	—
Cement masons, concrete finishers, and terrazzo workers	95	556	—	—	95	556	—
Construction laborers	986	492	21	*	965	492	*
Operating engineers and other construction equipment operators	335	689	4	*	331	689	*
Drywall installers, ceiling tile installers, and tapers	156	529	—	—	156	529	—
Electricians	668	719	14	*	655	718	*
Painters, construction and maintenance	410	494	15	*	395	495	*
Pipelayers, plumbers, pipefitters, and steamfitters	483	690	2	*	480	690	*
Roofers	188	480	3	*	184	482	*
Sheet metal workers	132	606	6	*	126	614	*
Structural iron and steel workers	53	694	—	—	53	695	—
Helpers, construction trades	99	386	4	*	94	386	*
Construction and building inspectors	87	718	10	*	77	724	*
Highway maintenance workers	81	565	2	*	79	572	*
Installation, maintenance, and repair occupations	4,330	704	190	611	4,140	707	86.4
First-line supervisors/managers of mechanics, installers, and repairers	326	876	22	*	304	877	*
Computer, automated teller, and office machine repairers	309	723	38	*	271	735	*
Radio and telecommunications equipment installers and repairers	221	877	31	*	190	891	*
Electronic home entertainment equipment installers and repairers	52	668	2	*	50	676	*
Security and fire alarm systems installers	52	661	2	*	51	666	*
Aircraft mechanics and service technicians	116	856	3	*	113	856	*
Automotive body and related repairers	107	630	5	*	102	638	*
Automotive service technicians and mechanics	735	637	12	*	723	639	*
Bus and truck mechanics and diesel engine specialists	298	706	1	*	297	707	*
Heavy vehicle and mobile equipment service technicians mechanics	189	708	2	*	188	708	*
Heating, air conditioning, and refrigeration mechanics and installers	298	682	5	*	293	683	*
Industrial and refractory machinery mechanics	419	707	11	*	408	708	*
Maintenance and repair workers, general	281	665	10	*	270	668	*
Millwrights	59	839	1	*	58	844	*

TABLE 5.3

Median usual weekly earnings of full-time wage and salary workers, by occupation and sex, 2004 [CONTINUED]

[Numbers in thousands]

Occupation	Both sexes		Women		Men		Women's earnings as percent of men's
	Total employed	Median weekly earnings	Total employed	Median weekly earnings	Total employed	Median weekly earnings	
Electrical power-line installers and repairers	112	$804	2	*	111	$813	*
Telecommunications line installers and repairers	134	755	7	*	127	771	*
Production, transportation, and material moving occupations	15,082	523	3,296	406	11,786	578	70.2
Production occupations	8,478	526	2,454	405	6,024	597	67.8
First-line supervisors/managers of production and operating workers	874	726	169	546	706	765	71.4
Electrical, electronics, and electromechanical assemblers	213	443	117	397	96	515	77.1
Bakers	126	410	53	364	73	454	80.2
Butchers and other meat, poultry, and fish processing workers	260	454	51	369	209	488	75.6
Food batchmakers	68	466	30	*	39	*	*
Cutting, punching, and press machine setters, operators and tenders	139	517	42	*	97	557	*
Grinding, lapping, polishing, and buffing machine tool setters, operators and tenders, metal and plastic	78	516	8	*	70	527	*
Machinists	408	670	16	*	392	679	*
Molders and molding machine setters, operators, and tenders, metal and plastic	69	459	19	*	50	489	*
Tool and die makers	80	764	2	*	78	769	*
Welding, soldering, and brazing workers	539	606	26	*	513	614	*
Job printers	54	563	12	*	42	*	*
Printing machine operators	174	592	32	*	142	622	*
Laundry and dry-cleaning workers	136	360	74	23	62	460	70.2
Pressers, textile, garment, and related materials	67	293	42	*	24	*	*
Sewing machine operators	242	327	186	319	56	381	83.7
Tailors, dressmakers, and sewers	50	376	33	*	17	*	*
Cabinetmakers and bench carpenters	61	498	3	*	58	503	*
Stationary engineers and boiler operators	102	704	1	*	101	701	*
Chemical processing machine setters, operators, and tenders	65	790	7	*	58	809	*
Crushing, grinding, polishing, mixing, and blending workers	107	587	20	*	87	600	*
Cutting workers	73	519	17	*	56	563	*
Inspectors, testers, sorters, samplers, and weighers	638	585	240	474	398	663	71.5
Medical, dental, and ophthalmic laboratory technicians	76	524	41	*	35	*	*
Packaging and filling machine operators and tenders	299	368	168	341	131	410	83.2
Painting workers	180	509	27	*	154	530	*
Transportation and material moving occupations	6,604	520	842	410	5,762	549	74.7
Supervisors, transportation and material moving workers	180	655	33	*	147	688	*
Aircraft pilots and flight engineers	95	1,418	5	*	90	1,472	*
Bus drivers	366	500	152	440	215	588	74.8
Driver/sales workers and truck drivers	2,587	610	93	476	2,494	613	77.7
Taxi drivers and chauffeurs	165	486	22	*	143	494	*
Railroad conductors and yardmasters	57	881	5	*	52	903	*
Parking lot attendants	52	378	8	*	44	*	*
Service station attendants	78	319	2	*	76	319	*
Crane and tower operators	66	732	2	*	64	721	*

standards of living. The official poverty measure used by the United States is an absolute measure.

The official poverty rate in 2003 was 12.5%. (See Table 5.9.) More than 35.9 million Americans (up from 32.9 million in 2001) were living in poverty, of which 56% were female; 13.7% of all American females were impoverished. More than 7.6 million families (10%) were in poverty, up from 6.8 million (9.2%) in 2001. Only 5.4% of married-couple families lived in poverty in 2003,

compared to 28% of families headed by a woman with no spouse present.

Because the Census Bureau made significant changes in the way data are collected in regard to race, there is no one method to compare racial statistics for recent years (from 2002 forward) to those from past years. In 2003 African-Americans had the highest percentage of people living in poverty (24.4%); 22.5% of Hispanics, 11.8% of Asian-Americans, and 8.2% of non-Hispanic whites lived in poverty.

TABLE 5.3

Median usual weekly earnings of full-time wage and salary workers, by occupation and sex, 2004 [CONTINUED]

[Numbers in thousands]

Occupation	Both sexes		Women		Men		Women's earnings as percent of men's
	Total employed	Median weekly earnings	Total employed	Median weekly earnings	Total employed	Median weekly earnings	
Dredge, excavating, and loading machine operators	57	$607	—	—	57	$607	—
Industrial truck and tractor operators	525	486	40	*	485	487	*
Cleaners of vehicles and equipment	258	384	28	*	230	387	*
Laborers and freight, stock, and material movers, hand	1,342	443	196	402	1,146	457	88.0
Packers and packagers, hand	349	349	206	333	143	373	89.3
Refuse and recyclable material collectors	67	508	5	*	62	512	*

*Data not shown where base is less than 50,000.
— Dash indicates no data or data that do not meet publication criteria.

SOURCE: "Table 18. Median Usual Weekly Earnings of Full-Time Wage and Salary Workers by Detailed Occupation and Sex, 2004 Ànnual Averages," in *Women in the Labor Force: A Databook*, U.S. Department of Labor, Bureau of Labor Statistics, May 2005, http://www.bls.gov/cps/wlf-table18-2005.pdf (accessed June 10, 2005)

FIGURE 5.2

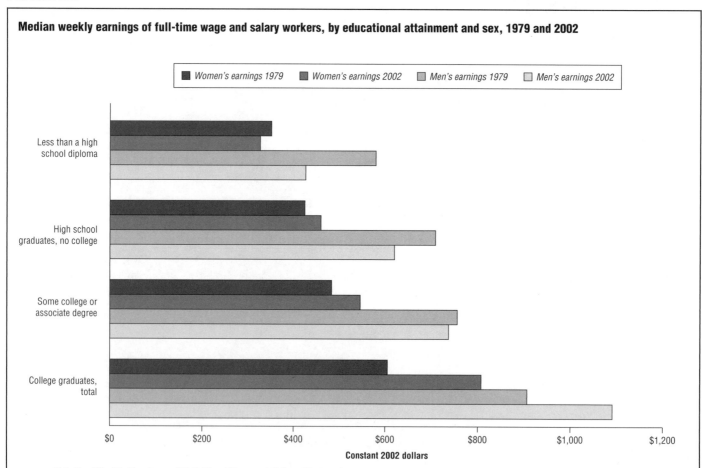

Median weekly earnings of full-time wage and salary workers, by educational attainment and sex, 1979 and 2002

SOURCE: "Median Weekly Earnings of Full-Time Wage and Salary Workers by Educational Attainment and Sex, 1979 and 2002," in *Earnings by Educational Attainment and Sex, 1979 and 2002*, U.S. Department of Labor, Bureau of Labor Statistics, October 23, 2003, http://www.bls.gov/opub/ted/2003/oct/wk3/art04.htm (accessed June 10, 2005)

FIGURE 5.3

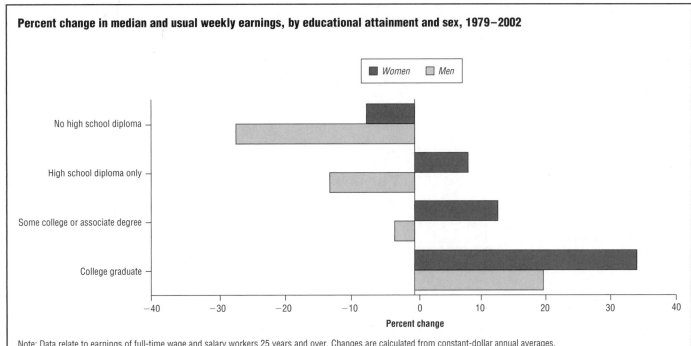

Percent change in median and usual weekly earnings, by educational attainment and sex, 1979–2002

Note: Data relate to earnings of full-time wage and salary workers 25 years and over. Changes are calculated from constant-dollar annual averages.

SOURCE: "Chart 3. Percent Change in Median Usual Weekly Earnings from 1979 to 2002 by Educational Attainment and Sex," in *Highlights of Women's Earnings in 2002*, U.S. Department of Labor, Bureau of Labor Statistics, September 2003, http://bls.gov/cps/cpswom2002.pdf (accessed June 6, 2005)

Single Mothers

More than one-third of families headed by single mothers (35.5%) in 2003 lived below the poverty threshold, compared with 19.1% of families headed by single fathers and 7% of married-couple families with children. Families headed by a white, non-Hispanic single mother (28.1%) were less likely than families headed by an African-American single mother (42.8%), an Asian-American single mother (29%), or a Hispanic single mother (43%) to live in poverty, although a substantial proportion of all families headed by a single mother, regardless of race or ethnicity, lived in poverty.

In 2003 the number of children under age eighteen in poverty was 12.9 million, up from 11.7 million in 2001. The poverty rate also increased from 16.7% to 17.6%. Children under the age of five are particularly vulnerable to poverty. The rate for this age group in 2003 was 20.3%. Four out of ten children (41.7%) living in a family headed by a single mother were in poverty, compared with only 8.6% of children living in married couple families (*Annual Social and Economic Supplement*, "Poverty," Current Population Survey, Bureau of Labor Statistics and Bureau of the Census, 2004).

The Working Poor

In 2003, 70.7% of poor and near-poor families (within 200% of the poverty level) had at least one working member, and 61% of families below 100% of poverty had at least one working member. Only 4% of married-couple families with at least one working member were below the poverty line, but 19.7% of families headed by a female householder with at least one working member were below the poverty line, and 25.6% of families including children headed by a single mother with at least one working member were below the poverty line. The vast majority of poor and near-poor (within 200% of the poverty level) families include at least one adult working most of the year (*Annual Social and Economic Supplement*, "Poverty").

Unemployment in 2000 reached its lowest level in more than three decades, according to the CBPP, and poverty rates dropped to the lowest level since 1979. But by 2003 the unemployment rate average was 6%, up from 4% in 2000. The rate dropped again in 2004 to 5.5%.

Welfare Reform and Government Benefits

The Personal Responsibility and Work Opportunity Reconciliation Act (PRWORA) was designed to move people, primarily single mothers, off welfare and into the workforce. A 2001 study by the CBPP found that although earnings by single working mothers increased in the late 1990s because of a strong economy, the earned income tax credit, and improved child care options, these gains were completely offset by declines in government benefits. As a group, single working mothers were no better off than before, and those who were already poor became poorer. The proportion of single mothers who worked increased from 68% in

TABLE 5.4

Median usual weekly earnings of full-time wage and salary workers, by sex, marital status, and presence and age of own children under 18 years old, 2003

Characteristic	Number of workers (in thousands)	Median weekly earnings
Women		
Total, all marital statuses	**44,076**	**$552**
With children under 18 years old	16,772	539
With children 6 to 17, none younger	10,663	554
With children under 6 years old	6,109	515
With no children under 18 years old	27,304	561
Total, married, spouse present	**23,230**	**588**
With children under 18 years old	11,238	582
With children 6 to 17, none younger	7,009	581
With children under 6 years old	4,230	583
With no children under 18 years old	11,992	594
Total, other marital statuses*	**20,845**	**512**
With children under 18 years old	5,534	476
With children 6 to 17, none younger	3,655	511
With children under 6 years old	1,879	404
With no children under 18 years old	15,312	526
Men		
Total, all marital statuses	**56,227**	**695**
With children under 18 years old	22,021	767
With children 6 to 17, none younger	11,732	806
With children under 6 years old	10,289	727
With no children under 18 years old	34,206	646
Total, married, spouse present	**34,997**	**786**
With children under 18 years old	20,344	786
With children 6 to 17, none younger	10,764	823
With children under 6 years old	9,580	750
With no children under 18 years old	14,653	786
Total, other marital statuses*	**21,229**	**561**
With children under 18 years old	1,676	587
With children 6 to 17, none younger	968	669
With children under 6 years old	709	497
With no children under 18 years old	19,553	558

*Includes never-married, divorced, separated, and widowed persons.
Note: Children refer to "own" children and include sons, daughters, stepchildren, and adopted children. Excluded are other related children such as grandchildren, nieces, nephews, and cousins, and unrelated children.

SOURCE: "Table 8. Median Usual Weekly Earnings of Full-Time Wage and Salary Workers by Sex, Marital Status, and Presence and Age of Own Children Under 18 Years Old, 2003 Annual Averages," in *Highlights of Women's Earnings in 2003*, U.S. Department of Labor, Bureau of Labor Statistics, September 2004, http://www.bls.gov/cps/cpswom2003.pdf (accessed June 6, 2005)

1993 to 82% in 1999. But the study found that the poverty rate for working single mothers in 1999 was just as high as in 1995, before PRWORA, even after government benefits were figured in. The poverty gap also increased for working single-mother families between 1995 and 1999. (The poverty gap is the total amount of money needed to lift all families that are below the poverty line up to the poverty line. The poverty gap, therefore, is a measure of not only the numbers in poverty but the depth of their poverty.) In contrast, both the poverty status and the poverty gap of other types of working families with children improved. The report concluded that since 1995 government safety-net programs for the poor have been less effec-

tive in improving the poverty status of working single-mother families. With the slowing of the economy and the rise in unemployment in 2001, the number of women in poverty was expected to increase (Kathryn H. Porter and Allen Dupree, "Table 2. Poverty Rates for People in Families with Children," in *Poverty Trends for Families Headed by Working Single Mothers: 1993 to 1999*, Center on Budget and Policy Priorities, August 2001).

After taking into consideration government benefits and taxes, the poverty rate for all single-mother families was 27.7% in 1999, down from 41% in 1993. The poverty rate for single mothers was back up to 35.5% in 2003. The poverty rate for families headed by single working mothers, taking into account benefits and taxes, remained at 19.4% in 1999, up slightly from 19.2% in 1995. It increased slightly again to 19.5% in 2003.

A 2005 review of the issue by the Office of the Assistant Secretary for Planning and Evaluation, U.S. Department of Health and Human Services, found that unemployment rates fell in the late 1990s among the general population and among single mothers with children because of the strong economic growth. This was in part responsible for the decline in the proportion of families with children under eighteen receiving Temporary Assistance for Needy Families (TANF) from 12.8% in 1996 to 6% in 2003. (See Figure 5.4.)

But during the period of economic downturn after 2000, TANF rates remained relatively stable, despite the increase in the poverty rate of female-headed families and the increase in the percentage of the population receiving food stamps. (See Figure 5.4.) In part this was because the TANF program provided federal aid for a lifetime maximum of five years to families transitioning from welfare to work. Recipients had to be in work-related activities within two years, and states could be penalized for having too few welfare recipients transitioning to work. In some states work or schooling to prepare for work were conditions for receiving the benefits, and mothers with children under age six had to work at least twenty hours per week to qualify. Beginning in 2000 mothers of children over age six were required to work thirty hours per week.

These mothers instead turned to unemployment insurance. Between 2000 and 2003 the proportion of single women with children receiving unemployment insurance increased from 4.6% to 6.7%. Since the employment rates of never-married mothers with children rose from 45% in 1990 to 63% in 2003, rising numbers of them qualified for unemployment insurance. And since potential unemployment insurance benefits are often twice as high as TANF benefits, these mothers prefer it as a safety net over welfare payments.

TABLE 5.5

Median hourly earnings of wage and salary workers paid hourly rates, by selected characteristics, 2003

	Both sexes		Women		Men		
Characteristic	Number of workers (in thousands)	Median hourly earnings	Number of workers (in thousands)	Median hourly earnings	Number of workers (in thousands)	Median hourly earnings	Women's earnings as percent of men's[a]
Age							
Total, 16 years and over	**72,946**	**$10.85**	**37,093**	**$10.08**	**35,853**	**$11.89**	**84.8**
16 to 24 years	15,871	7.90	7,841	7.59	8,031	8.14	93.2
16 to 19 years	5,412	6.93	2,804	6.85	2,608	7.02	97.6
20 to 24 years	10,460	8.66	5,037	8.19	5,423	9.00	91.1
25 years and over	57,075	12.05	29,252	11.01	27,823	13.25	83.1
25 to 34 years	16,499	11.25	7,734	10.51	8,765	12.01	87.6
35 to 44 years	16,827	12.46	8,604	11.17	8,224	14.13	79.0
45 to 54 years	14,544	12.97	7,852	11.79	6,691	14.93	79.0
55 to 64 years	7,130	12.19	3,928	11.05	3,202	14.09	78.4
65 years and over	2,075	9.19	1,134	8.84	941	9.79	90.4
Race and Hispanic or Latino ethnicity							
White	59,109	10.97	29,668	10.11	29,441	12.03	84.1
Black or African American	9,419	10.15	5,173	9.91	4,246	10.81	91.6
Asian	2,528	11.12	1,320	10.68	1,208	11.89	89.8
Hispanic or Latino	11,462	9.76	4,687	8.88	6,775	10.03	88.5
Marital status							
Never married	24,737	8.93	11,633	8.37	13,104	9.42	88.9
Married, spouse present	35,963	12.33	17,802	11.09	18,162	13.97	79.4
Other marital status	12,246	11.12	7,658	10.46	4,587	12.32	84.9
Divorced	7,840	11.91	4,858	11.06	2,983	13.23	83.6
Separated	2,881	10.07	1,576	9.82	1,305	10.59	92.7
Widowed	1,524	9.99	1,224	9.71	300	11.83	82.1
Union affiliation[b]							
Members of unions[c]	9,906	15.73	3,638	13.58	6,267	17.16	79.1
Represented by unions[d]	10,802	15.32	4,091	13.45	6,711	16.98	79.2
Not represented by a union	62,145	10.18	33,002	9.89	29,143	10.95	90.3
Educational attainment							
Total, 25 years and over	**57,075**	**12.05**	**29,252**	**11.01**	**27,823**	**13.25**	**83.1**
Less than a high school diploma	8,014	9.16	3,213	8.05	4,801	10.02	80.3
High school graduates, no college	22,114	11.77	10,854	10.19	11,260	13.42	75.9
Some college or associate degree	17,838	12.90	9,872	11.87	7,967	14.77	80.4
Bachelor's degree and higher	9,109	16.20	5,314	16.14	3,795	16.38	98.5

[a]These figures are computed using unrounded medians and may differ slightly from percents computed using the rounded medians displayed in this table.
[b]Differences in earnings levels between workers with and without union affiliation reflect a variety of factors in addition to coverage by a collective bargaining agreement, including the distribution of male and female employees by occupation, industry, firm size, or geographic region.
[c]Data refer to members of a labor union or an employee association similar to a union.
[d]Data refer to members of a labor union or an employee association similar to a union as well as workers who report no union affiliation but whose jobs are covered by a union or an employee association contract.
Note: Hourly-paid workers account for approximately three-fifths of all wage and salary workers. Estimates for the above race groups (white, black or African American, and Asian) include persons who selected this race group only; persons who selected more than one race group are not included. Estimates for the race groups will not sum to totals because data are not presented for all races. Persons whose ethnicity is identified as Hispanic or Latino may be of any race and, therefore, are classified by ethnicity as well as by race.

SOURCE: "Table 9. Median Hourly Earnings of Wage and Salary Workers Paid Hourly Rates by Selected Characteristics, 2003 Annual Averages," in *Highlights of Women's Earnings in 2003*, U.S. Department of Labor, Bureau of Labor Statistics, September 2004, http://www.bls.gov/cps/cpswom2003.pdf (accessed June 6, 2005)

FOOD PROGRAMS. Government expenditures for food programs such as school breakfasts and lunches, child and adult care, and the Special Supplemental Nutrition Program for Women, Infants, and Children (WIC) increased between fiscal year 2002 and 2003. (See Table 5.10.) Participation in WIC increased from less than two million in 1980 to more than eight million in 2002. (See Table 5.11.) Half of all WIC participants in 2003 were children, while 24% were women and 26% were infants. Spending for WIC totaled $2.2 billion by mid-year 2003, a 2% increase from FY 2002. According to *The Food Assistance Landscape*, published in September 2003 by the Department of Agriculture, participation in the Food Stamp Program was up 10% in 2003 from 2002, an average increase of 20.6 million people per month. More than half of USDA annual spending went to the program's 2002 expenditures. The National School Lunch Program provides free or low-cost lunches to needy children. As of September 2003, 59% of all children attending a participating school were in the program.

Overall, 11.2% of families were food insecure in 2003; 7.7% were food insecure without hunger, and 3.5% were food insecure with hunger. (See Table 5.12.) Households with children under the age of eighteen were more likely than households with no children to be food

TABLE 5.6

Wage and salary workers paid hourly rates with earnings at or below the prevailing federal minimum wage, by sex, age, race/ethnicity, and full- or part-time status, 2004

[Numbers in thousands]

Characteristic	2004				
	Workers paid hourly rates			Total at or below prevailing federal minimum wage	
	Total	Below prevailing federal minimum wage	At prevailing federal minimum wage	Number	Percent of hourly-paid workers
Sex and age					
Total, 16 years and over	73,939	1,483	520	2,003	2.7
16 to 24 years	16,174	750	272	1,021	6.3
25 years and over	57,765	733	249	982	1.7
Men, 16 years and over	36,806	470	210	680	1.8
16 to 24 years	8,305	239	127	366	4.4
25 years and over	28,500	231	83	314	1.1
Women, 16 years and over	37,133	1,013	310	1,323	3.6
16 to 24 years	7,869	510	145	655	8.3
25 years and over	29,265	502	166	668	2.3
Race, sex and Hispanic or Latino ethnicity					
White, 16 years and over	59,877	1,286	395	1,681	2.8
Men	30,255	393	161	555	1.8
Women	29,621	892	234	1,126	3.8
Black or African American, 16 years and over	9,417	128	99	228	2.4
Men	4,243	49	40	89	2.1
Women	5,174	79	59	138	2.7
Asian, 16 years and over	2,672	30	8	38	1.4
Men	1,295	12	3	15	1.2
Women	1,378	18	5	23	1.7
Hispanic or Latino, 16 years and over	12,073	168	82	250	2.1
Men	7,183	66	32	99	1.4
Women	4,890	102	49	151	3.1
Full- and part-time status and sex*					
Full-time workers	55,739	583	177	760	1.4
Men	30,951	223	77	300	1.0
Women	24,788	360	100	460	1.9
Part-time workers	18,046	897	343	1,240	6.9
Men	5,770	246	132	378	6.6
Women	12,276	651	210	861	7.0

*The distinction between full- and part-time workers is based on hours usually worked. These data will not sum to totals because full- or part-time status on the principal job is not identifiable for a small number of multiple jobholders.

Note: The prevailing Federal minimum wage was $5.15 per hour in 2004. Data are for wage and salary workers, excluding the incorporated self-employed. They refer to a person's earnings on their sole or principal job, and pertain only to workers who are paid hourly rates. Salaried workers and other nonhourly workers are not included. The presence of workers with hourly earnings below the minimum wage does not necessarily indicate violations of the Fair Labor Standards Act, as there are exceptions to the minimum wage provisions of the law. In addition, some survey respondents might have rounded hourly earnings to the nearest dollar, and, as a result, reported hourly earnings below the minimum wage even though they earned the minimum wage or higher. Beginning in January 2004, data reflect revised population controls used in the household survey.

SOURCE: "Table 44. Wage and Salary Workers Paid Hourly Rates with Earnings at or Below the Prevailing Federal Minimum Wage by Selected Characteristics," U.S. Department of Labor, Bureau of Labor Statistics, http://www.bls.gov/cps/cpsaat44.pdf (accessed June 6, 2005)

insecure (16.7% and 8.2%, respectively). Single-mother families were particularly vulnerable to food insecurity; 31.7% of these families were food insecure. Not surprisingly, households under the poverty line were more likely to be food insecure than other families, but families under 1.85 of the poverty line still had an 18.8% rate of food insecurity. African-American and Hispanic households were much more likely than white non-Hispanic households to be food insecure.

CHILD SUPPORT. Children living in single-parent families are far more likely to be poor than children living in two-parent households, and the number of children living with only one parent—usually the mother—is increasing. According to a report by the

U.S. Census Bureau, *Custodial Mothers and Fathers and Their Child Support, 2001*, in spring 2002, 13.4 million parents had custody of 21.5 million children under the age of twenty-one whose other parent lived elsewhere. Mothers accounted for 84.4% of all custodial parents; 15.6% of custodial parents were fathers. These proportions have not statistically changed since 1994.

When President Bill Clinton signed PRWORA in 1996, he stated, "If every parent paid the child support that he or she owes legally today, we could move 800,000 women and children off welfare immediately." The IWPR, in *How Much Can Child Support Provide? Welfare, Family Income, and Child Support* (1999), examined the role of child support in helping welfare

TABLE 5.7

Households by total money income, 1967–2003

[Income in 2003 adjusted dollars. Households as of March of the following year.]

Race and Hispanic origin of householder and year	Number (thousands)	Percent distribution										Median income (dollars)	Mean income (dollars)
		Total	Under $5,000	$5,000 to $9,999	$10,000 to $14,999	$15,000 to $24,999	$25,000 to $34,999	$35,000 to $49,999	$50,000 to $74,999	$75,000 to $99,999	$100,000 and over		
All races													
2003	112,000	100.0	3.4	5.6	6.9	13.1	11.9	15.0	18.0	11.0	15.1	43,318	59,067
2002	111,278	100.0	3.1	5.7	6.9	12.9	12.2	14.9	18.2	11.2	14.7	43,381	59,177
2001	109,297	100.0	3.0	5.5	6.8	12.9	12.1	15.2	18.4	11.2	14.9	43,882	60,488
2000a	108,209	100.0	2.8	5.5	6.7	12.5	12.3	15.2	18.6	11.3	15.2	44,853	61,031
1999b	106,434	100.0	2.7	5.5	6.5	13.0	12.1	15.2	18.5	11.4	15.0	44,922	60,420
1998	103,874	100.0	2.9	5.8	6.8	13.1	12.2	15.0	19.1	11.0	13.9	43,825	58,443
1997	102,528	100.0	3.0	6.2	7.2	13.4	12.3	15.5	18.7	10.7	12.9	42,294	56,794
1996	101,018	100.0	2.8	6.6	7.3	13.8	12.2	15.9	18.9	10.5	11.9	41,431	55,008
1995c	99,627	100.0	2.9	6.5	7.4	14.2	12.4	16.2	18.7	10.4	11.3	40,845	53,865
1994d	98,990	100.0	3.2	7.0	7.7	14.2	12.6	16.1	18.0	10.2	11.0	39,613	52,958
1993e	97,107	100.0	3.3	7.2	7.5	14.0	13.1	16.0	18.4	9.9	10.6	39,165	51,935
1992f	96,426	100.0	3.2	7.3	7.5	14.3	12.8	16.1	19.0	9.7	9.9	39,364	49,905
1991	95,669	100.0	2.9	7.4	7.3	13.7	13.2	16.4	19.1	9.9	10.0	39,679	49,947
1990	94,312	100.0	2.9	7.1	7.0	13.6	12.9	17.0	19.2	10.0	10.3	40,865	51,046
1989	93,347	100.0	2.8	6.7	7.3	13.5	12.4	16.5	19.9	10.2	10.9	41,411	52,319
1988	92,830	100.0	2.9	7.4	7.0	13.6	12.4	16.6	19.6	10.4	10.0	40,678	50,826
1987	91,124	100.0	3.0	7.4	7.1	13.8	12.7	16.5	19.5	10.3	9.7	40,357	50,189
1986	89,479	100.0	3.3	7.6	7.0	13.9	12.6	17.0	19.4	10.1	9.1	39,868	49,255
1985g	88,458	100.0	3.2	7.7	7.5	14.3	13.3	17.2	19.0	9.7	8.2	38,510	47,394
1984	86,789	100.0	3.1	7.6	8.0	14.4	13.6	17.3	19.2	9.1	7.8	37,767	46,274
1983h	85,290	100.0	3.4	7.9	7.9	15.0	13.4	17.9	19.0	8.5	7.0	36,826	44,870
1982	83,918	100.0	3.3	8.0	8.2	14.7	13.7	18.2	18.7	8.5	6.7	36,811	44,362
1981	83,527	100.0	3.1	8.2	7.9	15.2	13.6	17.7	19.6	8.6	6.3	36,868	44,045
1980	82,368	100.0	2.8	8.0	8.0	14.3	14.0	17.9	20.0	8.8	6.3	37,447	44,537
1979i	80,776	100.0	2.8	7.8	7.4	14.3	13.2	18.2	20.7	8.8	6.9	38,649	45,912
1978	77,330	100.0	2.5	7.8	7.8	14.3	13.6	17.9	20.7	9.0	6.5	38,693	45,540
1977	76,030	100.0	2.7	8.4	8.3	15.0	14.0	18.5	19.9	7.9	5.3	36,359	43,132
1976	74,142	100.0	2.8	8.5	8.1	15.1	14.1	19.1	19.9	7.5	4.9	36,155	42,528
1975	72,867	100.0	2.9	8.6	8.3	15.4	14.3	19.4	19.3	7.3	4.5	35,559	41,523

TABLE 5.7

Households by total money income, 1967–2003 [CONTINUED]

[Income in 2003 adjusted dollars. Households as of March of the following year.]

Race and Hispanic origin of householder and year	Number (thousands)	Total	Under $5,000	$5,000 to $9,999	$10,000 to $14,999	$15,000 to $24,999	$25,000 to $34,999	$35,000 to $49,999	$50,000 to $74,999	$75,000 to $99,999	$100,000 and over	Median income (dollars)	Mean income (dollars)
						Percent distribution							
1974[i]	71,163	100.0	2.8	8.2	7.7	14.8	14.5	19.7	19.7	7.6	5.0	36,537	42,727
1973	69,859	100.0	3.2	7.7	8.0	13.7	13.8	19.3	20.7	7.9	5.6	37,700	43,599
1972[k]	68,251	100.0	3.7	7.9	7.6	14.5	14.0	19.9	19.7	7.5	5.2	36,953	43,009
1971[l]	66,676	100.0	4.2	8.4	7.5	14.8	14.6	20.9	18.9	6.4	4.2	35,463	40,786
1970	64,778	100.0	4.3	8.3	7.2	14.3	14.9	21.1	19.1	6.5	4.2	35,832	41,030
1969	63,401	100.0	4.2	8.3	6.9	14.0	15.6	21.2	19.5	6.3	4.1	36,074	41,041
1968	62,214	100.0	4.6	8.2	7.3	14.7	15.7	22.4	18.3	5.4	3.3	34,746	39,310
1967	60,813	100.0	5.3	8.6	7.8	14.9	16.2	22.3	16.7	4.8	3.4	33,338	37,287

aImplementation of a 28,000 household sample expansion.
bImplementation of Census 2000-based population controls.
cFull implementation of 1990 census-based sample design and metropolitan definitions, 7,000 household sample reduction, and revised editing of responses on race.
dIntroduction of 1990 census sample design.
eData collection method changed from paper and pencil to computer-assisted interviewing. In addition, the 1994 Annual Social and Economic Supplement (ASEC) was revised to allow for the coding of different income amounts on selected questionnaire items. Limits either increased or decreased in the following categories: earnings limits increased to $999,999; social security limits increased to $49,999; supplemental security income and public assistance limits increased to $24,999; veterans' benefits limits increased to $99,999; child support and alimony limits decreased to $49,999.
fImplementation of 1990 census population controls.
gRecording of amounts for earnings from longest job increased to $299,999. Full implementation of 1980 census-based sample design.
hImplementation of Hispanic population weighting controls and introduction of 1980 census-based sample design.
iImplementation of 1980 census population controls. Questionnaire expanded to show 27 possible values from a list of 51 possible sources of income.
jQuestionnaire expanded to ask 11 income questions.
kFull implementation of 1970 census-based sample design.
lIntroduction of 1970 census sample design and population controls.

SOURCE: Adapted from Carmen DeNavas-Walt, Bernadette D. Proctor, and Robert J. Mills, "Table A-1. Households by Total Money Income, Race, and Hispanic Origin of Householder: 1967–2003," in *Income, Poverty, and Health Insurance Coverage in the United States: 2003*, U.S. Census Bureau, Current Population Reports, P60-226, August 2004, http://www.census.gov/prod/2004pubs/p60-226.pdf (accessed June 6, 2005)

TABLE 5.8

Poverty thresholds by size of family and number of related children under 18 years, 2004

[In dollars]

Size of family unit	Related children under 18 years								
	None	One	Two	Three	Four	Five	Six	Seven	Eight or more
One person (unrelated individual)									
Under 65 years	9,827								
65 years and over	9,060								
Two persons									
Householder under 65 years	12,649	13,020							
Householder 65 years and over	11,418	12,971							
Three persons	14,776	15,205	15,219						
Four persons	19,484	19,803	19,157	19,223					
Five persons	23,497	23,838	23,108	22,543	22,199				
Six persons	27,025	27,133	26,573	26,037	25,241	24,768			
Seven persons	31,096	31,290	30,621	30,154	29,285	28,271	27,159		
Eight persons	34,778	35,086	34,454	33,901	33,115	32,119	31,082	30,818	
Nine persons or more	41,836	42,039	41,480	41,010	40,240	39,179	38,220	37,983	36,520

SOURCE: "Poverty Thresholds for 2004 by Size of Family and Number of Related Children Under 18 Years," in *Poverty Thresholds 2004*, U.S. Census Bureau, January 28, 2005, http://www.census.gov/hhes/poverty/threshld/thresh04.html (accessed June 7, 2005)

TABLE 5.9

Poverty of people, by sex, 1966–2003

[Numbers in thousands]

Year	All people	Male			Female		
		Total	Below poverty		Total	Below poverty	
			Number	Percent		Number	Percent
2003	287,699	140,931	15,783	11.2	146,768	20,078	13.7
2002	285,317	139,558	15,162	10.9	145,759	19,408	13.3
2001	281,475	137,558	14,327	10.4	143,917	18,580	12.9
2000	278,944	136,274	13,536	9.9	142,670	18,045	12.6
1999	276,208	134,823	14,079	10.4	141,385	18,712	13.2
1998	271,059	132,408	14,712	11.1	138,652	19,764	14.3
1997	268,480	131,376	15,187	11.6	137,105	20,387	14.9
1996	266,218	130,353	15,611	12.0	135,865	20,918	15.4
1995	263,733	128,852	15,683	12.2	134,880	20,742	15.4
1994	261,616	127,838	16,316	12.8	133,778	21,744	16.3
1993	259,278	126,668	16,900	13.3	132,610	22,365	16.9
1992	256,549	125,288	16,222	12.9	131,261	21,792	16.6
1991	251,192	122,418	15,082	12.3	128,774	20,626	16.0
1990	248,644	121,073	14,211	11.7	127,571	19,373	15.2
1989	245,992	119,704	13,366	11.2	126,288	18,162	14.4
1988	243,530	118,399	13,599	11.5	125,131	18,146	14.5
1987	240,890	117,123	14,029	12.0	123,767	18,518	15.0
1986	238,554	115,915	13,721	11.8	122,640	18,649	15.2
1985	236,594	114,970	14,140	12.3	121,624	18,923	15.6
1984	233,816	113,391	14,537	12.8	120,425	19,163	15.9
1983	231,700	112,280	15,182	13.5	119,332	20,084	16.8
1982	229,412	111,175	14,842	13.4	118,237	19,556	16.5
1981	227,157	110,010	13,360	12.1	117,147	18,462	15.8
1980	225,027	108,990	12,207	11.2	116,037	17,065	14.7
1979	222,903	105,542	10,535	10.0	112,306	14,810	13.2
1978	215,656	104,480	10,017	9.6	111,175	14,480	13.0
1977	213,867	103,629	10,340	10.0	110,238	14,381	13.0
1976	212,303	102,955	10,373	10.1	109,348	14,603	13.4
1975	210,864	102,211	10,908	10.7	108,652	14,970	13.8
1974	209,343	101,523	10,313	10.2	107,743	13,881	12.9
1973	207,621	100,694	9,642	9.6	106,898	13,316	12.5
1972	206,004	99,804	10,190	10.2	106,168	14,258	13.4
1971	204,554	99,232	10,708	10.8	105,298	14,841	14.1
1970	202,489	98,228	10,879	11.1	104,248	14,632	14.0
1969	199,848	96,802	10,292	10.6	103,037	13,978	13.6
1968	197,618	95,681	10,793	11.3	101,919	14,578	14.3
1967	195,677	94,796	11,813	12.5	100,861	15,951	15.8
1966	193,390	93,718	12,225	13.0	99,637	16,265	16.3

SOURCE: "Table 7. Poverty of People, by Sex: 1966 to 2003," in *Historical Poverty Tables*, U.S. Census Bureau, August 26, 2004, http://www.census.gov/hhes/poverty/histpov/hstpov7.html (accessed June 7, 2005)

FIGURE 5.4

Trends in TANF receipt, unemployment rates, food stamps, and poverty rate, 1990–2003

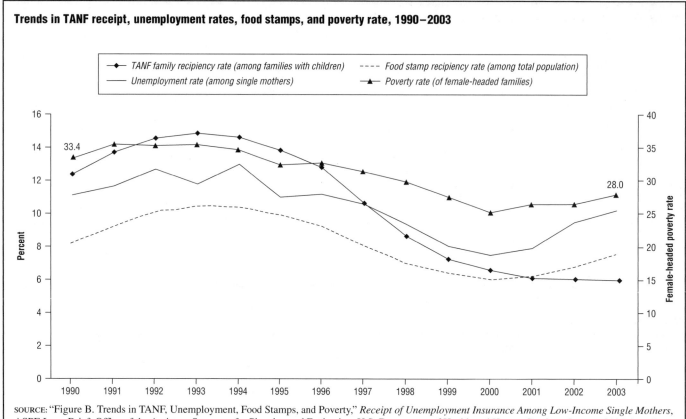

SOURCE: "Figure B. Trends in TANF, Unemployment, Food Stamps, and Poverty," *Receipt of Unemployment Insurance Among Low-Income Single Mothers*, ASPE Issue Brief, Office of the Assistant Secretary for Planning and Evaluation, U.S. Department of Health and Human Services, January 2005, http://aspe .hhs.gov/hsp/05/unemp-receipt/ib.pdf (accessed June 10, 2005)

TABLE 5.10

Federal nutrition assistance, fiscal years 2002 and first half of 2003

Program		Fiscal year 2002		Fiscal year 2003
		Full year	1st half	1st half
Food stamp program	Average monthly participation (millions)	19.1	18.8	20.6
	Average benefit per person (dollars/month)	79.62	80.0	83.32
	Total expenditures ($ billions)	20.7	10.1	11.4
WIC	Average monthly participation (millions)	7.5	7.5	7.5
	Total expenditures ($ billions)	4.3	2.1	2.2
National school lunch program	Average daily participation (millions)	28.0	28.2	28.4
	Total expenditures ($ billions)	6.9	4.1	4.3
School breakfast program	Average daily participation (millions)	8.1	8.2	8.4
	Total expenditures ($ millions)	1,567	927	962
Child and adult care food program	Meals served in:			
	• Child care centers (millions)	984	497	515
	• Family child care homes (millions)	708	346	340
	• Adult day care centers (millions)	45	21	23
	Total expenditures ($ millions)	1,855	922	957
Total program expenditures	Total expenditures ($ billions)	38.0	19.5	20.9

SOURCE: "Federal Nutrition Assistance At-a-Glance," in "The Food Assistance Landscape," *Food Assistance and Nutrition Research Report*, no. 28-3, September 2003

recipients and other low-income single-mother families to become self-sufficient. The study found that child support generally provided only a small portion of the income of single-mother families.

More than half (59.1%) of the 13.4 million custodial parents in April 2002 had a child support agreement with the other parent. Most of these agreements required child support payments from the noncustodial parent. In 2001,

TABLE 5.11

Distribution of Women, Infants and Children (WIC) participants, by participant category, 2000 and 2002

Participant category	Number of participants 2000	Number of participants 2002	Percent change 2000–2002
Women			
Pregnant women	898,210	878,619	−2.18%
Breastfeeding women	417,850	458,131	+9.64
Postpartum women	579,291	597,451	+3.13
Total women	**1,895,353**	**1,934,203**	**+2.05**
Infants	2,062,759	2,062,682	+0.00
Children	3,897,425	4,020,032	+3.15
US WIC	7,855,537	8,016,918	+2.05

SOURCE: "Exhibit 2.1. Distribution of WIC Participants by Participant Category in 2000 and 2002," in "WIC Participant and Program Characteristics 2002," *Nutrition Assistance Program Report Series*, no. WIC-03-PC, September 2003

74% of custodial parents due support received at least some payments. Almost half (44.8%) received all the payments they were due, up from only a little more than a third (36.9%) in 1993. Noncustodial parents who had visitation rights to their children were more likely to pay child support (77.1%) than parents who did not (55.8%) (Timothy S. Grall, *Custodial Mothers and Fathers and Their Child Support: 2001*, U.S. Census Bureau, Current Population Reports, P602–25, 2003).

Receipt of child support payments made a significant difference in the household incomes of single-parent families. In 2001 the average family income of custodial parents who received the total amount of child support owed them was $32,300, and their poverty rate was 14.6%. In contrast, custodial parents who either had no child support agreements or had agreements but received only part or none of the amount due had an average family income of about $25,000, and their poverty rates were significantly higher, at about 25%.

Elderly Women

Poverty among older Americans has declined since the establishment of Medicare in 1965 and later increases in Social Security benefits. In addition, Supplemental Security Income (SSI) has become available to more people. During the rapid economic expansion following World War II, Americans accumulated pensions and built equity in their homes, which led to unprecedented wealth among the middle class in the United States.

In 2003 the poverty rate for people age sixty-five and older was 9%, slightly lower than in 2002 (10.4%). The poverty rates of older African-Americans (23.7%) and Hispanics (19.5%) were substantially higher than that of non-Hispanic whites (8%). The poverty rate of women was substantially higher than that of men (12.5% and 7.3%, respectively). Much of this can be attributed to the wage earnings gap, which allowed men to save more

during their working years and to earn larger pensions. The recent trend of young children residing with grand-parents—usually the grandmother—is another reason the poverty rates for elderly women are so much higher. Yet another reason is the greater likelihood that older women will become widowed and live alone.

According to a May 2001 study by the IWPR, *The Gender Gap in Pension Coverage: What Does the Future Hold?*, there is a substantial gender gap in all forms of retirement income, including Social Security, pensions, savings, and earnings from post-retirement employment. Despite the growing participation of women in the labor force, they continue to receive fewer traditional pension and Social Security benefits than men. Furthermore, women in general live longer than men and therefore require more retirement income.

In 2003 President George W. Bush signed into law a bill that gave those on Medicare the ability to buy prescription drugs through Medicare for the first time. The bill, which was expected to cost an estimated $395 billion over ten years, covers less than one-fourth of the nation's prescription drug costs of the elderly and disabled, according to CBPP. The controversial law was opposed by many citizens because while it increased assistance for some, many of the nation's poorest and sickest Medicare beneficiaries found themselves with less drug coverage than they previously had through Medicaid. These people would be required to pay more for drugs while also losing coverage for specific drugs altogether. By 2006, when the law takes effect, approximately 6.4 million seniors would be affected. Seniors with disabilities whose incomes are barely above the poverty line would face rising co-payments with which their incomes cannot keep up. Some may lose coverage for necessary drugs, thereby finding it impossible to afford them.

SOCIAL SECURITY. Social Security was developed to protect senior citizens from a drastic reduction in income at retirement and intended to be supplemented by other sources of income, like pensions and income from assets. Social Security has over time become a bigger share of many older Americans' income. According to the CBPP, Social Security has been more effective in lifting people out of poverty than all other government programs combined. More women than men depend on Social Security as their only income, and many of these women live at or just above the poverty level. According to *Older Americans 2004: Key Indicators of Well-Being* (Federal Interagency Forum on Aging and Related Statistics, November 2004), in 2002 more than one in ten older Americans (10.4%) were living in poverty, and another 28% lived just above the poverty threshold. While Social Security accounted for 39% of the income of seniors overall in 2002, it accounted for 82.6% of the income of the

TABLE 5.12

Prevalence of food security, food insecurity, and food insecurity with hunger, by selected household characteristics, 2003

| | Total[a] | Food secure | | Food insecure | | | | | |
| | | | | All | | Without hunger | | With hunger | |
Category	1,000	1,000	Percent	1,000	Percent	1,000	Percent	1,000	Percent
All households	112,214	99,631	88.8	12,583	11.2	8,663	7.7	3,920	3.5
Household composition:									
With children <18	40,286	33,575	83.3	6,711	16.7	5,165	12.8	1,546	3.8
With children <6	18,110	14,933	82.5	3,177	17.5	2,516	13.9	661	3.6
Married-couple families	27,484	24,503	89.2	2,981	10.8	2,446	8.9	535	1.9
Female head, no spouse	9,623	6,572	68.3	3,051	31.7	2,210	23.0	841	8.7
Male head, no spouse	2,475	1,937	78.3	538	21.7	401	16.2	137	5.5
Other household with child[b]	704	563	80.0	141	20.0	108	15.3	33	4.7
With no children <18	71,928	66,057	91.8	5,871	8.2	3,498	4.9	2,373	3.3
More than one adult	42,553	39,753	93.4	2,800	6.6	1,840	4.3	960	2.3
Women living alone	16,724	15,032	89.9	1,692	10.1	964	5.8	728	4.4
Men living alone	12,651	11,271	89.1	1,380	10.9	694	5.5	686	5.4
With elderly	25,946	24,391	94.0	1,555	6.0	1,105	4.3	450	1.7
Elderly living alone	10,574	9,921	93.8	653	6.2	430	4.1	223	2.1
Race/ethnicity of households:									
White non-Hispanic	81,080	74,733	92.2	6,347	7.8	4,169	5.1	2,178	2.7
Black non-Hispanic	13,156	10,251	77.9	2,905	22.1	2,010	15.3	895	6.8
Hispanic[c]	12,034	9,347	77.7	2,687	22.3	2,034	16.9	653	5.4
Other non-Hispanic	5,944	5,301	89.2	643	10.8	450	7.6	193	3.2
Household income-to-poverty ratio:									
Under 1.00	12,739	8,266	64.9	4,473	35.1	2,863	22.5	1,610	12.6
Under 1.30	18,143	12,245	67.5	5,898	32.5	3,845	21.2	2,053	11.3
Under 1.85	27,104	19,357	71.4	7,747	28.6	5,107	18.8	2,640	9.7
1.85 and over	62,145	59,116	95.1	3,029	4.9	2,274	3.7	755	1.2
Income unknown	22,965	21,160	92.1	1,805	7.9	1,281	5.6	524	2.3
Area of residence:									
Inside metropolitan area	90,708	80,611	88.9	10,097	11.1	6,903	7.6	3,194	3.5
In central city[d]	27,682	23,581	85.2	4,101	14.8	2,804	10.1	1,297	4.7
Not in central city[d]	47,243	42,996	91.0	4,247	9.0	2,879	6.1	1,368	2.9
Outside metropolitan area	21,505	19,020	88.4	2,485	11.6	1,760	8.2	725	3.4
Census geographic region:									
Northeast	21,306	19,267	90.4	2,039	9.6	1,343	6.3	696	3.3
Midwest	25,941	23,360	90.1	2,581	9.9	1,752	6.8	829	3.2
South	40,554	35,541	87.6	5,013	12.4	3,472	8.6	1,541	3.8
West	24,412	21,463	87.9	2,949	12.1	2,096	8.6	853	3.5

[a]Totals exclude households whose food security status is unknown because they did not give a valid response to any of the questions in the food security scale. In 2003, these represented 381,000 households (0.3 percent of all households.)
[b]Households with children in complex living arrangements—e.g., children of other relatives or unrelated roommate or boarder.
[c]Hispanics may be of any race.
[d]Metropolitan area subtotals do not add to metropolitan area totals because central-city residence is not identified for about 17 percent of households in metropolitan statistical areas.

SOURCE: Mark Nord, et al., "Table 2. Prevalence of Food Security, Food Insecurity, and Food Insecurity with Hunger, by Selected Household Characteristics, 2003," in *Household Food Security in the United States, 2003*, U.S. Department of Agriculture, Food Assistance and Nutrition Research Report Number 42, October 2004, http://www.ers.usda.gov/publications/fanrr42/ (accessed June 7, 2005)

poorest quintile and 84% of the income of the second lowest income quintile. Without Social Security, these senior citizens would have almost no income at all.

Although women pay only 38% of all Social Security payroll taxes, they receive 53% of the benefits because they live longer than men and Social Security benefits increase annually to keep up with inflation. In addition, more women than men receive spousal Social Security benefits, regardless of their labor force participation.

The U.S. Government Accountability Office (GAO) conducted a study on Social Security benefits in 2003 and found that African-American and Hispanic workers tend to benefit more from current Social Security laws than do non-Hispanic whites. This is due to differences in lifetime earnings, rates of disability, and mortality rates among each group. The Institute for Women's Policy Research found that women's patterns of labor force participation resulted in their receiving only about 70% of the Social Security that men do (Sunwha Lee and Lois Shaw, *Gender and Economic Security in Retirement*, Institute for Women's Policy Research, 2003).

THE PENSION GAP. According to the Institute for Women's Policy Research, only 29.5% of women age sixty-five and older in the 1998–2000 period received pension income, compared with 46.7% of men. The average amount paid to women who did receive pensions, $5,600, was only 54% of what was paid to men. Women who are dependent on their husbands' pensions may lose them through divorce or have them reduced if their husbands die. The study also noted that the median annual income of women between fifty and sixty-one ($29,000) is just two-thirds that of men. In other words, the pension gap is even greater than the earnings gap.

More women than ever before are participating in employee-sponsored pension plans, and for women who work full-time the plans are nearly equal to those of men. Still, less than one-third of part-time workers, primarily women, have pension plans. Of women age thirty-five to sixty-four, 35% work too few hours to participate in their employers' pension plans, compared with only 20% of men. Approximately half of all women leave the work-force at some point to care for children. During these absences, women workers cannot contribute to their pensions and retirement savings plans.

Women do not stay at the same jobs as long as men, either. According to the Bureau of Labor Statistics, women averaged only 3.8 years at their current jobs. Many employers do not offer pension benefits until an employee has worked for five years. The IWPR study found that for women whose employers offered pension plans, the most common reason for not participating was that the women had not worked long enough for that employer. The second most common reason for nonparticipation was that they worked part-time and so did not qualify.

When employees leave a job, they often receive a lump-sum distribution of their pension fund assets. The IWPR study found that women are much less likely than men to roll over their distribution into another retirement fund. Rather, they use the distribution to pay off bills or loans or for their children's education. In part this is because women average only about one-half of the lump-sum distributions that men receive.

Homeless Women

The U.S. Conference of Mayors' annual twenty-seven-city survey, *Hunger and Homeless Survey: A Status Report on Hunger and Homelessness in America's Cities* (Washington, DC, December 2004), found that families with children accounted for 40% of the homeless population, up from 36% in 1989. (See Table 5.13.) Single parents, the vast majority of them mothers, headed 66% of these families. Requests for shelter from families with children increased by an average of 7% over the previous year, and 32% of the requests went unmet. Two-parent families were often forced to separate to obtain shelter because some shelters do not admit teenage boys or fathers. As a result, many families stayed together on the streets rather than split up to get into shelters. Other families must separate because only some members are eligible for state-funded assistance.

In the Conference of Mayors' survey, single women accounted for 14% of the homeless population, compared with just 3% in 1963. Other surveys of homelessness have found higher proportions of single women, although the proportion remained fairly constant after 1984. Homeless single women may find it difficult to obtain shelter and other services because most programs that serve women are designed for families.

The Association of Gospel Rescue Missions found in 2004 that 23% of the homeless population was female, while the Urban Institute, in a study conducted in 1996, found that 32% of the homeless population was female. All studies agree, however, that the majority of the homeless population is male.

Lack of affordable housing was identified as a primary cause of homelessness in twenty-four of the twenty-seven cities surveyed in the Conference of Mayors report; twenty-one cities cited mental illness and lack of needed mental health services as the primary cause. Twenty other cities cited substance abuse as a primary cause. Unemployment was identified as a main cause of homelessness by thirteen cities; eleven listed domestic violence as a main reason for homelessness.

TABLE 5.13

Hunger and homelessness in America's cities, 1989–2004

Indicator	1989	1990	1991	1992	1993	1994	1995	1996	1997	1998	1999	2000	2001	2002	2003	2004
Hunger																
Increase in demand for emergency food	19%	22%	26%	18%	13%	12%	9%	11%	16%	14%	18%	17%	23%	19%	17%	14%
Cities in which demand for food increased	96%	90%	93%	96%	83%	83%	72%	83%	86%	78%	85%	83%	93%	100%	88%	96%
Increase in demand by families for food assistance	14%	20%	26%	14%	13%	14%	10%	10%	13%	14%	15%	16%	19%	17%	18%	13%
Portion of those requesting food assistance who are families with children	61%	75%	68%	68%	67%	64%	63%	62%	58%	61%	58%	62%	54%	48%	59%	56%
Demand for emergency food unmet	17%	14%	17%	21%	16%	15%	18%	18%	19%	21%	21%	13%	14%	16%	14%	20%
Cities in which food assistance facilities must turn people away	73%	86%	79%	68%	68%	73%	59%	50%	71%	47%	54%	46%	33%	32%	56%	48%
Cities which expect demand for emergency food to increase next year	89%	100%	100%	89%	100%	81%	96%	96%	92%	96%	84%	71%	100%	100%	87%	88%
Homelessness																
Increase in demand for emergency shelter	25%	24%	13%	14%	10%	13%	11%	5%	3%	11%	12%	15%	13%	19%	13%	6%
Cities in which demand increased	89%	80%	89%	88%	81%	80%	63%	71%	59%	72%	69%	76%	81%	88%	80%	70%
Demand for emergency shelter unmet	22%	19%	15%	23%	25%	21%	19%	20%	27%	26%	25%	23%	37%	30%	30%	23%
Cities in which shelters must turn people away	59%	70%	74%	75%	77%	72%	82%	81%	88%	67%	73%	56%	44%	56%	84%	81%
Cities which expect demand for shelter to increase next year	93%	97%	100%	93%	88%	71%	100%	100%	100%	93%	92%	72%	100%	100%	88%	88%
Composition of homeless population																
Single men	46%	51%	50%	55%	43%	48%	46%	45%	47%	45%	43%	44%	40%	41%	41%	41%
Families with children	36%	34%	35%	32%	34%	39%	36%	38%	36%	38%	36%	36%	40%	41%	40%	40%
Single women	14%	12%	12%	11%	11%	11%	14%	14%	14%	14%	13%	13%	14%	13%	14%	14%
Unaccompanied youth	4%	3%	3%	2%	4%	3%	4%	3%	4%	3%	4%	7%	4%	5%	5%	5%
Children	25%	23%	24%	22%	30%	26%	25%	27%	25%	25%	NA	NA	NA	NA	NA	NA
Severely mentally ill	25%	28%	29%	28%	27%	26%	23%	24%	27%	24%	19%	22%	22%	23%	23%	23%
Substance abusers	44%	38%	40%	41%	48%	43%	46%	43%	43%	38%	31%	37%	34%	32%	30%	30%
Employed	24%	24%	18%	17%	18%	19%	20%	18%	17%	22%	21%	26%	20%	22%	17%	17%
Veterans	26%	26%	23%	18%	21%	23%	23%	19%	22%	22%	14%	15%	11%	10%	10%	10%

SOURCE: "Hunger and Homelessness in America's Cities: A Sixteen-Year Comparison of Data," in *Hunger and Homeless Survey: A Status Report on Hunger and Homelessness in America's Cities, A 27-City Survey,* United States Conference of Mayors-Sodexho USA, December 2004, http://www.usmayors.org/uscm/hungersurvey/2004/onlinereport/HungerAndHomelessnessReport2004.pdf (accessed May 25, 2005)

CHAPTER 6
WOMEN AND THEIR CHILDREN

Although more and more women are joining the workforce and pursuing educational opportunities and new careers, raising children remains a focal point of life for many. The development of effective methods of contraception (including birth control pills), the legalization of abortion, the "morning-after" pill, and increased condom use to combat the spread of the human immunodeficiency virus (HIV) and other sexually transmitted diseases (STDs) have contributed to falling fertility and birth rates and have enabled women to time their childbearing. Increases in maternal age, in single motherhood, and in labor force participation by women have affected many aspects of women's relationships with their children.

FERTILITY AND BIRTH RATES

American women are having fewer children than in the past. The fertility rate is defined as the total number of live births per one thousand women ages fifteen to forty-four. The fertility rate increased dramatically during the post–World War II baby boom of the 1940s and 1950s. By 1960, when far fewer women were active in the labor force and larger families were more common, the fertility rate was 118. (See Table 6.1.) But the fertility rate declined in the 1960s and early 1970s to 65. Between 1977 and 2002 the fertility rate remained between 63.6 and 70.9. After 1997 the fertility rate increased slightly. In 2002 it was 64.8. Table 6.2 shows 2003 fertility rates by age and race of mother. The highest rate (126) was found among African-American twenty- to twenty-four-year-olds. African-American women also had the highest fertility rates for ages ten to twenty-four. After age twenty-four, the African-American fertility rate dropped below that of whites.

Crude birth rates are defined as the number of live births per one thousand population. Table 6.1 lists birth rates for selected years between 1940 and 2002. The U.S. Census Bureau indicates that more than four million women between the ages of fifteen and forty-four gave birth in 2002, for a birth rate of 13.9. According to the Census Bureau, this is the lowest birth rate on record since 1909 (when birth rates were first officially tracked). It also represents a 3.3% drop in the total number of births since 1990.

Increasing Maternal Age

The rising rate of births to older mothers was a remarkable feature of the late twentieth century. Although the teenage birth rate declined and the rates for women in their twenties remained fairly stable between 1980 and 2003, birth rates for women thirty-five and over increased steadily. According to the National Center for Health Statistics (NCHS) of the Centers for Disease Control and Prevention (CDC), the birth rate for women ages thirty to thirty-four increased by about 1% annually from 1991 to 2003, when it was 95.2. The birth rate for women thirty-five to thirty-nine increased from less than twenty in 1990 to 43.8 in 2003. (See Table 6.2.) Women of this age group gave birth to 467,520 babies in 2003, a record high.

The 2003 birth rate was 8.7 for those ages forty to forty-four and 0.5 for those ages forty-five to fifty-four. (See Table 6.2.) Both figures have more than doubled since 1990. The number of births to women in their late forties (5,845) was at a record high, in part because of the increased numbers of women in this age group, a result of the postwar baby boom, and in part because recent advances in reproductive technologies have enabled more women in this age group to give birth.

Despite the increases in birth rates among older women, 51.8% of all births in 2003 were to women in their twenties. This is a drop from 1980, when about two-thirds of all births were to this age group.

Racial and Ethnic Differences

Between 2002 and 2003 the number of births to non-Hispanic whites increased by only 1%, after decreasing

TABLE 6.1

Live births, birth rates, and fertility rates, by race, selected years 1940–55 and all years 1960–2002

[Birth rates are live births per 1,000 population in specified group. Fertility rates are live births per 1,000 women aged 15–44 years in specified group. Population enumerated as of April 1 for census years and estimated as of July 1 for all other years. Beginning with 1970, excludes births to nonresidents of the United States.]

Year	Number All races[a]	White	Black	American Indian[b]	Asian or Pacific Islander	Birth rate All races[a]	White	Black	American Indian[b]	Asian or Pacific Islander	Fertility rate All races[a]	White	Black	American Indian[b]	Asian or Pacific Islander
Race of mother:						Registered births									
2002	4,021,726	3,174,760	593,691	42,368	210,907	13.9	13.5	15.7	13.8	16.5	64.8	64.8	65.8	58.0	64.1
2001	4,025,933	3,177,626	606,156	41,872	200,279	14.1	13.7	16.3	13.7	16.4	65.3	65.0	67.6	58.1	64.2
2000	4,058,814	3,194,005	622,598	41,668	200,543	14.4	13.9	17.0	14.0	17.1	65.9	65.3	70.0	58.7	65.8
1999	3,959,417	3,132,501	605,970	40,170	180,776	14.2	13.7	16.8	14.2	15.9	64.4	64.0	68.5	59.0	60.9
1998	3,941,553	3,118,727	609,902	40,272	172,652	14.3	13.8	17.1	14.8	15.9	64.3	63.6	69.4	61.3	60.1
1997	3,880,894	3,072,640	599,913	38,572	169,769	14.2	13.7	17.1	14.7	16.2	63.6	62.8	69.0	60.8	61.3
1996	3,891,494	3,093,057	594,781	37,880	165,776	14.4	13.9	17.3	14.9	16.5	64.1	63.3	69.2	61.8	62.3
1995	3,899,589	3,098,885	603,139	37,278	160,287	14.6	14.1	17.8	15.3	16.7	64.6	63.6	71.0	63.0	62.6
1994	3,952,767	3,121,004	636,391	37,740	157,632	15.0	14.3	19.1	16.0	17.1	65.9	64.2	75.9	65.8	63.9
1993	4,000,240	3,149,833	658,875	38,732	152,800	15.4	14.6	20.2	17.0	17.3	67.0	64.9	79.6	69.7	64.3
1992	4,065,014	3,201,678	673,633	39,453	150,250	15.8	15.0	21.1	17.9	17.9	68.4	66.1	82.4	73.1	66.1
1991	4,110,907	3,241,273	682,602	38,841	145,372	16.2	15.3	21.8	18.3	18.3	69.3	66.7	84.8	73.9	67.1
1990	4,158,212	3,290,273	684,336	39,051	141,635	16.7	15.8	22.4	18.9	19.0	70.9	68.3	86.8	76.2	69.6
1989	4,040,958	3,192,355	673,124	39,478	133,075	16.4	15.4	22.3	19.7	18.7	69.2	66.4	86.2	79.0	68.2
1988	3,909,510	3,102,083	638,562	37,088	129,035	16.0	15.0	21.5	19.3	19.2	67.3	64.5	82.6	76.8	70.2
1987	3,809,394	3,043,828	611,173	35,322	116,560	15.7	14.9	20.8	19.1	18.4	65.8	63.3	80.1	75.6	67.1
1986	3,756,547	3,019,175	592,910	34,169	107,797	15.6	14.8	20.5	19.2	18.0	65.4	63.1	78.9	75.9	66.0
1985	3,760,561	3,037,913	581,824	34,037	104,606	15.8	15.0	20.4	19.8	18.7	66.3	64.1	78.8	78.6	68.4
1984[c]	3,669,141	2,967,100	568,138	33,256	98,926	15.6	14.8	20.1	20.1	18.8	65.5	63.2	78.2	79.8	69.2
1983[c]	3,638,933	2,946,468	562,624	32,881	95,713	15.6	14.8	20.2	20.6	19.5	65.7	63.4	78.7	81.8	71.7
1982[c]	3,680,537	2,984,817	568,506	32,436	93,193	15.9	15.1	20.7	21.1	20.3	67.3	64.8	80.9	83.6	74.8
1981[c]	3,629,238	2,947,679	564,955	29,688	84,553	15.8	15.0	20.8	20.0	20.1	67.3	64.8	82.0	79.6	73.7
1980[c]	3,612,258	2,936,351	568,080	29,389	74,355	15.9	15.1	21.3	20.7	19.9	68.4	65.6	84.7	82.7	73.2
Race of child:															
1980[c]	3,612,258	2,898,732	589,616	36,797	—	15.9	14.9	22.1	—	—	68.4	64.7	88.1	—	—
1979[c]	3,494,398	2,808,420	577,855	34,269	—	15.6	14.5	22.0	—	—	67.2	63.4	88.3	—	—
1978[c]	3,333,279	2,681,116	551,540	33,160	—	15.0	14.0	21.3	—	—	65.5	61.7	86.7	—	—
1977[c]	3,326,632	2,691,070	544,221	30,500	—	15.1	14.1	21.4	—	—	66.8	63.2	88.1	—	—
1976[c]	3,167,788	2,567,614	514,479	29,009	—	14.6	13.6	20.5	—	—	65.0	61.5	85.8	—	—
1975[c]	3,144,198	2,551,996	511,581	27,546	—	14.6	13.6	20.7	—	—	66.0	62.5	87.9	—	—
1974[c]	3,159,958	2,575,792	507,162	26,631	—	14.8	13.9	20.8	—	—	67.8	64.2	89.7	—	—
1973[c]	3,136,965	2,551,030	512,597	26,464	—	14.8	13.8	21.4	—	—	68.8	64.9	93.6	—	—
1972[c]	3,258,411	2,655,558	531,329	27,368	—	15.6	14.5	22.5	—	—	73.1	68.9	99.9	—	—
1971[d]	3,555,970	2,919,746	564,960	27,148	—	17.2	16.1	24.4	—	—	81.6	77.3	109.7	—	—
1970[d]	3,731,386	3,091,264	572,362	25,864	—	18.4	17.4	25.3	—	—	87.9	84.1	115.4	—	—
1969[d]	3,600,206	2,993,614	543,132	24,008	—	17.9	16.9	24.4	—	—	86.1	82.2	112.1	—	—
1968[e]	3,501,564	2,912,224	531,152	24,156	—	17.6	16.6	24.2	—	—	85.2	81.3	112.7	—	—
1967[e]	3,520,959	2,922,502	543,976	22,665	—	17.8	16.8	25.1	—	—	87.2	82.8	118.5	—	—
1966[d]	3,606,274	2,993,230	558,244	23,014	—	18.4	17.4	26.2	—	—	90.8	86.2	124.7	—	—
1965[d]	3,760,358	3,123,860	581,126	24,066	—	19.4	18.3	27.7	—	—	96.3	91.3	133.2	—	—
1964[d]	4,027,490	3,369,160	607,556	24,382	—	21.1	20.0	29.5	—	—	104.7	99.8	142.6	—	—
1963[d,f]	4,098,020	3,326,344	580,658	22,358	—	21.7	20.7	—	—	—	108.3	103.6	—	—	—
1962[c,f]	4,167,362	3,394,068	584,610	21,968	—	22.4	21.4	—	—	—	112.0	107.5	—	—	—
1961[d]	4,268,326	3,600,864	611,072	21,464	—	23.3	22.2	—	—	—	117.1	112.3	—	—	—
1960[d]	4,257,850	3,600,744	602,264	21,114	—	23.7	22.7	31.9	—	—	118.0	113.2	153.5	—	—

TABLE 6.1

Live births, birth rates, and fertility rates, by race, selected years 1940–55 and all years 1960–2002 [CONTINUED]

[Birth rates are live births per 1,000 population in specified group. Fertility rates are live births per 1,000 women aged 15–44 years in specified group. Population enumerated as of April 1 for census years and estimated as of July 1 for all other years. Beginning with 1970, excludes births to nonresidents of the United States.]

	Number					Birth rate					Fertility rate				
Year	All races[a]	White	Black	American Indian[b]	Asian or Pacific Islander	All races[a]	White	Black	American Indian[b]	Asian or Pacific Islander	All races[a]	White	Black	American Indian[b]	Asian or Pacific Islander
								Births adjusted for underregistration							
Race of child:															
1955	4,097,000	3,485,000	—	—	—	25.0	23.8	—	—	—	118.3	113.7	—	—	—
1950	3,632,000	3,108,000	—	—	—	24.1	23.0	—	—	—	106.2	102.3	—	—	—
1945	2,858,000	2,471,000	—	—	—	20.4	19.7	—	—	—	85.9	83.4	—	—	—
1940	2,559,000	2,199,000	—	—	—	19.4	18.6	—	—	—	79.9	77.1	—	—	—

—Data not available.
[a]For 1960–91 includes births to races not shown separately. For 1992 and later years, unknown race of mother is imputed.
[b]Includes births to Aleuts and Eskimos.
[c]Based on 100 percent of births in selected states and on a 50-percent sample of births in all other states.
[d]Based on a 50-percent sample of births.
[e]Based on a 20- to 50-percent sample of births.
[f]Figures by race exclude New Jersey.
Note: Race and Hispanic origin are reported separately on birth certificates. Race categories are consistent with the 1977 Office of Management and Budget guidelines. In this table all women (including Hispanic women) are classified only according to their race. Rates for 1991–2001 may differ from those published in "Births: Final Data for 2001" but are consistent with those published in "Revised Birth and Fertility Rates for the 1990s and New Rates for Hispanic Populations, 2000 and 2001: United States."

SOURCE: "Table 1. Live Births, Birth Rates, and Fertility Rates, by Race: United States, Specified Years 1940–55 and Each Year, 1960–2002," in "Births: Final Data for 2002," *National Vital Statistics Reports*, vol. 52, no. 10, December 17, 2003, http://www.cdc.gov/nchs/data/nvsr/nvsr52/nvsr52_10.pdf (accessed June 9, 2005)

TABLE 6.2

Births and birth rates, by age, race, and Hispanic origin of mother, 2002–03

[Data for 2003 are based on a continuous file of records received from the states. Figures for 2003 are based on weighted data rounded to the nearest individual, so categories may not add to totals. Rates per 1,000 women in specified age and racial/Hispanic origin group.]

Age and race/ Hispanic origin	2003 Number	2003 Rate	2002 Number	2002 Rate
All races				
Total[a]	4,091,063	66.1	4,021,726	64.8
10–14 years	6,665	0.6	7,315	0.7
15–19 years	414,961	41.7	425,493	43.0
15–17 years	134,617	22.4	138,731	23.2
18–19 years	280,344	70.8	286,762	72.8
20–24 years	1,032,337	102.6	1,022,106	103.6
25–29 years	1,086,898	115.7	1,060,391	113.6
30–34 years	975,964	95.2	951,219	91.5
35–39 years	467,520	43.8	453,927	41.4
40–44 years	100,873	8.7	95,788	8.3
45–54 years[b]	5,845	0.5	5,487	0.5
White total[c]				
Total[a]	3,227,755	66.2	3,174,760	64.8
10–14 years	3,682	0.5	3,884	0.5
15–19 years	298,821	38.3	305,988	39.4
15–17 years	92,807	19.8	95,864	20.5
18–19 years	206,014	66.3	210,124	68.0
20–24 years	791,106	100.6	783,000	101.6
25–29 years	872,288	119.6	851,142	117.4
30–34 years	796,520	99.4	779,535	95.5
35–39 years	379,703	44.8	369,833	42.4
40–44 years	80,929	8.7	76,928	8.2
45–54 years[b]	4,706	0.5	4,450	0.5
Non-Hispanic white[c]				
Total[a]	2,320,778	58.5	2,298,156	57.4
10–14 years	1,402	0.2	1,493	0.2
15–19 years	172,727	27.5	179,511	28.5
15–17 years	46,899	12.4	49,756	13.1
18–19 years	125,827	50.1	129,755	51.9
20–24 years	521,712	83.5	519,153	84.3
25–29 years	627,373	110.9	614,909	109.3
30–34 years	626,245	97.7	620,173	94.4
35–39 years	303,008	43.2	297,436	40.9
40–44 years	64,414	8.1	61,853	7.6
45–54 years[b]	3,897	0.5	3,628	0.5
Black total[c]				
Total[a]	599,414	66.2	593,691	65.8
10–14 years	2,722	1.6	3,188	1.8
15–19 years	100,865	63.7	103,795	66.6
15–17 years	36,855	38.2	37,889	40.0
18–19 years	64,009	103.6	65,906	107.6
20–24 years	196,112	126.0	194,704	127.1
25–29 years	139,853	100.3	136,591	99.0
30–34 years	97,526	66.5	95,006	64.4
35–39 years	49,810	33.1	48,388	31.5
40–44 years	11,880	7.7	11,443	7.4
45–54 years[b]	645	0.5	576	0.4
Non-Hispanic black[c]				
Total[a]	576,347	67.1	578,335	67.4
10–14 years	2,642	1.6	3,132	1.9
15–19 years	97,534	64.8	101,494	68.3
15–17 years	35,582	38.8	37,017	41.0
18–19 years	61,952	105.3	64,477	110.3
20–24 years	189,063	128.2	190,241	131.0
25–29 years	133,959	102.2	132,824	102.1
30–34 years	93,459	67.5	92,155	66.1
35–39 years	47,657	33.5	46,831	32.1
40–44 years	11,416	7.7	11,097	7.5
45–54 years[b]	616	0.5	561	0.4

TABLE 6.2

Births and birth rates, by age, race, and Hispanic origin of mother, 2002–03 [CONTINUED]

[Data for 2003 are based on a continuous file of records received from the states. Figures for 2003 are based on weighted data rounded to the nearest individual, so categories may not add to totals. Rates per 1,000 women in specified age and racial/Hispanic origin group.]

Age and race/ Hispanic origin	2003 Number	2003 Rate	2002 Number	2002 Rate
American Indian total[c,d]				
Total[a]	42,647	57.9	42,368	58.0
10–14 years	156	1.0	133	0.9
15–19 years	7,617	52.6	7,707	53.8
15–17 years	2,648	30.3	2,663	30.7
18–19 years	4,969	86.5	5,044	89.2
20–24 years	14,480	108.8	14,343	112.6
25–29 years	10,421	92.6	10,139	91.8
30–34 years	6,372	57.0	6,338	56.4
35–39 years	2,900	25.4	2,976	25.4
40–44 years	660	5.5	701	5.8
45–54 years[b]	43	0.4	31	0.3
Asian or Pacific Islander total[c]				
Total[a]	221,247	66.3	210,907	64.1
10–14 years	105	0.2	110	0.3
15–19 years	7,658	17.6	8,003	18.3
15–17 years	2,307	8.9	2,315	9.0
18–19 years	5,351	30.1	5,688	31.5
20–24 years	30,639	59.9	30,059	60.4
25–29 years	64,336	108.4	62,519	105.4
30–34 years	75,546	114.4	70,340	109.6
35–39 years	35,107	59.9	32,730	56.5
40–44 years	7,405	13.4	6,716	12.5
45–54 years[b]	451	0.9	430	0.9
Hispanic[e]				
Total[a]	912,256	96.9	876,642	94.4
10–14 years	2,349	1.3	2,421	1.4
15–19 years	128,472	82.2	127,900	83.4
15–17 years	46,949	49.7	46,740	50.7
18–19 years	81,523	131.9	81,160	133.0
20–24 years	273,258	163.4	265,235	164.3
25–29 years	246,388	144.4	236,143	139.4
30–34 years	169,056	102.0	157,887	95.1
35–39 years	75,812	50.8	71,480	47.8
40–44 years	16,169	12.2	14,809	11.5
45–54 years[b]	753	0.7	767	0.7

[a]The total number includes births to women of all ages, 10–54 years. The rate shown for all ages is the fertility rate, which is defined as the total number of births, regardless of age of mother, per 1,000 women aged 15–44 years.

[b]The number of births shown is the total for women aged 45–54 years. The birth rate is computed by relating the number of births to women aged 45–54 years to women aged 45–49 years, because most of the births in this group are to women aged 45–49 years.

[c]Race and Hispanic origin are reported separately on the birth certificate. Race categories are consistent with the 1977 Office of Management and Budget standards. California, Hawaii, Ohio (for December), Pennsylvania, Utah, and Washington reported multiple-race data in 2003. The multiple-race data for these states were bridged to the single race categories of the 1977 Office of Management and Budget standards for comparability with other states. Data for persons of Hispanic origin are included in the data for each race group according to the mother's reported race.

[d]Includes births to Aleuts and Eskimos.

[e]Includes all persons of Hispanic origin of any race.

SOURCE: "Table 1. Births and Birth Rates, by Age, Race and Hispanic Origin of Mother: United States, Final 2002 and Preliminary 2003," in "Births: Preliminary Data for 2003," *National Vital Statistics Reports*, vol. 53, no. 9, November 23, 2004, http://www.cdc.gov/nchs/data/nvsr/nvsr53/nvsr53_09 .pdf (accessed June 9, 2005)

TABLE 6.3

Total births and percent of births with selected characteristics, by race and Hispanic origin of mother, 2002–03

[Figures for 2003 are based on weighted data rounded to the nearest individual]

Characteristic	All races and origins		Non-Hispanic white[a]		Non-Hispanic black[a]		Hispanic[b]		American Indian total[a]		Asian or Pacific Islander total[a]	
	2003	2002	2003	2002	2003	2002	2003	2002	2003	2002	2003	2002
	Number											
Births	4,091,063	4,021,726	2,320,778	2,298,156	576,347	578,335	912,256	876,642	42,647	42,368	221,247	210,907
	Rate											
Birth rate	14.1	13.9	11.8	11.7	15.9	16.1	22.9	22.6	13.7	13.8	16.8	16.5
Fertility rate	66.1	64.8	58.5	57.4	67.1	67.4	96.9	94.4	57.9	58.0	66.3	64.1
Total fertility rate	2,044.0	2,013.0	1,858.0	1,828.5	2,030.0	2,047.0	2,785.0	2,718.0	1,716.5	1,735.0	1,873.5	1,819.5
Maternal	**Percent**											
Births to unmarried mothers	34.6	34.0	23.5	23.0	68.5	68.4	45.0	43.5	61.2	59.7	15.1	14.9
Prenatal care beginning in first trimester[c]	84.1	83.7	89.0	88.7	76.0	75.3	77.4	76.8	70.9	69.6	85.4	84.9
Prenatal care beginning in third trimester or no care[c]	3.5	3.6	2.1	2.2	6.0	6.2	5.3	5.5	7.6	8.1	3.1	3.1
Smoker[d]	11.0	11.4	14.5	15.0	8.5	8.8	2.8	3.0	18.3	19.7	2.3	2.5
Total cesarean delivery rate[e]	27.6	26.1	27.7	26.2	29.3	27.7	26.6	25.2	24.2	23.1	26.7	25.0
Primary cesarean rate[e]	19.1	18.0	19.6	18.3	20.7	19.4	16.9	16.1	15.8	15.1	19.9	18.5
VBAC rate[e]	10.6	12.6	10.7	12.8	11.3	13.2	9.4	11.5	14.1	17.0	12.2	14.1
Infant												
Preterm[f]	12.3	12.1	11.3	11.0	17.8	17.7	11.9	11.6	13.5	13.1	10.6	10.4
Low birthweight[g]	7.9	7.8	7.0	6.9	13.5	13.4	6.7	6.5	7.4	7.2	7.8	7.8
Very low birthweight[g]	1.4	1.5	1.2	1.2	3.1	3.1	1.2	1.2	1.3	1.3	1.1	1.1

[a]Race and Hispanic origin are reported separately on the birth certificate. Race categories are consistent with the 1977 Office of Management and Budget standards. California, Hawaii, Ohio (for December), Pennsylvania, Utah, and Washington reported multiple-race data in 2003. The multiple-race data for these states were bridged to the single race categories of the 1977 Office of Management and Budget standards for comparability with other states. Data for persons of Hispanic origin are included in the data for each race group according to the mother's reported race.

[b]Includes all persons of Hispanic origin of any race.

[c]Excludes data for Pennsylvania and Washington, which implemented the 2003 Revision to the U.S. Standard Certificate of Live Birth for data year 2003.

[d]Excludes data for California, which did not report tobacco use on the birth certificate.

[e]Total cesarean delivery rate is the total number of births by cesarean as percent of all births. Primary cesarean rate is the number of primary cesareans per 100 live births to women who have not had a previous cesarean. Vaginal births after previous cesarean (VBAC) rate is the number of VBAC delivery per 100 live births to women with a previous cesarean delivery.

[f]Percent of births less than 37 completed weeks of gestation.

[g]Low birthweight is birthweight of less than 2,500 grams (5 lb 8 oz). Very low birthweight is birthweight of less than 1,500 grams (3 lb 4 oz).

SOURCE: "Table A. Total Births and Percent of Births with Selected Demographic and Health Characteristics, by Race and Hispanic Origin of Mother: United States, Final 2002 and Preliminary 2003," in "Births: Preliminary Data for 2003," *National Vital Statistics Reports*, vol. 53, no. 9, November 23, 2004, http://www.cdc.gov/nchs/data/nvsr/nvsr53/nvsr53_09.pdf (accessed June 9, 2005)

the previous year. The number of births to non-Hispanic African-Americans decreased by less than one percentage point. However, number of births to both Hispanic women and Asian/Pacific Islander women increased significantly—Hispanic births increased by 4.1% and Asian-American/Pacific Islander births increased by 4.9%. (See Table 6.3.) Hispanic women had by far the highest fertility rate at 94.4, though this was down from 96.0 in 2001, 95.9 in 2000, and 107.7 in 1990. Native Americans had the lowest fertility rate in 2003 of 57.9. Non-Hispanic white women had a fertility rate of 58.5, up slightly from the previous year. African-American women had a fertility rate of 67.1, lower than the previous year but higher than the rate of non-Hispanic white women.

Births to Foreign-Born Women

According to the Census Bureau's *Fertility of American Women: June 2002* (October 2003), 15% of women of childbearing age (8.9 million) were foreign-born in 2002. Foreign-born women had a higher fertility rate than native-born women (71.3 versus 59.7). (See Table 6.4.) As of June 2002 native-born women ages fifteen to forty-four had birthed an average of 1.2 children, while foreign-born women had birthed an average of 1.5 children.

Childbearing among Teenagers

Birth rates among teenagers declined by 57% between 1991 and 2003, reaching a record low. (See Table 6.5.) Among young girls ages ten to fourteen the rate declined from 1.4 in 1991 to an all-time low of 0.6 in 2003. Asian-American and native-Pacific Islander girls (0.2) had the lowest birth rates in this age group in 2002; African-American girls had the highest (1.6).

Among teens ages fifteen to nineteen the birth rate also declined throughout the 1990s to its lowest point ever in 2003. (See Figure 6.1 and Table 6.5.) At its peak in 1957 the rate was 96.3 per one thousand, more than twice the rate of 41.7 in 2003. Despite a decrease in the number of teenagers, the birth rate increased between

TABLE 6.4

Fertility indicators for women 15–44 years old, by selected characteristics, June 2002

[Numbers in thousands]

Characteristic	Number of women	Percent childless	Women who had a child in the last year			Children ever born per 1,000 women
			Number	Births per 1,000 women	First births per 1,000 women	
Total	**61,361**	**43.5**	**3,766**	**61.4**	**23.1**	**1,211**
Marital status						
Currently married	30,275	18.7	2,505	82.8	28.6	1,792
Married—husband present	27,828	18.5	2,382	85.6	29.6	1,784
Married—husband absent*	2,446	21.1	124	50.5	17.0	1,878
Divorced or widowed	5,303	21.1	143	26.9	6.6	1,724
Never married	25,782	77.2	1,118	43.3	19.9	423
Educational attainment						
Not a high school graduate	13,096	58.8	812	62.0	20.1	1,043
High school graduate	16,644	30.7	1,005	60.4	22.8	1,478
College, 1 or more years	31,621	43.9	1,949	61.6	24.4	1,140
No degree	12,451	45.9	750	60.2	24.0	1,124
Associate degree	5,113	33.0	221	43.2	15.5	1,374
Bachelor's degree	10,592	46.6	683	64.5	25.1	1,059
Graduate or professional degree	3,465	44.6	294	84.9	36.8	1,100
Labor force status						
In labor force	43,360	44.0	2,056	47.4	19.5	1,165
Employed	40,150	43.2	1,867	46.5	18.4	1,178
Unemployed	3,210	52.8	189	58.8	32.9	1,011
Not in labor force	18,001	42.4	1,710	95.0	31.6	1,320
Annual family income						
Under $10,000	4,203	40.0	355	84.5	30.5	1,449
$10,000 to $19,999	5,760	39.9	472	81.9	34.8	1,334
$20,000 to $24,999	3,348	38.2	215	64.3	21.9	1,338
$25,000 to $29,999	3,464	41.9	194	56.1	15.9	1,221
$30,000 to $34,999	3,612	43.7	264	73.2	23.1	1,206
$35,000 to $49,999	8,477	43.0	457	53.9	19.0	1,204
$50,000 to $74,999	10,613	43.6	554	52.2	23.3	1,176
$75,000 and over	13,771	47.2	826	60.0	21.4	1,098
Not ascertained	8,114	44.7	428	52.8	21.1	1,188
Region of residence						
Northeast	11,616	46.1	694	59.7	21.2	1,148
Midwest	14,041	43.8	780	55.6	21.6	1,212
South	21,680	40.9	1,453	67.0	25.9	1,234
West	14,024	45.1	838	59.8	21.7	1,226
Metropolitan residence						
Metropolitan	50,755	44.8	3,032	59.7	22.6	1,180
In central cities	18,804	46.4	1,163	61.8	22.9	1,167
Outside central cities	31,950	43.8	1,869	58.5	22.5	1,188
Nonmetropolitan	10,606	37.3	734	69.2	25.1	1,357
Nativity and Hispanic origin						
Native	52,428	44.8	3,129	59.7	22.0	1,169
Hispanic (of any race)	4,739	43.7	371	78.3	28.5	1,285
Not Hispanic	47,689	45.0	2,758	57.8	21.3	1,157
White, not Hispanic	38,485	45.7	2,170	56.4	21.1	1,127
Foreign born	8,933	35.6	637	71.3	29.3	1,456
Hispanic (of any race)	4,402	27.4	379	86.0	32.5	1,755
Not Hispanic	4,531	43.5	258	56.9	26.2	1,166
White, not Hispanic	1,533	42.4	92	59.7	26.8	1,195

*Includes separated women.

Note: Since the number of women who have had a birth during the 12-month period was tabulated and not the actual numbers of births themselves, a small under estimation of fertility for this period may exist because of the omission of: (1) multiple births; (2) more than one live birth occurring to a woman in a 12-month period (the woman is only counted once); (3) women who had births in the period and who died by the survey date; (4) women who were in institutions and therefore not in the survey universe; (5) 2 percent of births in a 12-month period; only 51 weeks of data are tabulated in the CPS (Current Population Survey) due to the mid- to late-June interview schedule. These losses may be somewhat offset by the inclusion in the CPS of births to immigrants who did not have their children born in the United States and births to nonresident women who had their children born in the United States. These births would not have been recorded in the vital registration system. The ages of the women in this table and similar tables in this report refer to the age of women at the time of the survey and not at the birth of the child.

SOURCE: Barbara Downs, "Table 3. Fertility Indicators for Women 15 to 44 Years Old by Selected Characteristics: June 2002," in *Fertility of American Women: June 2002*, U.S. Census Bureau, Current Population Reports, P20-548, October 2003, http://www.census.gov/prod/2003pubs/p20-548.pdf (accessed June 9, 2005)

TABLE 6.5

Birth rates for women under 20 years of age, by age, race, and Hispanic origin, 1991, 2001, 2002, and 2003

[Rates per 1,000 women in specified group]

Age and race and Hispanic origin of mother	2003	2002	2001	1991	Percent change, 1991–2003
			10–14 years		
All races[a]	0.6	0.7	0.8	1.4	−57
Non-Hispanic white[b]	0.2	0.2	0.3	0.5	−60
Non-Hispanic black[b]	1.6	1.9	2.1	4.9	−67
American Indian total[b]	1.0	0.9	1.0	1.6	−38
Asian or Pacific Islander total[b]	0.2	0.3	0.2	0.8	−75
Hispanic[c]	1.3	1.4	1.6	2.4	−46
			15–19 years		
All races[a]	41.7	43.0	45.3	61.8	−33
Non-Hispanic white[b]	27.5	28.5	30.3	43.4	−37
Non-Hispanic black[b]	64.8	68.3	73.5	118.2	−45
American Indian total[b]	52.6	53.8	56.3	84.1	−37
Asian or Pacific Islander total[b]	17.6	18.3	19.8	27.3	−36
Hispanic[c]	82.2	83.4	86.4	104.6	−21
			15–17 years		
All races[a]	22.4	23.2	24.7	38.6	−42
Non-Hispanic white[b]	12.4	13.1	14.0	23.6	−47
Non-Hispanic black[b]	38.8	41.0	44.9	86.1	−55
American Indian total[b]	30.3	30.7	31.4	51.9	−42
Asian or Pacific Islander total[b]	8.9	9.0	10.3	16.3	−45
Hispanic[c]	49.7	50.7	52.8	69.2	−28
			18–19 years		
All races[a]	70.8	72.8	76.1	94.0	−25
Non-Hispanic white[b]	50.1	51.9	54.8	70.6	−29
Non-Hispanic black[b]	105.3	110.3	116.7	162.2	−35
American Indian total[b]	86.5	89.2	94.8	134.2	−36
Asian or Pacific Islander total[b]	30.1	31.5	32.8	42.2	−29
Hispanic[c]	131.9	133.0	135.5	155.5	−15

[a]Includes data for white and black Hispanic women, not shown separately.
[b]Race and Hispanic origin are reported separately on the birth certificate. Race categories are consistent with the 1977 Office of Management and Budget standards. California, Hawaii, Ohio (for December), Pennsylvania, Utah, and Washington reported multiple-race data in 2003. The multiple-race data for these states were bridged to the single race categories of the 1977 Office of Management and Budget standards for comparability with other states. Data for persons of Hispanic origin are included in the data for each race group according to the mother's reported race.
[c]Includes all persons of Hispanic origin of any race.

SOURCE: "Table B. Birth Rates for Women Under 20 Years of Age, by Age, Race, and Hispanic Origin: United States, Final 1991, 2001 and 2002, and Preliminary 2003, and Percent Change in Rates, 1991–2003," in "Births: Preliminary Data for 2003," *National Vital Statistics Reports*, vol. 53, no. 9, November 23, 2004, http://www.cdc.gov/nchs/data/nvsr/nvsr53/nvsr53_09.pdf (accessed June 9, 2005).

FIGURE 6.1

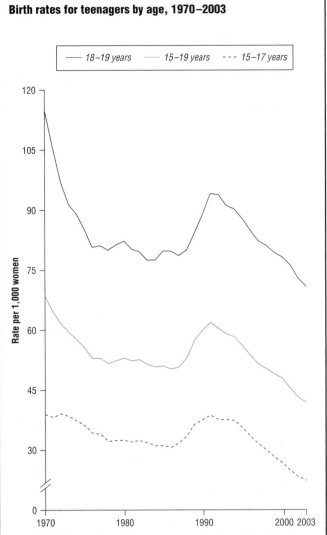

Birth rates for teenagers by age, 1970–2003

SOURCE: "Figure 2. Birth Rates for Teenagers by Age: United States, 1970–2003," in "Births: Preliminary Data for 2003," *National Vital Statistics Reports*, vol. 53, no. 9, November 23, 2004, http://www.cdc.gov/nchs/data/nvsr/nvsr53/nvsr53_09.pdf (accessed June 9, 2005)

1986 and 1991, when it was 61.8, then declined by 33% from 1991 to 2003. Those in their mid-teens accounted for much of the decline. From 1991 to 2003 the birth rate for fifteen- to seventeen-year-olds declined 42%.

Although birth rates for African-American teenagers declined steeply in the 1990s, African-Americans and Hispanics continued to have the highest teen birth rates. (See Table 6.5.) The birth rate for African-American teenagers ages fifteen to nineteen declined 45% from 1991 to 2003. The birth rate for Hispanic teens ages fifteen to nineteen declined 21% in the same period. The birth rate

for non-Hispanic whites of the same age fell 37% from 1991 to 2003, and the rates for Native American and Asian-American/Pacific Islander teens fell 37% and 36%, respectively. Asian-American and Pacific Islander teenagers had the lowest overall birth rate. In each racial/ethnic group the rates fell more sharply among teens fifteen to seventeen than among teens eighteen and nineteen.

Education, Income, Employment, and Residence

The Census Bureau's *Fertility of American Women: June 2002* lists demographic statistics for American women who had given birth in the last year. (See Table 6.4.) In 2002 women with an associate degree had the lowest birth rate (43.2 births per one thousand women), and those with a graduate or professional degree had the highest (84.9 per one thousand). According to the

NCHS, 78.5% of women who gave birth in 2002 had at least twelve years of schooling—that is, a high school education.

On the other hand, the fertility rate (the number of pregnancies per one thousand women) was highest for those with family incomes under $10,000 (84.5) and lowest for those with incomes of $50,000 to $74,999 (52.2). Women who were not in the labor force had the highest fertility rate (95), and unemployed women in the labor force had a higher fertility rate than employed women (58.8 versus 46.5). Women who lived outside of metropolitan areas (69.2) had a higher fertility rate than those living in cities (61.8) and suburbs (58.5).

Family Size and Marital Status

Families are becoming smaller. According to data from the Census Bureau's Current Population Survey, the average number of children in families with their own children under eighteen had shrunk to 1.83 in 2003 from 2.19 in 1965. Family households headed by women had slightly more children (1.72) than family households headed by men (1.50), although neither had as many as married couples (1.89).

The fertility rate in 2002 was highest for women who were currently married, 82.8 births per one thousand women ages fifteen to forty-four. The fertility rate for never-married women was 43.3. (See Table 6.4.) The birth rate for unmarried women ages fifteen to forty-four in 2002 was 43.7, down from 46.2 in 1994. (See Table 6.6.) Unmarried Hispanic women had the highest birth rate, at 87.9, compared with 27.8 for non-Hispanic white women and 21.3 for Asian-Americans/Pacific Islanders. The highest birth rate for unmarried women by age was for those ages twenty to twenty-four, at 70.5. In 2002 nearly 1.4 million births, or 34% of all births, were to unmarried women. Births to unmarried women represented 43.5% of births to Hispanic mothers, 68.4% of all births to African-American mothers, 23% of births to non-Hispanic white mothers, and 14.9% of births to Asian-American or Pacific Islander mothers.

Multiple Births

One of the most striking developments in childbearing has been the increase in multiple births since 1980. From 1995 to 2002 the twin birth rate (twin births per one thousand live births) rose from 26.1 to 33 (*Statistical Abstract of the United States*, U.S. Census Bureau, 2004–05). There were 125,134 twin births in 2002, compared with 96,736 reported in 1995. The twin birth rate rose steadily with the age of the mother, with the highest twinning rate (199 per one thousand births) among women forty-five to fifty-four years of age. The number of triplets or greater multiple births also rose dramatically between 1995 and 2002, from 4,973 to 7,401.

Increasing maternal age is a factor in the number of multiple births, since, as women age, they often begin to release multiple eggs during a single ovulation. (According to the NCHS, the average age at first birth rose from 21.4 in 1970 to 25.1 in 2002.) But most of the increase in triplet and higher-order births results from assisted reproductive techniques and ovulation-inducing (fertility) drugs. Ovulation-inducing drugs often result in women releasing multiple eggs for fertilization during a single cycle.

UNMARRIED CHILDBEARING

Since the 1970s increasing percentages of women of all ages, races, and ethnicities have been giving birth outside marriage. In 1970 only 10.7% of births were to unmarried women, compared with 18.4% in 1980. Increases from 1996–97 to 2002 were slower, from 32.4% of all births to unmarried women in 1996–97 to 34% in 2002. Of the births to unmarried women in 2002, the rate was highest among women ages twenty to twenty-four. (See Table 6.6.) About half (51.6%) of all births to women in this age group were out of wedlock. In total, there were nearly 1.4 million births to unmarried women in 2002.

Pregnant women often no longer feel that they have to marry, and the likelihood that a pregnant woman will marry before giving birth has declined sharply since the early 1960s. There are several reasons for this change. Unmarried women are more sexually active than in the past, and many of them have put their education and careers ahead of marriage. The stigma that was formerly attached to unmarried motherhood has largely disappeared. In addition, many women feel that being single is preferable to living in an unhappy, unstable, or abusive marriage, and some prefer to raise their children by themselves. Furthermore, many women who are having children without being married live with their partners in families that may be traditional in every way except for the marriage license. Some unmarried mothers are lesbians who have chosen to conceive a child with a male friend or by artificial insemination with sperm from a sperm bank. Finally, part of the increase in unmarried childbearing is attributable to the decrease in the birth rate for married women and to the increasing proportion of unmarried women of childbearing age. The NCHS's *Births: Final Data for 2002* (December 17, 2003) notes that while the number of nonmarital births had increased since 1995, the birth rate for unmarried women has stayed relatively constant.

Age and Race

There were 43.7 births to every one thousand unmarried women in 2002. (See Table 6.6.) Figure 6.2 traces the birth rate per one thousand unmarried women from 1980 to 2002. The rate climbed for all age groups in the decade 1980 to 1990, but since then different age groups have shown different trends. Rates for those twenty to

TABLE 6.6

Number, birth rate, and percent of births to unmarried women, by age, race, and Hispanic origin of mother, 2002

Measure and age of mother	All races[a]	White Total[b]	White Non-Hispanic	Black Total[b]	Black Non-Hispanic	American Indian[b,c]	Asian or Pacific Islander[b]	Hispanic[d]
Number								
All ages	1,365,966	904,461	528,535	404,864	395,538	25,297	31,344	381,466
Under 15 years	7,093	3,683	1,446	3,174	3,119	129	107	2,266
15–19 years	340,186	228,407	135,313	99,375	97,282	6,678	5,726	94,483
15 years	17,629	10,672	4,811	6,293	6,150	399	265	5,970
16 years	38,888	25,531	12,816	12,015	11,728	774	568	12,954
17 years	66,274	44,829	25,344	19,053	18,637	1,329	1,063	19,774
18 years	95,259	64,580	39,359	27,131	26,589	1,880	1,668	25,547
19 years	122,136	82,795	52,983	34,883	34,178	2,296	2,162	30,238
20–24 years	527,657	349,161	214,529	158,276	155,080	9,548	10,672	136,369
25–29 years	268,312	176,055	94,304	79,946	77,952	4,993	7,318	83,035
30–34 years	139,208	91,688	50,150	40,375	39,193	2,475	4,670	42,254
35–39 years	66,036	43,684	25,472	18,958	18,299	1,176	2,218	18,566
40 years and over	17,474	11,783	7,321	4,760	4,613	298	633	4,493
Rate per 1,000 unmarried women in specified group								
15–44 years[e]	43.7	38.9	27.8	66.2	—	—	21.3	87.9
15–19 years	35.4	30.4	22.1	64.8	—	—	13.4	66.1
15–17 years	20.8	17.5	11.5	39.9	—	—	7.5	43.0
18–19 years	58.6	51.0	38.8	104.1	—	—	22.2	105.3
20–24 years	70.5	61.6	46.1	119.2	—	—	26.5	131.4
25–29 years	61.5	56.8	38.5	85.9	—	—	27.5	123.1
30–34 years	40.8	38.3	26.0	49.9	—	—	28.6	88.1
35–39 years	20.8	19.4	13.5	24.9	—	—	18.7	51.3
40–44 years[f]	5.4	5.0	3.7	6.3	—	—	6.8	12.7
Percent of births to unmarried women								
All ages	34.0	28.5	23.0	68.2	68.4	59.7	14.9	43.5
Under 15 years	97.0	94.8	96.9	99.6	99.6	97.0	97.3	93.6
15–19 years	80.0	74.6	75.4	95.7	95.9	86.6	71.5	73.9
15 years	94.3	91.5	93.8	99.3	99.3	98.3	89.5	89.8
16 years	90.1	86.5	88.9	99.0	99.0	96.1	81.3	84.6
17 years	86.2	82.0	83.9	98.2	98.2	91.5	80.5	79.8
18 years	80.3	75.1	76.9	96.0	96.1	86.9	73.6	72.7
19 years	72.7	66.7	67.4	92.7	92.8	79.7	63.2	65.7
20–24 years	51.6	44.6	41.3	81.3	81.5	66.6	35.5	51.4
25–29 years	25.3	20.7	15.3	58.5	58.7	49.2	11.7	35.2
30–34 years	14.6	11.8	8.1	42.5	42.5	39.1	6.6	26.8
35–39 years	14.5	11.8	8.6	39.2	39.1	39.5	6.8	26.0
40 years and over	17.3	14.5	11.2	39.6	39.6	40.7	8.9	28.8

—Data not available.

[a]Includes races other than white and black and origin not stated.

[b]Race and Hispanic origin are reported separately on the birth certificate. Race categories are consistent with the 1977 Office of Management and Budget guidelines. Data for persons of Hispanic origin are included in the data for each race group according to the mother's reported race.

[c]Includes births to Aleuts and Eskimos.

[d]Includes all persons of Hispanic origin of any race.

[e]Birth rates computed by relating total births to unmarried mothers, regardless of age of mother, to unmarried women aged 15–44 years.

[f]Birth rates computed by relating births to unmarried mothers aged 40 years and over to unmarried women aged 40–44 years.

Note: For 48 states and the District of Columbia, marital status is reported on the birth certificate; for Michigan and New York, mother's marital status is inferred. Rates cannot be computed for unmarried non-Hispanic black women or for American Indian women because the necessary populations are not available.

SOURCE: "Table 17. Number, Birth Rate, and Percent of Births to Unmarried Women by Age, Race, and Hispanic Origin of Mother: United States, 2002," in "Births: Final Data for 2002," *National Vital Statistics Reports*, vol. 52, no. 10, December 17, 2003, http://www.cdc.gov/nchs/data/nvsr/nvsr52/nvsr52_10.pdf (accessed June 9, 2005)

thirty-four have increased only slightly, while those for women thirty-five to thirty-nine have increased by a larger amount. Rates for teens, particularly fifteen- to seventeen-year-olds, have dropped significantly. Nevertheless, the vast majority of teens fifteen to nineteen who gave birth in 2002 were unmarried (80%). This percentage generally dropped with age.

In 2002, 68.2% of African-American women who gave birth were single; 59.7% of all Native American women, 43.5% of all Hispanic women, and 28.5% of all white women who gave birth were single. (See Table 6.6.) Only 14.9% of Asian-American and Pacific Islander births were to unmarried mothers. Almost all women ages fifteen and under who gave birth were unmarried. Almost three-quarters of Asian-American/Pacific Islander teens ages fifteen to nineteen who gave birth were unmarried (71.5%); a higher percentage of Hispanic teens (73.9%), non-Hispanic white teens (75.4%), Native American teens (86.6%), and African-American teens (95.9%) who gave

FIGURE 6.2

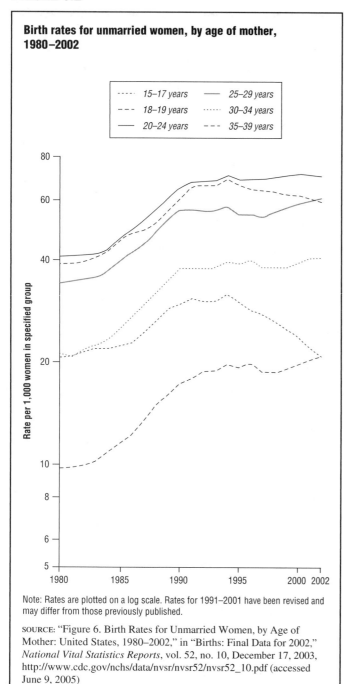

Birth rates for unmarried women, by age of mother, 1980–2002

Note: Rates are plotted on a log scale. Rates for 1991–2001 have been revised and may differ from those previously published.

SOURCE: "Figure 6. Birth Rates for Unmarried Women, by Age of Mother: United States, 1980–2002," in "Births: Final Data for 2002," *National Vital Statistics Reports*, vol. 52, no. 10, December 17, 2003, http://www.cdc.gov/nchs/data/nvsr/nvsr52/nvsr52_10.pdf (accessed June 9, 2005)

had 36.6% of those between the ages of forty and forty-four, compared with only 7.8% of never-married teenagers (fifteen to nineteen). Among never-married African-American women, 45% had given birth, as had nearly one-third of Hispanic women (30.6%) and 17% of non-Hispanic white women. Among births to unmarried women in 2002, 38% were to women who had earned only their high school diploma; 18% were to those who had earned their associate degree, and nearly two-thirds (63%) were to women who had not graduated from high school. Only 6% of births to unwed mothers in 2002 were to women who had earned a bachelor's degree.

TEENAGE MOTHERHOOD

Although the teenage birth rate has been declining steadily, there were 347,279 births to women under twenty in 2002 (see Table 6.6), and according to *Teenagers' Sexual and Reproductive Health* (New York: Alan Guttmacher Institute, January 2002), the birth rate remained much higher for American teens than for teens in other developed countries. Furthermore, the proportion of teen births to unmarried mothers increased steadily from 14% in 1957 to 80% in 2002, although the birth rate for unmarried teens declined beginning in 1994. This reflects the overall trend toward nonmarital childbearing.

Sexually Active Teenagers

According to the NCHS, after increasing steadily for twenty years, the proportion of sexually active teenagers stabilized in the mid-1990s. From 1995 to 2001 this percentage dropped slightly, from about 38% of teens to 35%. But in 2003, 46.7% of high school students reported having had sexual intercourse—and 14.4% had had four or more sex partners during their lifetimes. (See Table 6.7.) Most disturbingly, 37% had not used a condom at the last occurrence of intercourse. (See Table 6.8.)

Early sexual activity results in many unintended pregnancies. According to the NCHS, however, in addition to the teen birth rate, the pregnancy rate of young women fifteen to nineteen—which is based on the number of live births, legally induced abortions, and estimated fetal losses—declined by 25% from 1990 to 1999 (the latest year for which statistics are available). But the NCHS also reports that 34% of young women become pregnant at least once as a teen—approximately 820,000 each year.

Health Risks of Teen Pregnancy

In 2002 mothers ages fifteen to nineteen were less likely to receive first-trimester prenatal care (only 70% did, compared with 83.7% of all women), were more likely to smoke during pregnancy (16.7% versus 11.4% of all women), were more likely to have a preterm birth, and were more likely to have a low-birth-weight baby (9.6% versus 7.8% of all mothers). Teenage mothers

birth were unmarried. In general, African-American mothers and Native American mothers had the highest birth rates to unmarried women in each age group.

Never-Married Mothers

According to the Census Bureau, mothers who have never been married tend to be younger and less able to support themselves and their children than other groups of unmarried mothers who may be divorced or widowed. In 2002, 22.8% of women who had never married were mothers. (See Table 6.4.) Among never-married women ages thirty-five to thirty-nine, 44.2% had given birth, as

TABLE 6.7

Percent of high school students who engaged in sexual behaviors, by sex, race/ethnicity, and grade, 2003

Category	Ever had sexual intercourse			Had first sexual intercourse before age 13 years			Had ≥ 4 sex partners during lifetime		
	Female	Male	Total	Female	Male	Total	Female	Male	Total
	%	%	%	%	%	%	%	%	%
Race/ethnicity									
White*	43.0	40.5	41.8	3.4	5.0	4.2	10.1	11.5	10.8
Black*	60.9	73.8	67.3	6.9	31.8	19.0	16.3	41.7	28.8
Hispanic	46.4	56.8	51.4	5.2	11.6	8.3	11.2	20.5	15.7
Grade									
9	27.9	37.3	32.8	5.3	13.2	9.3	6.4	14.2	10.4
10	43.1	45.1	44.1	5.7	11.2	8.5	8.8	16.4	12.6
11	53.1	53.4	53.2	3.2	7.5	5.4	13.4	18.6	16.0
12	62.3	60.7	61.6	1.9	8.8	5.5	17.9	22.2	20.3
Total	**45.3**	**48.0**	**46.7**	**4.2**	**10.4**	**7.4**	**11.2**	**17.5**	**14.4**

*Non-Hispanic.

SOURCE: Jo Anne Grunbaum, et al., "Table 42. Percentage of High School Students Who Engaged in Sexual Behaviors, by Sex, Race/Ethnicity, and Grade—United States, Youth Risk Behavior Survey, 2003," *Morbidity and Mortality Weekly Report*, vol. 53, no. SS-2, Department of Health and Human Services, Centers for Disease Control and Prevention, May 21, 2004, http://www.cdc.gov/mmwr/PDF/SS/SS5302.pdf (accessed June 15, 2005)

TABLE 6.8

Percent of high school students who were currently sexually active and who used a condom during or birth control pills before last sexual intercourse, by sex, race/ethnicity, and grade, 2003

Category	Currently sexually active			Condom use during last sexual intercourse			Birth control pill use before last sexual intercourse		
	Female	Male	Total	Female	Male	Total	Female	Male	Total
	%	%	%	%	%	%	%	%	%
Race/ethnicity									
White*	33.1	28.5	30.8	56.5	69.0	62.5	26.5	17.3	22.3
Black*	44.2	54.0	49.0	63.6	81.2	72.8	11.7	4.4	7.9
Hispanic	35.8	38.5	37.1	52.3	62.5	57.4	12.1	10.3	11.2
Grade									
9	18.3	24.0	21.2	66.1	71.2	69.0	11.6	6.6	8.7
10	31.2	30.0	30.6	66.4	71.8	69.0	13.5	11.8	12.7
11	42.9	39.2	41.1	55.5	66.7	60.8	24.1	14.8	19.6
12	51.0	46.5	48.9	48.5	67.0	57.4	27.2	17.5	22.6
Total	**34.6**	**33.8**	**34.3**	**57.4**	**68.8**	**63.0**	**20.6**	**13.1**	**17.0**

*Non-Hispanic

SOURCE: Jo Anne Grunbaum, et al., "Table 44. Percentage of High School Students Who Were Currently Sexually Active and Who Used a Condom During or Birth Control Pills Before Last Sexual Intercourse, by Sex, Race/Ethnicity, and Grade—United States, Youth Risk Behavior Survey, 2003," in *Morbidity and Mortality Weekly Report*, vol. 53, no. SS-2, Department of Health and Human Services, Centers for Disease Control and Prevention, May 21, 2004, http://www.cdc.gov/mmwr/PDF/SS/SS5302.pdf (accessed June 15, 2005)

were more likely to defer prenatal care until the third trimester or not get any prenatal care (6.6% for those ages fifteen to nineteen versus 3.6% of all mothers). Low-birth-weight babies are at higher risk for serious and long-term illness, developmental delays, and infant mortality. Teenagers are usually emotionally, psychologically, and financially unprepared for parenthood, and their children may suffer from lack of attention and stimulation.

Social Consequences of Teen Childbearing

Unmarried mothers, particularly teenagers, often have their educational plans disrupted, sometimes permanently. According to a February 2002 report from the National Campaign to Prevent Teen Pregnancy, *Not Just Another Single Issue: Teen Pregnancy Prevention's Link to Other Critical Social Issues*, not only are teenage mothers less likely to finish high school (only 41% of teens who give birth before age eighteen ever receive a diploma), but their children are also less likely to be successful in school (they are 50% more likely to repeat a grade). About 52% of mothers on welfare had their first child as a teenager, and about three-quarters of unmarried teen mothers begin receiving welfare within five years of giving birth to their first child. Sons of teen mothers are 13% more likely to go to prison, while daughters are 22% more likely to have a child as a teenager themselves.

Teenage mothers are more likely to depend on their families and on public assistance than are older mothers. In response to calls for welfare reform, the Personal Responsibility and Work Opportunity Reconciliation Act of 1996 (PRWORA) abolished the sixty-year-old Aid to Families with Dependent Children (AFDC) program and established the Temporary Assistance for Needy Families (TANF) block grant program. To qualify for TANF benefits, unmarried minor parents are required to remain in high school or its equivalent and to live at home or in an adult-supervised setting. PRWORA provided for the establishment of homes for teen parents and their children. These homes require that all residents either enroll in school or participate in a job-training program. They also provide parenting and life-skills classes, counseling, and support services.

A June 15, 2003, report from the Urban Institute (Paul Offner, *Teenagers and Welfare Reform*) notes that due to other changes over the period, it is hard to isolate what part of the reduction in teen pregnancy rates were attributable to PRWORA. Still, in analyzing welfare reform more generally (including pre-PRWORA reform), the author finds it "seems to have significantly reduced the school drop-out rate of low-income teenage girls, had little effect on living arrangements (with the exception of young low-income mothers), and reduced the number of never-married girls who have children."

HEALTH ISSUES DURING PREGNANCY, CHILDBIRTH, AND INFANCY

Smoking, Alcohol, and Illegal Drugs

According to the Child Trends Data Bank, the percentage of women who smoked during pregnancy declined from 19.5% in 1989 to 11.4% in 2002. (See Table 6.9.) In general, except for the group with the very least education (eight years or less), the more years of education the mother had, the less likelihood the expectant mother would smoke. In 2003 Native American/Alaskan Native expectant mothers were the most likely to smoke (18.3%), followed by non-Hispanic white mothers (14.5%), African-American mothers (8.5%), Hispanic mothers (2.8%), and Asian-American or Pacific Islander mothers (2.3%). Smoking during pregnancy has been linked to miscarriages, premature births, stillbirths,

low birth weight, infant mortality, and sudden infant death syndrome (SIDS). Although some women stop smoking during pregnancy and resume smoking after they give birth, their children may still be exposed to dangerous secondhand smoke.

More women are becoming aware of the dangers of alcohol consumption during pregnancy. Nevertheless, many women continue to drink while they are pregnant. According to the Substance Abuse and Mental Health Services Administration (SAMHSA), 9% of pregnant women ages fifteen to forty-four polled in 2002 had used alcohol in the past thirty days, and 3% reported binge drinking (consuming five or more drinks on the same occasion at least once within the past thirty days) (*Pregnancy and Substance Use*, January 2, 2004). The binge drinking rate for younger pregnant women (fifteen to twenty-five) was more than twice that for older women (twenty-six to forty-four).

There is no level of alcohol consumption that is considered safe during pregnancy. Alcohol consumption during pregnancy has been associated with low birth weight and birth defects. Excessive consumption of alcohol by pregnant women can lead to fetal alcohol syndrome, a condition that may include mental retardation and growth deficiencies in the child.

Prenatal Care

According to *Health, United States, 2004*, published by the CDC's U.S. Department of Health and Human Services (HHS), of the more than four million births in 2002, 83.7% of mothers began receiving prenatal care in their first trimester, up from 68% in 1970. From 1980 to 2002 the proportion of women receiving first-trimester prenatal care rose from 75.8% to 83.7%. Early prenatal care for African-American and Hispanic women increased from 60.7% to 75.2% and from 60.2% to 76.7%, respectively, over the same period. Non-Hispanic white women (88.6%) were more likely to receive first-trimester prenatal care in 2002 than either African-American (75.2%) or Hispanic (76.7%) women.

As Table 6.10 shows, the percentage of women receiving late or no prenatal care has generally decreased since 1990. Overall, 3.5% of women who gave birth in 2003 did not receive prenatal care until the third trimester of their pregnancies or received no prenatal care at all. African-American (6%) and Hispanic (5.3%) women were most likely to receive care only late in their pregnancies or not at all.

Preterm and Cesarean Births

According to the NCHS, the total cesarean rate in 2002 was 26.1%, or more than one-fourth of all births, the highest percentage ever recorded. Although the cesarean rate declined from 1989 through 1996, it rose from 1996 through

TABLE 6.9

Percent of total births to mothers who smoked during pregnancy, by mother's detailed race, Hispanic origin, and education, selected states, 1989–2003

	Percent of mothers who smoked[a]														
	1989	1990	1991	1992	1993	1994	1995	1996	1997	1998	1999	2000	2001	2002	2003[f]
All races	19.5	18.4	17.8	16.9	15.8	14.6	13.9	13.6	13.2	12.9	12.6	12.2	12.0	11.4	11.0
Age															
Under 15 years	7.7	7.5	7.6	6.9	7.0	6.7	7.3	7.7	8.1	7.7	7.8	7.1	6.0	5.8	—
15–19 years	22.2	20.8	19.7	18.6	17.5	16.7	16.8	17.2	17.6	17.8	18.1	17.8	17.5	16.7	—
15–17 years	19.0	17.6	16.6	15.6	14.8	14.4	14.6	15.4	15.5	15.5	15.5	15.0	14.4	13.4	—
18–19 years	23.9	22.5	21.5	20.3	19.1	18.1	18.1	18.3	18.8	19.2	19.5	19.2	19.0	18.2	—
20–24 years	23.5	22.1	21.2	20.3	19.2	17.8	17.1	16.8	16.6	16.5	16.7	16.8	17.0	16.7	—
25–29 years	19.0	18.0	17.2	16.1	14.8	13.5	12.8	12.3	11.8	11.4	11.0	10.5	10.3	9.9	—
30–34 years	15.7	15.3	15.1	14.5	13.4	12.3	11.4	10.9	10.0	9.3	8.6	8.0	7.6	7.1	—
35–39 years	13.6	13.3	13.3	13.4	12.8	12.2	12.0	11.7	11.1	10.6	9.9	9.1	8.6	7.8	—
40–54 years[d]	13.2	12.3	11.9	11.6	11.0	10.3	10.1	10.1	10.1	10.0	9.5	9.5	9.3	8.4	—
Race and Hispanic origin of mother															
White non-Hispanic[c]	21.7	21.0	20.5	19.7	18.6	17.7	17.1	16.9	16.5	16.2	15.9	15.6	15.5	15.0	14.5
Black non-Hispanic[c]	17.2	15.9	14.6	13.8	12.7	11.5	10.6	10.3	9.8	9.6	9.4	9.2	9.1	8.8	8.5
Asian or Pacific Islander[b]	5.7	5.5	5.2	4.8	4.3	3.6	3.4	3.3	3.2	3.1	2.9	2.8	2.8	2.5	2.3
Chinese	2.7	2.0	1.9	1.7	1.1	0.9	0.8	0.7	1.0	0.8	0.5	0.6	0.7	0.5	—
Japanese	8.2	8.0	7.5	6.6	6.7	5.4	5.2	4.8	4.7	4.8	4.5	4.2	3.8	4.0	—
Filipino	5.1	5.3	5.3	4.8	4.3	3.7	3.4	3.5	3.4	3.3	3.3	3.2	3.2	2.9	—
Hawaiian and part Hawaiian	19.3	21.0	19.4	18.5	17.2	16.0	15.9	15.3	15.8	16.8	14.7	14.4	14.8	13.7	—
Other Asian or Pacific Islander	4.2	3.8	3.8	3.6	3.2	2.9	2.7	2.7	2.5	2.4	2.3	2.3	2.3	2.1	—
American Indian or Alaska Native	23.0	22.4	22.6	22.5	21.6	21.0	20.9	21.3	20.8	20.2	20.2	20.0	19.9	19.7	18.3
Hispanic[c]	8.0	6.7	6.3	5.8	5.0	4.6	4.3	4.3	4.1	4.0	3.7	3.5	3.2	3.0	2.8
Mexican	6.3	5.3	4.8	4.3	3.7	3.4	3.1	3.1	2.9	2.8	2.6	2.4	2.4	2.2	—
Puerto Rican	14.5	13.6	13.2	12.7	11.2	10.9	10.4	11.0	11.0	10.7	10.5	10.3	9.7	9.0	—
Cuban	6.9	6.4	6.2	5.9	5.0	4.8	4.1	4.7	4.2	3.7	3.3	3.3	3.0	2.8	—
Central and South American	3.6	3.0	2.8	2.6	2.3	1.8	1.8	1.8	1.8	1.5	1.4	1.5	1.3	1.3	—
Other and unknown Hispanic	12.1	10.8	10.7	10.1	9.3	8.1	8.2	9.1	8.5	8.0	7.7	7.4	6.8	6.5	—
Education of mother[e]	Percent of mothers 20 years of age and over who smoked[b]														
0–8 years	18.9	17.5	16.8	15.5	13.9	12.1	11.0	10.3	9.9	9.5	8.9	7.9	7.2	8.3	—
9–11 years	42.2	40.5	39.1	37.8	36.1	33.6	32.0	31.1	30.2	29.3	29.0	28.2	27.6	24.1	—
12 years	22.8	21.9	21.2	20.7	19.9	18.7	18.3	18.0	17.5	17.1	16.9	16.6	16.5	15.8	—
13–15 years	13.7	12.8	12.5	12.1	11.4	10.8	10.6	10.4	9.9	9.6	9.4	9.1	9.2	8.7	—
16 years or more	5.0	4.5	4.2	3.9	3.1	2.8	2.7	2.6	2.4	2.2	2.1	2.0	1.9	1.7	—

[a]Excludes live births for whom smoking status of mother is unknown.
[b]Maternal tobacco use during pregnancy was not reported on the birth certificates of California, which in 1999 accounted for 32 percent of the births to Asian or Pacific Islander mothers.
[c]Includes data for 42 states and DC in 1989, 44 states and DC in 1990, 45 states and DC in 1991–92, 46 states and DC in 1993, 46 states, DC, and NYC in 1994–98, and 48 states, DC, and NYC in 1999. Excludes data for California, and South Dakota (1989–99), New Hampshire (1989–92), Oklahoma (1989–90), Louisiana and Nebraska (1989), NYC (1989–93), and Indiana and NY (1989–98), which did not require the reporting of either Hispanic origin of mother or tobacco use during pregnancy on the birth certificate.
[d]Prior to 1997 data are for live births to mothers 45–49 years of age.
[e]Includes data for 42 states and DC in 1989, 44 states and DC in 1990, 45 states and DC in 1991, 46 states and DC in 1992–93, 46 states, DC, and NYC in 1994–98 and 48 states, DC, and NYC in 1999. Excludes data for California and South Dakota (1989–99), Washington (1989–91), Oklahoma (1989–90), Louisiana and Nebraska (1989), NYC (1989–93), and Indiana and NY (1989–98), which did not require the reporting of either mother's education or tobacco use during pregnancy on the birth certificate.
[f]Estimates for 2003 are preliminary.
Notes: Unless otherwise specified, the race groups white, black, American Indian or Alaska Native, and Asian or Pacific Islander include persons of Hispanic and non-Hispanic origin. Conversely, persons of Hispanic origin may be of any race. All data are based on the National Vital Statistics System.

SOURCE: "Table 1. Percent of Total Births to Mothers Who Smoked During Pregnancy, by Mother's Detailed Race, Hispanic Origin, Age, and Education: Selected States, 1989–2003," in *Mothers Who Smoke While Pregnant*, Child Trends Data Bank, 2003, http://www.childtrendsdatabank.org/pdf/11_PDF.pdf (accessed June 9, 2005)

2002. This increase was the result of both an increase in the rate of cesarean first births and a decrease in the rate of vaginal births following a previous cesarean delivery. African-American women were somewhat more likely to have cesarean deliveries (27.6%). The percentage of preterm babies (born before thirty-seven weeks gestation) increased slightly from 11.9% in 2001 to 12.1% in 2002.

Low Birth Weight

In 2002, 7.8% of all births resulted in low-birth-weight babies. This figure had generally increased since the mid-1980s. The low-birth-weight percentage among African-Americans in 2002 was 13.3%, while the percentages among non-Hispanic whites and Hispanics were 6.8% and 6.6%, respectively.

The percentage of low- and very low-birth-weight babies was significantly higher for mothers who smoked (12.2%) than for those who did not (7.5%). Although low-birth-weight babies are more commonly born to heavy smokers, the NCHS found that more than twice as many babies born to "light smokers" (those who smoked fewer than six cigarettes daily) as babies born to nonsmokers suffered from low birthweight.

TABLE 6.10

Percent of all births to women receiving late or no prenatal care, by race and Hispanic origin of mother and age, selected years 1970–2003

	Percent of live births[a]													
	1970	1975	1980	1985	1990	1995	1996	1997	1998	1999	2000	2001	2002	2003[d]
All races	**7.9**	**6.0**	**5.1**	**5.7**	**6.1**	**4.2**	**4.0**	**3.9**	**3.9**	**3.8**	**3.9**	**3.7**	**3.6**	**3.5**
White	6.3	5.0	4.3	4.8	4.9	3.5	3.3	3.2	3.3	3.2	3.3	3.2	3.1	—
Non-Hispanic white[b]	—	—	3.5	4.0	3.4	2.5	2.4	2.4	2.4	2.3	2.3	2.2	2.2	2.1
Black	16.6	10.5	8.9	10.2	11.3	7.6	7.3	7.3	7.0	6.6	6.7	6.5	6.2	—
Non-Hispanic black[b]	—	—	9.7	10.9	11.2	7.6	7.3	7.3	7.0	6.6	6.7	6.5	6.2	6.0
Hispanic origin[b,c]	—	—	12.0	12.4	12.0	7.4	6.7	6.2	6.3	6.3	6.3	5.9	5.5	5.3
Mexican	—	—	11.8	12.9	13.2	8.1	7.2	6.7	6.8	6.7	6.9	6.2	5.8	—
Puerto Rican	—	—	16.2	15.5	10.6	5.5	5.7	5.4	5.1	5.0	4.5	4.6	4.1	—
Cuban	—	—	3.9	3.7	2.8	2.1	1.6	1.5	1.2	1.4	1.4	1.3	1.3	—
Central and South American	—	—	13.1	12.5	10.9	6.1	5.5	5.0	4.9	5.2	5.4	5.7	4.9	—
Other and unknown Hispanic	—	—	9.2	9.4	8.5	6.0	5.9	5.3	6.0	6.3	5.9	5.4	5.3	—
Asian or Pacific Islander	—	—	6.5	6.5	5.8	4.3	3.9	3.8	3.6	3.5	3.3	3.4	3.1	3.1
Chinese	6.5	4.4	3.7	4.4	3.4	3.0	2.5	2.4	2.2	2.0	2.2	2.4	2.1	—
Japanese	4.1	2.7	2.1	3.1	2.9	2.3	2.2	2.7	2.1	2.1	1.8	2.0	2.1	—
Filipino	7.2	4.1	4.0	4.8	4.5	4.1	3.3	3.3	3.1	2.8	3.0	3.0	2.8	—
Hawaiian and part Hawaiian	—	—	6.7	7.4	8.7	5.1	5.0	5.4	4.7	4.0	4.2	4.8	4.7	—
Other Asian or Pacific Islander	—	—	9.3	8.2	7.1	5.0	4.6	4.4	4.2	4.1	3.8	3.8	3.5	—
American Indian or Alaska Native	28.9	22.4	15.2	12.9	12.9	9.5	8.6	8.6	8.5	8.2	8.6	8.2	8.0	7.6
Age														
Under 15 years	—	—	—	—	—	—	—	—	—	—	16.3	16.8	14.8	—
15–19 years	—	—	—	—	—	—	—	—	—	—	7.2	6.9	6.6	—
15–17 years	—	—	—	—	—	—	—	—	—	—	8.6	8.4	8.0	—
18–19 years	—	—	—	—	—	—	—	—	—	—	6.4	6.2	6.0	—
20–24 years	—	—	—	—	—	—	—	—	—	—	5.1	4.9	4.7	—
25–29 years	—	—	—	—	—	—	—	—	—	—	3.1	3.1	3.0	—
30–34 years	—	—	—	—	—	—	—	—	—	—	2.4	2.3	2.3	—
35–39 years	—	—	—	—	—	—	—	—	—	—	2.6	2.6	2.5	—
40 years and over	—	—	—	—	—	—	—	—	—	—	3.5	3.4	3.3	—

"—" Indicates data not available.

Notes: Data for 2000 and later years are based on decennial census 2000 data. Data for 1970 and 1975 exclude births that occurred in states not reporting prenatal care. The race groups, white, black, American Indian or Alaska Native, and Asian or Pacific Islander, include persons of Hispanic and non-Hispanic origin. Conversely, persons of Hispanic origin may be of any race. All data are based on the National Vital Statistics System.

[a]Excludes live births for whom trimester when prenatal care began is unknown.

[b]Trend data for Hispanics and non-Hispanics are affected by expansion of the reporting area for an Hispanic-origin item on the birth certificate and by immigration. These two factors affect numbers of events, composition of the Hispanic population, and maternal and infant health characteristics. The number of states in the reporting area increased from 22 in 1980, to 23 and the District of Columbia (DC) in 1983–87, 30 and DC in 1988, 47 and DC in 1989, 48 and DC in 1990, 49 and DC in 1991–92, and 50 and DC in 1993 and later years.

[c]Includes mothers of all races.

[d]Estimates for 2003 are preliminary.

SOURCE: "Table 1. Percent of All Births to Mothers Receiving Late or No Prenatal Care by Detailed Race and Hispanic Origin of Mother and Age, Selected Years 1970–2003," in *Late or No Prenatal Care*, Child Trends Data Bank, 2003, http://www.childtrendsdatabank.org/pdf/25_PDF.pdf (accessed June 9, 2005)

Breast-feeding

In *Breast-feeding: HHS Blueprint for Action on Breast-feeding* (2000), HHS's Office on Women's Health declared "that breast-feeding is the best method for feeding most newborns, and that breast-feeding is beneficial to the infant's and the mother's health." The report recommends that infants should be exclusively breast-fed for at least four months, and preferably for their entire first year of life. Extensive research has shown that human breast milk is superior to infant formulas. Breast-fed infants experience fewer and less severe cases of both infectious and noninfectious diseases, including diarrhea and respiratory and ear infections. This is because of the transfer of immunological agents from mother to child. In addition, human breast milk provides the most balanced nutrition for infants.

Breast-feeding is beneficial for mothers as well. Mothers who breast-feed experience less postpartum bleeding, earlier return to prepregnancy weight, and are at lowered risk for ovarian and premenopausal breast cancers. Furthermore, breast-feeding may promote mother–infant bonding.

Many more women are breast-feeding their infants than in previous years. According to *Women's Health USA 2004* (HHS, Health Resources and Services Administration, Maternal and Child Health Bureau, 2004), through the 1970s and early 1980s the prevalence of women who breast-fed their infants in the hospital rose, decreased in the later 1980s, and then rose again between 1990 and 2002. In 2002 breast-feeding rates in hospitals were 73.4% for white mothers, 70.7% for Hispanic mothers, 80.2% for Asian-American mothers, and 53.9% for African-American mothers. These rates were the highest recorded since data began being collected. Women in the western United States were significantly more likely to breast-feed in 2002 than women in other parts of the country. Mothers twenty-five and over and those with a college education were also more likely to breast-feed.

The percentage of women who were continuing to breast-feed at six months postpartum (33.2%) reached a record high in 2002. Almost half of Asian-American women (46.2%), 36% of white women, 32.7% of Hispanic women, and 19.2% of African-American women were still breast-feeding at that time.

Unfortunately, breast-feeding can be difficult for working mothers. Some employers are beginning to address this issue by providing lactation rooms where mothers can pump their breasts to store milk for their babies. Employees with on-site child care may be able to breast-feed their babies throughout the work day.

ALTERNATIVES TO CHILDBEARING

Contraceptive Use

Contraceptive use rose significantly during the 1990s. According to a fact sheet (*Contraceptive Use*, 2005) from the Alan Guttmacher Institute (AGI), nearly all women (98%) who have ever had sexual intercourse have used at least one contraceptive method, and 62% of the sixty-two million women of childbearing age currently use a contraceptive method. About 31% of the sixty-two million women do not need contraception because they are infertile, pregnant, have just had a baby, are trying to become pregnant, or are not sexually active. Almost nine out of ten (89%) fertile, sexually active women who do not want to become pregnant use contraception. During the 1999–2002 period, 79% of women used contraception at their first intercourse, compared with 43% in the 1970s.

In 2002, among women who used contraception, 64% used reversible methods, such as condoms and birth control pills. The birth control pill was the most widely used form of contraception (used by 30.6% of contraceptive users), followed by surgery to block the fallopian tubes (27%). Sterilization is most likely to be used by women over thirty-four, women who have been married, women with less than a high school education, and low-income women. African-American and Hispanic women are more likely than white women to have undergone sterilization, whereas white women are more likely to use oral contraceptives. Although most medical plans cover prenatal care, delivery, abortions, and sterilization, most do not cover the costs of contraception other than sterilization.

Among women ages forty to forty-four who practiced contraception, 50% have been sterilized and 18% had a male partner who had had a vasectomy. Among teenage

women who used contraception, 53% (more than 1.5 million) used birth control pills, and 27% used condoms.

Abortion

DECLINING ABORTION RATES. Abortion has been a legal option for American women since the Supreme Court ruling in *Roe v. Wade* (410 U.S. 113, 1973). The number of abortions generally increased from 1973 until they reached a high in 1990, when the CDC reported 1.4 million abortions and the AGI estimated that there were 1.6 million. (See Table 6.11.) From 1990 to 2001 the number of legal abortions in the United States generally declined, to about 853,000 in 2001. The ratio of legal abortions to live births dropped from 35.9 abortions per one hundred live births in 1980 to 24.6 abortions per one hundred births in 2001.

The youngest pregnant teenagers were most likely to choose abortion in 2001 (74.4 abortions per one hundred live births). Among teens ages fifteen to nineteen, there were 36.6 abortions per one hundred live births in 2001, down from 71.4 in 1980. The ratio of abortions to live births declined with age up to the thirty-five to thirty-nine age group. Among women ages forty and over there were 30.4 abortions per one hundred live births in 2001, compared with 80.7 per one hundred live births among women of the same age in 1980. Women in their forties may be concerned about increased health risks for the mother and child because of maternal age, although the development of methods such as amniocentesis that enable physicians to test the fetus for abnormalities has alleviated some of these concerns. In addition, women over forty may not want to begin raising children, particularly if they already have older children. According to a 2003 fact sheet called *Women Who Have Abortions* from the National Abortion Federation (NAF), an organization of abortion providers, by the age of forty-five, 35% of American women will have had an abortion.

Among unmarried women the ratio of abortions to live births declined from 161 per one hundred births in 1975 to 57.2 in 2001, reflecting the increasing trend toward childbearing among unmarried women. (See Table 6.11.) Among women who had already had three or more children, the ratio of abortions to live births also declined significantly from highs in 1973 and 1975.

According to the CDC, a number of factors have contributed to the dropping abortion rate. *Abortion Surveillance—United States, 2000* (*Morbidity and Mortality Weekly Report*, Vol. 52, No. SS-12, November 28, 2003) states:

> The overall declines . . . may reflect multiple factors, including a decrease in the number of unintended pregnancies; a shift in the age distribution of women toward the older and less fertile ages; reduced or limited access to abortion services, including the passage of abortion laws that affect adolescents (e.g., parental consent or notification laws and mandatory waiting periods); and

TABLE 6.11

Legal abortions and legal abortion ratios, according to selected patient characteristics, selected years, 1973–2001

[Data are based on reporting by state health departments and by hospitals and other medical facilities]

Characteristic	1973	1975	1980	1985	1990	1995	1997	1998[a]	1999[a]	2000[b]	2001[b]
					Number of legal abortions reported in thousands						
Centers for Disease Control and Prevention (CDC)	616	855	1,298	1,329	1,429	1,211	1,186	884	862	857	853
Alan Guttmacher Institute[c]	745	1,034	1,554	1,589	1,609	1,359	1,335	1,319	1,315	1,313	—
					Abortions per 100 live births[d]						
Total	**19.6**	**27.2**	**35.9**	**35.4**	**34.4**	**31.1**	**30.6**	**26.4**	**25.6**	**24.5**	**24.6**
Age											
Under 15 years	123.7	119.3	139.7	137.6	81.8	66.4	72.9	75.0	70.9	70.8	74.4
15–19 years	53.9	54.2	71.4	68.8	51.1	39.9	40.7	39.1	37.5	36.1	36.6
20–24 years	29.4	28.9	39.5	38.6	37.8	34.8	34.5	32.9	31.6	30.0	30.4
25–29 years	20.7	19.2	23.7	21.7	21.8	22.0	22.4	21.6	20.8	19.8	20.0
30–34 years	28.0	25.0	23.7	19.9	19.0	16.4	16.1	15.7	15.2	14.5	14.7
35–39 years	45.1	42.2	41.0	33.6	27.3	22.3	20.9	20.0	19.3	18.1	18.0
40 years and over	68.4	66.8	80.7	62.3	50.6	38.5	35.2	33.8	32.9	30.1	30.4
Race											
White[e]	32.6	27.7	33.2	27.7	25.8	20.3	19.4	18.9	17.7	16.7	16.5
Black or African American[f]	42.0	47.6	54.3	47.2	53.7	53.1	54.3	51.2	52.9	50.3	49.1
Hispanic origin[g]											
Hispanic or Latino	—	—	—	—	—	27.1	26.8	27.3	26.1	22.5	23.0
Not Hispanic or Latino	—	—	—	—	—	27.9	27.2	27.1	25.2	23.3	23.2
Marital status											
Married	7.6	9.6	10.5	8.0	8.7	7.6	7.4	7.1	7.0	6.5	6.5
Unmarried	139.8	161.0	147.6	117.4	86.3	64.5	65.9	62.7	60.4	57.0	57.2
Previous live births[h]											
0	43.7	38.4	45.7	45.1	36.0	28.6	26.4	25.5	24.3	22.6	26.4
1	23.5	22.0	20.2	21.6	22.7	22.0	22.3	21.4	20.6	19.4	18.0
2	36.8	36.8	29.5	29.9	31.5	30.6	31.0	30.0	29.0	27.4	25.5
3	46.9	47.7	29.8	18.2	30.1	30.7	31.1	30.5	29.8	28.5	26.4
4 or more[i]	44.7	43.5	24.3	21.5	26.6	23.7	24.5	24.3	24.2	23.7	21.9
					Percent distribution[j]						
Total	**100.0**	**100.0**	**100.0**	**100.0**	**100.0**	**100.0**	**100.0**	**100.0**	**100.0**	**100.0**	**100.0**
Period of gestation											
Under 9 weeks	36.1	44.6	51.7	50.3	51.6	54.0	55.4	55.7	57.6	58.1	59.1
9–10 weeks	29.4	28.4	26.2	26.6	25.3	23.1	22.0	21.5	20.2	19.8	19.0
11–12 weeks	17.9	14.9	12.2	12.5	11.7	10.9	10.7	10.9	10.2	10.2	10.0
13–15 weeks	6.9	5.0	5.1	5.9	6.4	6.3	6.2	6.4	6.2	6.2	6.2
16–20 weeks	8.0	6.1	3.9	3.9	4.0	4.3	4.3	4.1	4.3	4.3	4.3
21 weeks and over	1.7	1.0	0.9	0.8	1.0	1.4	1.4	1.4	1.5	1.4	1.4
Previous induced abortions											
0	—	81.9	67.6	60.1	57.1	55.1	53.4	53.8	53.7	54.7	55.5
1	—	14.9	23.5	25.7	26.9	26.9	27.5	27.0	27.1	26.4	25.8
2	—	2.5	6.6	9.8	10.1	10.9	11.5	11.4	11.5	11.3	11.0
3 or more	—	0.7	2.3	4.4	5.9	7.1	7.6	7.8	7.7	7.6	7.7

— Data not available.

[a]In 1998 and 1999 Alaska, California, New Hampshire, and Oklahoma did not report abortion data to CDC. For comparison, in 1997 the 48 corresponding reporting areas reported about 900,000 legal abortions.

[b]In 2000 and 2001 Alaska, California, and New Hampshire did not report abortion data to CDC.

[c]No surveys were conducted in 1983, 1986, 1989, 1990, 1993, 1994, 1997, or 1998. Data for these years were estimated by interpolation.

[d]For calculation of ratios by each characteristic, abortions with characteristic unknown were distributed in proportion to abortions with characteristic known.

[e]For 1989 and later years, white race includes women of Hispanic ethnicity.

[f]Before 1989 black race includes races other than white.

[g]Reporting area increased from 20–22 states, the District of Columbia (DC), and New York City (NYC) in 1991–95 to 31 states and NYC in 2001. California, Florida, Illinois, and Arizona, states with large Hispanic populations, do not report Hispanic ethnicity.

[h]For 1973–75 data indicate number of living children.

[i]For 1975 data refer to four previous live births, not four or more. For five or more previous live births, the ratio is 47.3.

[j]For calculation of percent distribution by each characteristic, abortions with characteristic unknown were excluded.

SOURCE: "Table 16. Legal Abortions and Legal Abortion Ratios, according to Selected Patient Characteristics: United States, Selected Years 1973–2001," in *Health, United States, 2004*, U.S. Department of Health and Human Services, Centers for Disease Control and Prevention, National Center for Health Statistics, September 2004, http://www.cdc.gov/nchs/data/hus/hus04trend.pdf (accessed June 9, 2005)

changes in contraceptive practices, including an increased use of contraception, such as condoms, and, among young women, of long-acting hormonal contraceptive methods that were introduced in the early 1990s.

According to the CDC, slightly more than half (55.5%) of the women who chose abortion in 2001 had not had a previous abortion. (See Table 6.11.) This was about the same percentage as in 1995 (55.1%). The majority of abortions in 2001 (59.1%) were performed when the fetus was less than nine weeks old. Only 1.4% of abortions that year occurred after more than twenty weeks of gestation. Most abortions were obtained by unmarried women; in this group, there were 57.2 abortions per every one hundred live births. Conversely, among married women, there were 6.5 abortions per every one hundred live births.

ABORTION DRUGS. Mifepristone, formerly known as RU-486, is an abortion-inducing drug that has been used in Europe and China since the late 1980s. In September 2000 the U.S. Food and Drug Administration approved mifepristone for use in the United States. According to the NAF, mifepristone, when used in combination with the drug misoprostol, is 95 to 98% effective in inducing abortion up to sixty-three days after the start of the last menstrual period. Some women are now choosing this method of "medical abortion," as opposed to more traditional surgical abortions. According to the CDC, there were 6,895 medical abortions in 2002.

REPRODUCTIVE RIGHTS. Judicial rulings since *Roe v. Wade* have weakened abortion rights in at least some states. As of May 2005, according to the AGI, thirty-three states and the District of Columbia followed minimal federal guidelines to fund through Medicaid only those abortions in which the pregnancy resulted from rape or incest or the woman's life was in danger. The U.S. Supreme Court has upheld the right of states to require parental consent before a minor can obtain an abortion (which thirty-three states did as of May 2005), provided that the minor has the right to appeal in court. These restrictions have made it more difficult for some women to obtain abortions.

Particularly controversial is the procedure known as partial-birth abortion, or Intact Dilation and Extraction (D&X), in which a fetus is delivered to the point where only the head remains inside the womb; a physician then pierces the back of the skull to remove the brain. Partial birth abortion accounts for less than 1% of all abortions performed and is typically used only in cases where the mother's life is in danger. In *Stenberg v. Carhart* in 2002, the Supreme Court struck down a Nebraska law that criminalized partial-birth abortions because it did not include protections for women's health. In 2003 President George W. Bush signed into law a bill banning these abortion procedures. Although President Bill Clinton had vetoed this ban twice, a January 2003 Gallup poll indicated that 70% of the public favored the bill. Opponents of the bill claim it violates the rights provided by *Roe v. Wade*. They also criticize the fact that the ban allows no exceptions. Some believe the bill is the first step toward the outlawing of all abortions. Others believe the ban protects

the lives of viable fetuses (those that can survive outside the womb). One day after the bill was signed into law, federal judges in New York and California blocked it.

In addition, by 2004 some pharmacists were refusing to fill prescriptions for either the "morning after pill" or birth control pills, stating that dispensing such medication violated their moral beliefs. In some cases pharmacists refused to release the prescription to another pharmacy, preventing women from obtaining prescribed medicines until they could get a new prescription. The *Washington Post* reported cases in California, Washington, Georgia, Illinois, Louisiana, Massachusetts, Texas, New Hampshire, Ohio, and North Carolina, and the trend was spreading. The refusals of basic health care to women, in the opinion of Rachel Laser of the National Women's Law Center, constituted sex discrimination and represented the growing conservative political climate in the United States (Rob Stein, "Pharmacists' Rights at Front of New Debate," WashingtonPost.com, March 28, 2005).

Childlessness

With the development of fertility drugs and assisted reproductive techniques, many previously infertile couples are now able to have children. Nevertheless, as is shown in Table 6.12, women are not only postponing childbearing but are increasingly choosing not to have children. In 2002, among women ages forty to forty-four, 15.8% had not had at least one live birth, compared with 16.6% of women in that age group in 1996–97 and only 9% in 1980. The percentage of women ages thirty-five to thirty-nine who had not had at least one live birth dropped from a high of nearly 19% from 1990 to 1996 to 17.2% in 2002.

Marriage is no longer synonymous with childbearing. Although fewer women are marrying, more unmarried women are having children and more married women are choosing not to have children. According to the Census Bureau, in 2002, 77.2% of never-married women and 18.7% of currently married women ages fifteen to forty-four had never had children. (See Table 6.4.) Of all women in that age group, 43.5% had no children. About 26.7 million women between the ages of fifteen and forty-four were childless in the United States in 2002.

Adoption

No public agency or private organization collects current, comprehensive adoption statistics. In part this is because, at least until recent years, it was widely believed that adoptions should be kept indefinitely secret. Legal records of adoptions are sealed, and in the past many children were never even told that they were adopted.

TABLE 6.12

Women 15–44 years of age who have not had at least one live birth, by age, selected years, 1960–2002

[Data are based on birth certificates]

Year*	15–19 years	20–24 years	25–29 years	30–34 years	35–39 years	40–44 years
			Percent of women			
1960	91.4	47.5	20.0	14.2	12.0	15.1
1965	92.7	51.4	19.7	11.7	11.4	11.0
1970	93.0	57.0	24.4	11.8	9.4	10.6
1975	92.6	62.5	31.1	15.2	9.6	8.8
1980	93.4	66.2	38.9	19.7	12.5	9.0
1985	93.7	67.7	41.5	24.6	15.4	11.7
1986	93.8	68.0	42.0	25.1	16.1	12.2
1987	93.8	68.2	42.5	25.5	16.9	12.6
1988	93.8	68.4	43.0	25.7	17.7	13.0
1989	93.7	68.4	43.3	25.9	18.2	13.5
1990	93.3	68.3	43.5	25.9	18.5	13.9
1991	93.0	67.9	43.6	26.0	18.7	14.5
1992	92.7	67.3	43.7	26.0	18.8	15.2
1993	92.6	66.7	43.8	26.1	18.8	15.8
1994	92.6	66.1	43.9	26.2	18.7	16.2
1995	92.5	65.5	44.0	26.2	18.6	16.5
1996	92.5	65.0	43.8	26.2	18.5	16.6
1997	92.8	64.9	43.5	26.2	18.4	16.6
1998	93.1	65.1	43.0	26.1	18.2	16.5
1999	93.4	65.5	42.5	26.1	18.1	16.4
2000	93.7	66.0	42.1	25.9	17.9	16.2
2001	94.0	66.5	41.6	25.4	17.6	16.0
2002	94.3	66.5	41.3	24.8	17.2	15.8

*As of January 1.

Notes: Data are based on cohort fertility. Percents are derived from the cumulative childbearing experience of cohorts of women, up to the ages specified. Data on births are adjusted for underregistration and population estimates are corrected for underregistration and misstatement of age. Beginning in 1970 births to persons who were not residents of the 50 states and the District of Columbia are excluded.

SOURCE: "Table 5. Women 15–44 Years of Age Who Have Not Had at Least 1 Live Birth, by Age: United States, Selected Years 1960–2002," in *Health, United States, 2004*, U.S. Department of Health and Human Services, Centers for Disease Control and Prevention, National Center for Health Statistics, September 2004, http://www.cdc.gov/nchs/data/hus/hus04trend.pdf (accessed June 9, 2005)

Birth mothers never again heard of their children after relinquishing them for adoption.

According to Adam Pertman (*Adoption Nation: How the Adoption Revolution Is Transforming America*, New York: Basic Books, 2000), there are estimated to be five to six million adoptees in the United States. This is far higher than previous estimates. The National Adoption Information Clearinghouse (NAIC) estimates that during the 1990s there were about 120,000 adoptions per year, up from a low of about 50,000 adoptions in 1944 and down from a high of about 175,000 in 1970. As of 1993 there were estimated to be one million children living with adoptive parents in the United States, with 2 to 4% of American families having at least one adopted child.

The NAIC reported that in 2000 and 2001, about 127,000 children were adopted annually in the United States, a number that had remained fairly constant since 1987 ("How Many Children Were Adopted in 2000 and 2001?" U.S. Department of Health and Human Services, 2004). Although the demand for adoption has remained stable, the adoption rate has fallen significantly since 1973. This is because there are far fewer infants—at least healthy white infants—available for adoption in the United States than in the past. The decline in the pregnancy rate, particularly among teenagers, the availability of abortion, and the increased numbers of unmarried women who are choosing to bear and raise children have all contributed to the reduced number of infants being placed for adoption. Most adoptions were either intercountry adoptions or done through public agencies; less than half of all adoptions were of infants through private agencies.

Unmarried women are not being pressured into relinquishing their babies, at least to the extent that they were in the past. According to the NAIC, from 1952 to 1972, 8.7% of all births to never-married mothers, 19.3% of births to never-married white mothers, and 1.5% of births to never-married African-American mothers were relinquished for adoption. From 1973 to 1981 the rate fell to 4.1% of all never-married mothers, 7.6% of never-married white mothers, and 0.2% of never-married African-American mothers. From 1982 to 1988 (the most recent data provided by the NAIC), 2% of all unmarried mothers, 3.2% of white unmarried mothers, and 1.1% of African-American unmarried mothers placed their children for adoption.

FOSTER CARE ADOPTIONS. The Adoption and Safe Families Act of 1997 included provisions for collecting state data on children in foster care and public adoptions, so this is one area in which more recent statistics are available. From 1986 to 1995 there was a 72% increase in the number of children in foster care; but public agencies have been placing more children in the homes of relatives, and in many cases the relatives adopt these children. As of September 30, 2002, an estimated 532,000 children were in foster care in the United States. The median age of the children was 10.8 years. Slightly more boys (52%) than girls (48%) were in foster care. Most children in foster care were non-Hispanic white (46%), 28% were non-Hispanic African-American, and 17% were Hispanic. About 126,000 of these children were waiting to be adopted. In fiscal year 2002, of the estimated 281,000 children who exited foster care, 17% (almost 49,000 children) were adopted and 10% went to live with a relative.

INTERNATIONAL ADOPTION. International adoptions first became common after the Korean War, when Americans began adopting South Korean children who had been fathered by American GIs. Most international adoptions were from South Korea until the 1990s, when China began allowing the foreign adoption of girls. With the breakup of the Soviet Union, Americans began adopting Russian children in large numbers. The U.S. State Department tracks the numbers of immigrant visas issued to orphans coming to the United States. These children are intended for adoption by U.S. citizens. Though not all may eventually be adopted, some organizations use these numbers to represent total numbers of foreign adoptions by U.S. citizens. The number of such visas increased from 4,472 in 1992 to almost 22,000 in 2004. Of the children granted visas in 2004, 7,044 were from China, 5,865 were from Russia, 3,264 were from Guatemala, 1,716 were from South Korea, and 826 were from Kazakhstan.

ADOPTION BY SINGLE MOTHERS. Both domestic and international adoptions by single parents increased from an estimated 0.5–4% in the 1970s to an estimated 8–34% in the 1980s. The NAIC noted that as of 1993 (the latest data available), the increase was continuing. As of the same year, most single adoptive parents were women who had not been foster parents to the child they adopted. Single adopters were more likely to adopt "special needs" children—those who are older, minority, and/or handicapped.

ADOPTION BY GAYS AND LESBIANS. A 1999–2000 survey conducted by the Evan B. Donaldson Adoption Institute (David M. Brodzinsky et al., *Adoption by Lesbians and Gays: A National Survey of Adoption Agency Policies, Practices, and Attitudes*, October 29, 2003) indicated that 60% of the nation's adoption agencies accept applications from gays and lesbians. Approximately 39% placed at least one child with a known gay or lesbian applicant (though the number is likely higher, as less than half of agencies asked applicants

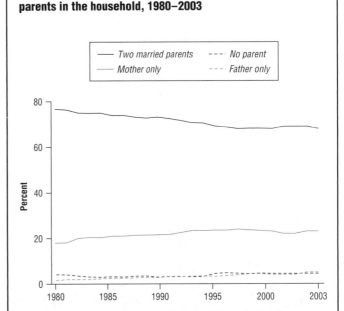

FIGURE 6.3

Percentage of children under age 18, by presence of married parents in the household, 1980–2003

Note: The category "two married parents" includes children who live with a biological, step, or adoptive parent who is married with his or her spouse present. If a second parent is present and not married to the first parent, then the child is identified as living with a single parent.

SOURCE: "Figure 1. Percentage of Children Under Age 18 by Presence of Married Parents in the Household, 1980–2003," in *America's Children in Brief: Key National Indicators of Well-Being, 2004*, Federal Interagency Forum on Child and Family Statistics, July 2004, http://www.childstats.gov/americaschildren/pdf/ac04brief.pdf (accessed June 10, 2005)

about their sexual orientation). About half of the agencies (47%) routinely informed birth parents when placing a child with a gay adoptive parent. About one-fourth of the agencies said some birth parents had objected to such a placement, while others specifically asked that their child not be placed in a gay household. In August 2003 the American Bar Association issued a position supporting state laws and decisions allowing unmarried couples of any sexual orientation to adopt children together.

CHANGING ATTITUDES TOWARD ADOPTION. Since 1997 adoptive families have been able to take a federal tax credit to help cover adoption expenses. More employers are offering adoption benefits to their employees, often in the form of cash to help cover medical costs for the birth mother and legal and other adoption fees. Employers are also beginning to grant the same leaves to new adoptive parents that they grant to birth parents.

FAMILY AND WORK ARRANGEMENTS FOR MOTHERS AND CHILDREN

Single Mothers

In 2003, 23% of children lived with a single mother, and 5% lived with a single father. (See Figure 6.3.)

FIGURE 6.4

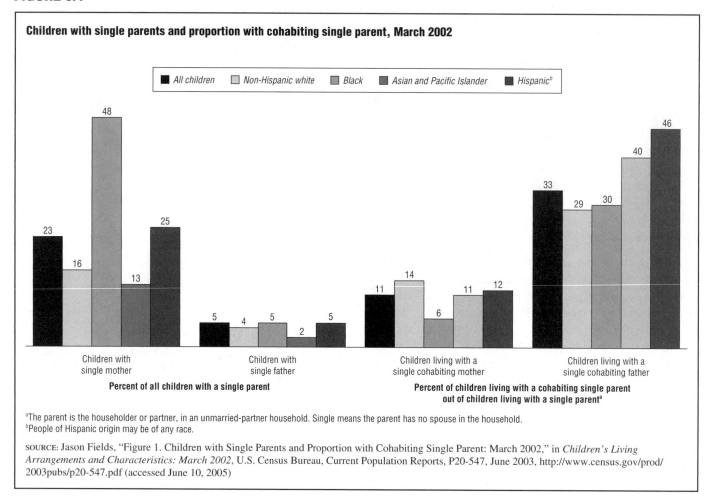

Children with single parents and proportion with cohabiting single parent, March 2002

Legend: ■ All children □ Non-Hispanic white ▨ Black ▨ Asian and Pacific Islander ■ Hispanic[b]

Children with single mother: 23, 16, 48, 13, 25
Children with single father: 5, 4, 5, 2, 5

Percent of all children with a single parent

Children living with a single cohabiting mother: 11, 14, 6, 11, 12
Children living with a single cohabiting father: 33, 29, 30, 40, 46

Percent of children living with a cohabiting single parent out of children living with a single parent[a]

[a]The parent is the householder or partner, in an unmarried-partner household. Single means the parent has no spouse in the household.
[b]People of Hispanic origin may be of any race.

SOURCE: Jason Fields, "Figure 1. Children with Single Parents and Proportion with Cohabiting Single Parent: March 2002," in *Children's Living Arrangements and Characteristics: March 2002*, U.S. Census Bureau, Current Population Reports, P20-547, June 2003, http://www.census.gov/prod/2003pubs/p20-547.pdf (accessed June 10, 2005)

Among non-Hispanic white children in 2002, 16% lived with their mothers only, compared with 48% of African-American children and 25% of Hispanic children. About 6% of African-American children and 14% of non-Hispanic white children living with single mothers also had the mother's partner present. (See Figure 6.4.) Although the percentage of children living with two married parents declined from 1980 to 1995, it remained stable between 1995 and 2003. In 2002, 77% of non-Hispanic white children lived with two married parents, compared with 38% of African-American children and 65% of Hispanic children.

Working Mothers

The majority of American mothers are in the labor force. Figure 6.5 shows that in 2004, 77.3% of women with children ages six to seventeen years worked, compared with 93.1% of men; 61.8% of women with children under six years worked, compared with 95.4% of men. Table 6.13 shows that in 2004, 57.5% of mothers with children under three years old worked,

and 67.7% of them worked full-time; 52.9% of women with children under one year worked, and 65.7% of them worked full-time. Single women with young children were more likely than married women to be in the labor force.

In 2002 a mother's educational attainment was correlated with the likelihood that she was employed full-time. Among mothers with graduate or professional degrees and children under one year, 46.2% were employed full-time, compared with 31.6% of mothers with only a high school diploma. (See Table 6.14.)

Older and more educated women are more likely to have greater career commitments and to have salaries that justify continuing to work outside the home. Child care may also be more accessible and more affordable for these women. But women with more than one child are less likely to be employed. (See Table 6.14.) Not only is it more difficult to raise multiple children while working, but arranging and affording child care for more than one child may be an obstacle.

FIGURE 6.5

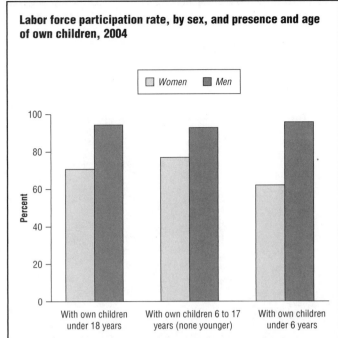

Labor force participation rate, by sex, and presence and age of own children, 2004

SOURCE: "Labor Force Participation Rate by Sex, and Presence and Age of Own Children, 2004 Annual Averages," in "Labor Force Participation of Mothers and Fathers," *Monthly Labor Review*, U.S. Department of Labor, Bureau of Labor Statistics, June 10, 2005, http://www.bls.gov/opub/ted/2005/jun/wk1/art05.htm (accessed June 15, 2005)

TABLE 6.13

Employment status of mothers with own children under three years old, by single year of youngest child and marital status, 2003–04

[Numbers in thousands]

| | Civilian noninstitutional population | Civilian labor force | | | | | | Unemployed | |
| | | Total | Percent of population | Employed | | | | | |
				Total	Percent of population	Full-time workers[a]	Part-time workers[b]	Number	Percent of labor force
2003									
Total mothers									
With own children under 3 years old	9,450	5,563	58.9	5,115	54.1	3,430	1,685	446	8.0
2 years	2,987	1,896	63.5	1,752	58.7	1,205	547	143	7.5
1 year	3,353	1,997	59.6	1,842	54.9	1,223	619	154	7.7
Under 1 year	3,110	1,670	53.7	1,521	48.9	1,002	519	149	8.9
Married, spouse present									
With own children under 3 years old	7,165	4,068	56.8	3,872	54.0	2,529	1,342	197	4.8
2 years	2,243	1,350	60.2	1,281	57.1	853	428	69	5.1
1 year	2,541	1,458	57.4	1,395	54.9	906	488	64	4.4
Under 1 year	2,381	1,260	52.9	1,196	50.2	770	426	64	5.1
Other marital status[c]									
With own children under 3 years old	2,287	1,495	65.4	1,244	54.4	902	341	250	16.7
2 years	744	546	73.4	471	63.3	352	118	75	13.7
1 year	813	539	66.3	448	55.1	317	131	91	16.9
Under 1 year	730	410	56.2	325	44.5	233	92	84	20.5
2004									
Total mothers									
With own children under 3 years old	9,345	5,377	57.5	4,964	53.1	3,360	1,604	414	7.7
2 years	2,813	1,746	62.1	1,630	57.9	1,152	477	116	6.6
1 year	3,273	1,906	58.2	1,759	53.7	1,172	587	147	7.7
Under 1 year	3,259	1,725	52.9	1,575	48.3	1,035	540	151	8.7
Married, spouse present									
With own children under 3 years old	7,071	3,910	55.3	3,740	52.9	2,513	1,227	170	4.4
2 years	2,111	1,246	59.0	1,200	56.8	839	361	46	3.7
1 year	2,519	1,401	55.6	1,337	53.1	877	459	65	4.6
Under 1 year	2,441	1,262	51.7	1,203	49.3	797	406	59	4.7
Other marital status[c]									
With own children under 3 years old	2,274	1,467	64.5	1,224	53.8	847	377	243	16.6
2 years	702	499	71.1	430	61.2	314	116	70	13.9
1 year	754	505	66.9	422	56.0	295	127	82	16.3
Under 1 year	818	463	56.6	372	45.4	238	134	91	19.7

[a]Usually work 35 hours or more a week at all jobs.
[b]Usually work less than 35 hours a week at all jobs.
[c]Includes never-married, divorced, separated, and widowed persons.

SOURCE: "Table 6. Employment Status of Mothers with Own Children Under 3 Years Old by Single Year of Youngest Child and Marital Status, 2003–04 Averages," in "Employment Characteristics of Families in 2004," Press Release, U.S. Department of Labor, Bureau of Labor Statistics, June 9, 2005, http://www.bls.gov/news.release/pdf/famee.pdf (accessed June 9, 2005)

TABLE 6.14

Labor force participation among mothers 15–44 years old, by fertility status and selected characteristics, June 2002

[Numbers in thousands. Limited to women with at least one child ever born.]

Characteristic	Mothers who had a child in the last year					Mothers who did not have a child in the last year				
	Number of mothers	Percent in labor force				Number of mothers	Percent in labor force			
		Total	Full-time	Part-time	Unemployed		Total	Full-time	Part-time	Unemployed
Total	3,766	54.6	33.8	15.7	5.0	30,905	72.0	51.3	16.4	4.3
Age										
15 to 19 years	549	38.9	12.6	18.4	7.9	318	56.9	23.7	20.1	13.0
20 to 24 years	872	54.7	32.3	14.5	7.9	2,327	66.4	43.5	15.1	7.8
25 to 29 years	897	54.0	38.5	11.9	3.6	4,156	69.0	47.1	16.2	5.8
30 to 44 years	1,449	60.9	39.9	17.9	3.1	24,104	73.2	53.1	16.5	3.6
Children ever born and age of woman										
On child	1,415	59.8	37.0	15.3	7.5	9,298	75.2	56.4	14.7	4.1
15 to 19 years	272	48.3	15.4	20.7	12.2	242	56.9	23.8	19.1	13.9
20 to 24 years	438	58.3	34.6	12.8	10.8	1,455	68.2	44.7	16.8	6.7
25 to 29 years	306	59.6	41.0	14.6	4.0	1,746	76.1	55.9	16.3	3.9
30 to 44 years	399	69.5	51.3	15.0	3.2	5,855	77.5	60.8	13.6	3.1
Two or more children	2,351	51.5	31.9	16.0	3.5	21,607	70.6	49.1	17.1	4.4
15 to 19 years	277	29.7	9.9	16.1	3.7	76	56.7	23.4	23.1	10.2
20 to 24 years	433	51.0	30.0	16.2	4.9	872	63.3	41.6	12.1	9.6
25 to 29 years	591	51.1	37.2	10.5	3.4	2,410	64.0	40.7	16.1	7.1
30 to 44 years	1,050	57.6	35.6	19.0	3.0	18,249	71.9	50.7	17.5	3.7
Race and ethnicity										
White	2,958	53.8	33.0	16.9	3.9	24,230	71.5	49.4	18.3	3.8
White non-Hispanic	2,262	56.8	34.0	19.5	3.4	19,516	73.2	50.1	19.7	3.4
Black	571	57.4	36.7	10.0	10.6	4,823	76.4	60.0	9.1	7.3
Asian and Pacific Islander	181	51.1	35.2	11.7	4.1	1,426	66.3	52.2	10.7	3.4
Hispanic (of any race)	750	45.2	29.9	8.7	6.6	5,115	64.2	46.3	12.6	5.2
Marital status										
Married-husband present	2,382	55.4	36.4	16.3	2.7	20,297	69.1	48.0	18.3	2.8
Married-husband absent, separated										
divorced, or widowed	266	62.9	44.8	9.8	8.4	5,848	80.3	62.0	11.9	6.5
Never married	1,118	51.0	25.8	16.0	9.2	4,760	73.8	51.9	13.9	8.0
Educational attainment										
Not a high school graduate	812	32.2	13.0	11.0	8.1	4,590	55.4	34.4	14.0	7.0
High school, 4 years	1,005	56.1	31.6	17.4	7.1	10,527	73.0	53.0	15.0	5.1
College, 1 or more years	1,949	63.2	43.7	16.9	2.6	15,789	76.1	55.1	18.1	3.0
No degree	750	60.8	41.4	16.0	3.4	5,983	75.8	54.5	17.0	4.4
Associate degree	221	70.0	43.7	19.4	7.0	3,205	80.0	55.6	20.6	3.8
Bachelor's degree	683	63.2	45.0	17.0	1.2	4,975	73.3	54.1	17.7	1.5
Graduate or professional degree	294	64.1	46.2	17.0	0.9	1,626	78.2	59.1	18.3	0.8
Annual family income										
Under $10,000	355	50.1	20.7	14.1	15.4	2,167	55.0	25.8	16.5	12.7
$10,000 to $19,999	472	43.2	26.2	12.7	4.4	2,992	66.2	42.7	16.0	7.5
$20,000 to $24,999	215	48.5	26.8	13.0	8.7	1,853	70.9	53.3	12.6	5.0
$25,000 to $29,999	194	42.7	22.9	13.9	5.9	1,819	72.2	52.4	12.3	7.4
$30,000 to $34,999	264	57.1	41.3	10.6	5.2	1,768	74.1	54.5	15.7	3.9
$35,000 to $49,999	457	60.9	37.2	18.9	4.8	4,371	75.2	54.6	16.7	3.9
$50,000 to $74,999	554	58.6	38.3	17.1	3.2	5,429	78.8	59.2	17.5	2.2
$75,000 and over	826	65.0	44.2	18.8	2.0	6,448	75.5	53.6	20.1	1.8
Not ascertained	428	45.9	27.7	14.9	3.3	4,056	66.6	50.5	13.0	3.2
Nativity										
Native born	3,129	57.2	35.0	17.4	4.9	25,787	74.4	52.9	17.2	4.3
Foreign born	637	41.6	28.3	7.8	5.6	5,118	59.8	43.2	12.5	4.1

SOURCE: Barbara Downs, "Table 6. Labor Force Participation among Mothers 15 to 44 Years Old by Fertility Status and Selected Characteristics: June 2002," in *Fertility of American Women: June 2002*, U.S. Census Bureau, Current Population Reports, P20-548, October 2003, http://www.census.gov/prod/2003pubs/p20-548.pdf (accessed June 10, 2005)

CHAPTER 7
CHILD CARE AND ELDER CARE

Far more women than ever before, including mothers with infants and small children, have entered the labor force and are working full-time outside of the home. Women are increasingly pursuing education and embarking on careers that may require long hours and extensive travel. Unprecedented numbers of women are raising children on their own. But one element of women's lives has not changed: women remain the primary caregivers for both children and elderly family members.

WORKING MOTHERS

How Many American Mothers Work Outside the Home?

In 2004, 70.4% of women with children under the age of eighteen were in the labor force, and all but 5.5% of women in the labor force were employed. (See Table 3.3 in Chapter 3.) Overall, 66.5% of American women with children younger than eighteen were working, and 68.6% of those worked full-time. More than three-quarters (77.1%) of women with children under eighteen who did not live with a spouse were in the labor force; 69.6% were working. More than four-fifths (80.9%) of these employed women were working full-time.

Among all mothers with children under the age of six in 2004, 57.4% were employed and 69.8% of them worked full-time. (See Table 7.1.) In 2004, 53.1% of all mothers with children under age three were employed, and 67.7% of these women were employed full-time. (See Table 6.13 in Chapter 6.) Of mothers with children under one year old in 2004, 48.3% were employed, and 65.7% of these mothers were employed full-time. This is a substantial increase from earlier decades. In 1978, according to the Women's Research and Education Institute, only 44% of mothers with children under age six and 39.4% of mothers with children under age three were in the labor force. But the labor force participation rate for mothers of children under age eighteen has been declining

since 2000 ("Employment Characteristics of Families Summary," Bureau of Labor Statistics, June 9, 2005).

Juggling Work and Child Care

Child-care arrangements are a major concern for working mothers, at least until their children reach about the age of twelve, since full-time working mothers may need before- and after-school care for their school-age children. Part-time workers and those with irregular working hours require child-care arrangements that fit their work schedules and may often need to make last-minute arrangements. Child-care arrangements must be made for school closures and vacations. Leaving work to give birth, to care for a newborn, or to nurse a sick child may cost a mother her job. According to a May 2001 fact sheet by the Institute for Women's Policy Research ("Today's Women Worker: Shut Out of Yesterday's Unemployment Insurance System"), many states consider child care to be a "voluntary" reason for leaving a job, so mothers who are forced to quit work to care for a child may not be eligible for unemployment insurance.

Summer vacations present a big challenge for working mothers. According to the Urban Institute, more than one in ten school-age children regularly take care of themselves during the summer; 11% of six- to twelve-year-olds regularly spend time in self-care ("Summer Child Care Arrangements," The Urban Institute, April 29, 2004). About one-third of these children are in organized child care during the summer months; 24% spend time in summer camps, and 6% attend summer school. Another one-third (34%) regularly spend time in the care of relatives. Smaller percentages spend time in family child care (6%) or with nannies or babysitters (8%). A higher proportion of low-income children (14%) than higher-income children (2%) attend summer school and are also in the care of relatives (45% of low-income children and 27% of

TABLE 7.1

Employment status of the population, by sex, marital status, and presence and age of own children under 18, 2003–04 annual averages

[Numbers in thousands]

Characteristic	2003			2004		
	Total	Men	Women	Total	Men	Women
With own children under 18 years						
Civilian noninstitutional population	64,932	28,402	36,530	64,758	28,272	36,486
Civilian labor force	52,727	26,739	25,988	52,288	26,607	25,681
Participation rate	81.2	94.1	71.1	80.7	94.1	70.4
Employed	50,103	25,638	24,466	49,957	25,696	24,261
Employment-population ratio	77.2	90.3	67.0	77.1	90.9	66.5
Full-time workers[a]	42,880	24,762	18,118	42,758	24,794	17,964
Part-time workers[b]	7,223	876	6,347	7,200	902	6,298
Unemployed	2,624	1,101	1,523	2,331	911	1,420
Unemployment rate	5.0	4.1	5.9	4.5	3.4	5.5
Married, spouse present						
Civilian noninstitutional population	52,476	26,049	26,427	52,109	25,852	26,258
Civilian labor force	42,776	24,638	18,138	42,247	24,449	17,798
Participation rate	81.5	94.6	68.6	81.1	94.6	67.8
Employed	41,128	23,712	17,416	40,847	23,703	17,144
Employment-population ratio	78.4	91.0	65.9	78.4	91.7	65.3
Full-time workers[a]	35,315	22,954	12,360	35,141	22,935	12,206
Part-time workers[b]	5,813	757	5,056	5,706	768	4,938
Unemployed	1,648	926	722	1,400	747	653
Unemployment rate	3.9	3.8	4.0	3.3	3.1	3.7
Other marital status[c]						
Civilian noninstitutional population	12,455	2,354	10,102	12,649	2,420	10,229
Civilian labor force	9,950	2,100	7,850	10,042	2,158	7,883
Participation rate	79.9	89.2	77.7	79.4	89.2	77.1
Employed	8,975	1,926	7,050	9,110	1,993	7,117
Employment-population ratio	72.1	81.8	69.8	72.0	82.4	69.6
Full-time workers[a]	7,566	1,807	5,759	7,617	1,859	5,757
Part-time workers[b]	1,411	118	1,291	1,494	134	1,360
Unemployed	976	175	800	931	165	766
Unemployment rate	9.8	8.3	10.2	9.3	7.6	9.7
With own children 6 to 17 years, none younger						
Civilian noninstitutional population	35,943	15,653	20,290	35,874	15,597	20,277
Civilian labor force	30,362	14,572	15,790	30,182	14,516	15,666
Participation rate	84.5	93.1	77.8	84.1	93.1	77.3
Employed	29,040	14,008	15,032	29,013	14,056	14,957
Employment-population ratio	80.8	89.5	74.1	80.9	90.1	73.8
Full-time workers[a]	25,116	13,558	11,557	25,069	13,597	11,473
Part-time workers[b]	3,925	450	3,475	3,944	459	3,485
Unemployed	1,322	564	758	1,170	460	709
Unemployment rate	4.4	3.9	4.8	3.9	3.2	4.5
With own children under 6 years						
Civilian noninstitutional population	28,988	12,749	16,240	28,884	12,675	16,210
Civilian labor force	22,365	12,167	10,198	22,106	12,091	10,014
Participation rate	77.2	95.4	62.8	76.5	95.4	61.8
Employed	21,063	11,630	9,433	20,944	11,640	9,304
Employment-population ratio	72.7	91.2	58.1	72.5	91.8	57.4
Full-time workers[a]	17,764	11,203	6,561	17,689	11,197	6,491
Part-time workers[b]	3,299	426	2,872	3,256	443	2,813
Unemployed	1,302	538	765	1,162	451	710
Unemployment rate	5.8	4.4	7.5	5.3	3.7	7.1

higher-income children). Higher-income children are more likely than lower-income children to care for themselves during the summer months (15% and 5%, respectively).

According to a 2000 report by the National Center for Children in Poverty, *Better Strategies for Babies: Strengthening the Caregivers and Families of Infants and Toddlers*, the number of infants and toddlers in child care increased significantly in the 1990s, particularly among low-income working families and those transitioning from welfare. Infant care poses special challenges for working mothers, especially women who are breast-feeding their infants. In 2004 mothers of infants—particularly unmarried mothers—were more likely to be unemployed than other mothers. (See Table 6.13 in Chapter 6.) Single mothers in the labor force were more likely to be unemployed, and child-care arrangements can make the difference between employment and unemployment. Sunhwa Lee wrote in a

TABLE 7.1

Employment status of the population, by sex, marital status, and presence and age of own children under 18, 2003–04 annual averages [CONTINUED]

[Numbers in thousands]

Characteristic	2003			2004		
	Total	Men	Women	Total	Men	Women
With no own children under 18 years						
Civilian noninstitutional population	154,714	76,510	78,204	156,900	77,739	79,160
Civilian labor force	92,319	50,036	42,284	93,511	50,771	42,740
Participation rate	59.7	65.4	54.1	59.6	65.3	54.0
Employed	86,233	46,294	39,939	87,748	47,282	40,467
Employment-population ratio	55.7	60.5	51.1	55.9	60.8	51.1
Full-time workers[a]	69,073	39,245	29,827	70,244	40,134	30,110
Part-time workers[b]	17,160	7,049	10,111	17,505	7,148	10,357
Unemployed	6,087	3,741	2,345	5,763	3,489	2,274
Unemployment rate	6.6	7.5	5.5	6.2	6.9	5.3

[a]Usually work 35 hours or more a week at all jobs.
[b]Usually work less than 35 hours a week at all jobs.
[c]Includes never-married, divorced, separated, and widowed persons.

SOURCE: "Table 5. Employment Status of the Population by Sex, Marital Status, and Presence and Age of Own Children Under 18, 2003–04 Annual Averages," in *Employment Characteristics of Families in 2004*, News, U.S. Bureau of Labor Statistics, USDL 05-876, June 9, 2005, http://www.bls.gov/news.release/famee.t05.htm (accessed June 15, 2005)

study for the Institute for Women's Policy Research, "Having any type of regular child care—whether it be relative care, non-relative care, or center-based care—is important for job retention among low-income mothers who have preschool children" ("Women's Work Supports, Job Retention, and Job Mobility: Child Care and Employer-Provided Health Insurance Help Women Stay on Jobs," November 2004).

CHILD-CARE ARRANGEMENTS

How Are Children Cared For?

Parents want their children to be cared for in a safe, stable, and attentive environment. The choice of child-care arrangements depends on availability, work schedules, transportation, affordability, and, in particular, the age of the child. Child care is categorized as parental or nonparental. Parental care means that the child is cared for on a regular basis only by the parents. Nonparental care may be child care by relatives, by nonrelatives, or in a child-care center. Some children have more than one type of regular nonparental care.

According to an October 1999 study by the Center for Law and Social Policy (Rachel Schumacher and Mark Greenberg, *Child Care after Leaving Welfare: Early Evidence from State Studies*), the majority of families who left welfare for work relied on friends and relatives for child care. Lack of child care was consistently identified as one of the reasons for unemployment among parents who had left welfare. Child-care arrangements also appeared to affect the type of job that the parent could accept, the hours worked, and absences from work.

Sunhwa Lee, in "Work Supports, Job Retention, and Job Mobility among Low-Income Mothers" (Institute for Women's Policy Research, November 2004), found that for working mothers whose youngest child was under age six, the child was most likely to be cared for by relatives, especially grandparents and the child's other parent. Care by nonrelatives, such as a babysitter or family day care, was also common. Center care was more likely to be used by higher-income mothers. For working mothers with a youngest child age six to fourteen, parental care and relative care were again the most common child-care arrangements. Low-income mothers were less likely than higher-income mothers to use organized care arrangements like center care and organized enrichment activities. Only about a third of low-income mothers paid for child care, and very few received child-care subsidies, despite the expansion of subsidy programs after welfare reform.

Types of Child-Care Arrangements

PARENTAL CARE. As Figure 7.1 shows, about 48% of children up to age two and 26% of children ages three to six received primarily parental child care in 2001. Although 52% of children up to age two received nonparental care, only 17% were in center-based care situations. On the other hand, 74% of children ages three to six received primarily nonparental care. More than half of three- to six-year-olds (approximately 56%) were in a center-based program.

Since the average workday is longer than the average school day, many mothers need to find before- and after-school care for children ages six and older enrolled in school. According to *The Condition of Education 2004* by the National Center for Education Statistics (NCES),

FIGURE 7.1

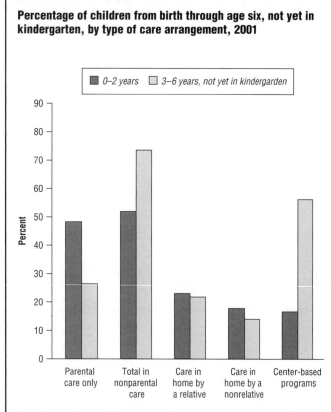

Percentage of children from birth through age six, not yet in kindergarten, by type of care arrangement, 2001

Note: Some children participate in more than one type of arrangement, so the sum of all arrangement types exceeds the total percentage in nonparental care. Center-based programs include day care centers, prekindergartens, nursery schools, Head Start programs, and other early childhood education programs. Relative and nonrelative care can take place in either the child's own home or another home.

SOURCE: "Figure POP8.A. Percentage of Children from Birth through Age Six, Not Yet in Kindergarten by Type of Care Arrangement, 2001," in *America's Children: Key National Indicators of Well-Being, 2003*, Federal Interagency Forum on Child and Family Statistics, July 2003, http://www.nichd.nih.gov/publications/pubs/childstats/report2003.pdf (accessed June 15, 2005)

in 2001 non-Hispanic white children in kindergarten through eighth grade were most likely to have only parental care (53.7%) after school, and African-American children (34.1%) were least likely. (See Table 7.2.) About half (49.6%) of all children in this age group were cared for after school by a parent, and the other half (50.4%) were in nonparental care. Although children living below the poverty level were more likely than others to have parental care only (52%), even among poor children, 48% were cared for by nonparents at least part of the time. In general, the more educated the mother, the more likely she was to be in the workforce and the less likely her children were to receive only parental care. Although some working mothers are able to arrange schedules with their spouses and take advantage of flexible work arrangements to accommodate child care, only about one-third (32.1%) of children whose mothers worked full-time received primarily parental care, compared with 57.4% of children whose mothers

worked part-time and 72.1% whose mothers did not participate in the labor force.

HOME-BASED CHILD CARE BY RELATIVES. Almost one-quarter (23%) of children under age two were primarily cared for by relatives in 2001. That percentage was only slightly lower (19%) for children ages three to six. (See Figure 7.1.) Grandparents, older siblings, or other family members may care for children in their home or in the child's home.

Younger children are more likely than older children to be cared for by relatives. According to a 2005 report from the Urban Institute, *Who's Caring for Our Youngest Children? Child Care Patterns of Infants and Toddlers*, in 2002, 33% of children under three years old were regularly cared for by a relative when a parent worked, as were 31.4% of three- and four-year-olds, 25.6% of six- to nine-year-olds, and 20.2% of ten- to twelve-year-olds. (See Table 7.3.) *The Condition of Education 2003* found that for children in grades one through eight whose mothers worked full-time, more than one-quarter (26.1%) were cared for by relatives after school in 2001. (See Table 7.2.) What emerges from the research is a clear picture of the importance of extended families for working mothers with young children.

HOME-BASED CHILD CARE BY NONRELATIVES. In 2001, 18% of children from birth through age two were cared for in-home by someone other than a relative, as were 14% of children ages three to six. (See Figure 7.1.) Some working parents can afford to hire a babysitter or nanny to care for children in their own home, and some parents rely on their friends for child care. Groups of parents may form a child-care cooperative, using parent volunteers or a hired caregiver or preschool teacher.

But most home-based or family day care is provided by an adult, usually a mother, who cares for several children in her own home. These home-based day-care businesses may or may not be licensed by the state and often are more affordable than center-based day care. According to the Urban Institute report noted above, small home-based child-care providers cared for 13% of infants less than one year old with employed mothers, 16% of one-year-olds, and 21% of two-year-olds. Only 7% of children under age three were cared for by nannies or babysitters while their mothers were at work.

CHILD-CARE CENTERS. According to Figure 7.1, 17% of children age two and under were cared for in a center-based program; that number jumped to 56% for children ages three to six. A 2001 Urban Institute report found that two-year-old children of employed mothers were more likely to be in a child-care center than in other types of nonparental arrangements—15% of children under the age of one with employed mothers were in

TABLE 7.2

Percentage of children in kindergarten through eighth grade who participated in various care arrangements after school, by child, family, and community characteristics, 2001

Child, family, and community characteristics	Number of children (thousands)	Parental care	Nonparental care	Type of nonparental care arrangement				
				Relative care	Nonrelative care	Center- or school-based programs	Extra-curricular activities[a]	Self-care
Total	35,743	49.6	50.4	16.9	6.5	18.7	7.3	13.3
Child's grade								
K–2	11,778	51.7	48.3	19.5	9.6	21.4	5.0	1.6*
3–5	12,343	50.9	49.1	17.9	6.5	20.3	8.2	8.4
6–8	11,622	46.2	53.8	13.2	3.2	14.2	8.8	30.5
Child's race/ethnicity[b]								
Black	5,822	34.1	65.9	25.3	6.3	28.9	9.6	18.2
White	22,144	53.7	46.3	14.8	6.5	15.2	6.7	12.6
Other	2,091	47.8	52.2	14.4	3.8*	22.5	11.8	13.3
Hispanic	5,686	50.3	49.7	17.3	7.3	20.5	5.6	11.2
Parents' language spoken most at home								
Both parents speak English	32,606	48.8	51.2	17.4	6.6	18.6	7.5	13.8
One parent speaks English	636	53.6	46.4	12.1*	6.9*	21.9	7.4*	11.6*
Neither parent speaks English	2,502	59.3	40.7	12.0	4.2	19.3	5.1*	7.5
Mother's employment status[c]								
Full-time	16,067	32.1	67.9	26.1	9.5	23.1	8.7	18.3
Part-time	7,459	57.4	42.6	12.3	6.3	14.1	6.3	11.7
Not in a labor force	10,952	72.1	27.9	5.6	1.8*	14.3	5.9	6.3
Family type								
Two-parent household	24,809	56.4	43.6	12.9	5.5	16.2	6.7	11.9
One-parent household	9,924	33.4	66.6	26.4	9.0	24.6	8.7	16.8
Nonparent guardians	1,010	43.1	56.9	21.6	3.7*	23.0	9.9*	15.3
Household income								
$25,000 or less	10,671	47.8	52.2	19.3	6.3	20.8	6.9	13.7
$25,001–50,000	9,542	48.7	51.3	19.6	5.7	17.3	6.7	14.0
$50,001–75,000	7,608	51.6	48.4	15.6	6.3	17.4	6.8	12.9
More than $75,000	7,922	51.3	48.7	11.7	7.7	18.8	9.0	12.4
Poverty status								
Poor	7,940	52.0	48.0	17.1	5.7	20.6	7.2	11.3
Nonpoor	27,803	49.0	51.0	16.8	6.7	18.2	7.4	13.9
Community type								
Urban	22,673	48.3	51.7	16.6	6.2	21.2	7.2	13.2
Outside of urbanized areas	4,465	52.9	47.1	17.1	6.0	13.9	6.2	15.5
Rural	8,605	51.5	48.5	17.6	7.2	14.6	8.3	12.7

*Interpret data with caution (estimates are unstable).

[a]Includes organized activities such as sports, arts, and clubs that were used to cover period when parents needed adult supervision for their children.

[b]Black includes African American and Hispanic includes Latino. Race categories exclude Hispanic unless specified.

[c]Children without mothers (birth, adoptive, step, or foster) residing in the household are not included in estimates of mother's employment status. Detail may not sum to totals because of the exclusion.

Note: Home-schooled children are excluded. Since some children participate in more than one type of nonparental care arrangement after school, the sum of all arrangement types exceeds the total percentage of nonparental care arrangements. Detail may not sum to totals because of rounding.

SOURCE: "Table 33–1. Percentage of Children in Kindergarten through 8th Grade Who Participated in Various Care Arrangements After School, by Child, Family, and Community Characteristics: 2001," in *The Condition of Education, 2004*, U.S. Department of Education, National Center of Education Statistics, NCES 2004-077, June 2004, http://nces.ed.gov/programs/coe/2004/pdf/33_2004.pdf (accessed June 15, 2005)

child-care centers, as were 23% of one-year-olds and 27% of two-year-olds. These center-based programs include day-care centers, nursery schools, preschools, Head Start programs, and other early-childhood education and school-based programs such as prekindergartens. These child-care facilities may operate as commercial businesses, private nonprofit organizations, or publicly funded programs (like Head Start and public prekindergartens). Some businesses have child-care facilities for their employees, and many schools and universities have child-care facilities for students and staff. Some centers

care for only one age group of children; others care for all children from infancy through school age.

The NCES reported in 2004 that 21.4% of children in kindergarten through second grade, 20.3% of children in third through fifth grades, and 14.2% of children in sixth through eighth grades were placed in center-based programs for after-school care in 2001. (See Table 7.2.) African-American children were more likely to be in center-based programs (28.9%) than white children (15.2%) or Hispanic children (20.5%). Almost one-quarter of

TABLE 7.3

Children under age 13 regularly in relative care while a parent works, by age of child, 1999 and 2002

[Percent]

Age (years)	Any relative care		Only relative care		Relative care in combination		Sample size	
	1999	2002	1999	2002	1999	2002	1999	2002
Under 3	34.7	33.0	28.0	25.7	6.5	7.2	3,511	3,379
3 to 4	31.7	31.4	18.2	17.2	13.1	14.0	2,907	2,812
6 to 9	26.7	25.6	21.5	20.2	5.1	5.3	5,361	4,991
10 to 12	24.1	20.2[b]	20.9	16.7[b]	3.1	3.4	3,816	3,856

Notes: "Any relative care" includes children in relative care as their only regular arrangement ("only relative care") and children in relative care as part of a combination of arrangements ("relative care in combination"). The sums of the only relative care and relative care in combination columns may not equal the percentage shown in the any relative care column because of rounding.

[a] Analysis excludes children age 5.

[b] Decrease between 1999 and 2002 is significant at the 0.10 level.

SOURCE: Kathleen Snyder, Timothy Dore, and Sarah Adelman, "Table 1. Children Under Age 13 Regularly in Relative Care While a Parent Works, by Age of Child (Percent)," in *Use of Relative Care by Working Parents,* Snapshots of America's Families III, No. 23, The Urban Institute, April 2005, www.urban.org/UploadedPDF/311161_snapshots3_No23.pdf (accessed June 27, 2005)

children in one-parent households (24.6%) and families with full-time working mothers (23.1%) were enrolled in center-based child care.

PRESCHOOLS. According to the Federal Interagency Forum on Child and Family Statistics, early-childhood education programs improve the likelihood of a child's success in school. Studies have shown that high-quality preschool education improves school achievement in the short term and increases the likelihood that low-income minority children will complete school.

The number of three- and four-year-olds attending preschool (also known as nursery school), increased between 1964 and 2003, from about half a million to five million. (See Figure 7.2.) The percentage of preschool-age children enrolled in nursery school grew from about 6% in 1964 to about 60% in 2003. In 2003 more than half of eligible non-Hispanic white children (55%) were enrolled in nursery school, compared with 49% of African-American children, 43% of Asian-American children, and 39% of Hispanic children.

The likelihood of nursery school attendance is linked to family income and the mothers' education and labor force participation. Although some public nursery school programs like Head Start are available to low-income families, children from families with incomes over $50,000 were more likely to attend nursery school (62%), and children from families with incomes less than $20,000 were less likely to attend (41%). Children whose mothers had graduated from college were twice as likely as children whose mothers lacked a high school degree to attend nursery school (64% and 34%, respectively). Nursery school provides child care for families whose mothers work; although only half of nursery school students attended full-time, among children whose mothers worked

full-time, 64% attended nursery school full-time (Hyon B. Shin, *School Enrollment—Social and Economic Characteristics of Students: October 2003*, Current Population Reports, P20–554, U.S. Census Bureau, May 2005).

Kindergarten enrollment also rose between 1967 and 2003, but the percentage of kindergarteners attending full-day kindergartens rose even more dramatically during that period. (See Figure 7.3.) In 2003, 3.7 million children were enrolled in kindergarten. Race and ethnic groups were represented in numbers comparable to their numbers in the general population of five-year-olds; 60% of kindergarteners were non-Hispanic whites, 20% were Hispanic, 14% were African-American, and 4% were Asian-American. The percentage of children attending kindergarten full-time rose from 20% in 1973 to 65% in 2003, reflecting the expansion of public full-day kindergarten programs during that period. Such full-day programs provide child care for working mothers.

Child-Care Breakdowns

Mothers who work nonstandard hours or weekends, or are called in to work unexpectedly, may struggle to find child care. Working mothers also must arrange for child care during school closures and vacations. Centers may have extended hours for working parents and extra staff to cover for absent employees, but mothers who depend on relatives or home-based child care may have to find alternative arrangements if their regular caregiver becomes ill or is otherwise unavailable. Married working women may be able to rely on their husbands when child care breaks down or if a child becomes ill and cannot go to school or to a regular caregiver. But many mothers—especially single mothers—may have to stay home from work under such circumstances. Any disruption of the normal child-care routine can result in loss of working hours and productivity for mothers.

FIGURE 7.2

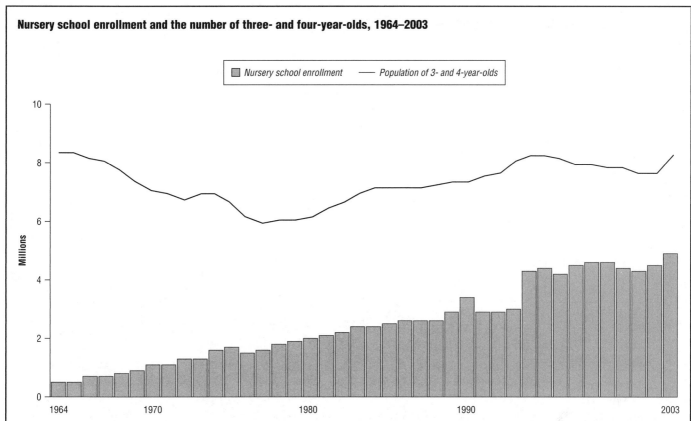

Nursery school enrollment and the number of three- and four-year-olds, 1964–2003

SOURCE: Hyon B. Shin, "Figure 2. Nursery School Enrollment and the Number of 3- and 4-Year-Olds: 1964 to 2003," in *School Enrollment—Social and Economic Characteristics of Students: October 2003*, U.S. Census Bureau, Current Population Reports, P20-554, May 2005, http://www.census.gov/prod/2005pubs/p20-554.pdf (accessed June 26, 2005)

In its April 2003 report *Women, Work and Family Health: A Balancing Act*, the Henry J. Kaiser Family Foundation reported that in 2001, 49% of employed mothers said they would have to take time off work to care for a sick child, while only 30% of working fathers would have to do so. Of mothers who miss work to care for a sick child, about half do not get paid for their absence—42% of full-time workers and 65% of part-time workers. The report attributes this to the fact that women tend to work part-time and/or low-paying jobs that do not afford them sick leave or vacation time.

CHILD-CARE COSTS

According to a February 2003 study by the Urban Institute (Linda Giannarelli et al., *Getting Help with Child Care Expenses*), about half (48%) of all working families with children under age thirteen paid for child care in 1999. For many working families, child care is the fourth-largest expense after food, housing, and taxes. The *Wall Street Journal* reported that in 2004 the cost of child care had been rising 3% to 8% annually for several years (Sue Shellenbarger, "As Cost of Child Care Rises Sharply, Here's How Some Families Are Coping," October 21, 2004). Family child-care homes averaged $9,100 per year per child; child-

care centers averaged $7,020 per year per child. These costs are impossible for low-income families to meet. In 2005 one person earning the federal minimum wage of $5.15 per hour working full-time, year-round, earned only $10,712.

CHILD-CARE ASSISTANCE

Employee Benefits

FAMILY LEAVE. On February 5, 1993, President Bill Clinton signed the Family and Medical Leave Act (FMLA) (PL 103–3), which provides for up to twelve weeks of unpaid leave annually for illness, at the birth or adoption of a child or a foster-care placement, or to care for a seriously ill immediate family member. The law applies to all public agencies and all private companies with fifty or more employees and to employees who worked 1,250 hours in the previous year. Employers are required to maintain the employee's health coverage and to reinstate the returning employee in the same or an equivalent job. As of 2000, the FMLA applied to 58.3% of U.S. employees and 10.8% of U.S. private-sector establishments.

In *Balancing the Needs of Families and Employers: Family and Medical Leave Surveys* (David Cantor et al., 2001), the Department of Labor found that the second

FIGURE 7.3

Kindergarten enrollment and the percent attending full day, 1967–2003

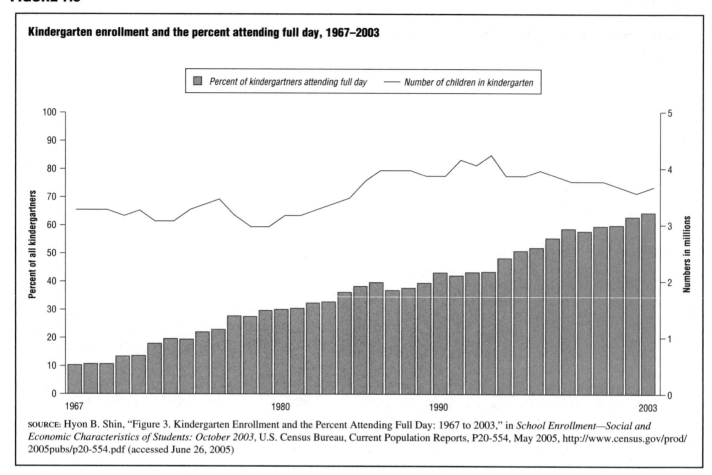

SOURCE: Hyon B. Shin, "Figure 3. Kindergarten Enrollment and the Percent Attending Full Day: 1967 to 2003," in *School Enrollment—Social and Economic Characteristics of Students: October 2003*, U.S. Census Bureau, Current Population Reports, P20-554, May 2005, http://www.census.gov/prod/2005pubs/p20-554.pdf (accessed June 26, 2005)

most popular reason for taking FMLA leave in 2000, given by 18.5% of leave-takers, was to care for a newborn or newly adopted child. The fourth most popular reason, given by 11.5%, was to care for a sick child. (The primary reason given for taking leave, given by 52.4% of leave-takers, was the employee's own health.) The percentage of all FMLA-covered and eligible employees who took leave in 2000 was 18.3%, an increase from 1995's 11.6% figure.

The Families and Work Institute's 1998 Business Work-Life Study (BWLS), being updated in 2005 by author Ellen Galinsky, surveyed 1,057 for-profit and not-for-profit companies with more than one hundred employees. Although many companies provided more than the required twelve weeks of leave, 7 to 10% of the companies with more than one hundred employees did not provide twelve weeks, although the BWLS concluded that most of these companies were not out of compliance with the FMLA. Many of the companies (53%) provided at least some replacement pay during maternity leave, but only 13% provided paid paternity leave and only 12.5% provided paid adoption/foster-care leave. Almost half of the companies (49%) allowed employees paid time off to care for a mildly ill child, although they were not required by law to do so. Among

the companies surveyed, 81% allowed parents to return to work gradually following childbirth or adoption. Larger companies were more likely than smaller companies to provide long maternity, paternity, and adoption leaves, paid maternity leave, flexible hours, and child- and elder-care resources.

CHILD-CARE-FRIENDLY COMPANY POLICIES. Among other policies to accommodate family responsibilities, the most common were to allow workers to take time off for school and child-care functions (88% of companies) and to allow employees to periodically change their starting and quitting work times (68%), although only 24% allowed changing hours on a daily basis. More than half of the companies allowed employees to switch back and forth between full- and part-time work (57%) and to occasionally work at home (55%); however, only 37.5% allowed job sharing, and just 33% allowed employees to work at home on a regular basis.

The 1998 BWLS survey found that only 9% of companies provided on-site or close-by child care, and only 5% provided child-care subsidies to employees. But 50% provided dependent care assistance plans (DCAPs) that enabled employees to pay for child care with pretax dollars. Only a small percentage of the companies

TABLE 7.4

Percent of workers with access to employer assistance for child care, by selected characteristics, private industry, March 2004

Characteristics	Total*	Employer-provided funds	On-site and off-site child care	Child care resource and referral services
		Employer assistance for child care		
All workers	14	3	5	10
Worker characteristics:				
White-collar occupations	19	4	7	14
Blue-collar occupations	8	2	2	6
Service occupations	9	2	4	4
Full time	16	4	6	11
Part time	8	1	3	5
Union	16	3	6	15
Nonunion	13	3	5	9
Average wage less than $15 per hour	8	2	3	5
Average wage $15 per hour or higher	22	5	8	16
Establishment characteristics:				
Goods-producing	12	3	3	10
Service-producing	14	3	6	10
1–99 workers	4	1	2	3
100 workers or more	25	5	9	18
Geographic areas:				
Metropolitan areas	15	3	5	11
Nonmetropolitan areas	8	2	4	3
New England	17	2	9	14
Middle Atlantic	16	4	5	11
East North Central	15	3	6	11
West North Central	16	2	9	7
South Atlantic	11	4	4	8
East South Central	9	3	4	5
West South Central	14	2	4	10
Mountain	16	3	3	13
Pacific	11	3	3	9

*The total is less than the sum of individual child care provisions because many employees have access to more than one of the benefits.
Note: Because of rounding, sums of individual items may not equal totals. Where applicable, dash indicates no employees in this category or data do not meet publication criteria.

SOURCE: Adapted from "Table 19. Percent of Workers with Access to Selected Benefits, by Selected Characteristics, Private Industry, National Compensation Survey, March 2004," in *National Compensation Survey: Employee Benefits in Private Industry in the United States, March 2004,* U.S. Department of Labor, Bureau of Labor Statistics, November 2004, http://www.bls.gov/ncs/ebs/sp/ebsm0002.pdf (accessed June 15, 2005).

provided sick child care (5%), school vacation care (6%), or backup child care (4%), or reimbursed employees for child care when they worked late (4%) or were traveling on business (6%). More than one-third (36%) of companies provided information to help parents locate child care.

EMPLOYER-PROVIDED CHILD CARE. According to the National Compensation Survey of the Bureau of Labor Statistics (BLS), 5% of all U.S. private industry employees had access to employer-provided on-site or off-site child care in March 2004. (See Table 7.4.) White-collar workers (7%) were much more likely than blue-collar workers (2%) to have this benefit, and those

whose wages were $15 per hour or higher (8%) were also more likely than those with lower wages (3%) to receive this benefit. More companies with one hundred workers or more (9%) than fewer workers (2%) offered employer-provided child care.

Bright Horizons Family Solutions, a Massachusetts-based company that provides child-care facilities for businesses, hospitals, universities, and government offices, conducted an Investment Impact Study on some of its large clients (including Bank of America, Chick-Fil-A, Georgia Pacific, and Staples) in 2002. It concluded that employer-sponsored child-care centers have "a direct and significant impact" on retaining employees. Employees who used their workplace's child-care facility were just over half as likely to leave their jobs as all employees (3.7% versus 7.2%). This resulted in $3.4 million in savings to the companies surveyed.

The Economic Growth and Tax Relief Reconciliation Act of 2001 provided a number of economic incentives to U.S. companies effective in 2002. One such incentive is a new tax credit of up to one-quarter of expenses for providing child care for employees. There is also a 10% tax credit on providing employees with resources and referrals regarding child care. Proponents believe this will encourage more companies to provide child-care facilities.

BACKUP CHILD CARE. An October 2001 research brief by the Institute for Women's Policy Research (*The Widening Gap: A New Book on the Struggle to Balance Work and Caregiving*) reported that 53% of employed mothers cannot take paid time off when their child is sick. In 2003, 70% of the workforce do not have paid sick leave to take time off to care for sick family members and risk losing their jobs in addition to losing pay for taking time off (Vicky Lovell et al., "Expanded Sick Leave Would Yield Substantial Benefits to Business, Employers, and Families," Institute for Women's Policy Research, Fact Sheet, June 15, 2004). Although some day-care centers will make arrangements to care for mildly ill children, many will not. Some hospitals and physician groups have set up "sick day care" centers, but these arrangements tend to be considerably more expensive than regular day care.

Some employers are beginning to establish backup care programs for the children of workers whose regular child-care arrangements break down. According to the 1998 BWLS, 4% of companies provided such programs, and an additional 4.5% were considering doing so. A 2000 survey of "major" U.S. companies by Hewitt Associates LLC, a human resources consulting and outsourcing firm, found that 46% offered sick/emergency child care.

ChildrenFirst Inc. began operating employer-sponsored backup child-care facilities in 1992. As of year-end 2004, it operated backup child-care centers in more than 260 companies and had been used more than five hundred thousand times since 1992. ChildrenFirst estimated that by the end of 2004, the backup child-care centers had saved more than six hundred thousand employee days for its clients, who include firms such as American Express, Deloitte & Touche, General Electric, Prudential, and Target. On June 28, 2005, Bright Horizons Family Solutions announced plans to acquire Children First, uniting the two leading providers of backup child care.

RESOURCE AND REFERRAL SERVICES. The BLS found that in March 2004, 10% of private-industry workers had access to employer-provided child-care resource and referral services. (See Table 7.4.) Workers in companies with one hundred workers or more (18%), those making $15 per hour or more (16%), and white-collar workers (14%) were most likely to have such access. The 1998 BWLS survey, which surveyed 1,057 for-profit and not-for-profit companies, found that 36% of companies provided child-care resource services to their employees. Although 56% of the companies had an Employee Assistance Program to help with various types of problems, only 25% provided workshops or seminars on parenting, child development, elder care, or other work–family issues.

PROGRAMS FOR OLDER CHILDREN AND TEENAGERS. The October 2003 issue of Working Mother magazine listed programs for teens and "tweens" (children between the ages of ten and twelve) as a fast-growing trend. According to the magazine, some of the best companies to work for are those that offer such programs in acknowledgment of employees' family needs. The article cited an Indianapolis-based pharmaceutical company, Eli Lilly, that offered an on-site, YMCA-managed all-day summer science camp to employees' families for $100 a week. The company also allowed for flex-time scheduling so that parents could spend more time with their families. As a result of its innovative strategies, Eli Lilly was voted one of the ten best companies to work for and the best in its industry by Working Mother.

MILITARY CHILD CARE. The U.S. military has the largest employer-sponsored child-care program in the country, offering full- and part-time child care, drop-in and extended-hours child care, and before- and after-school programs. The Military Child Care Act of 1989 made the Department of Defense (DOD) Child Development Program a leader in training and compensating child-care workers. But the DOD meets only 58% of its child-care requirements. Therefore, the DOD program provides training and certification for the family-care homes that provide about one-third of the military's child care. Child-care costs to families are on a sliding scale that depends on family income. In 2003 the average fee was $81 per week, with costs for lower- and higher-range incomes from $42 to $124 per week. This covered fifty hours of care, plus breakfast, lunch, and two snacks for each child. An October 1999 Government Accountability Office (GAO) study (Child Care: How Do Military and Civilian Costs Compare?) found that the DOD child-care costs were about 7% higher than civilian costs, primarily because of higher pay for workers, accreditation of the centers, and the large numbers of infants and toddlers served by the military centers.

The DOD's child-care program has been lauded as an example for others to follow. Be All That We Can Be: Lessons from the Military for Improving Our Nation's Child Care System, an April 2000 report from the National Women's Law Center, identifies six lessons for policy makers. These include recognizing and acknowledging the problem of child care, continually reassessing unmet needs, and committing quality resources. A July 2003 Urban Institute report (Improving Child Care Quality: A Comparison of Military and Civilian Approaches) also found aspects of the military child-care programs that could be used to improve civilian child care. The factors the report identified included training and educating care providers, subsidizing care, and establishing accountability.

Government Benefits

In 1976 changes to the federal tax code granted a tax credit for child-care expenses for working families. In 2005 the federal government provided a tax credit of up to 35% of working parents' child-care costs. But many low-income families cannot receive the credit because they do not earn enough income to pay taxes, making the tax credit worthless. Other tax subsidies, although not tied to child-care expenses, provide some help to low-income families. The Earned Income Tax Credit is refundable, which means that even families with no tax liability get the credit, and the Child Tax Credit is partially refundable (Leonard E. Burman et al., "Tax Subsidies to Help Low-Income Families Pay for Child Care," Discussion Paper No. 23, Urban Institute, June 2005).

CHILD CARE AND DEVELOPMENT FUND. The Personal Responsibility and Work Opportunity Reconciliation Act of 1996 (PRWORA) recognized that moving single mothers off welfare and into the workforce would increase the need for affordable child care. The Act established the Child Care and Development Fund (CCDF), to be administered by the Child Care Bureau of the Department of Health and Human Services (HHS). It provided for more than $20 billion in block grants to the states from 1997 to 2002. A portion of the money was to be used to increase the quality and availability of child care for all families. In fiscal year (FY) 2004, the CCDF provided $2.717 billion to assist with child care for low-income families, families receiving Temporary Assistance for Needy Families (TANF) benefits, and those in transition from welfare to work. This was approximately the same level as the previous year under a temporary extension while Congress worked to reauthorize CCDF.

According to the Child Care Bureau, in FY 2004 the CCDF served an average of 1.75 million children in more than one million families per month. Most of the children (78%) were cared for while their parents worked. Another 12% of the children's parents were in education or training programs. Most of the CCDF assistance (84%) was in the form of certificates or vouchers to parents to help cover child-care expenses. Another 13% of the assistance was in the form of contracts with child-care centers, and 3% was cash assistance to parents. Most CCDF-assisted child care (59%) occurred in centers; 29% was for care in a family home, and 7% was for care in the child's home.

A February 2001 study by the GAO found that between FY 1994–95 and FY 1999–2000 state spending on child care for low-income families increased significantly. But a more recent GAO report, *Child Care: Recent State Policy Changes Affecting the Availability of Assistance for Low-Income Families* (May 2003), found that from January 2001 to April 2003 thirty-five states made changes that affected child-care availability. Of these thirty-five states, twenty-three made changes "tending to decrease the availability of assistance." Although most states made families receiving TANF, families transitioning off welfare, and other low-income working families eligible for assistance, TANF and transitioning families often received priority when funds were not adequate to cover all eligible applicants. Only half the states reported they served all eligible applicants. Lower-priority families were more likely to be put on waiting lists, to be subject to enrollment freezes, or to lose benefits while still eligible. The GAO suggested that state budget crunches, steady or growing TANF caseloads, and reevaluation of TANF and state spending might account for the drop in coverage.

After several years of flat funding for child care, in March 2005 the Senate Finance Committee passed its TANF reauthorization bill that included $6 billion in new federal funds for child-care assistance. The $6 billion was a modest increase in child-care funds—it would keep child-care payments in line with inflation between 2005 and 2010 and meet the cost of the increase in work participation requirements for TANF recipients, but it would not provide any funding to expand access to child care or improve the quality of child care (Danielle Ewen, "The Senate's $6 Billion Child Care Provision: A Critical, but Modest, Investment," Center for Law and Social Policy, April 2005).

ELDER CARE

If the creation of high-quality, affordable child care has not kept up with the needs of a changing workforce, issues surrounding elder care are even further behind. In 1900 the over-sixty-five population was just 4% of the total U.S. population; as of July 1, 2004, the Census Bureau estimated it at 12.4%. The American population is aging, and people with chronic diseases are living longer. According to Census Bureau projections, by the year 2030, 19.6% of the population—almost 71.5 million people—will be age sixty-five or older ("U.S. Interim Projects by Age, Sex, Race, and Hispanic Origin," U.S. Census Bureau, March 18, 2004). Seniors eighty-five years and older are expected to be the fastest-growing group, with the population increasing from 4.2 million in 2000 to 20.9 million in 2050.

Family members, primarily women, have traditionally cared for elderly relatives. According to a 2004 report by the National Alliance for Caregiving and AARP (formerly known as the American Association of Retired Persons), *Caregiving in the U.S.*, "The typical caregiver is a 46 year old woman who has at least some college experience and provides more than 20 hours of care each week to her mother." Although a substantial portion of caregivers are men (39%), most are women (61%), and female caregivers tend to give more hours of care and a higher level of care than male caregivers. Women who provide care are also more likely than men to feel that they had no choice in taking on the caregiving role (42% and 34%, respectively).

Older Americans may suffer from failing vision or hearing, infirmity, loneliness, financial difficulties, and general loss of control over their lives. The elderly often need a wide variety of services, and their needs are constantly changing. Whereas children require less care as they get older, the elderly usually need more care. Most elderly prefer to remain at home and avoid institutionalization, putting the burden of care on nearby relatives, often a daughter or daughter-in-law.

The "Sandwich Generation"

A July 2001 study by AARP, *In the Middle: A Report on Multicultural Boomers Coping with Family and Aging Issues*, found that members of the "sandwich generation," baby boomers between the ages of forty-five and fifty-five, often had both child-care and elder-care responsibilities:

- About 70% had at least one living parent.

- Nearly 40% had children living at home: 32% had children under twenty-one, and 7% had adult children at home.

- Asian-Americans were most likely to have both children at home and aging parents.

- About one-fifth reported that their caregiving had caused strain between themselves and their spouses (20%) or siblings (18%).

- African-Americans were most likely to feel over-whelmed by these family responsibilities.

Among the elder-care providers, AARP found that:

- More than 80% provided social interaction.

- 46% provided transportation.

- 45% performed housework.

- 44% shopped.

- 36% talked to doctors.

- 33% handled paperwork or bills.

- 27% helped with expenses.

- 17% hired nurses or aides.

- 12% handled intimate care.

AARP found that among women ages forty-five to fifty-five, 37% had both children under twenty-one and living parents and/or in-laws; 54% of all people in this age group were caring for children, parents, or both; and 22% were caring for a parent or in-law. *Caregiving in the U.S.* found that 33.9 million people, or 16% of the population in the United States, provide unpaid care to a person age fifty or older.

According to the May 2003 AARP publication *These Four Walls . . . Americans 45+ Talk about Home and Community*, 68% of Americans age forty-five and over believe family members or friends will assist them with tasks that will allow them to stay in their homes as they age. But only 35% of this population are counting on their children to provide this help.

Racial/Ethnic Differences among Elder-Care Providers

Caregivers in the U.S. found that non-Hispanic whites were most likely to be caring for a person over age fifty (17%), followed by Asian-Americans (15%), African-Americans (15%), and Hispanics (12%). *In the Middle* found that only 19% of non-Hispanic whites wanted their children to care for them in their later years, compared with 23% of African-Americans, 31% of Hispanics, and 38% of Asian-Americans. Asian-Americans reported the most care-related stress on their interpersonal relationships, as well as the most feelings that they should provide more care.

Caregiving in the U.S. reported that African-American caregivers tend to provide a very high level of care compared to other racial and ethnic groups. For example, African-American caregivers are more likely than white caregivers to spend nine to twenty hours per week providing care (31% and 21%, respectively). African-American caregivers (53%) are also more likely than white (35%), Hispanic (39%), or Asian-American (34%) caregivers to also be caring for children under eighteen. African-American caregivers are more likely than white caregivers to be employed (68% and 56%, respectively) and also more likely to provide more than $100 in cash support per month for the person they care for.

Women as Caregivers for the Elderly

Caregiving in the U.S. found that most caregivers (61%) are women. Women caregivers, on average, spend more time providing care than male caregivers and also provide a higher level of care. Women taking care of older relatives can suffer from depression, anxiety, and stress, along with other ailments. These problems may be especially acute for women who are also employed. Employed caregivers may suffer financial hardships (if they must take unpaid time off), or may even lose or be unable to maintain a job.

According to an October 2001 research brief from the Institute for Women's Policy Research (*The Widening Gap: A New Book on the Struggle to Balance Work and Caregiving*), more employed women (27%) than employed men (23%) had cared for someone over age sixty-five in the past year. Among employed caretakers, more men than women were likely to be providing one to four hours of unpaid assistance or emotional support to parents. But employed female caretakers were twice as likely as male ones to provide more than thirty hours of such care.

The Family Caregiver Alliance noted in a December 2003 report (*Caregiving and Retirement Planning: What Happens to Family Caregivers Who Leave the Work Force*) that most informal caregivers are married women in their mid-forties to mid-fifties. Nearly three-quarters of all informal caregivers are women, and caregiving can have a serious impact on these women's retirement savings in several ways. First, workers with lower lifetime earnings from working in low-paying jobs or spending time out of the workforce earn less Social Security. Second, access to employer-sponsored pensions is less common in part-time and low-paying jobs. Third, many caregivers' schedules do not allow them to work full-time, so they must choose part-time jobs or take extended leaves. Finally, caregivers often apply their own personal savings toward the expenses of those they are caring for.

Business Involvement

According to the 1998 BWLS, 23% of companies with more than one hundred employees offered elder-care resource and referral services. In addition, 9% offered long-term-care insurance for family members, and 5% offered direct financial support for local elder-care programs. Of companies offering such programs, about equal percentages felt the benefits outweighed the costs (21%) as felt the costs outweighed the benefits (19%); most companies (60%) felt their elder-care programs were cost-neutral.

The American Business Collaboration for Quality Dependent Care (ABC) is a national initiative by American corporations, such as Deloitte & Touche, Exxon Mobil, General Electric, IBM, and Johnson & Johnson, to improve dependent-care programs for young and school-aged children as well as the elderly. Since 1992, ABC had invested $125 million in child, school-age, and elder-care programs, funding more than fifteen hundred programs, including adult day care, elder-care information fairs and support groups, and respite programs.

In 2000 Congress enacted a law offering long-term-care insurance (LTCI) to all federal employees, the military, and their retirees. According to *The MetLife Study of Employed Caregivers: Does Long Term Care Insurance Make a Difference?* (March 2001), employees caring for disabled elders with LTCI are nearly twice as likely to remain in the workforce than those caring for noninsured elders. LTCI typically covers a broad range of services including nursing home coverage and adult day care.

Government Assistance

The Older Americans Act of 2000 established the National Family Caregiver Support Program (NFCSP), a grant program to help states provide various caregiver services to those caring for people sixty and older or children eighteen and younger. According to *The Older Americans Act: National Family Caregiver Support Program (Title III-E and Title VI-C): Compassion in Action* (HHS, Administration on Aging, 2004), the program had Title III-E funding of $55.2 million in FY 2003, with $7.5 million designated to support thirty-nine research projects. The NFCSP provides caregivers with information, counseling/training, help gaining access to services, respite care, and supplemental caregiving services.

About 2.2% of all employees took advantage of the FMLA to care for an ill parent in 2000, according to the Department of Labor in *Balancing the Needs of Families and Employers: Family and Medical Leave Surveys.* About one out of every six leave-takers that year (13%) used their leave for parental care. Parental care was the third most common use of the FMLA, following care for the employee's own health and care for a newborn or newly adopted child. In 2000 about 3.5 million people said they had needed leave time but had not been able to take it because they were worried such a leave might have negative financial or career repercussions, or for other reasons. Among the employees who needed leave but did not take it, 22.6% wanted to use the leave to care for an ill parent.

CHAPTER 8
WOMEN IN AMERICAN POLITICS

THE POLITICAL POWER OF WOMEN

On August 26, 1920, Tennessee became the thirty-sixth state to ratify the Nineteenth Amendment to the Constitution. With three-quarters of the states having ratified the amendment, all American women were granted the right to vote. On the advice of his mother, Henry Thomas Burn cast the deciding vote in the Tennessee House of Representatives. Previously he had sided with the anti-suffragists, who were opposed to women voting. Allegedly, the anti-suffragists were so angry at Burn that they chased him from the chamber, forcing him to climb out a window of the Capitol and inch along a ledge to safety.

The passage of the Nineteenth Amendment marked the end of a long and bitter struggle for the suffragists, led by Susan B. Anthony, Elizabeth Cady Stanton, and Lucretia Mott. From 1838 to 1910, twenty-five states passed laws allowing women to vote on school issues. In 1893 Colorado became the first state to allow women's suffrage, and by 1920 thirty states, primarily in the West and Midwest, had already granted women full suffrage. In the years since 1920, American women have exercised their right to vote, helped to elect their government, influenced legislation, and helped determine the direction of the nation.

More recently, the terrorist attacks on America of September 11, 2001, influenced women's interest in and involvement with politics. According to a January 2002 poll ("A First Look at the 2002 Election," *Women's Monitor*, EMILY's List, January 23, 2002), both men and women reported that they were paying more attention to the news than in the past, but women were more likely to be doing so (64% of women versus 57% of men). Nearly half of women (46%) reported a higher level of interest in politics than previously, compared with 38% of men, and a full 10% more women than men felt more interest in governmental policies than they had in the past (62% versus 52%).

A Note on the Sources of Data on Women's Political Activity

A great deal of data on voting patterns in the United States is collected by the U.S. Census Bureau. But much information specific to women's involvement in voting and other political behaviors is compiled by the Center for American Women and Politics (CAWP), a unit of the Eagleton Institute of Politics of Rutgers, The State University of New Jersey. Since 1971 CAWP has provided research and data on women in political office and has also conducted educational programs and worked to increase the political impact and effectiveness of women. EMILY's List, the nation's largest political action committee, which supports Democratic pro-choice women candidates, also conducts its own research on the behavior and attitudes of women voters in the United States. The bulk of the data in this chapter comes from these three sources.

WOMEN VOTERS
Registration and Voter Turnout

Any discussion of American elections is usually broken down into two categories: presidential elections and nonpresidential or congressional elections. Each takes place every four years, but alternating, so that 2000 was a presidential election, 2002 a nonpresidential election, and 2004 another presidential election. Although some congressional seats are up for election in years when there are presidential elections, the Census Bureau generally compares nonpresidential elections with other nonpresidential elections and presidential elections with other presidential elections. Voting and registration rates are generally higher in presidential election years than in nonpresidential years.

NONPRESIDENTIAL ELECTIONS. In the 2002 nonpresidential (congressional) elections, 47.1 million women voted, compared with 41.8 million men. (See Table 8.1.)

TABLE 8.1

Sex differences in voter turnout in nonpresidential elections, 1966–2002

Non-presidential election year	% of voting age population who reported voting		Number who reported voting	
	Women	Men	Women	Men
2002	43.0	41.4	47.1 million	41.8 million
1998	42.4	41.4	43.7 million	39.3 million
1994	45.3	44.7	44.9 million	40.7 million
1990	45.4	44.6	43.3 million	38.7 million
1986	46.1	45.8	42.2 million	37.7 million
1982	48.4	48.7	42.3 million	38.0 million
1978	45.3	46.6	36.3 million	33.3 million
1974	43.4	46.2	32.5 million	30.7 million
1970	52.7	56.8	33.8 million	32.0 million
1966	53.0	58.2	31.8 million	30.7 million

SOURCE: "Voter Turnout in Non-Presidential Elections," in "Sex Differences in Voter Turnout," Center for American Women and Politics, Eagleton Institute of Politics, Rutgers University, June 2005, http://www.cawp .rutgers.edu/Facts/sexdiff.pdf (accessed June 16, 2005)

A higher proportion of the female voting age population voted than the male voting age population (43% compared with 41.4%). In that year female registered voters (75.6 million) outnumbered male registered voters (66.4 million) by almost ten million. Since 1986, the proportion of eligible female voters who voted has exceeded the proportion of eligible male voters who voted, and that disparity seems to be growing.

Among citizens eligible to vote in 2002, 76% were non-Hispanic whites; 69.4% of this group was registered and 49.1% voted, a higher proportion than in any other group. (See Table 8.2.) Asian-American and Pacific Islanders were least likely to be registered (49.2%), followed by Hispanics (52.5%) and African-Americans (62.4%). Hispanics were least likely to vote (30.4%), followed by Asian-Americans and Pacific Islanders (31.2%) and African-Americans (42.3%). The majority of registered voters in each group voted; 70.7% of non-Hispanic whites, followed by 67.8% of African-Americans, 63.4% of Asian-Americans and Pacific Islanders, and 57.9% of Hispanics. (See Figure 8.1.) Within every racial/ethnic group except for Asian-Americans and Pacific Islanders, women were more likely than men to be registered and to have voted—although these percentages were much closer for non-Hispanic whites than African-Americans or Hispanics.

In 1972 the voting age was lowered from twenty-one to eighteen nationwide, thereby increasing the voting-age population. From 1966 to 2002 the number of women voting in nonpresidential elections increased 48.1%, whereas the numbers of voting men increased 36.2%. (See Table 8.1.) But in 1966, 53% of the female voting-age population voted, compared with only 43% in 2002. The percentage of the male voting-age population who

voted decreased from 58.2% in 1966 to 41.4% in 2002. The overall rate of voting in 2002 was 42.2%, up from a voter turnout of 41.9% in 1998, but still at historically low levels.

PRESIDENTIAL ELECTIONS. In 2004, a presidential election year, American women made up 52.2% of the voting-age U.S. citizen population. (See Table 8.3.) About 91.3% of voting-age U.S. residents in 2004 were citizens and therefore eligible to vote. The voting-age population does not include U.S. citizens living abroad who may vote.

Not only did women outnumber men in the voting-age population, but a higher proportion of women than men registered to vote. In 2004, 65.9% of voting age residents and 72.1% of U.S. citizens age eighteen and over were registered to vote—73.6% of eligible women and 70.5% of eligible men. (See Table 8.3.) Nearly 75.7 million women were registered to vote in 2004, compared with 66.4 million men. The voting rate of women eighteen and over has surpassed that of men in every presidential election from 1980 through 2004. Prior to 1980 men had been more likely to vote than women. Experts attribute this shift to a change in social climate—educational attainment and labor force participation increased among women in the second half of the twentieth century; both factors are strong correlates of voting.

In the 2004 presidential election between John Kerry and George W. Bush, 56.3% of the male voting-age population voted and 60.1% of the female voting-age population voted. (See Table 8.4.) Smaller percentages of voting-age men and women voted in the 2000 presidential election between Al Gore and George W. Bush.

THE POLITICAL GENDER GAP
The Opinion Gap

Differences in the political opinions of men and women may reflect differences in their lives. Since women generally earn less, have fewer employee benefits, and live longer than men, they tend to be more concerned about health care reform, Social Security, and other social programs. As the primary caregivers for children and the elderly, women are more likely to support programs that would help these groups.

In the 2004 presidential election, women were more likely to prefer the Democratic candidate, John Kerry, while men were more likely to prefer the Republican incumbent, George W. Bush. While both men and women viewed the war on terrorism and in Iraq as well as jobs and the economy as the most important issues, women and men differed in their perspectives. Women were less likely than men to think that the country was safer from terrorism than it had been before the terrorist attacks on

TABLE 8.2

Reported rates of voting and registration, by selected characteristics, November 2002

[Numbers in thousands]

Characteristic	Total population	Total citizen	Total citizen Reported registered Number	Total citizen Reported registered Percent	Total citizen Reported voted Number	Total citizen Reported voted Percent
Total, 18 years and over	**210,421**	**192,656**	**128,154**	**66.5**	**88,903**	**46.1**
Sex						
Men	100,939	91,644	59,422	64.8	41,801	45.6
Women	109,481	101,011	68,732	68.0	47,102	46.6
Race, Hispanic origin, and sex						
White	174,099	161,694	109,808	67.9	76,730	47.5
Men	84,466	77,850	51,769	66.5	36,784	47.2
Women	89,633	83,844	58,039	69.2	39,946	47.6
White non-Hispanic	150,499	147,171	102,154	69.4	72,259	49.1
Men	72,368	70,735	48,198	68.1	34,668	49.0
Women	78,132	76,438	53,957	70.6	37,591	49.2
Black	24,445	22,912	14,304	62.4	9,695	42.3
Men	10,811	9,998	5,758	57.6	3,815	38.2
Women	13,634	12,914	8,546	66.2	5,879	45.5
Asian and Pacific Islander	9,631	6,009	2,955	49.2	1,873	31.2
Men	4,569	2,827	1,428	50.5	931	32.9
Women	5,062	3,182	1,527	48.0	941	29.6
Hispanic (of any race)	25,162	15,601	8,196	52.5	4,747	30.4
Men	12,855	7,594	3,783	49.8	2,225	29.3
Women	12,307	8,007	4,413	55.1	2,522	31.5
Nativity status of citizens						
Total citizens	**192,656**	**192,656**	**128,154**	**66.5**	**88,903**	**46.1**
Native	180,473	180,473	121,526	67.3	84,490	46.8
Naturalized	12,183	12,183	6,628	54.4	4,413	36.2
Age						
18 to 24 years	27,377	24,334	10,470	43.0	4,697	19.3
25 to 34 years	38,512	32,854	19,339	58.9	10,450	31.8
35 to 44 years	43,716	39,241	26,214	66.8	17,569	44.8
45 to 54 years	40,043	37,593	27,006	71.8	20,088	53.4
55 to 64 years	26,881	25,679	19,424	75.6	15,432	60.1
65 to 74 years	17,967	17,415	13,681	78.6	11,339	65.1
75 years and over	15,925	15,540	12,020	77.3	9,328	60.0
Marital status						
Married-spouse present	117,772	107,702	79,524	73.8	59,214	55.0
Married-spouse absent	2,761	1,855	1,013	54.6	617	33.3
Widowed	14,080	13,538	9,677	71.5	6,864	50.7
Divorced	20,835	20,045	12,321	61.5	7,941	39.6
Separated	4,597	4,008	2,238	55.8	1,203	30.0
Never married	50,376	45,508	23,381	51.4	13,064	28.7
Educational attainment						
Less than 9th grade	12,333	8,004	3,999	50.0	2,393	29.9
9th to 12th grade, no diploma	20,908	18,238	8,699	47.7	4,875	26.7
High school graduate or GED	68,866	64,503	39,315	61.0	25,565	39.6
Some college or associate degree	57,343	54,752	38,236	69.8	26,239	47.9
Bachelor's degree	34,095	31,669	24,985	78.9	19,165	60.5
Advanced degree	16,877	15,490	12,919	83.4	10,667	68.9
Annual family income[a]						
Total family members	**157,892**	**144,287**	**98,797**	**68.5**	**69,768**	**48.4**
Less than $5,000	2,159	1,801	975	54.1	476	26.4
$5,000 to $9,999	4,051	3,420	1,680	49.1	837	24.5
$10,000 to $14,999	6,696	5,691	3,325	58.4	2,041	35.9
$15,000 to $24,999	14,665	12,175	7,521	61.8	4,699	38.6
$25,000 to $34,999	16,868	14,741	9,485	64.3	6,459	43.8
$35,000 to $49,999	21,945	19,904	13,605	68.4	9,369	47.1
$50,000 to $74,999	28,921	27,253	20,190	74.1	14,496	53.2
$75,000 and over	40,309	38,433	30,434	79.2	22,796	59.3
Income not reported	22,278	20,868	11,582	55.5	8,595	41.2

September 11, 2001, and they had more reservations about the Iraq war. Women were more likely than men to think that the country was moving in the wrong direction. And while men and women are very concerned about jobs, women are also very concerned about health care and retirement security (Susan Carroll, "Women Voters and the Gender Gap," American Political Science Association, 2004, http://www.apsanet.org/content_5270.cfm).

TABLE 8.2

Reported rates of voting and registration, by selected characteristics, November 2002 [CONTINUED]

[Numbers in thousands]

Characteristic	Total population	Total citizen	Total citizen			
			Reported registered		Reported voted	
			Number	Percent	Number	Percent
Employment status						
In the civilian labor force	142,635	130,221	86,904	66.7	58,918	45.2
Employed	134,900	123,429	83,186	67.4	56,813	46.0
Unemployed	7,735	6,792	3,718	54.7	2,105	31.0
Not in the labor force	67,785	62,434	41,250	66.1	29,985	48.0
Tenure						
Owner-occupied units	151,777	144,534	103,290	71.5	75,416	52.2
Renter-occupied units	55,994	45,736	23,442	51.3	12,627	27.6
No cash rent units	2,649	2,415	1,422	58.9	861	35.7
Duration of residence[b]						
Less than 1 month	3,323	2,805	1,355	48.3	576	20.5
1 to 6 months	18,022	15,179	8,097	53.3	4,030	26.5
7 to 11 months	8,929	7,482	4,054	54.2	2,189	29.3
1 to 2 years	30,448	26,037	16,435	63.1	9,980	38.3
3 to 4 years	27,200	24,199	17,489	72.3	11,842	48.9
5 years or longer	104,047	100,275	79,773	79.6	59,692	59.5
Not reported	18,451	16,677	952	5.7	594	3.6
Region and race and Hispanic origin						
Northeast	41,109	37,405	24,997	66.8	17,027	45.5
White	34,520	32,304	22,050	68.3	15,136	46.9
White non-Hispanic	31,402	30,260	21,057	69.6	14,547	48.1
Black	4,585	3,947	2,413	61.1	1,615	40.9
Asian and Pacific Islander	1,499	837	384	45.9	199	23.8
Hispanic (of any race)	3,751	2,510	1,234	49.2	712	28.4
Midwest	48,842	46,784	32,467	69.4	22,986	49.1
White	42,951	41,536	29,192	70.3	20,761	50.0
White non-Hispanic	40,880	40,306	28,553	70.8	20,401	50.6
Black	4,467	4,356	2,806	64.4	1,976	45.4
Asian and Pacific Islander	892	476	236	49.6	123	25.8
Hispanic (of any race)	2,183	1,286	671	52.2	375	29.2
South	74,208	68,769	45,706	66.5	30,857	44.9
White	58,216	54,325	36,802	67.7	24,958	45.9
White non-Hispanic	49,474	48,722	33,663	69.1	23,194	47.6
Black	13,330	12,628	7,973	63.1	5,323	42.2
Asian and Pacific Islander	1,669	961	459	47.8	287	29.9
Hispanic (of any race)	9,178	5,889	3,302	56.1	1,846	31.3
West	46,261	39,697	24,983	62.9	18,033	45.4
White	38,412	33,529	21,765	64.9	15,875	47.3
White non-Hispanic	28,744	27,884	18,881	67.7	14,117	50.6
Black	2,063	1,981	1,113	56.2	780	39.4
Asian and Pacific Islander	4,424	3,038	1,537	50.6	1,052	34.6
Hispanic (of any race)	10,050	5,916	2,989	50.5	1,815	30.7

[a]Limited to people in families.
[b]Data on duration of residence were obtained from responses to the question "How long has (this person) lived at this address?"

SOURCE: Jennifer Cheeseman Day and Kelly Holder, "Table B. Reported Rates of Voting and Registration by Selected Characteristics: November 2002," in *Voting and Registration in the Election of November 2002*, U.S. Census Bureau, Current Population Reports, P20-552, July 2004, http://www.census.gov/prod/2004pubs/p20-552.pdf (accessed June 16, 2005).

In "Women at the Center of Political Change," EMILY's List found that by May 2005 the Republican party had failed to hold the support that won them the 2004 presidential election; one-third of women who voted for Bush in the presidential election were not planning on voting Republican in the 2006 congressional elections. This shift occurred in part because domestic issues, rather than terrorism and foreign policy, began to take precedence. While women continued to believe that Republicans were stronger on issues of terrorism, in most domestic issues as well as the war in Iraq, women had more confidence in Democrats. (See Table 8.5.) In addition, while issues of morality and religion were very important to women voters, they viewed themselves as the arbiters of moral values. They felt that they did not want government to dictate religion or morality, and that the Republican government had overstepped its bounds in that regard.

The Voting Gap

The political opinion gap between men and women is reflected in their voting patterns. Women tend to be more likely than men to vote for Democratic candidates. The gender gap is defined as the difference between the proportion of women and the proportion of men voting

FIGURE 8.1

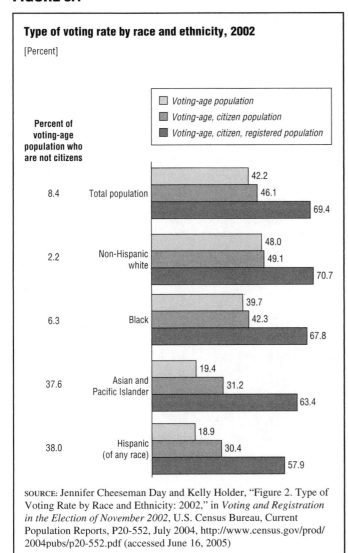

Type of voting rate by race and ethnicity, 2002

[Percent]

Legend:
- □ Voting-age population
- ▨ Voting-age, citizen population
- ▪ Voting-age, citizen, registered population

Percent of voting-age population who are not citizens

Total population (8.4)
- 42.2
- 46.1
- 69.4

Non-Hispanic white (2.2)
- 48.0
- 49.1
- 70.7

Black (6.3)
- 39.7
- 42.3
- 67.8

Asian and Pacific Islander (37.6)
- 19.4
- 31.2
- 63.4

Hispanic (of any race) (38.0)
- 18.9
- 30.4
- 57.9

SOURCE: Jennifer Cheeseman Day and Kelly Holder, "Figure 2. Type of Voting Rate by Race and Ethnicity: 2002," in *Voting and Registration in the Election of November 2002*, U.S. Census Bureau, Current Population Reports, P20-552, July 2004, http://www.census.gov/prod/2004pubs/p20-552.pdf (accessed June 16, 2005)

support of only 44% of white women, compared with the 48% who voted for Gore in 2000. The gender gap was apparent across all demographic groups, including traditionally Republican-leaning groups like white voters ("Gender Gap Persists in the 2004 Election," Votes for Women 2004, November 5, 2004).

A survey by Lake Snell Perry & Associates, commissioned by Votes for Women 2004, found that the gender gap was evident across marital categories, racial groups, and within every age group ("The Gender Gap and Women's Agenda for Moving Forward," November 9, 2004, http://votesforwomen2004.org/Election%20 Pol-l%20Analysis%2011-04.pdf). Among Democratic women who widely favored Kerry, 38% thought the economy and jobs were the most important issues, followed by health care and prescription drugs (14%) and Iraq (11%). On the other hand, Republican women, most of whom voted for Bush, were most concerned with terrorism and homeland security (24%), moral values (15%), and jobs and the economy (13%). Most women of both parties thought that the presidential campaign did not pay enough attention to issues important to them, like equal pay for women, prevention of violence against women, and women's equality under the law.

EMILY's List noted in its June 2005 report, "Women at the Center of Political Change," that the increased support of women for the Republican candidate George W. Bush in the 2004 presidential election that helped his reelection had eroded in the six months following the election. "The gender gap has reemerged strongly, as 43% of women say they would vote Democratic and only 32% would vote Republican," the report states. Important defectors from the Republican party included social conservatives (who viewed the Republicans as intruding into moral decisions), noncollege-educated whites, Midwestern whites, Catholics, white married women without children at home, women in the ideological middle, and women who identified themselves as weak Republicans. EMILY's List views these defections as an opportunity for Democrats to gain ground in the Congressional elections of 2006.

WOMEN AS ELECTED OFFICIALS

The number of women holding elective office at all levels of government increased steadily between 1979 and 2005. (See Table 8.6.) In 2005 the U.S. Congress was 15% female, up from 10.3% in 1995 and 3% in 1979. Women held 25.7% of statewide elective offices in 2005, down from 27.6% in 2001 but up from 11% in 1979. Women accounted for 22.5% of state legislators in 2005, up from 20.6% in 1995 and 10% in 1979. The majority of female elected officials are Democrats.

for the winning candidate. In 2004 the gap was seven percentage points—48% of women and 55% of men voted to reelect George W. Bush. But the Democratic candidate John Kerry won only a slight majority of women's votes (51%), down from the 54% of women who voted for Al Gore in the 2000 presidential election ("Gender Gap Persists in the 2004 Election," Votes for Women 2004, November 5, 2004, http://www.votesfor-women2004.org/gender.htm). The gender gap was consistent with the average gap of 7.7 points since 1980.

Although the 2000 presidential election was the closest in history, the voting gender gap was particularly large at ten percentage points. The EMILY's List survey "The Women's Vote and the 2000 Elections" found that 54% of women voted for Vice President Al Gore, a Democrat, and 43% voted for Governor George W. Bush, a Republican; 53% of men voted for Bush and 42% for Gore.

In 2004 Kerry won a smaller majority of working women than Gore had won in 2000. He also won the

TABLE 8.3

Reported voting and registration, by sex and age, November 2004

[In thousands]

Race, Hispanic origin, sex, and age	Total	Total population								U.S. citizen		
		Reported registered		Not registered		Reported voted		Did not vote		Reported registered	Not registered	Not a citizen
		Number	Percent	Number	Percent	Number	Percent	Number	Percent	Number	Number	Number
All races												
Both sexes												
Total 18 years and over	215,694	142,070	65.9	73,624	34.1	125,736	58.3	89,958	41.7	142,070	54,936	18,688
18 to 24 years	27,808	14,334	51.5	13,474	48.5	11,639	41.9	16,169	58.1	14,334	10,564	2,910
25 to 44 years	82,133	49,371	60.1	32,763	39.9	42,845	52.2	39,288	47.8	49,371	21,860	10,902
45 to 64 years	71,014	51,659	72.7	19,355	27.3	47,327	66.6	23,688	33.4	51,659	15,524	3,831
65 to 74 years	18,363	14,125	76.9	4,239	23.1	13,010	70.8	5,354	29.2	14,125	3,635	604
75 years and over	16,375	12,581	76.8	3,794	23.2	10,915	66.7	5,459	33.3	12,581	3,352	442
Male												
Total 18 years and over	103,812	66,406	64.0	37,406	36.0	58,455	56.3	45,357	43.7	66,406	27,741	9,665
18 to 24 years	13,960	6,731	48.2	7,229	51.8	5,415	38.8	8,545	61.2	6,731	5,642	1,587
25 to 44 years	40,618	23,403	57.6	17,215	42.4	19,913	49.0	20,705	51.0	23,403	11,435	5,780
45 to 64 years	34,471	24,676	71.6	9,795	28.4	22,520	65.3	11,951	34.7	24,676	7,922	1,873
65 to 74 years	8,438	6,534	77.4	1,904	22.6	6,119	72.5	2,319	27.5	6,534	1,635	269
75 years and over	6,325	5,062	80.0	1,263	20.0	4,489	71.0	1,836	29.0	5,062	1,107	156
Female												
Total 18 years and over	111,882	75,663	67.6	36,219	32.4	67,281	60.1	44,601	39.9	75,663	27,195	9,024
18 to 24 years	13,848	7,603	54.9	6,245	45.1	6,224	44.9	7,624	55.1	7,603	4,922	1,323
25 to 44 years	41,515	25,967	62.5	15,548	37.5	22,932	55.2	18,583	44.8	25,967	10,425	5,123
45 to 64 years	36,544	26,984	73.8	9,560	26.2	24,807	67.9	11,737	32.1	26,984	7,603	1,957
65 to 74 years	9,926	7,591	76.5	2,335	23.5	6,891	69.4	3,034	30.6	7,591	2,000	335
75 years and over	10,049	7,519	74.8	2,531	25.2	6,426	63.9	3,623	36.1	7,519	2,245	286

Note: 'Not registered' includes 'did not register to vote,' 'do not know,' and 'not reported.' 'Did not vote' includes 'did not vote,' 'do not know,' and 'not reported.'

SOURCE: "Table 2. Reported Voting and Registration, by Race, Hispanic Origin, Sex, and Age, for the United States: November 2004," in *Voting and Registration in the Election of November 2004*, U.S. Census Bureau, April 8, 2005, http://www.census.gov/population/www/socdemo/voting/cps2004.html (accessed July 1, 2005)

TABLE 8.4

Sex differences in voter turnout in presidential elections, 1964–2004

Presidential election year	% of voting age population who reported voting		Number who reported voting	
	Women	Men	Women	Men
2004	60.1	56.3	67.3 million	58.5 million
2000	56.2	53.1	59.3 million	51.5 million
1996	55.5	52.8	56.1 million	48.9 million
1992	62.3	60.2	60.6 million	53.3 million
1988	58.3	56.4	54.5 million	47.7 million
1984	60.8	59.0	54.5 million	47.4 million
1980	59.4	59.1	49.3 million	43.8 million
1976	58.8	59.6	45.6 million	41.1 million
1972	62.0	64.1	44.9 million	40.9 million
1968	66.0	69.8	41.0 million	38.0 million
1964	67.0	71.9	39.2 million	37.5 million

SOURCE: "Voter Turnout in Presidential Elections," in "Sex Differences in Voter Turnout," Center for American Women and Politics, Eagleton Institute of Politics, Rutgers University, June 2005, http://www.cawp.rutgers.edu/Facts/sexdiff.pdf (accessed June 16, 2005)

Women in Congress

The number of women in the U.S. Congress has either increased or stayed the same every session between the 96th (1979–81) and 109th (2005–07) Congresses. Since 1917 only the 66th Congress (1919–1921) had no female representation. In 2005 there were sixty-nine female representatives and fourteen female senators for a total of eighty-three congresswomen, the highest number ever, out of 540 total congressional seats. (See Table 8.7.) As of the same date, 228 women had served in Congress (144 Democrats and eighty-four Republicans); 195 had served only in the House, twenty-six had served only in the Senate, and seven had served in both houses. California had sent the most women to Congress (thirty), and five states (Delaware, Iowa, Mississippi, New Hampshire, and Vermont) had never been represented by a congresswoman. (See Table 8.8.) Nearly four-fifths of the states (thirty-eight) and the District of Columbia had elected five or fewer congresswomen.

Out of the one hundred senators in 2005, fourteen were women—nine Democrats and five Republicans, representing eleven states. Four states have been represented by two women senators in the same Congress (California, Kansas, Maine, and Washington). In 2005 both of the senators from three states—California, Washington, and Maine—were women.

TABLE 8.5

Women's trust of Democratic Party and Republican Party on selected issues on a scale of 1 to 10, 2005

[PLEASE TELL ME HOW MUCH YOU TRUST THE DEMOCRATIC OR REPUBLICAN PARTY TO HANDLE EACH OF THESE ISSUES ON A SCALE FROM 1 TO 10, ON WHICH A 10 MEANS THAT YOU COMPLETELY TRUST THE PARTY TO HANDLE THAT ISSUE AND A 1 MEANS THAT YOU DO NOT TRUST THE PARTY AT ALL TO HANDLE THAT ISSUE.*]

	Democrats (mean)	Republicans (mean)	Difference +/−
Having the right approach to protecting the environment	6.3	4.6	1.7
Addressing the needs of families on issues such as health care and education	6.1	4.7	1.4
Having the right approach on Social Security	5.7	4.3	1.4
Understanding the challenges that you face in making ends meet	5.7	4.4	1.3
Being fiscally responsible in dealing with the budget, taxes, and spending	5.4	4.3	1.1
Respecting the privacy of individuals and families	6.1	5.1	1
Promoting economic opportunity, so that people have a chance to get ahead	5.9	4.9	1
Having the right approach on taxes	5.3	4.7	0.6
Having the right approach to the situation in Iraq	5.2	4.7	0.5
Supporting the right kind of justices to serve on the Supreme Court	5.6	5.2	0.4
Representing your values on issues such as abortion and gay marriage	5.2	5.0	0.2
Having solid and consistent ideas, policies, and principles	5.3	5.4	−0.1
Keeping America safe from terrorism	5.4	5.8	−0.4

*Among all women voters.

SOURCE: "Table 1," in *Women at the Center of Political Change*, EMILY'S List Women's Monitor, June 2005, http://www.emilyslist.org/newsroom/monitor/full_report.pdf (accessed July 1, 2005)

TABLE 8.6

Percentages of women in elective offices, selected years 1979–2005

Year	U.S. Congress	Statewide elective	State legislatures
1979	3%	11%	10%
1981	4%	11%	12%
1983	4%	11%	13%
1985	5%	14%	15%
1987	5%	14%	16%
1989	5%	14%	17%
1991	6%	18%	18%
1993	10.1%	22.2%	20.5%
1995	10.3%	25.9%	20.6%
1997	11.0%	25.4%	21.6%
1999	12.1%	27.6%	22.4%
2001	13.6%	27.6%	22.4%
2003	13.6%	26.0%	22.4%
2004	13.8%	26.0%	22.5%
2005	15.0%	25.7%	22.5%

SOURCE: "Percentages of Women in Elective Offices," in *Women in Elective Office 2005*, Center for American Women in Politics, Eagleton Institute of Politics, Rutgers University, July 2005, http://www.cawp.rutgers.edu/Facts/Officeholders/elective.pdf (accessed June 16, 2005)

As of 2005, a total of thirty-three women had served in the Senate—twenty Democrats and thirteen Republicans—and the number of female senators climbed every session from the 101st (1989–91) to the 108th. The first woman senator was Rebecca Latimer Felton (D-GA), appointed in 1922 to fill the remainder of the term of a senator who had died, an eighty-seven-year-old who served for only one day. Hattie Wyatt Caraway (D-AR) became the first woman elected to the Senate, first finishing out her late husband's term starting in 1931, then winning two additional terms. Margaret Chase Smith (R-ME) served in the House from 1940 through 1949,

then served in the Senate from 1949 through 1973, a record for a female senator's term. Fourteen women had first entered the Senate through appointments to unexpired terms, and five women had won special elections to fill unexpired terms. Of the eight women who had been elected to the Senate without first having been elected to the House or elected/appointed to fill a vacant Senate seat, five were members of the 108th Congress.

Of the 435 seats in the House of Representatives in 2005, sixty-nine were held by women (forty-six Democrats and twenty-three Republicans), representing twenty-six states. Three of the Democratic women were delegates from Guam, the Virgin Islands, and Washington, D.C. According to CAWP, a record 141 women (eighty-eight Democrats, fifty-three Republicans), were major-party candidates for regular House seats in 2004, along with the three Democratic women and one Republican for delegates.

MINORITY WOMEN IN CONGRESS. Twenty-four African-American women, seven Hispanic women, and two Asian-American women have served in Congress. Fourteen African-American women and seven Hispanic women served in the 109th Congress.

Patsy Takemoto Mink (D-HI), the first of the two Asian-American/Pacific Islander women who have served in Congress, served in the House from 1965 until 1977, was reelected in 1990, and continued to serve until her death in 2002. The other Asian-American congresswoman was Patricia Saiki (D-HI), who served from 1987 to 1991.

Ileana Ros-Lehtinen (R-FL) was the first Cuban-American and the first Hispanic woman to serve in

TABLE 8.7

Number of women in Congress, 1917–2007

Congress	Years	Total number of women in Congress	Number of women in House	Number of women in Senate
65th	1917–1919	1	1	0
66th	1919–1921	0	0	0
67th	1921–1923	4	3	1
68th	1923–1925	1	1	0
69th	1925–1927	3	3	0
70th	1927–1929	5	5	0
71st	1929–1931	9	9	0
72nd	1931–1933	8	7	1
73rd	1933–1935	8	7	1
74th	1935–1937	8	6	2
75th	1937–1939	9	6	3
76th	1939–1941	9	8	1
77th	1941–1943	10	9	1
78th	1943–1945	9	8	1
79th	1945–1947	11	11	0
80th	1947–1949	8	7	1
81st	1949–1951	10	9	1
82nd	1951–1953	11	10	1
83rd	1953–1955	15	12	3
84th	1955–1957	18	17	1
85th	1957–1959	16	15	1
86th	1959–1961	19	17	2
87th	1961–1963	20	18	2
88th	1963–1965	14	12	2
89th	1965–1967	13	11	2
90th	1967–1969	12	11	1
91st	1969–1971	11	10	1
92nd	1971–1973	15	13	2
93rd	1973–1975	16	16	0
94th	1975–1977	19	19	0
95th	1977–1979	20	18	2
96th	1979–1981	17	16	1
97th	1981–1983	23	21	2
98th	1983–1985	24	22	2
99th	1985–1987	25	23	2
100th	1987–1989	25	23	2
101st	1989–1991	31	29	2
102nd	1991–1993	33	30	3
103rd	1993–1995	55	48	7
104th	1995–1997	59	50	9
105th	1997–1999	65	56	9
106th	1999–2001	67	58	9
107th	2001–2003	75	62	13
108th	2003–2005	77	63	14
109th	2005–2007	83	69	14

SOURCE: Mildred L. Amer, "Table 3. Number of Women in Congress, 65th–109th Congresses (1917–2005)," in *Women in the United States Congress, 1917–2005*, The Library of Congress, Congressional Research Service, June 21, 2005, http://www.fas.org/sgp/crs/misc/RL30261.pdf (accessed July 1, 2005)

TABLE 8.8

Number of women ever sent to Congress, by state, 1917–2007

State/DC, VI, GU*	Number of women sent to Congress, 65th–109th Congresses
California	30
New York	20
Illinois	12
Florida	10
Washington	8
Maryland	7
Michigan	7
Connecticut	6
Missouri	6
Ohio	6
Georgia	6
Texas	6
Pennsylvania	6
Arkansas	5
Indiana	5
Kansas	5
Louisiana	5
New Jersey	5
Oregon	5
South Carolina	5
Tennessee	5
North Carolina	5
Alabama	3
Hawaii	3
Maine	3
Massachusetts	3
Minnesota	3
Nebraska	3
Utah	3
South Dakota	3
Colorado	3
Virginia	3
Arizona	2
Idaho	2
Kentucky	2
New Mexico	2
Nevada	2
West Virginia	2
Wisconsin	2
District of Columbia	1
Montana	1
North Dakota	1
Oklahoma	1
Rhode Island	1
Virgin Islands	1
Wyoming	1
Alaska	1
Guam	1
Delaware	0
Iowa	0
Mississippi	0
New Hampshire	0
Vermont	0

*VI is Virgin Islands and GU is Guam

SOURCE: Adapted from Mildred L. Amer, "Table 2. Women in Congress, 65th–109th Congresses, by State," in *Women in the United States Congress, 1917–2005*, The Library of Congress, Congressional Research Service, June 21, 2005, http://www.fas.org/sgp/crs/misc/RL30261.pdf (accessed July 1, 2005)

Congress. She was elected to the House in a special August 1989 election. Lucille Roybal-Allard (D-CA), who began her term in 1993, was the first Mexican-American congresswoman. Hispanic representatives Loretta Sanchez (D-CA) and Linda Sanchez (D-CA) were the first sisters to serve in Congress.

Shirley Chisholm (D-NY) was the first African-American woman in Congress. She was elected to the House in 1968 and served until 1983. In 1992 Carol Moseley-Braun (D-IL) became the only African-American woman to ever be elected to the Senate. She lost her bid for reelection in 1998. Although fourteen black women served in the 109th Congress, this was one fewer than the record number of fifteen who served in the 107th Congress (2001–03).

CONGRESSIONAL POSITIONS OF POWER. In the 109th Congress women held more leadership positions and committee chairs than ever before, according to CAWP

("Women in Congress: Leadership Roles and Committee Chairs," March 2005). In the Senate, seven women held leadership roles and two more were committee chairs:

- Barbara Boxer (D-CA)—Chief Deputy Whip

- Hillary Rodham Clinton (D-NY)—Chair, Steering and Outreach Committee

- Elizabeth Dole (R-NC)—Chair, National Republican Senatorial Committee

- Kay Bailey Hutchison (R-TX)—Republican Conference Secretary

- Blanche L. Lincoln (D-AR)—Chair of Rural Outreach

- Patty Murray (D-WA)—Assistant Floor Leader

- Debbie Stabenow (D-MI)—Democratic Conference Secretary

- Susan Collins (R-ME)—Chair, Committee on Homeland Security and Governmental Affairs

- Olympia J. Snowe (R-ME)—Chair, Committee on Small Business and Entrepreneurship

In the 103rd and 104th Congresses (1993–95 and 1995–97), only two women senators held positions of leadership, and prior to the 90th Congress (1967–69), no woman had done so. Nancy Landon Kassebaum (R-KS) became the first woman to chair a major Senate committee when she became head of the Committee on Labor and Human Resources of the 104th Congress. The only previous female Senate committee chair was Hattie Caraway, who chaired the Committee on Enrolled Bills from 1933 to 1945 for the 73rd to 78th Congresses.

Women also hold important roles in the U.S. House of Representatives. Representative Nancy Pelosi (D-CA) was elected House Democratic Leader, the highest leadership position ever held by a woman in the House in the 108th and 109th Congresses. She was also the first woman to be nominated to be Speaker of the House. Although no women chaired House committees in the 109th Congress (and had not done so since the 104th Congress), CAWP notes that seven female representatives did have leadership roles:

- Nancy Pelosi (D-CA)—House Democratic Leader

- Barbara Cubin (R-WY)—Secretary, House Republican Conference

- Diana DeGette (D-CO)—Chief Deputy Whip

- Rosa De Lauro (D-CT)—Co-Chair, House Democratic Steering Committee

- Deborah Pryce (R-OH)—Chair, House Republican Conference

- Jan Schakowsky (D-IL)—Chief Deputy Whip

- Maxine Waters (D-CA)—Chief Deputy Whip

State Executive Offices

As of April 2005, eighty-one women held statewide elective executive posts, 25.7% of the 315 available posts; more were Republicans (forty-three) than Democrats (thirty-five), and three had no party affiliation. The posts held by women were:

- Governor (8)
- Lieutenant Governor (15)
- Attorney General (5)
- Secretary of State (12)
- State Treasurer (8)
- State Auditor (7)
- State Comptroller/Controller (3)
- Chief Agricultural Official (2)
- Chief State Education Official (10)
- Commissioner of Insurance (2)
- Commissioner of Labor (2)
- Corporation Commissioner (2)
- Public Service Commissioner (4)
- Railroad Commissioner (1)

The number of women in statewide elective office in 2004 was lower than it was in 1995 and from 1997 to 2001, but higher than all other previous years. In 1969 only twenty-three women held statewide elective executive offices (6.6%). According to CAWP, every state but Maine had elected women to executive offices as of April 2005.

GOVERNORS. There were six Democratic and two Republican women governors as of February 2004. Of these, one took office in 2001, two in 2002, two in 2003, two in 2004, and one in 2005. The 2005 total of eight is the highest-ever number of simultaneous female governors.

As of July 2005, a total of twenty-eight women had served as state governors—eighteen Democrats and ten Republicans. Of these women, eighteen were first elected in their own right, seven became governors by constitutional succession, and three replaced their husbands as governor.

MINORITY WOMEN. Five women of color held statewide elective executive offices in 2005. Jennette Bradley (R-OH) was state treasurer of Ohio and Denise Nappier (D-CT) was state treasurer of Connecticut; both are African-American. Three Hispanic women also served: Susan Castillo (NP-OR) was superintendent of public instruction in Oregon; Patricia Madrid (D-NM) was attorney general in New Mexico; and Rebecca Vigil-Giron (D-NM) was secretary of state in New Mexico.

State Legislators

According to CAWP ("Women in State Legislatures 2005," June 2005), women accounted for 22.5% of state legislators in 2005. These 1,662 women held 401 (20.3%) of the state senate seats and 1,281 (23.3%) of the state house or assembly seats. The majority (62.8%) were Democrats; a little more than a third (36.3%) were Republicans. A third or more of state legislators were women in Maryland (34%), Delaware (33.9%), Arizona (33.3%), Nevada (33.3%), Vermont (33.3%), and Washington (33.3%). One of ten or fewer state legislators were women in South Carolina (8.8%) and Alabama (10%).

The number of women serving in state legislatures increased nearly fivefold between 1971 (when 344 women served) and 2005. The first women state legislators were three Republicans elected to the Colorado House of Representatives in 1894. The first female state senator was a Utah Democrat elected in 1896.

MINORITY WOMEN. According to CAWP ("Women of Color in Elective Office 2005," June 2005), among the women in the 2005 state legislatures—320, or 19.2%—were women of color; these were overwhelmingly Democratic. African-American women held 218 seats in thirty-seven state legislatures—fifty-eight senators and 160 representatives—all but four of them Democrats. Asian-American/Pacific Islander women held twenty-four seats in eight state legislatures—six senators and eighteen representatives—all but six of them Democrats. Hispanic women held sixty-nine seats in seventeen state legislatures—nineteen senators and fifty representatives—all but eight of them Democrats. Native American women held nine seats in five state legislatures—two senators and seven representatives—all but one of them Democrats.

LEADERSHIP POSITIONS. In 2005 three women served as presidents of state senates: Joan Fitz-Gerald (D-CO), Beth Edmonds (D-ME), and Rosa Franklin (D-WA). Two women were speakers of state houses: Karen Minnis (R-OR) and Gaye R. Symington (D-VT).

As of August 2003, forty-six state legislators in leadership positions (13.6%) were women ("Women State Legislators: Leadership Positions and Committee Chairs 2003," CAWP, August 2003). They held twenty-one of the 167 leadership positions in state senates (12.5%) and twenty-five of the 170 leadership positions in state houses (14.7%). In state legislatures, 18.9% of committee chairs were women as of August 2003.

Municipal Offices

In 1887 Susanna Salter of Argonia, Kansas, became the first elected woman mayor in the United States. According to "Women in Elective Office 2005" (CAWP, June 2005), as of January 2005, thirteen of the one hundred largest American cities had women mayors.

Dallas, Texas, the ninth-largest city in the nation, was the largest city with a woman mayor, Laura Miller. One mayor, Shirley Franklin of Atlanta, Georgia, was African-American, and Heather Fargo, mayor of Sacramento, California, was Hispanic. Of the 243 mayors of cities with more than one hundred thousand people, 15.6% were women (down from 19% in 2001), including three African-Americans and six Latinas. Of the 1,135 mayors of cities with more than thirty thousand residents in 2005, 15.9% were women (down from 21.2% in 2001).

FINANCING WOMEN'S POLITICAL CAMPAIGNS

Political campaigns are expensive, and political action committees (PACs) are a major source of campaign financing. Lack of campaign funds has been an obstacle for women candidates. According to CAWP ("Women's PACs and Donor Networks: A Contact List," March 2005), in 2005 there were forty-one political action committees (PACs) or donor networks (thirteen national and twenty-nine state/local) that either gave money primarily to women candidates or received the majority of their donations from women. This was a decrease of four PACs since the previous year. In addition, PACs that raise money for specific issues of concern to women, such as abortion rights, may donate to women candidates who support those issues.

EMILY's List is a donor network founded in 1985 with the goal of electing more Democratic congresswomen and women governors who support abortion rights. "EMILY" stands for "early money is like yeast"—it makes the "dough" rise. The network raises money for women candidates, helps with their campaigns, and encourages women to vote. According to information available on the EMILY's List Web site in July 2005, EMILY's List is the largest PAC in the United States, with more than one hundred thousand members, and has provided the most funds to federal candidates since 1994. For the 2004 elections, members of EMILY's List contributed $10.7 million to candidates, and every EMILY's List incumbent seeking reelection won.

PRESIDENTIAL AND VICE-PRESIDENTIAL CANDIDATES

Presidential Hopefuls

Although several First Ladies, including Eleanor Roosevelt and Hillary Rodham Clinton, played important political roles during their husbands' presidencies, no woman has yet served as president of the United States. However, according to CAWP ("Women Presidential and Vice Presidential Candidates," May 2003), at least twenty-one women have made a bid for the presidency or vice-presidency. In 1872 Victoria Claflin Woodhull ran against Republican Ulysses S. Grant and Democrat Horace Greeley as the candidate of the suffragist Equal

Rights Party. Belva Ann Bennett Lockwood was the Equal Rights Party presidential candidate in 1884 and 1888. She was also the first woman lawyer to practice before the U.S. Supreme Court.

In 1964 Margaret Chase Smith (R-ME) became the first woman to run in presidential primary elections. In 1972 Shirley Chisholm became the first African-American woman to run in the presidential primaries. In 1988 Patricia S. Schroeder (D-CO) became the first woman to initiate a serious bid for the presidency, although she dropped out before the primaries because of a lack of money. In 1996 three women Democrats and six women Republicans entered presidential primaries; three third-party women also ran that year. Elizabeth Hanford Dole initiated a bid for the Republican Party presidential nomination in 1999 but dropped out of the race before the primaries. Lenora Fulani ran as the New Alliance Party presidential candidate in the 1992 general election, becoming the first African-American and the first woman to appear on ballots in all fifty states.

2004. In early 2004, while no Republicans were challenging incumbent President George W. Bush in the primaries, a number of Democrats vied for their party's nomination. One of those was Carol Moseley-Braun (D-IL), who entered the race in September 2004. Braun was the first female senator from Illinois, the first black female senator, and the first black Democratic senator. Her candidacy was endorsed by both the National Organization for Women and the National Women's Political Caucus, and by January 9, 2004, according to the Feminist Daily News Wire, her name had appeared on primary ballots in twenty states. But in January 2004 Braun withdrew from the race, noting in a January 15 press statement that "the funding and organizational disadvantages of a nontraditional campaign could not be overcome" ("Carol Moseley Braun Withdraws from Presidential Race and Endorses Howard Dean").

Vice-Presidential Candidates

Two women have sought major party vice-presidential nominations. The first, Frances "Sissy" Farenthold, received four hundred votes at the 1972 Democratic National Convention, finishing second. In 1984 Geraldine Anne Ferraro became the only woman to run for vice-president on a major-party ticket when Walter F. Mondale picked her as his running mate. The Mondale-Ferraro ticket lost to Ronald Reagan and Dan Quayle in a landslide election. In addition to these two women, Libertarian Toni Nathan won one electoral vote in 1972 when a Virginia elector voted for Richard M. Nixon but would not support Nixon's running mate, Spiro T. Agnew. In 1996 and 2000 Winona LaDuke of the White Earth Reservation in Minnesota was Ralph Nader's running mate on the Green Party ticket.

PRESIDENTIAL CABINETS

The first woman to serve in a cabinet post was Frances Perkins, appointed by President Franklin D. Roosevelt as Secretary of Labor in 1933. She remained in that post until 1945, one of only two cabinet members to serve throughout the entire Roosevelt administration. Perkins was instrumental in the design and implementation of the New Deal legislation. As of 2005, according to CAWP's "Women Appointed to Presidential Cabinets," thirty women had been appointed by presidents to cabinet or cabinet-level posts. Of these women, sixteen were appointed by three Democratic presidents and fourteen by five Republican presidents.

President Dwight D. Eisenhower named Oveta Culp Hobby as Secretary of Health, Education, and Welfare in 1953, and President Gerald Ford named Carla Anderson Hills as Secretary of Housing and Urban Development (HUD) in 1975. Since then many more women have been named to cabinet-level positions. Patricia R. Harris was appointed secretary of HUD by President Jimmy Carter in 1977 and Secretary of Health and Human Services (HHS) in 1979. She was the first African-American woman to serve in a presidential cabinet. Carter also appointed Shirley M. Hufstedler as Secretary of Education. President Ronald Reagan had three women cabinet members, including Elizabeth Dole, who was Secretary of Transportation under Reagan and Secretary of Labor under President George H. W. Bush. Reagan also named Jeane J. Kirkpatrick as United Nations ambassador, and President Bush named Carla Hills as special trade representative.

Under President Bill Clinton, Hazel R. O'Leary served as energy secretary, Carol M. Browner was head of the Environmental Protection Agency (EPA), Janet Reno was attorney general, Donna E. Shalala was Secretary of HHS, and Alexis Herman was Secretary of Labor. Madeleine K. Albright served Clinton first as U.N. ambassador and then as Secretary of State, the highest-ranking woman in the U.S. government. Clinton also named women as chairs of the National Economic Council and the Council of Economic Advisors, as U.S. trade representative, and as director of the Office of Personnel Management. Clinton appointed Alice M. Rivlin as director of the Office of Management and Budget (OMB) in 1994 and named her to the Federal Reserve Board in February 1996. Aida Alvarez became administrator of the Small Business Administration in 1997, the first Hispanic woman to hold a cabinet-level position.

In 2001 George W. Bush appointed Elaine Chao as Secretary of Labor, the first Asian-American woman to hold a cabinet-level post. Bush also named Gale Norton as Secretary of the Interior, Condoleezza Rice as National Security Advisor, Anne Veneman as Secretary of Agriculture, and Christie Todd Whitman as administrator of the EPA. (Whitman resigned her post in June 2003.) In 2005 Bush appointed Condoleezza Rice as Secretary of State and Margaret Spellings as Secretary of Education.

By 2005 six women had headed the Department of Labor, and HHS had had three women heads. Women had never been appointed heads of the Defense, Treasury, or Veterans Affairs Departments. Among the cabinet-level appointees, twelve women were attorneys and ten were academics. Prior to being named to cabinet-level posts, twenty-one women had held other federal offices. Margaret M. Heckler, Reagan's secretary of HHS and later ambassador to Ireland, and Lynn Morley Martin, Secretary of Labor from 1991 to 1993 under President George H. W. Bush, were former congresswomen.

CHAPTER 9
WOMEN AS VICTIMS

CRIME

Since 1973 the Bureau of Justice Statistics (BJS) of the U.S. Department of Justice (DOJ) has conducted an annual survey to measure rates of criminal victimization. Each year the National Crime Victimization Survey (NCVS) questions forty-two thousand households containing nearly seventy-six thousand people on the frequency, characteristics, and consequences of criminal victimization and estimates the likelihood of rape, sexual assault, robbery, assault, theft, household burglary, and motor vehicle theft for the population as a whole, as well as for segments of the population, including women. Much of the data in this chapter is derived from BJS analyses of the NCVS.

Falling Crime Rates

According to *Criminal Victimization 2002* (August 2003) from the BJS, the rate of violent crime dropped from 51.2 victimizations per one thousand people age twelve and over in 1994 to less than half that (22.6) in 2003. Overall, violent victimization rates for 2003 were approximately the same as in 2002, indicating that crime rates had stabilized. The rates were the lowest ever recorded since such rates began to be measured in 1973. There were 5.4 million violent crimes (rape, sexual assault, robbery, and simple and aggravated assault), 18.6 million property crimes (theft, burglary, and motor vehicle theft), and 185,000 personal thefts (pocket picking and purse snatching) committed against U.S. residents age twelve and over in 2003.

VIOLENT CRIMES. Violent crime rates have been dropping for both genders since 1994. (See Figure 9.1.) In fact, the violent crime rate decreased 55.9% between 1994 and 2003. The rate of violent victimizations, excluding murder, in 2003 was 22.6 per one thousand people age twelve and over, down from 25.1 per one thousand in 2001. The violent crime rate fell slightly from 2002 to 2003 because assault rates fell slightly (from 19.8 to 19.3 per one thousand households) and rape/sexual assault rates fell slightly (from 1.1 to 0.8 per one thousand households).

PROPERTY CRIMES. The property crime rate generally fell between 1974 and 2003, falling steadily from 1993 (319 victimizations per one thousand households) to 2002 (159 victimizations per one thousand households), and stabilizing somewhat from 2002 to 2003, when the rate was 163 per one thousand households. This drop represented a 49% decrease in property crimes over the decade. The 2002 rate had been the lowest level since such data were measured beginning in 1974.

Female Victims of Crime

Fewer women than men are victims of violent crime, including homicide, although in recent years the rates have become much more even. (See Figure 9.1.) In 1973 more than twice as many men (sixty-eight per one thousand) were victimized as women (31.4 per one thousand), but 2003 figures show that only a little more than a third (38.4%) more men were victimized than women (26.3 males per one thousand individuals versus nineteen females per one thousand individuals). (See Table 9.1.) Although violent crime rates have been generally falling for both genders, men's rates have fallen more than have women's.

Assaults were the most common violent crime committed against both males and females in 2003. (See Table 9.1.) During 2001 a slightly higher percentage of males than females were victims of simple assault (16.7 men per one thousand versus 15.1 per one thousand); in 2003 this gap widened (17.1 men per one thousand versus 12.4 women per one thousand). A far higher proportion of females than males were raped or sexually assaulted in 2002 (1.5 per one thousand women versus 0.2 per one thousand men), and females experienced more personal

FIGURE 9.1

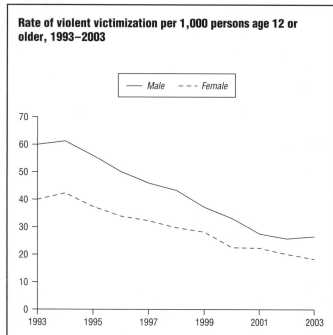

Rate of violent victimization per 1,000 persons age 12 or older, 1993–2003

— Male - - - Female

SOURCE: Shannan M. Catalano, "Figure 3. Violent Crime and Gender," in "Criminal Victimization, 2003," *National Crime Victimization Survey*, U.S. Department of Justice, Bureau of Justice Statistics, NCJ 205455,b September 2004, http://www.ojp.usdoj.gov/bjs/pub/pdf/cv03 .pdf (accessed June 16, 2005)

theft (1.1 victimizations per one thousand women versus 0.4 per one thousand men). A higher proportion of males (3.2 per one thousand) than females (1.9 per one thousand) were robbed in 2003.

Victims of robbery and assault are often young, and the rates for these crimes decline sharply among older age groups. (See Table 9.1.) Overall, sixteen- to nineteen-year-olds had the highest rate of violent victimizations in 2003 (fifty-three per one thousand). But rape/sexual assault rates were highest among twenty- to twenty-four-year-olds (1.7 per one thousand), second-highest among twenty-five- to thirty-four-year-olds (1.6 per one thousand), and third-highest among sixteen- to nineteen-year-olds (1.3 per one thousand). Robbery rates were also higher among twenty- to twenty-four-year-olds (6.4 per one thousand) and twelve- to fifteen-year-olds (5.2 per one thousand) than among sixteen- to nineteen-year-olds (5.1 per one thousand).

Victimization rates also differed by race and ethnic group in 2003. Violent victimization rates were highest among African-Americans (29.1 per one thousand). Hispanics followed, with a violent victimization rate of 24.2 per one thousand. Whites had the lowest rate of 21.5 per one thousand.

TABLE 9.1

Violent crime and personal theft, by sex, race, Hispanic origin, and age, 2003

		Victimizations per 1,000 persons age 12 or older						
		Violent crimes						
					Assault			
Characteristic of victim	Population	All	Rape/sexual assault	Robbery	Total	Aggravated	Simple	Personal theft
Gender								
Male	116,041,090	26.3	0.2[a]	3.2	23.0	5.9	17.1	0.4
Female	123,264,890	19.0	1.5	1.9	15.7	3.3	12.4	1.1
Race[b]								
White	197,577,400	21.5	0.8	1.9	18.8	4.2	14.7	0.6
Black	28,561,780	29.1	0.8[a]	5.9	22.3	6.0	16.3	1.7
Other race	11,120,220	16.0	0.2[a]	3.4	12.4	5.4	7.0	0.9[a]
Two or more	2,046,590	67.7	5.8[a]	8.1[a]	53.7	21.3	32.4	2.7[a]
Hispanic origin[b]								
Hispanic	30,275,550	24.2	0.4[a]	3.1	20.8	4.6	16.1	1.1[a]
Non-Hispanic	207,263,340	22.3	0.9	2.4	19.0	4.6	14.4	0.7
Age								
12–15	17,084,330	51.6	1.2[a]	5.2	45.3	8.9	36.4	1.5[a]
16–19	16,210,780	53.0	1.3[a]	5.1	46.6	11.9	34.7	1.4[a]
20–24	19,786,270	43.3	1.7	6.4	35.3	9.8	25.5	1.6
25–34	39,449,790	26.4	1.6	2.5	22.3	6.0	16.3	1.0
35–49	65,780,190	18.5	0.6	1.7	16.1	3.8	12.3	0.5
50–64	46,736,200	10.3	0.4[a]	1.4	8.5	1.6	7.0	0.3[a]
65 or older	34,258,430	2.0	0.1[a]	0.7[a]	1.2	0.1[a]	1.1	0.5[a]

Note: The National Crime Victimization Survey includes as violent crime rape, sexual assault, robbery, and assault. Because the NCVS interviews persons about their victimizations, murder and manslaughter cannot be included.
[a]Based on 10 or fewer sample cases.
[b]Racial and ethnic categories in 2003 are not comparable to those in previous years.

SOURCE: Shannan M. Catalano, "Table 6. Rates of Violent Crime and Personal Theft, by Gender, Race, Hispanic Origin, and Age, 2003," in "Criminal Victimization, 2003," *National Crime Victimization Survey*, U.S. Department of Justice, Bureau of Justice Statistics, NCJ 205455, September 2004, http://www .ojp.usdoj.gov/bjs/pub/pdf/cv03.pdf (accessed June 16, 2005)

TABLE 9.2

Victim and offender relationship, by sex, 2003

Relationship with victim	Violent crime		Rape/sexual assault		Robbery		Aggravated assault		Simple assault	
	Number	Percent	Number	Percent	Number	Percent	Number	Percent	Number	Percent
Male victims										
Total	3,056,160	100%	19,670	100%	365,590	100%	688,420	100%	1,982,480	100%
Nonstranger	1,287,960	42%	14,500	74%*	118,300	32%	266,770	39%	888,400	45%
Intimate	83,750	3	5,940	30*	6,130	2*	21,910	3*	49,780	3
Other relative	138,310	5	0	0*	17,250	5*	12,490	2*	108,570	6
Friend/acquaintance	1,065,900	35	8,560	44*	94,910	26	232,370	34	730,050	37
Stranger	1,658,160	54%	5,170	26%*	226,110	62%	399,240	58%	1,027,630	52%
Relationship unknown	110,050	4%	0	0%*	21,180	6%*	22,420	3%*	66,450	3%
Female victims										
Total	2,345,550	100%	179,170	100%	230,540	100%	412,690	100%	1,523,150	100%
Nonstranger	1,562,010	67%	125,370	70%	110,670	48%	274,430	67%	1,051,540	69%
Intimate	437,990	19	21,440	12*	30,990	13*	101,400	25	284,170	19
Other relative	230,850	10	13,930	8*	17,430	8*	40,320	10	159,180	11%
Friend/acquaintance	893,170	38	90,000	50	62,260	27	132,720	32	608,190	40%
Stranger	745,930	32%	53,800	30%	103,630	45%	131,850	32%	456,640	30%
Relationship unknown	37,610	2%	0	0%*	16,240	7%*	6,400	2%*	14,970	1%*

Note: Percentages may not total to 100% because of rounding.
*Based on 10 or fewer sample cases.

SOURCE: Shannan M. Catalano, "Table 9. Victim and Offender Relationship, 2003," in "Criminal Victimization, 2003," *National Crime Victimization Survey*, U.S. Department of Justice, Bureau of Justice Statistics, NCJ 205455, September 2004, http://www.ojp.usdoj.gov/bjs/pub/pdf/cv03.pdf (accessed June 16, 2005)

ARMED CRIMINALS AND SELF-PROTECTION. According to the BJS, 24% of violent crime victims faced an armed offender in 2003 (down from 33.3% in 2001). Robbery victims were most likely to face an armed criminal in 2003 (45%), whereas only 11% of rape/sexual assault victims faced an armed offender. Firearms were used in 7% of violent crimes but were most common in robberies (25%).

VICTIM–OFFENDER RELATIONSHIP. In contrast to violent crimes committed against men, most violent crimes against women are not committed by strangers. In 2003 only 32% of violent crimes against women were committed by a stranger, compared with 54% of violent crimes against men. (See Table 9.2.) Strangers committed 45% of robberies of females and 62% of robberies of males. Strangers committed only 30% of all rape/sexual assault crimes against women, 32% of aggravated assaults, and 30% of simple assaults.

Among violent crimes against females in 2003, 38% were committed by a friend or acquaintance and 19% were committed by an intimate—a current or former spouse, boyfriend, or girlfriend—of the victim. (See Table 9.2.) In contrast, only 3% of violent crimes against males were committed by an intimate of the victim. Friends or acquaintances of the victims committed 50% of rape/sexual assault crimes against women.

In some cases the likelihood of a violent crime being committed by a stranger increases with the age of the female victim. For example, in 2002, 100% of completed or threatened rape/sexual assaults of women aged fifty to sixty-four reported by the NCVS were committed by strangers, as compared with only 22.8% of rape/sexual assaults against females ages sixteen to nineteen. (See Table 9.3. Note that the asterisked figures are based on very small sample sizes, so they may not be as accurate as larger samples.) Essentially all robberies of women sixty-five and over were committed by strangers as compared with 34.9% of robberies of girls ages twelve to fifteen. Among female victims ages sixty-five and over, 57.9% of assaults were committed by strangers.

According to the BJS, in 2002 strangers to the victim committed 6.4 violent crimes per every one thousand females age twelve and over, compared with seven violent crimes per one thousand females that were committed by a person well known to the victim. There were 3.2 violent crimes per one thousand females committed by casual acquaintances and 2.8 per one thousand committed by relatives. The rate of aggravated assaults against women by strangers (1.2 per one thousand) was slightly higher than the rate committed by someone well known to the victim (0.9 per one thousand), but simple assaults were somewhat more likely to have been committed by a well-known person (5.9 per one thousand) than by a stranger (5.2 per one thousand).

Of violent crime victims, white women were more likely than African-American women to have been the victim of a violent crime by a stranger in 2002 (37.6% versus 35.1%). About one-quarter (24.5%) of rape/sexual assault crimes against African-American women were committed by strangers, as compared with more than

TABLE 9.3

Percent of violent crime victimizations involving strangers, by gender and age of victims and type of crime, 2002

| | | Percent of victimizations involving strangers | | | | |
| | | | | Assault | | |
Gender and age	Crimes of violence	Rape/sexual assault[a]	Robbery	Total	Aggravated	Simple
Both genders	49.9%	33.9%	73.0%	48.1%	58.7%	45.2%
12–15	40.5	44.3*	66.6	38.3	38.7	38.3
16–19	42.2	24.9*	41.7*	44.3	65.2	37.5
20–24	55.8	30.6*	77.9	55.0	71.5	49.4
25–34	52.1	62.2*	70.7	49.5	59.3	46.6
35–49	51.3	32.2*	75.6	49.5	49.1	49.6
50–64	55.8	53.1*	90.6	49.7	56.2	48.2
65 and over	68.5	0.0*	93.4	61.0	67.0*	58.5*
Male	61.3%	47.8%*	82.4%	58.7%	66.3%	56.3%
12–15	46.5	0.0*	72.3	43.4	55.3*	41.6
16–19	56.6	50.2*	61.6*	56.3	66.7	51.6
20–24	67.2	100.0*	94.8	62.9	76.6	57.8
25–34	65.0	100.0*	83.5	62.5	74.8	58.3
35–49	64.2	23.9*	78.6	63.4	44.4	67.8
50–64	63.9	35.6*	100.0	58.7	66.7*	56.6
65 and over	68.4	0.0*	83.5*	63.4*	84.0*	48.3*
Female	36.7%	31.8%	56.9%	35.4%	47.6%	32.5%
12–15	33.6	44.3*	34.9*	32.4	17.5*	34.4
16–19	27.4	22.8*	10.1*	29.7	61.9	23.2
20–24	39.0	25.2*	23.1*	42.6	61.9	36.8
25–34	36.2	57.7*	53.7*	32.9	33.9*	32.6
35–49	37.8	37.6*	70.2*	35.7	52.9	30.2
50–64	47.2	100.0*	81.6*	40.3	42.1*	40.0
65 and over	68.6	0.0*	100.0*	57.9*	0.0*	67.5*

*Estimate is based on about 10 or fewer sample cases.
[a]Includes verbal threats of rape and threats of sexual assault.

SOURCE: "Table 29. Personal Crimes of Violence, 2002: Percent of Victimizations Involving Strangers, by Gender and Age of Victims and Type of Crime," in *Criminal Victimization in the United States, 2002 Statistical Tables*, U.S. Department of Justice, Bureau of Justice Statistics, December 2003, http://www.ojp.usdoj.gov/bjs/pub/pdf/cvus/current/cv0229.pdf (accessed June 20, 2005)

one-third (35.3%) of rape/sexual assaults against white women. Of assault victims, African-American women were less likely to get assaulted by a stranger (32.8%) than white women (36.6%).

REPORTING CRIMES

According to the BJS, 47.5% of violent crimes, 43.9% of personal thefts, and 38.4% of property crimes were reported to police in 2003. In general, males and females were approximately equally likely to report both violent and property victimizations to the police. Hispanic women (54.8%) were more likely than Hispanic men (40%) to report violent crime to the police, although both were about equally likely to report property crime. African-American women (60.2%) were also much more likely than African-American men (47.1%) to report violent crime to the police.

Crimes in which the victim was injured were much more likely to be reported in 2002 than those in which no injuries occurred. Whereas 59% of simple assaults of females in which an injury occurred were reported, only 42.3% of assaults without injury were reported. (See Table 9.4.) Similar statistics held true for completed robberies of women—85.3% of those resulting in an

injury were reported, compared with only 74.6% of those with no injury sustained.

Both men and women were more likely to report crimes committed by strangers in 2002. (See Table 9.4.) Female victims reported 49.7% of violent crimes committed by nonstrangers and 58.6% of crimes committed by strangers, whereas male victims reported 39.5% of violent crimes committed by nonstrangers and 47.9% of crimes committed by strangers. Female victims reported 65.7% of rape/sexual assault crimes committed by strangers but only 51.2% of those committed by nonstrangers. Likewise, they reported 78.6% of robbery attempts by strangers without injury, but only 61.5% of those without injury committed by nonstrangers.

RAPE AND SEXUAL ASSAULT

Because of the cultural and social stigma associated with sexual assault, statistics gathered about rape and sexual assault must be approached with caution. It is likely that the number of sexual crimes reported to police is only a small proportion of the total number of such crimes. Even data from the NCVS needs to be approached carefully, because while researchers ask about both reported and unreported sexual assaults,

TABLE 9.4

Percent of violent crime victimizations reported to the police, by type of crime, victim-offender relationship, and gender of victim, 2002

| | Percent of all victimizations reported to the police | | | | | | | | |
| Type of crime | All victimizations | | | Involving strangers | | | Involving nonstrangers | | |
	Both genders	Male	Female	Both genders	Male	Female	Both genders	Male	Female
Crimes of violence	**48.5%**	**44.6%**	**53.0%**	**51.5%**	**47.9%**	**58.6%**	**45.5%**	**39.5%**	**49.7%**
Completed violence	60.4	59.0	61.6	67.5	62.6	76.5	54.5	52.9	55.2
Attempted/threatened violence	42.7	38.9	47.8	44.8	41.7	50.7	40.4	34.5	45.7
Rape/sexual assault[1]	53.7	39.7*	55.8	57.9	22.8*	65.7	51.6	55.3*	51.2
Robbery	71.2	66.5	79.3	69.7	64.0	83.9	75.3	78.4	73.1
Completed/property taken	75.8	73.5	79.4	75.9	71.9	84.4	75.5	80.5	71.8
With injury	79.8	76.2	85.3	74.3	69.5	84.7*	88.7	91.9*	85.9*
Without injury	72.6	71.4	74.6	76.8	73.4	84.3	52.5*	51.0*	53.1*
Attempted to take property	57.4	47.4	78.7	50.1	42.4	81.3*	75.0*	72.2*	76.7*
With injury	92.6	90.0*	100.0*	87.9*	86.8*	100.0*	100.0*	100.0*	100.0*
Without injury	39.5	22.8*	70.6*	34.7*	20.5*	78.6*	54.5*	40.0*	61.5*
Assault	45.7	41.9	50.3	48.2	45.2	54.2	43.3	37.1	48.1
Aggravated	56.6	52.4	62.8	59.7	55.9	67.4	52.3	45.6	58.6
With injury	61.3	63.5	58.8	72.8	71.9	74.2	51.9	53.4	50.7
Threatened with weapon	54.5	48.1	65.2	55.5	51.1	64.9	52.6	40.7	65.5
Simple	42.7	38.6	47.3	44.1	41.3	49.6	41.5	35.1	46.2
With minor injury	54.8	49.6	59.0	58.4	52.4	72.6	52.9	46.3	55.8
Without injury	38.6	35.6	42.3	40.6	38.4	44.8	36.6	32.0	40.7

Note: Detail may not add to total shown because of rounding.
*Estimate is based on about 10 or fewer sample cases.
[1]Includes verbal threats of rape and threats of sexual assault.

SOURCE: "Table 93. Violent Crimes 2002: Percent of Victimizations Reported to the Police, by Type of Crime, Victim-Offender Relationship and Gender of Victims," in *Criminal Victimization in the United States, 2002 Statistical Tables*, U.S. Department of Justice, Bureau of Justice Statistics, December 2003, http://www.ojp.usdoj.gov/bjs/pub/pdf/cvus/current/cv0293.pdf (accessed June 20, 2005)

women may still not disclose these crimes. Because of historical insensitivity of the criminal justice system to rape victims, women fear that they may be further victimized by law enforcement authorities if they report the crime. Women also sometimes blame themselves for the sexual assault, or they may not identify a sexual assault as an assault at all.

The rape/sexual assault category of the NCVS covers a variety of crimes ranging from completed or attempted rape to verbal threats of sexual assault. Sexual assault ranges from grabbing or fondling a victim to attempted sexual intercourse. Rape/sexual assault includes the use of psychological coercion as well as physical force. Although men are sometimes raped, particularly in prison, rape is primarily a crime against women. Table 9.1 shows that according to the National Crime Victimization Survey, almost six times as many women were victims of rape in 2003 as men. Although rape was once believed to be a crime of sexual passion, it is now recognized as a crime of anger and hate, driven by the desire for power over others. The Violence against Women Act (PL 103–322), passed in 1994, categorized rape as a gender-based hate crime, punishable under federal civil rights laws as well as state criminal statutes. The Act increased penalties for violence against women and provided funding to police, prosecutors, and the courts to help protect women from violence.

There were 198,840 rapes/sexual assaults of men and women in 2003 (see Table 9.2), down from 247,730 in 2002. Detailed analysis of those numbers were not yet available for 2003, but in 2002 sexual assaults of women accounted for 28.6% of rapes/sexual assaults, attempted rape accounted for 23.8%, and rape accounted for 34.9%. In 2003 about 9.9% of rape/sexual assaults involved male victims, and 90.1% involved female victims. According to the BJS, in 84% of all rape/sexual assaults in 2003, the offender did not have a weapon.

The Uniform Crime Reporting Program of the Federal Bureau of Investigation (FBI) defines forcible rape as "the carnal knowledge of a female forcibly and against her will." It includes assaults or attempts to commit rape by force or threat of force but does not include rape without force (statutory rape) or other sexual offenses. Both the number and the rate of reported forcible rapes declined from 1993 to 1999 but then rose again through 2003. (See Figure 9.2, which shows how each year from 1999 to 2003 compares with 1999.) The number of forcible rape offenses in 2003 (93,433) was 1.9% lower than in 2002 (95,235). In 2003, 63.2 forcible rapes occurred per one hundred thousand females, a 2.7% decrease from the 2002 rate of sixty-five per one hundred thousand. The 2003 rate was 17.9% lower than the 1994 estimate of seventy-seven per one hundred thousand.

In 2003 more than half (55.8%) of the rapes and sexual assaults of women measured by the NCVS went

FIGURE 9.2

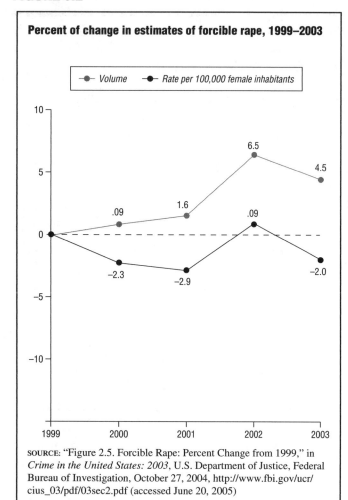

Percent of change in estimates of forcible rape, 1999–2003

SOURCE: "Figure 2.5. Forcible Rape: Percent Change from 1999," in *Crime in the United States: 2003*, U.S. Department of Justice, Federal Bureau of Investigation, October 27, 2004, http://www.fbi.gov/ucr/cius_03/pdf/03sec2.pdf (accessed June 20, 2005)

blackouts after ingesting Rohypnol with alcohol. A woman may be completely unaware of a sexual assault until she wakes up the next morning. The only way to determine if a victim has been given Rohypnol is to test for the drug within two or three days of the rape; few hospital emergency departments routinely screen for this drug. Health educators, high school guidance counselors, resident advisors at colleges, and scores of newspaper and magazine articles advise women not to accept drinks at parties or to leave drinks sitting unattended.

Although Rohypnol is legally prescribed outside of the United States for short-term treatment of severe sleep disorders, it is neither manufactured nor approved for sale in the United States. The importation of the drug was banned in March 1996, and the U.S. Customs Service began seizing quantities of Rohypnol at U.S. borders. In response to reported abuse, the manufacturers reformulated the drug as green tablets that can be detected in clear liquids and are visible in the bottom of a glass.

In October 1996 President Bill Clinton signed a bill amending the Controlled Substances Act to increase penalties for using drugs to disarm potential victims of violent crime. Anyone convicted of slipping a controlled substance, including Rohypnol, to an individual with intent to commit a violent act, such as rape, faces a prison term of up to twenty years and a fine as high as $2 million. The law also increased penalties for manufacturing, distributing, or possessing Rohypnol with the intent to distribute it.

Two other drugs are also used as date rape pills. Gamma hydroxybutyric acid (GHB, also known as "Liquid Ecstasy") enhances the effects of alcohol, which reduces the drinker's inhibitions. It also causes a form of amnesia. Ketamine hydrochloride (also known as "Special K") is an animal tranquilizer used to impair a person's natural resistance impulses. During 2002 anecdotal reports about another dangerous drug combination surfaced—3,4-methylenedioxymethamphetamine (known as "Ecstasy," "MDMA," or "crystal methamphetamine") and Viagra (a prescription drug used to treat erectile dysfunction)—dubbed "Sextasy." According to media reports, the drugs are taken together by male teens because Viagra offsets impotence, a potential side effect of methamphetamine use. Public health officials are alarmed by this use of Viagra and fear that it may contribute to increased rates of STDs and sexual assault.

Sexual Victimization on College Campuses

Many experts believe that college women are particularly vulnerable to sexual assault. In December 2000 the BJS and the National Institute of Justice (NIJ), another department of the DOJ, published *The Sexual Victimization of College Women* (NCWSV). The study

unreported—and the number was probably much higher. (See Table 9.4.) Women are often psychologically devastated by rape. They may be unwilling to talk about it, may feel responsible for it, or may believe that even if they do report it, nothing will happen to the offender.

Friends or acquaintances of the victim committed half (50%) of all rapes/sexual assaults of women in 2003. (See Table 9.2.) An additional 12% were committed by intimates of the victim and 8% by another relative of the victim. In 2002 women reported 51.2% of rape/sexual assaults involving nonstrangers, compared with 65.7% of rape/sexual assaults involving strangers.

"Date Rape" Drugs

While alcohol abuse remains a significant problem on college campuses, other substances, such as the drug Rohypnol, have made resistance to attacks practically impossible. A hypnotic sedative ten times more powerful than Valium, Rohypnol has been used to obtain nonconsensual sex from many women. Mixed in a drink, it causes memory impairment, confusion, and drowsiness—users often report eight- to twenty-four-hour

was based on a telephone survey of a randomly selected, national sample of 4,446 women attending colleges and universities in fall 1996. Respondents were asked between late February and early May 1997 if they had experienced sexual victimization "since school began in fall 1996"—the period covered, on average, 6.91 months.

The study found that in the nearly seven-month period, 2.8% of the women had experienced either an attempted or completed rape. The authors suggested that the data show that nearly 5% of women college students are victimized in a given calendar year, and that the percentage of attempted or completed rape victimizations of college women during their college careers approaches one in four. The authors concluded that although the 2.8% figure might "seem" low, "from a policy perspective, college administrators might be disturbed to learn that for every 1,000 women attending their institutions, there may well be 35 incidents of rape in a given academic year. . . . For a campus with 10,000 women, this would mean the number of rapes would exceed 350."

Researchers also asked respondents about other types of sexual victimization. They found that 1.7% of their sample had been victims of completed sexual coercion (unwanted sexual penetration with the threat of punishment or promise of reward), 1.3% had been victims of attempted sexual coercion, 1.9% had been victims of unwanted completed sexual contact with force or the threat of force, and 1.8% had been victims of completed sexual contact without physical force. Smaller percentages of women had been sexually threatened. The data revealed that 7.7% of college women surveyed had experienced sexual victimization involving physical force, 11% had experienced sexual victimization involving nonphysical force, and 15.5% had experienced any victimization since the start of the academic year.

The NCWSV also found that fewer than 5% of the rapes and attempted rapes had been reported to police, and even lower percentages of other types of sexual victimization were reported. A national study of college students reported by the CDC backed up this result, finding that 27.5% of women said they had suffered rape or attempted rape at least once since age fourteen, but just 5% of victims reported the incidents to the police.

A December 2003 BJS report by Timothy C. Hart, *Violent Victimization of College Students*, analyzed NCVS data for 1995–2000 for all types of violent crime against college students ages eighteen to twenty-four and nonstudents in the same age group. The report found that there was no statistical difference in the rate at which college women experienced rape/sexual assault (6.2 per one thousand eighteen- to twenty-four-year-olds) and the rate for female nonstudents (7.9 per one thousand). About three-quarters (74%) of college-student rape/sexual assault victims knew their attacker, and about equal per-

centages felt the attacker had been under the influence of drugs or alcohol (41%) as felt the attacker had not (40%). In nearly nine out of ten rapes/sexual assaults of students (89%), no weapon was used. The report found that of all college-age rape/sexual assault victims from 1995 to 2000, only 12% reported the crime to the police—86% did not. Of the reported crimes, 73% were reported by the victim and 27% by someone else.

These numbers confirm other researchers' findings that students overwhelmingly do not report acquaintance rapes or attempted rapes (Bonnie S. Fisher et al., "Reporting Sexual Victimization to the Police and Others: Results from a National-Level Study of College Women," *Criminal Justice and Behavior*, vol. 30, no. 1, February 2003). According to the CDC, the term "hidden rape" has been used to describe this finding of widespread unreported and underreported sexual assault. Anecdotal reports from college and university administrators suggest that many female students who have been raped not only fail to report the offense, but also drop out of school.

Some researchers have proposed that college rape is due in part to a difference between men's and women's abilities to read sexual cues. A 2003 study found that men are far more likely than women to interpret a woman's behavior as sexual and misconstrue it as an invitation to sexual intimacy. The study's authors wrote, "In conjunction with the finding that males significantly misperceived the female's sexual intent to engage in sexual intercourse, following the initial contact, this suggests that males, in a bid to calculate the probability of obtaining sexual intercourse, overestimate the predictive value of the female's initial consent to 'attend a party together.' This consequently leads to greater goal expectation, which, combined with hostile beliefs about women, might result in a greater likelihood of non-consensual sexual intercourse" (V. J. Willan and Paul Pollard, "Likelihood of Acquaintance Rape as a Function of Males' Sexual Expectations, Disappointment, and Adherence to Rape-Conducive Attitudes," *Journal of Social and Personal Relationships*, vol. 20, no. 5, 2003).

HOMICIDE

According to the FBI, there were 3,215 female homicide victims in 2003, 22.3% of total murder victims. (See Table 9.5.) Most female victims (84.6%) were age eighteen or over. Men committed 90.1% of all homicides, and 89.4% of all homicides of women. About 13.4% of murders of women were committed during the course of another felony, usually a robbery. (See Table 9.6.) Forty-three murders were committed during the course of a rape (1.3%). Other nonfelony circumstances, primarily arguments or brawls, accounted for 56.8% of the murders. (The murder circumstances were unknown for

TABLE 9.5

Murder victims, by age, sex, and race, 2003

Age	Total	Sex			Race			
		Male	Female	Unknown	White	Black	Other	Unknown
Total	14,408	11,167	3,215	26	6,913	6,887	408	200
Percent distribution[a]	100.0	77.5	22.3	0.2	48.0	47.8	2.8	1.4
Under 18[b]	1,333	905	424	4	660	617	40	16
Under 22[b]	3,445	2,724	716	5	1,556	1,749	100	40
18 and over[b]	12,811	10,083	2,721	7	6,133	6,189	358	131
Infant (under 1)	225	131	91	3	139	73	7	6
1 to 4	307	164	142	1	165	131	6	5
5 to 8	82	41	41	0	44	34	3	1
9 to 12	69	36	33	0	33	34	1	1
13 to 16	369	293	76	0	150	202	14	3
17 to 19	1,283	1,113	169	1	549	689	34	11
20 to 24	2,855	2,432	420	3	1,165	1,585	74	31
25 to 29	2,148	1,826	322	0	839	1,234	54	21
30 to 34	1,594	1,249	344	1	692	842	43	17
35 to 39	1,286	973	313	0	636	605	36	9
40 to 44	1,114	783	330	1	589	484	32	9
45 to 49	951	694	256	1	552	362	26	11
50 to 54	630	463	167	0	382	226	19	3
55 to 59	365	256	109	0	236	113	12	4
60 to 64	226	160	66	0	148	57	16	5
65 to 69	164	113	51	0	122	32	8	2
70 to 74	153	90	63	0	105	42	4	2
75 and over	323	171	152	0	247	61	9	6
Unknown	264	179	70	15	120	81	10	53

[a]Because of rounding, the percentages may not add to 100.0.
[b]Does not include unknown ages.

SOURCE: "Table 2.4. Murder Victims by Age, Sex, and Race, 2003," in *Crime in the United States: 2003*, U.S. Department of Justice, Federal Bureau of Investigation, October 27, 2004, http://www.fbi.gov/ucr/cius_03/pdf/03sec2.pdf (accessed June 20, 2005)

29.3% of female victims.) In 2003, 573 women were murdered by their husbands and 464 women were murdered by an intimate partner. In addition, 105 women were murdered by a son or daughter, 193 girls were murdered by a parent, and twenty-seven females were murdered by a sibling.

Special Circumstances: The Murders of 9/11

The FBI categorized the terrorist killings on September 11, 2001, as negligent manslaughter and murder in a special report on the events of 9/11 contained in the publication *Crime in the United States 2001*. According to the report, women comprised 24.3% of all deaths, or 739 deaths, in all locations of the attacks. (See Table 9.7.) Two of those females were under the age of five; 58.7% fell into the twenty-five- to forty-four-year-old age bracket. Most (71.3%) of the female victims were white and 15.7% were African-American, while other races comprised 8.1%, and the race for 4.9% of the victims was unknown. Most of the female victims (648; 87.8%) died at the New York City World Trade Center. The remainder were at the Pentagon in Washington, D.C. (seventy-one deaths), and in Somerset County, Pennsylvania (twenty deaths). Although the FBI conducted this analysis of 9/11 victims by age, gender, and race, the report stresses that "since the crimes were carried out indiscriminately to inflict the maximum pain on the

greatest number of people, these attributes must not be seen as factors that have contributed to these incidents."

INTIMATE PARTNER CRIME

The Extent of Domestic Violence

Aside from homicides, it has been very difficult to estimate the extent of domestic and intimate partner violence. The majority of victims of domestic violence are women who are abused by their intimate partners. The American Medical Association (AMA) and the National Coalition against Domestic Violence (NCADV) characterize domestic violence as a pattern of behavior that may include physical and/or sexual assault, psychological abuse, intimidation, and social isolation. The abuse is usually recurrent and escalates in frequency and severity as the abuser attempts to dominate the victim and control her activities.

DATA FROM THE NCVS. In a June 2005 publication the BJS reported that of the 32.2 million total victims of violent crimes between 1998 and 2002, 11% were victims of family violence, and 5.4% were victims of violence at the hands of a spouse (Matthew R. Durose et al., *Family Violence Statistics*, NCJ 207846). Women were disproportionately likely to be victims of family violence; they were 73.4% of the victims of family violence between 1998 and 2002, 84.3% of the victims of violence at the

TABLE 9.6

Murder circumstances, by victim sex, 2003

Circumstances	Total murder victims	Male	Female	Unknown
Total	14,408	11,167	3,215	26
Felony type total:	2,359	1,924	431	4
Rape	43	0	43	0
Robbery	1,056	908	145	3
Burglary	93	75	18	0
Larceny-theft	22	18	4	0
Motor vehicle theft	30	19	11	0
Arson	77	37	40	0
Prostitution and commercialized vice	16	3	13	0
Other sex offenses	10	4	6	0
Narcotic drug laws	666	611	54	1
Gambling	6	6	0	0
Other—not specified	340	243	97	0
Suspected felony type	88	71	17	0
Other than felony type total:	7,070	5,241	1,825	4
Romantic triangle	98	81	17	0
Child killed by babysitter	29	17	12	0
Brawl due to influence of alcohol	128	109	19	0
Brawl due to influence of narcotics	53	40	13	0
Argument over money or property	220	186	34	0
Other arguments	3,806	2,772	1,033	1
Gangland killings	115	111	4	0
Juvenile gang killings	819	782	37	0
Institutional killings	13	13	0	0
Sniper attack	2	1	1	0
Other—not specified	1,787	1,129	655	3
Unknown	4,891	3,931	942	18

SOURCE: "Table 2.14. Murder Circumstances by Victim Sex, 2003," in *Crime in the United States: 2003*, U.S. Department of Justice, Federal Bureau of Investigation, October 27, 2004, http://www.fbi.gov/ucr/cius_03/pdf/03sec2.pdf (accessed June 20, 2005)

hands of a spouse, and 85.9% of the victims of violence in dating couples. (See Table 9.8.) Victims from racial and ethnic groups were victimized in proportions approximately equal to their representation in the population as a whole.

The BJS, in a February 2003 report based on NCVS data (*Intimate Partner Violence, 1993–2001*), found that in 2001, 691,710 nonfatal violent crimes were committed against current or former spouses, boyfriends, or girlfriends (compared to about one million committed in 1998). Women were the victims of approximately 85% of these crimes. (See Table 9.9.) Intimate partner violence comprised 20% of all nonfatal violent crimes against women in 2001, whereas about 3% of the nonfatal violent crimes against men were committed by intimate partners.

From 1993 to 2001 the rate of nonfatal intimate partner violence against women fell 49.3%, from 9.8 victimizations per one thousand women to five per one thousand women; the rate of violence against males fell from 1.6 incidents per one thousand men to 0.9 per one thousand men over the same period. (See Figure 9.3.) The number of instances of intimate partner violence against

women declined from about 1.1 million in 1993 to about 588,490 in 2001, a drop of about 49%. In 2001 men were the victims of 103,220 violent crimes committed by intimates. (See Table 9.9.)

NATIONAL VIOLENCE AGAINST WOMEN (NVAW) SURVEY. In July 2000 the NIJ and the CDC published *Extent, Nature, and Consequences of Intimate Partner Violence* (Patricia Tjaden and Nancy Thoennes), which included findings from the National Violence against Women (NVAW) survey. This survey of eight thousand women and eight thousand men found that about 24.8% of women age eighteen and over had been raped and/or physically assaulted by a spouse, ex-spouse, cohabiting partner, or date at some point in their lives. In the twelve months preceding the survey, 1.5% of the women had been raped and/or assaulted by an intimate partner. These numbers were much higher than the numbers reported by the NCVS and mostly likely represent a truer picture of the extent of intimate partner violence.

About one in thirteen of the women surveyed (7.7%) reported that they had been raped at some point in their lives by an intimate partner; if that rate is extrapolated to the nation's population, about 7.8 million women in the United States have been raped by an intimate partner in their lifetimes. About one in five hundred (0.2%), representing 201,394 women in the United States, had been raped by an intimate partner in the previous twelve months. During their lifetimes, 22.1% of women (22.3 million) had been physically assaulted by an intimate partner, and 1.3% (1.3 million) of women had been assaulted by an intimate partner in the past twelve months. Since many individuals are victimized repeatedly, the total number of estimated victimizations is much higher.

The NVAW survey confirmed that intimate violence against women is usually chronic. Among women victims, 51.2% reported having been raped multiple times by their partner and 65.5% reported being physically assaulted multiple times. On average, women victims were raped by their partners 1.6 times per year and physically assaulted 3.4 times. The most common forms of physical assault were pushing, grabbing, or shoving (which 18.1% of women had experienced in their lifetimes) and slapping or hitting (which 16% of women had experienced in their lifetimes). About one in one hundred women (0.9%) had experienced assaults involving a knife, and 0.7% had been assaulted with a gun.

The NVAW survey also examined stalking as a form of intimate partner victimization. Stalking was defined as "a course of conduct directed at a specific person involving repeated visual or physical proximity; nonconsensual communication; verbal, written, or implied threats; or a combination thereof that would cause fear in a

TABLE 9.7

Murder victims of September 11, 2001 terrorist attacks, total all locations, by age, sex and race

Age	Total	Sex			Race			
		Male	Female	Unknown	White	Black	Other[a]	Unknown
Total	3,047	2,303	739	5	2,435	286	187	139
Percent distribution[b]	100.0	75.6	24.3	0.2	79.9	9.4	6.1	4.6
Under 18[c]	9	5	4	0	3	3		3
Under 22[c]	31	22	9	0	19	4	3	5
18 and over[c]	3,004	2,274	730	0	2,424	281	186	113
Infant (under 1)	0	0	0	0	0	0	0	0
1 to 4	5	3	2	0	2	0	0	3
5 to 8	1	0	1	0	1	0	0	0
9 to 12	3	2	1	0	0	3	0	0
13 to 16	0	0	0	0	0	0	0	0
17 to 19	3	3	0	0	1	0	1	1
20 to 24	117	78	39	0	95	8	10	4
25 to 29	341	241	100	0	273	26	30	12
30 to 34	503	388	115	0	401	40	47	15
35 to 39	578	467	111	0	469	66	24	19
40 to 44	510	402	108	0	420	43	28	19
45 to 49	369	277	92	0	299	39	16	15
50 to 54	272	200	72	0	218	28	12	14
55 to 59	177	128	49	0	139	18	12	8
60 to 64	79	54	25	0	62	8	4	5
65 to 69	29	20	9	0	25	2	1	1
70 to 74	15	10	5	0	13	2	0	0
75 and over	11	6	5	0	9	1	1	0
Unknown	34	24	5	5	8	2	1	23

[a]Includes 184 Asian or Pacific Islander and 3 American Indian or Alaskan Native victims.
[b]Because of rounding, the percentages may not add to total.
[c]Does not include unknown ages.

SOURCE: "Table 5.2. Murder Victims of 9/11/2001 Terrorist Attacks, Total All Locations by Age, Sex, and Race," in *Crime in the United States, 2001*, U.S. Department of Justice, Federal Bureau of Investigation, October 28, 2002, http://www.fbi.gov/ucr/cius_01/01crime5.pdf (accessed June 20, 2005)

reasonable person, with 'repeated' meaning on two or more occasions." The survey found that the incidence of stalking was much higher than previously believed. During their lifetimes, 4.8% of women had been victims of intimate partner stalking incidents. Over the twelve months preceding the survey, 0.5% of the surveyed women had been stalked by a current or former intimate partner. Among men, 0.6% had been stalked by a current or former intimate partner during their lifetime, and 0.2% had been stalked within the previous twelve months.

In total, taking into account rape, physical assault, and stalking, one in four surveyed women (25.5%), or 25.7 million women in the United States, had been victimized by an intimate partner during their lifetime, and 1.8% of women, or 1.8 million in the United States, had been victimized in the previous twelve months.

OTHER FACTS. According to information available in 2005 on the Web site of the CDC's National Center for Injury Prevention and Control:

- As many as 324,000 pregnant women are victims of intimate partner violence each year.

- Women who have experienced intimate partner violence have 60% higher rates of health problems than women with no history of abuse, including chronic pain, gastrointestinal disorders, and irritable bowel syndrome.

- The health costs for intimate partner rape, physical assault, and stalking totaled more than $5.8 billion each year, with nearly $4.1 billion going to direct medical and mental health care services.

- Each year, thousands of children witness intimate partner violence, which increases the likelihood that they will be victims or perpetrators of violence themselves later in life and can also cause long-term physical and mental health problems.

- Men who are physically violent toward women are more likely to be violent toward children as well.

MARITAL RAPE. One of the reasons for the wide disparity in estimates of intimate partner violence is that women may have difficulty recognizing or admitting that they have been victimized. This is particularly true for rape. Just as 30 to 60% of the college women in the NCWSV survey who had been raped were unsure if a crime had been committed or if harm was intended, many women may not identify their experiences with an intimate partner as rape or assault. Only recently has American society begun to accept that sexual relations must be consensual even in marriage.

TABLE 9.8

Demographic characteristics of family violence victims compared to nonfamily violence victims, by relationship, 1998–2002

		Percent of crimes in which the victim was the offender's —							
		Family member				Nonfamily member			
Victim characteristic	All violent crimes	Total	Spouse	Son or daughter	Other family	Total	Boyfriend or girlfriend	Friend or acquaintance	Stranger
All offenses	100%	100%	100%	100%	100%	100%	100%	100%	100%
Gender									
Male	54.9%	26.6%	15.7%	37.1%	37.1%	58.4%	14.1%	53.6%	68.3%
Female	45.1	73.4	84.3	62.9	62.9	41.6	85.9	46.4	31.7
Race/Hispanic origin									
White	72.3%	74.0%	76.8%	78.5%	69.5%	72.1%	71.0%	74.5%	70.3%
Black	14.3	13.6	10.9	12.6	17.1	14.3	17.2	14.6	13.7
Hispanic	10.5	10.1	9.8	8.0	11.1	10.6	9.0	8.9	12.2
Other	2.9	2.3	2.6	0.9	2.3	2.9	2.8	2.0	3.7
American Indian/Alaska Native	1.1	1.6	2.1	0*	1.4*	1.0	1.5	1.0	0.9
Asian/Pacific Islander	1.7	0.5*	0.4*	0.8*	0.5*	1.9	1.0*	0.9	2.7
Age									
Under 18	23.3%	10.8%	0.8%*	50.1%	12.6%	24.8%	9.4%	35.4%	18.5%
18–24	24.5	17.6	14.7	27.2	18.6	25.3	42.0	20.8	26.6
25–34	19.7	24.5	33.5	13.6	16.6	19.1	25.3	15.7	21.0
35–54	27.4	41.2	47.8	7.9	41.7	25.7	21.4	23.8	27.9
55 or older	5.1	6.0	3.2	1.3*	10.6	5.0	2.0	4.3	6.0
Total offenses	32,163,870	3,544,900	1,733,960	371,890	1,439,060	28,618,970	2,037,800	11,775,660	14,805,510
Percent of all offenses	100%	11.0%	5.4%	1.2%	4.5%	89.0%	6.3%	36.6%	46.0%

Note: Data identifying the victim's relationship to the offender were reported for 95.9% of 33,501,120 nonfatal violent crimes and for 58.4% of 80,319 murders. Of these 32,163,870 crimes with known relationships, victim characteristics were reported for virtually all victims. Detail may not add to total because of rounding.
*Estimate based on 10 or fewer sample cases.

SOURCE: Matthew R. Durose, et al., "Table 2.3. Demographic Characteristics of Family Violence Victims Compared to Nonfamily Violence Victims between 1998 and 2002, by Relationship," in *Family Violence Statistics*, U.S. Department of Justice, Bureau of Justice Statistics, NCJ 207846, June 2005, http:// www .ojp.usdoj.gov/bjs/pub/pdf/fvs.pdf (accessed July 1, 2005)

TABLE 9.9

Violence by Intimate partners, by type and gender of victim, 2001

	Intimate partner violence					
	Total		Female		Male	
	Number	Rate per 1,000 persons	Number	Rate per 1,000 females	Number	Rate per 1,000 males
Overall violent crime	691,710	3.0	588,490	5.0	103,220	0.9
Rape/sexual assault	41,740	0.2	41,740	0.4	—	—
Robbery	60,630	0.3	44,060	0.4	16,570	0.1
Aggravated assault	117,480	0.5	81,140	0.7	36,350	0.3
Simple assault	471,860	2.1	421,550	3.6	50,310	0.5

— Based on 10 or fewer sample cases.

SOURCE: Callie Marie Rennison, "Table 1. Violence by Intimate Partners, by Type of Crime and Gender of Victims, 2001," in *Crime Data Brief: Intimate Partner Violence, 1993–2001*, Bureau of Justice Statistics, February 2003, http://www.ojp.usdoj.gov/bjs/pub/pdf/ipv01.pdf (accessed June 20, 2005)

An analysis of data from the National Violence against Women Survey (NVAWS), sponsored jointly by the U.S. Departments of Justice and Health and Human Services and the Centers for Disease Control and Prevention (CDC), estimated that 1.5 million women and 834,700 men are raped and/or physically assaulted by an intimate partner each year. Of all surveyed women age eighteen and older, 1.5% said they were raped and/or physically assaulted by a current or former spouse, cohabiting partner, or date in the year preceding the interview, compared to 0.9% of all surveyed men. Of the women, 7.7% reported being raped by an intimate partner at some point in their lives. Although these estimates were developed in 1998, most researchers agree that these statistics are likely to remain unchanged until improved methods to respond to violence against women are instituted.

FIGURE 9.3

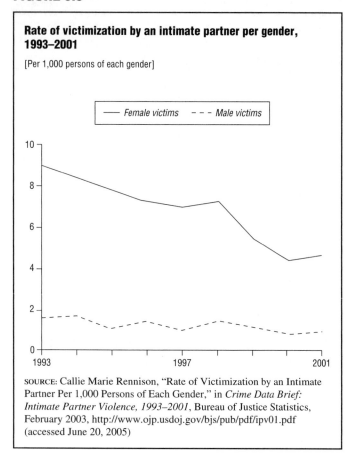

Rate of victimization by an intimate partner per gender, 1993–2001

[Per 1,000 persons of each gender]

— Female victims   - - - Male victims

SOURCE: Callie Marie Rennison, "Rate of Victimization by an Intimate Partner Per 1,000 Persons of Each Gender," in *Crime Data Brief: Intimate Partner Violence, 1993–2001*, Bureau of Justice Statistics, February 2003, http://www.ojp.usdoj.gov/bjs/pub/pdf/ipv01.pdf (accessed June 20, 2005)

Various research carried out through the 1990s showed that women who were raped by their husbands suffered from the same range of physical and psychological trauma as women who were raped by acquaintances or strangers and that marital rape may be just as violent as other rapes. However, although a woman now has the right to prosecute her husband for marital rape (it became a crime in all fifty states in 1993), it remains very difficult to prove in court. According to July 1998 data from the National Clearinghouse on Marital and Date Rape, thirty-three states have some type(s) of exemption for husbands from marital rape prosecution, and there is a tendency in the legal system to consider marital rape as far less serious than other forms of rape.

Who Are the Victims of Domestic Violence?

GENERAL DEMOGRAPHICS. According to the *Family Violence Statistics* (BJS, June 2005), from 1998 to 2002 the highest rates of spousal violence were among those ages thirty-five through fifty-four (47.8%); the highest rates of violence between dating couples were among those ages eighteen to twenty-four (42%). More than three-quarters of victims of spousal violence were white (76.8%), 10.9% were African-American, and 9.8% were Hispanic. Among dating partners, 71% of victims were white, 17.2% were African-American, and 9% were Hispanic.

The BJS found in an earlier survey that between 1993 and 1998 the highest rates of intimate partner violence against women were among couples with household incomes of less than $7,500 (20.3 incidents per one thousand women). Women who were divorced/separated (31.9 incidents per one thousand women) or never married (11.3 incidents per one thousand women) had higher rates of intimate partner violence than did married women (2.6 incidents per one thousand women). Women living in rental housing (16.2 incidents per one thousand women) and in urban areas (9.5 incidents per one thousand women) were at slightly higher risk than women who lived in owned homes (4.8 per one thousand) and those in rural (8.1 per one thousand) and suburban (7.8 per one thousand) areas.

The NVAW survey found that married women living apart from their husbands were almost four times more likely to have been raped, assaulted, or stalked by their husbands than women living with their husbands (20% versus 5.4%). Rape and physical assaults of females were most likely to occur either before or both before and after the relationship ended. Very few first rapes (6.3%) or physical assaults (4.2%) occurred only after the end of the relationship. In contrast, 42.8% of the stalking incidents against female victims first occurred after the relationship ended.

RACE/ETHNICITY AND INTIMATE PARTNER VIOLENCE. According to a September 2003 article published in *Alcoholism: Clinical & Experimental Research* (Craig A. Field and Raul Caetano, "Longitudinal Model Predicting Partner Violence among White, Black, and Hispanic Couples in the United States," vol. 27, no. 9), African-American and Hispanic couples were two to three times more likely to experience intimate partner violence five years after the study's initial survey than were white couples. Although not all cases studied involved alcohol consumption, the researchers indicated that heavy drinking and alcohol problems played an important role in the occurrence of intimate partner violence over time in couples of various ethnic groups. The BJS's 2005 report *Family Violence Statistics* confirmed that nonfatal violent incidents between spouses (41.8%) and between dating partners (41.4%) were more likely than average (30%) to involve drugs or alcohol.

These findings are similar to those reported in the BJS's *Intimate Partner Violence*, which noted that from 1993 to 1998 black women experienced intimate partner violence at a rate of 11.1 victims per one thousand population. In contrast, the rate for white women was 8.2 victims per one thousand. But the BJS did not find the difference in rates for Hispanic (7.7) and non-Hispanic (8.4) women to be statistically significant.

The NVAW survey also found that, as a group, nonwhite women experience significantly more intimate partner violence than do white females. It found that 28.6% of nonwhite women had been raped, sexually assaulted, or stalked by an intimate partner during their lifetime, while this figure for white women was 24.8%. The percentage of nonwhite women experiencing any of these incidents in the past year (10%) was also higher than that for white women (7.5%). Native American/Alaska Native women reported the highest lifetime rate of intimate partner violence (37.5%), and Asian-American/Pacific Islander women reported far lower rates (15%).

SAME-SEX VERSUS OPPOSITE-SEX PARTNERS. When comparing same-sex and opposite-sex intimate partners, the NVAW survey found that 30.4% of women with a woman partner had been victimized by a male partner during their lifetime, compared to 20.3% of women living with an opposite-sex partner. Only 11.4% of women with a same-sex partner had ever been victimized by a female partner.

Perpetrators of Domestic Violence

According to the NCADV, behaviors and characteristics of an abusive partner may include:

- Embarrassing or ridiculing a partner in front of others
- Intimidating or humiliating talk or behavior
- Grabbing, pushing, shoving, or hitting
- Abuse of alcohol or other drugs
- Sexual pressure
- Limiting a partner's activities or personal relationships
- Holding traditional ideas of a partner's role
- Moodiness, including extreme kindness at some times and extreme anger at other times
- Making demands of a partner and becoming enraged if they are not met
- A history of violence

Indications that a woman may be in an abusive relationship include:

- Fear of her partner
- Making excuses for her partner's behavior
- Feeling that she is the one who must change
- Avoiding conflict at all costs
- Avoiding angering her partner
- Trying to always do what her partner wants
- The presence of weapons in the home
- Fear of leaving the relationship
- Excessive jealousy or possessiveness by the partner

Why Women Don't Leave

One of the most frequently asked questions about abused women is: why do they stay? Some authors and advocates argue that the relevant questions for battered women themselves are very different, and that the very question implies there is something wrong with the woman for staying, rather than placing the blame where it belongs—on the batterer. Better questions, Ola W. Barnett argues, might be: "Why does he beat her?" or "Why does society let him get away with it?" or "What can be done to stop him?" ("Why Battered Women Do Not Leave," *Trauma, Violence, & Abuse*, vol. 1, October 2000).

But not all women do stay in abusive relationships. Many leave these situations without turning to the police or support organizations. While their number is unknown, most who leave without asking for help usually have strong personal support systems of friends and family or employment and earnings that enable them to live economically independent of their abusive partners. Yet there can be little question that a large percentage of women remain with their abusers.

Women stay in abusive relationships for a variety of reasons. One major reason is their economic dependency on their batterers. Many women feel they are better off with a violent partner than facing the challenge of raising children on their own. Some truly harbor deep feelings for their abusive partners and believe that over time they can change his or her behavior. Others mistakenly interpret their abusers' efforts to control their life as expressions of love. Other frequently reported considerations include:

- Most women have at least one dependent child who must be cared for.
- Many are unemployed.
- Their parents are distant, unable, or unwilling to help.
- The women may fear losing mutual friends and the support of family, especially in-laws.
- Many have no property that is solely their own.
- Some lack access to cash, credit, or any financial resources.
- If the woman leaves, she risks being charged with desertion and losing her children and other joint assets.
- She may face a decline in living standards for both herself and her children, and her children, especially older ones, might resent this decrease in living standard.
- The woman and/or children may be in poor health.
- The abuser had threatened or harmed her pets (Catherine A. Faver and Elizabeth B. Strand, "To Leave or To

Stay? Battered Women's Concern for Vulnerable Pets," *Journal of Interpersonal Violence*, vol. 18, December 2003).

Leaving an abusive partner is a process some therapists and counselors have termed an "evolution of separation," because many victimized women have to make several attempts before they depart from and remain parted from their abusive partners. According to Barnett, in order to separate from their abusers, women must first acknowledge their relationship is unhealthy and will not get better, experience a catalyst for leaving (for example, a particularly severe beating), give up their dreams for the relationship, and accept that some aspects of the relationship may continue (for example, child visitation arrangements). On average, women leave and return five times before separating for a final time.

Whether a separated woman will permanently leave her battering spouse largely depends on whether she has the economic resources to survive without him. Women who are economically dependent on their husbands are more likely to be battered, and also less likely to leave. Leaving will expose these women to the hazards of poverty: crime, more violence, lack of health care, lack of affordable housing and quality child care. Batterers also often interfere with their partners' finding and keeping employment.

Reporting or Not Reporting and Prosecuting Domestic Violence

NCVS. As part of the NCVS, the BJS reported in *Family Violence Statistics* that victims of spousal violence were somewhat more likely than average (61.7% versus 47.2%) to report the crimes to the police between 1998 and 2002. However, that varied by the type of crime. Victims reported their spouses for only 36.2% of sex offenses, 60.5% of aggravated assaults, 62% of simple assaults, and 75.1% of robberies. Victims of dating violence were even less likely to report sex offenses (29.8%) and simple assaults (53%) but more likely to report aggravated assaults (69.1%) and robberies (75.6%).

The BJS found that women (53%) were somewhat more likely than men (46%) to report intimate partner victimizations to the police from 1993 to 1998. Over this period, about 67% of African-American women reported intimate partner violence, compared with 50% of white women. About 65% of Hispanic females reported the violence, compared with about 52% of non-Hispanic women. The percentage of intimate partner violence against women that was reported to police increased from 48% in 1993 to 59% in 1998.

Among both men and women the most common reason for not reporting intimate partner violence was that they considered it to be a private or personal matter.

However, about 19% of women cited fear of reprisal as a reason for not reporting the violence. The BJS estimates that from 1993 to 1998 women experienced but did not report 480,060 intimate partner incidents.

NVAW. In the NVAW survey, 26.7% of female victims of physical assault by an intimate partner and 51.9% of female victims of stalking by an intimate partner reported the incident to police. In contrast, only 17.2% of female victims raped by an intimate partner reported their most recent rape to police. Most reports for all three categories were made by the victim herself within twenty-four hours of the crime.

The overwhelming reason given by female victims of intimate partner violence in the NVAW survey for not reporting their victimization was that the police could not do anything. Among women who did not report, 100% of the stalking victims, 99.7% of the assault victims, and 13.2% of the rape victims gave this as one reason for not reporting. Among female rape victims, 21.2% were afraid of the perpetrator; 20.3% believed it to be a minor, one-time incident; and 16.1% were ashamed and wanted to keep the incident private. Among female physical assault victims, 61.3% said that the police would not believe them, 37.9% said it was a minor incident, and 34.8% wanted to protect the attacker, the relationship, or children. In addition, 32% of the female assault victims did not want the police or the courts involved, 11.7% were afraid of the perpetrator, and 10.4% were ashamed and/or wanted to keep it quiet. Among female stalking victims who did not report to the police, 98.2% said the police would not believe them; 61.8% were ashamed and wanted to keep it quiet; 45.5% wanted to protect the attacker, relationship, or children; and 38.2% were afraid of the stalker.

For about two-thirds to three-quarters of the violent incidents against women that were reported to the police in the NVAW survey, police reports were taken. However, fewer than half of the reports resulted in the arrest or detention of the perpetrator (47.4% of reported rapes, 36.4% of reported physical assaults, and 28.7% of reported stalkings). Only one in ten (10.5%) reported rape cases were referred to the prosecutor or court, compared with 33% of physical assault cases and 28.1% of stalkings.

The NVAW survey found that only 7.5% of perpetrators of rape against intimate female partners were prosecuted. Of these, 41.9% were convicted; however, only two thirds of those convicted (69.2%) were sentenced to jail or prison. Among intimate partner perpetrators of physical assault against women, 7.3% were prosecuted, 47.9% of whom were convicted; but only one-third of the convicted (35.6%) were sentenced to jail or prison.

THE PREVALENCE AND ROLE OF PROTECTION ORDERS. A victim in any state in the nation may go to court to obtain a protection order forbidding the abuser from harming her. Also referred to as "restraining orders" or "injunctions," civil orders of protection are legally binding court orders that prohibit an individual who has committed an act of domestic violence from further abusing the victim. Although the terms are often used interchangeably, restraining orders usually refer to short-term or temporary sanctions, while protection orders have longer duration and may be permanent. These orders generally prohibit harassment, contact, communication, and physical proximity to the victim. Although protection orders are common and readily obtained, they are not always effective.

Protection orders give victims an option other than filing a criminal complaint. Issued immediately, usually within twenty-four hours, they provide safety for the victim by barring or evicting the abuser from the household. But this judicial protection has little meaning if the police do not maintain records and follow through with arrest should the abuser violate the order. Statutes in most states make violating a protection order a matter of criminal contempt, a misdemeanor, or even a felony.

According to the NVAW survey, women victims of a physical assault by an intimate were much more likely than male victims to obtain a temporary restraining order (17.1% of women versus 3.5% of men). Among female stalking victims, 36.6% obtained a temporary restraining order, as did 16.4% of rape victims. More than half of all female victims who obtained restraining orders (50.6% of physical assault victims, 67.6% of rape victims, and 69.7% of stalking victims) reported that the orders were violated.

An August 7, 2002, article in *JAMA: The Journal of the American Medical Association* (Victoria L. Holt et al., "Civil Protection Orders and Risk of Subsequent Police-Reported Violence," vol. 288, no. 5) found that women with a permanent protection order (duration of twelve months or more) were less likely to report physical abuse during the first six months and year after an intimate partner violence incident. On the other hand, temporary restraining orders (usually in effect for two weeks) had little effect on physical violence but actually increased the likelihood of psychological abuse six and twelve months after an incident. The study was based solely on Seattle Police Department records for 2,691 adult women who reported an incident of intimate partner violence between August 1, 1998, and December 31, 1999.

Another study by the same researchers ("Do Protection Orders Affect the Likelihood of Future Partner Violence and Injury?," *American Journal of Preventive Medicine*, vol. 24, no. 1, January 2003) examined 448 Seattle women who had experienced intimate partner violence between October 1997 and December 1998. The study concluded that protection orders decreased the likelihood of future violent and nonviolent intimate partner incidents. Women with protection orders were less likely to be contacted by the abuser, threatened with a weapon, injured, or to require abuse-related medical care. In addition to the items listed above, women who maintained the order for nine months following their incident of violence also had significantly decreased likelihood of experiencing psychological, sexual, and physical abuse.

SEXUAL HARASSMENT

Sexual harassment is pervasive in American society, and at one time or another nearly all women experience uninvited and unwanted attention of a sexual nature. But definitions of sexual harassment may range from a woman being whistled at on the street to losing her job for refusing to have sex with her boss. Stalking, sexual coercion, sexual assault, and rape are particularly severe forms of sexual harassment.

Scott Lindquist, in *The Date Rape Prevention Book: The Essential Guide for Girls and Women* (Naperville, IL: Sourcebooks, Inc., 2000), defines sexual harassment, in part, as:

- Catcalls, leering, ogling, whistling
- Suggestive or insulting gestures or noises
- Sexual innuendos or suggestive, offensive, or derogatory comments
- Jokes about sex or gender-specific traits
- Offensive remarks about physical characteristics, clothing, or sexual activity
- Sexual insults
- Requests or demands for sex
- Unwanted physical contact
- Physical assault or coerced sexual activity

Awareness of sexual harassment has increased in recent years, in part because of complaints and class-action lawsuits against large corporations and in part because of high-profile accusations of sexual harassment against such public officials as President Bill Clinton and Supreme Court Justice Clarence Thomas.

The Law

The government and the courts have focused primarily on issues of sexual harassment in the workplace. The U.S. Equal Employment Opportunity Commission (EEOC) defines sexual harassment as unwelcome sexual advances, requests for sexual favors, and other verbal or physical conduct of a sexual nature that affects an individual's employment, interferes with an individual's work performance, or creates an intimidating, hostile, or offensive work environment. According to the EEOC, the commission received 13,136 charges of sexual harassment in 2004, down from a high of 15,836 filed in 2000. The percentage of sexual harassment charges filed by men have increased substantially since 1992 (from 9.1% to 15.1%).

MERITOR SAVINGS BANK V. VINSON. The U.S. Supreme Court, in the landmark case *Meritor Savings Bank v. Vinson* (477 U.S. 57, 1986), ruled that sexual harassment is a violation of Title VII of the Civil Rights Act of 1964, which prohibited sexual discrimination. Mechelle Vinson claimed that her supervisor harassed her at work and outside of work and raped her. She did not file a complaint until a year after the harassment had ceased for fear of jeopardizing her employment. A lower court ruled against her, finding that sexual favors had not been a condition of her employment. The Supreme Court reversed the decision, ruling that "Title VII affords employees the right to work in an environment free from discriminatory intimidation, ridicule, and insult."

THE EMPLOYER'S RESPONSIBILITY. In 1998 the Supreme Court ruled that (1) employers could be held liable when a supervisor threatened to demote or take other action against an employee who refused a supervisor's sexual demands, even when the threats were not carried out (*Burlington Industries v. Ellerth* [66 LW 4643]), and (2) that companies were liable for the misconduct of their employees even though the company was unaware of the behavior (*Faragher v. Boca Raton* [118 S. Ct. 2275, 1998]). The Court's majority decision (seven to two) stated that employers could generally avoid liability for sexual harassment by showing that they had strong antiharassment programs, that the programs were communicated to all employees, and that systems were in place for submitting and reviewing complaints. Following these rulings, many companies reexamined their sexual harassment policies and revised them to meet the Court's tougher standards.

Harassment in the Military

During the twentieth century, women began to play an increasingly important role in the U.S. military. According to Women in Military Service for America Memorial Foundation (WIMSA), in May 2004, 215,331 women were serving in the armed services, 14.7% of the total military. But during the 1990s it became increasingly clear that sexual harassment of women was prevalent in the military and that it was often condoned and even perpetrated by high-ranking officers.

The Tailhook Association is a private group of Navy and marine aviators. During the group's 1991 annual convention in Las Vegas, Nevada, eighty-three women claimed they had been sexually assaulted as they made their way down a corridor filled with male personnel. More than one hundred officers faced Department of Defense (DOD) charges, and several high-ranking naval officers resigned as a result of the negative publicity brought by the Tailhook scandal.

As a result of charges brought against male drill sergeants by female recruits at Aberdeen Proving Ground in Maryland in 1996, the Army began an investigation of fifty-nine military installations around the world. Investigators found that sexual harassment was pervasive throughout the Army and that the Army leadership was, in large part, to blame. A 1997 Army survey found that about 47% of females had experienced unwanted sexual attention, 15% had experienced sexual coercion, and 7% had been victims of sexual assault. Most female soldiers were afraid to report sexual misconduct. Only 12% of recent sexual harassment victims had filed a formal complaint. Many female soldiers reported that they believed their commanders had little interest in enforcing the Army's rules against sexual harassment.

The DOD is congressionally mandated to conduct occasional surveys of gender relations within the armed services. Such surveys were conducted in 1988, 1995, and 2002 (Rachel N. Lipari and Anita R. Lancaster, *Armed Forces 2002 Sexual Harassment Survey*, Defense Manpower Data Center, Arlington, Virginia, November 2003). According to the 2002 survey, its purpose is "to document the extent to which Service members reported experiencing unwanted, uninvited sexual attention in the twelve months prior to filling out the survey, the details surrounding those events (e.g., where they occur), and Service members' perceptions of the effectiveness of sexual harassment policies, training, and programs." Nearly twenty thousand service members responded to the 2002 survey.

Figure 9.4 reports some of the survey's findings and compares those to results from the 1995 survey for both men and women. Women reported sexist behavior ("verbal/nonverbal behaviors that convey insulting, offensive, or condescending attitudes based on the gender of the member"), crude/offensive behavior ("verbal/nonverbal behaviors of a sexual nature that were offensive or embarrassing; whistling, staring, leering, ogling"), unwanted sexual attention ("attempts to establish a sexual relationship; touching, fondling"), sexual coercion ("classic *quid pro quo* instances or job benefits or losses conditioned on sexual cooperation"), and sexual assault ("attempted and/or actual sexual relations without the member's consent and against his or her will") at higher rates than did men in surveys from both years. The largest percentile difference between men and women in 2002 was for sexist behavior, which 50% of women reported, but only 17% of men reported. However, rates

FIGURE 9.4

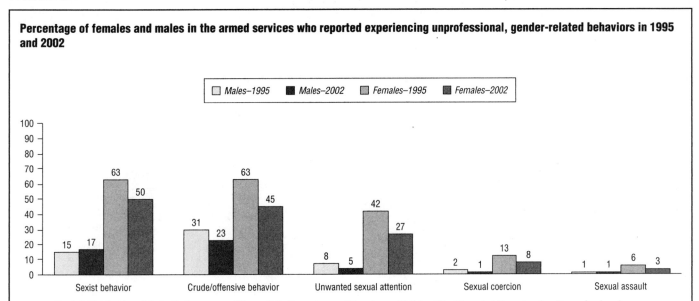

Percentage of females and males in the armed services who reported experiencing unprofessional, gender-related behaviors in 1995 and 2002

SOURCE: Rachel N. Lipari and Anita R. Lancaster, "Figure 3.2. Percentage of Females and Males Who Reported Experiencing Unprofessional, Gender-Related Behaviors in 1995 and 2002," in *Armed Forces 2002 Sexual Harassment Survey*, Defense Manpower Data Center, November 2003, http://stinet.dtic.mil/cgi-bin/fulcrum_main.pl?database=ft_u2&searchid=0&keyfieldvalue=ADA419817&filename=%2Ffulcrum%2Fdata%2FTR_fulltext%2Fdoc%2FADA419817.pdf (accessed July 19, 2005)

for all items, including sexist behavior, fell for women between the 1995 and 2002 surveys. The item with the highest percentage decline was crude/offensive behavior, which 63% of female service members reported in 1995 but only 45% reported in 2002.

Other 2002 survey findings include the fact that the overall rate of sexual harassment for both male and female service members fell from 1995 to 2002 (from 8 to 3% for men and from 46 to 24% for women). Women reported that 84% of the perpetrators of "unprofessional, gender-based behaviors" were other military personnel, and more than 60% were co-workers. Most (85%) were male. Three-quarters (76%) of the women noted that "their Service's training made them feel it is safe to complain about unwanted, sex-related attention," 30% of those who experienced such attention in the previous year had reported it, and 34% of those said they were satisfied by the outcome of their complaint. Reasons for not reporting given by females who failed to do so included not feeling the behavior was important enough to report (67%), taking care of it themselves (63%), fear of being labeled a troublemaker (29%), and fear of retaliation from the offender (18%).

STUDIES FROM THE IOWA CITY VA MEDICAL CENTER. A study by the University of Iowa and the Iowa City VA Medical Center was reported in *Journal of Occupational and Environmental Medicine* in April 2001 (Anne G. Sadler et al., "The Military Environment: Risk Factors for Women's Non-Fatal Assaults," vol. 43, no. 4). The researchers interviewed 537 women veterans who had

served in the military from the Vietnam era th Persian Gulf War. Among these women, abou reported having been sexually harassed during their m. tary service, 54% were subjected to unwanted sexua. contact, 23% were physically assaulted, and 21% were subjected to physical violence while being raped. Some women reported as many as twenty incidents of physical assault. Women who worked in military environments where sexual harassment occurred were five times more likely than other military women to have been physically assaulted. Women whose superior officers had made sexually demeaning comments or who tolerated such comments were three times more likely to have been victims of physical assault, and women who shared mixed-gender sleeping quarters and endured sexual harassment there were nearly seven times more likely to be physically assaulted.

The February 19, 2003, issue of *American Journal of Industrial Medicine* (Anne G. Sadler et al., "Factors Associated with Women's Risk of Rape in the Military Environment," vol. 43, no. 3) reported that 30% of 506 female U.S. military veterans surveyed reported having been raped or suffered a rape attempt during their military service. Participants in the survey ranged in age from twenty to eighty-three, with an average age of forty. The majority was white. Nearly half had served in the Army, 23% in the Air Force, and 22% in the Navy. More than three-fourths of participants reported some type of sexual harassment during their military experience. Just over half (54%) reported unwanted sexual contact. Of those respondents who reported having been raped, 37% had been raped more than once, while 14% of rape or rape attempt victims had been gang-raped. Three-fourths of the women who were raped failed to report the incident to a ranking officer; reasons for not reporting included not knowing how to (one-third) and believing rape was to be expected in the military (one-fifth). The only group who didn't expect rape to be part of military life was women who served during the Persian Gulf War era.

SEXUAL MISCONDUCT AT THE AIR FORCE ACADEMY (AFA). During the early 2000s, allegations of sexual misconduct at the U.S. Air Force Academy (AFA) in Colorado Springs, Colorado, began to surface. In February 2003 Congress requested that the inspector general of the DOD investigate allegations that the academy had suffered sexual assaults against female cadets and that academy officials had not taken appropriate measures to investigate and prosecute the cases. In response, the inspector general surveyed 579 of the 659 current female Air Force Academy cadets in May 2003; the results were published in *Report on the United States Air Force Academy Sexual Assault Survey* (September 11, 2003). The survey showed that 7.4% of participants (forty-three cadets) reported having been the victims of rape or attempted rape, and 18.8% (109 cadets) had been the victims of sexual assault. More than two-thirds (68.6%) of the respondents had experienced sexual teasing, jokes, remarks, or questions; 45.3% had experienced sexually suggestive looks, gestures, or body language; 38.9% received written or telephonic sexual communications; 35.2% experienced violations of personal space or unwanted touching; and 22.3% had experienced pressure to give sexual favors. Only thirty-three of 177 incidents (18.6%) were reported. Reasons given by cadets for not reporting incidents included embarrassment (53.8%), the fear of reprisal by peers (46.2%), a general fear of reprisal (42.7%), and a belief that nothing would be done (40.6%). The majority of offenders (86.1%) were fellow cadets.

Taking into account information provided by the DOD inspector general, a panel of seven private citizens appointed by the Secretary of Defense also conducted an investigation into the sexual misconduct, publishing their conclusions in *Report of the Panel to Review Sexual Misconduct Allegations at the U.S. Air Force Academy* (September 22, 2003). The panel reported that from January 1, 1993, to December 31, 2002, cadets made a total of 142 allegations of sexual abuse at the AFA. (See Figure 9.5.) The panel concluded that "the Academy and Air Force leadership had increasing cause for alarm" but "acted inconsistently and without a long-term plan." The panel noted that changes announced by senior leadership in March 2003 were a good start, but only "the initial step." Replacement of the AFA's leadership team in April 2003 marked another promising step. Changes that still needed to be addressed, the panel felt, included the following, particularly the first two items:

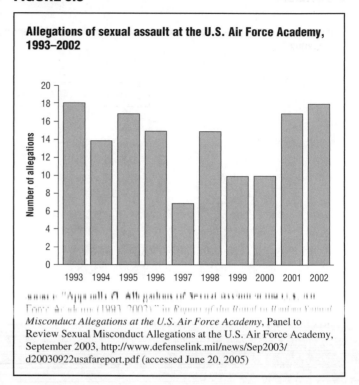

FIGURE 9.5

Allegations of sexual assault at the U.S. Air Force Academy, 1993–2002

SOURCE: "Appendix O. Allegations of Sexual Assault at the U.S. Air Force Academy (1993–2002)," in *Report of the Panel to Review Sexual Misconduct Allegations at the U.S. Air Force Academy*, Panel to Review Sexual Misconduct Allegations at the U.S. Air Force Academy, September 2003, http://www.defenselink.mil/news/Sep2003/d20030922usafareport.pdf (accessed June 20, 2005)

- "Enduring changes in the culture and gender climate at the Academy"
- "Permanent, consistent oversight by Air Force Headquarters leadership"
- "External oversight provided by the Academy's Board of Visitors"
- Availability of confidential reporting, counseling, and treatment

AFGHANISTAN AND IRAQ. Pamela Martineau and Steve Wiegand reported in 2005 that many female soldiers in Iraq and Afghanistan have said that they have faced unwelcome advances and demeaning comments, as well as the threat of rape, from male soldiers ("Military Women Say They Face Sex Harassment," *Sacramento Bee*, March 9, 2005). The authors reported that the Miles Foundation, a nonprofit organization that helps military victims of assault, had been contacted by 307 military personnel in Iraq and Afghanistan through February 2005. These numbers were likely to be far fewer than the numbers of women who actually experienced sexual harassment. Women interviewed for the article believed that all women in combat had been sexually harassed and made to feel "like second-class soldiers."

PENTAGON DRAFTS SEXUAL ASSAULT POLICIES. The 2005 Defense Authorization Act required the Pentagon to draft sexual assault policies by January 1, 2005, in response to repeated reports of sexual misconduct involving members of the military. On January 4, 2005, the

Pentagon announced it had drafted new policies to prevent and respond to sexual assaults in the military, including a standard definition of sexual assault, the creation of a sexual assault response coordinator and victim advocate position, and a checklist for commanders to follow when responding to reports of sexual assault.

Harassment in Prison

Amnesty International, a worldwide human rights organization, has been drawing attention to the sexual harassment and sexual abuse of women prisoners in the United States. As a result of the "war on drugs" and mandatory minimum sentences, the number of women in U.S. prisons has risen significantly in recent years. According to *Prisoners in 2003* (Paige M. Harrison and Allen J. Beck, U.S. Department of Justice, Bureau of Justice Statistics, November 2004), there were 101,179 women under the jurisdiction of state or federal correctional authorities at the end of 2003, a 3.6% increase over the previous year. Many of these women are at the mercy of male guards and correctional officers—women may be watched while dressing or showering, subject to verbal harassment, expected to exchange sexual favors for special privileges, or patted down by male guards. In a June 1999 report, *Women in Prison—Sexual Misconduct by Correctional Staff*, the U.S. Government Accountability Office admitted that sexual abuse of women prisoners does occur. The report examined the three largest female correctional systems—the Federal Bureau of Prisons and the state systems in California and Texas—as well as the District of Columbia correctional system.

In its 1999 report *"Not Part of My Sentence": Violations of the Human Rights of Women in Custody*, Amnesty International found widespread sexual abuse of women prisoners throughout the United States. Their follow-up 2001 study, *Abuse of Women in Custody: Sexual Misconduct and Shackling of Pregnant Women*, found that no state granted women prisoners full protection from sexual mistreatment by custodians. Most states allowed pat-down searches of women prisoners by male guards, and in some states cross-gender pat-down searches were routine.

On September 4, 2003, President George W. Bush signed into law the Prison Rape Elimination Act, the first U.S. law to deal with sexual assault among the incarcerated. The law requires that statistics on the problem be gathered, that guidelines for addressing prison rape be developed, that a review panel be created, and that grants be provided to states to help fight prison rape.

Hate Crimes

In addition to sexual harassment, women may be the victims of hate crimes because of their race, sexual orientation, ethnicity, religion, or disability. The U.S. government did not begin collecting data on hate crimes until the early 1990s and does not break its hate crimes data down by gender. According to the Anti-Defamation League, as of 2005 bias-motivated violence and intimidation was punishable by law in forty-six states and the District of Columbia. In its 2003 report on hate crimes, the FBI reported 7,489 incidents of hate crime with 9,100 victims in that year. Of the victims, 60.6% suffered crimes against their persons (including murder, rape, assault, and intimidation), and 38.7% suffered crimes against property (including robbery, burglary, motor vehicle theft, arson, and vandalism). Anti-lesbian bias accounted for 15% of the 1,239 offenses caused by a sexual-orientation bias; two lesbians were raped, twenty-one were victims of aggravated assault, sixty-six were victims of simple assault, and sixty-six were victims of intimidation. Because gender is not one of the biases listed in federal data, it is not possible to get an accurate reading of how many women are victims of hate crimes in any given year.

CHAPTER 10
WOMEN AS CRIMINALS

Women in the United States commit less than one out of every four crimes and even fewer violent crimes. In centuries past crimes by women were often committed out of desperation—for example, a woman might steal to feed her starving children. In Europe during the Middle Ages and up into the seventeenth and eighteenth centuries in both Europe and the United States, millions of women were tried and executed for the crime of witchcraft. These "witches" were scapegoats for the ills that befell society: infant deaths, disease, plague, crop failures, famine, and war. Pregnancy outside of marriage also was viewed as a crime that could be punishable by banishment or death.

Violent crimes by women in American culture today are often sensationalized. This is particularly true of mothers who murder their children. On October 24, 1994, Susan Smith of Union, South Carolina, strapped her two young sons in their car seats and then rolled her car into a lake. The little boys drowned. On June 6, 1996, Darlie Routier from Rowlett, Texas, allegedly stabbed two of her sons to death. She was tried and found guilty for the death of one of the boys. On June 20, 2000, Andrea Yates, a homemaker in Houston, Texas, called the police and told them that she had just drowned each of her five children in the bathtub. Yates was said to be suffering from a psychotic form of postpartum depression. Because women are the traditional caregivers and nurturers, acts such as these may be perceived as crimes against nature and, as such, are considered far more shocking than equivalent crimes committed by men.

ARRESTS OF WOMEN

According to the Federal Bureau of Investigation (FBI), there were more than 2.2 million arrests of women in 2003, about 23.5% of total arrests. (See Table 10.1 and Table 10.2.) Women eighteen and over accounted for 79.6% of arrests of women in 2003. In 2003 females were arrested for 65,492 aggravated assaults (2.9% of

all female arrests); 212,114 other assaults (9.5% of arrests); 302,958 larceny-thefts—the taking of property without force, violence, or fraud, including shoplifting and pocket picking (13.5% of arrests); 214,983 drug violations (9.7% of arrests); and 182,814 driving while under the influence (8.2% of arrests).

In 2003, 30.8% of those arrested for property crimes were female, and 17.8% of those arrested for violent crimes were female. Females accounted for 9.7% of all murder and nonnegligent manslaughter arrests, but only 1.1% of arrests for forcible rape. They accounted for 42% of all arrests for embezzlement, 60.5% of all arrests for prostitution and commercialized vice, and 57.1% of arrested runaways. Women accounted for only 7.9% of arrests for weapons violations.

More Women Are Being Arrested

Although crime rates have dropped significantly in recent years, more women than ever are being arrested. (See Table 10.2.) From 1994 to 2003 total arrests of males fell 6.7%. In contrast, total female arrests rose 12.3% over the same period.

Despite this increase in female arrests and the decrease in male arrests, males accounted for 76.8% of all arrests in 2003. Females younger than age eighteen accounted for 20.7% of all female arrests in 2003, compared with 24% in 1994. Males younger than age eighteen accounted for 15.3% of all male arrests in 2003, down from 18.4% in 1994. (See Table 10.2.)

VIOLENT CRIME ARRESTS. From 1994 to 2003 arrests of females for violent crimes (murder and nonnegligent manslaughter, forcible rape, robbery, and aggravated assault) rose 9.6%. Arrests for violent crimes dropped 11% for females under age eighteen. In contrast, arrests for violent crime fell 20% for all males and 36.1% for males under age eighteen. Male arrests for aggravated assault dropped 17.3% while female arrests rose 14%. (See Table 10.2.)

TABLE 10.1

Arrests of women, by age, 2003

[10,843 agencies; 2003 estimated population 204,034,545]

Offense charged	Total all ages	Ages under 15	Ages under 18	Ages 18 and over	Under 10	10–12	13–14	15	16	17	18	19	20	21
Total	2,225,730	155,234	453,284	1,772,446	3,299	30,352	121,583	95,829	103,373	98,848	99,692	100,391	95,443	83,279
Percent distribution[a]	100.0	7.0	20.4	79.6	0.1	1.4	5.5	4.3	4.6	4.4	4.5	4.5	4.3	3.7
Murder and nonnegligent manslaughter	941	10	73	868	0	2	8	11	21	31	39	38	41	41
Forcible rape	247	35	59	188	3	11	21	7	9	8	12	11	13	7
Robbery	7,849	455	1,585	6,264	10	73	372	355	360	415	482	449	406	340
Aggravated assault	65,492	3,926	10,187	55,305	70	895	2,961	1,992	2,111	2,158	2,200	2,246	2,305	2,466
Burglary	28,043	2,784	7,058	20,985	135	705	1,944	1,352	1,412	1,510	1,469	1,495	1,274	1,140
Larceny-theft	302,958	34,070	91,457	211,501	723	8,109	25,238	18,015	20,069	19,303	17,396	14,162	12,185	10,169
Motor vehicle theft	17,680	1,565	5,222	12,458	5	169	1,391	1,342	1,268	1,047	984	891	762	707
Arson	1,765	445	714	1,051	30	116	299	123	101	45	48	39	45	33
Violent crime[b]	74,529	4,426	11,904	62,625	83	981	3,362	2,365	2,501	2,612	2,733	2,744	2,765	2,854
Percent distribution[a]	100.0	5.9	16.0	84.0	0.1	1.3	4.5	3.2	3.4	3.5	3.7	3.7	3.7	3.8
Property crime[b]	350,446	38,864	104,451	245,995	893	9,099	28,872	20,832	22,850	21,905	19,897	16,587	14,266	12,049
Percent distribution[a]	100.0	11.1	29.8	70.2	0.3	2.6	8.2	5.9	6.5	6.3	5.7	4.7	4.1	3.4
Other assaults	212,114	23,289	55,263	156,851	448	5,323	17,518	11,430	10,907	9,637	8,064	7,318	7,415	7,573
Forgery and counterfeiting	31,942	125	1,181	30,761	7	13	105	173	282	601	1,142	1,447	1,679	1,542
Fraud	93,010	345	1,867	91,143	41	55	249	286	474	762	2,027	3,085	3,486	3,643
Embezzlement	5,975	17	331	5,644	0	2	15	11	102	201	370	402	329	342
Stolen property; buying, receiving, possessing	16,344	836	2,561	13,783	16	175	645	498	601	626	914	873	828	706
Vandalism	31,670	4,849	10,488	21,182	222	1,367	3,260	1,837	1,902	1,900	1,629	1,396	1,239	1,283
Weapons; carrying, possessing, etc.	9,652	1,335	3,043	6,609	31	313	991	612	586	510	385	380	366	353
Prostitution and commercialized vice	33,164	92	668	32,496	2	3	87	119	165	292	1,027	1,307	1,143	1,077
Sex offenses (except forcible rape and prostitution)	5,415	634	1,188	4,227	61	163	410	218	181	155	234	256	214	209
Drug abuse violations	214,983	5,281	22,671	192,312	67	689	4,525	4,284	5,628	7,478	10,512	10,505	9,970	9,175
Gambling	805	5	27	778	0	3	2	4	6	12	17	34	43	15
Offenses against the family and children	21,699	692	1,889	19,810	38	145	509	355	445	397	478	524	682	763
Driving under the influence	182,814	89	2,947	179,867	23	6	60	144	796	1,918	4,475	5,696	6,287	9,371
Liquor laws	111,422	4,490	33,793	77,629	31	302	4,157	6,210	9,472	13,621	20,334	19,760	15,859	2,241
Drunkenness	56,555	605	2,907	53,648	9	36	560	575	674	1,053	1,727	1,773	1,592	2,140
Disorderly conduct	113,902	18,534	42,474	71,428	256	3,888	14,390	9,351	8,164	6,425	4,869	4,157	3,935	4,166
Vagrancy	4,305	107	404	3,901	1	25	81	87	80	130	101	70	104	102
All other offenses (except traffic)	574,511	22,579	72,944	501,567	685	3,796	18,098	15,920	17,521	16,924	18,739	22,065	23,231	23,663
Suspicion	283	25	93	190	1	5	19	16	26	12	18	12	10	12
Curfew and loitering law violations	28,846	9,197	28,846	—	114	1,466	7,617	6,983	7,439	5,227	—	—	—	—
Runaways	51,344	18,818	51,344	—	270	2,497	16,051	13,519	12,571	6,436	—	—	—	—

[a]Because of rounding, the percentages may not add to 100.0.

[b]Violent crimes are offenses of murder, forcible rape, robbery, and aggravated assault. Property crimes are offenses of burglary, larceny-theft, motor vehicle theft, and arson.

SOURCE: "Table 40. Arrests, Females, by Age, 2003," in *Crime in the United States: 2003*, U.S. Department of Justice, Federal Bureau of Investigation, October 27, 2004, http://www.fbi.gov/ucr/cius_03/pdf/03sec4.pdf (accessed June 20, 2005)

TABLE 10.2

Arrests, by sex, 1994–2003

[7,592 agencies; 2003 estimated population 166,154,387; 1994 estimated population 149,051,209]

| | Male | | | | | | Female | | | | | |
| | Total | | | Under 18 | | | Total | | | Under 18 | | |
Offense charged	1994	2003	Percent change	1994	2003	Percent change	1994	2003	Percent change	1994	2003	Percent change
Total[a]	**6,364,846**	**5,958,949**	**−6.7**	**1,173,624**	**910,981**	**−22.4**	**1,628,948**	**1,828,638**	**+12.3**	**390,725**	**378,895**	**−3.0**
Murder and nonnegligent manslaughter	9,931	6,268	−36.9	1,798	560	−68.9	1,068	747	−30.1	115	59	−48.7
Forcible rape	18,910	14,651	−22.5	3,137	2,366	−24.6	215	212	−1.4	70	49	−30.0
Robbery	75,729	55,851	−26.2	23,510	13,262	−43.6	7,640	6,696	−12.4	2,222	1,383	−37.8
Aggravated assault	257,370	212,913	−17.3	39,028	26,923	−31.0	48,613	55,426	+14.0	8,460	8,298	−1.9
Burglary	200,801	148,373	−26.1	76,000	44,700	−41.2	25,420	24,688	−2.9	8,491	6,203	−26.9
Larceny-theft	587,473	425,990	−27.5	209,100	119,520	−42.8	296,766	256,322	−13.6	96,734	78,703	−18.6
Motor vehicle theft	101,422	71,364	−29.6	43,381	20,114	−53.6	15,165	14,374	−5.2	7,615	4,257	−44.1
Arson	10,679	7,547	−29.3	6,388	4,089	−36.0	1,771	1,351	−23.7	878	544	−38.0
Violent crime[b]	361,940	289,683	−20.0	67,473	43,111	−36.1	57,536	63,081	+9.6	10,867	9,789	−9.9
Property crime[b]	900,375	653,274	−27.4	334,872	188,423	−43.7	339,122	296,735	−12.5	113,718	89,707	−21.1
Other assaults	549,316	528,194	−3.8	90,771	91,865	+1.2	129,530	171,093	+32.1	32,413	44,043	+35.9
Forgery and counterfeiting	40,983	39,420	−3.8	3,384	1,813	−46.4	24,109	26,637	+10.5	1,971	1,043	−47.1
Fraud	109,546	86,978	−20.6	3,981	2,817	−29.2	83,323	73,668	−11.6	2,094	1,519	−27.5
Embezzlement	5,149	5,256	+2.1	401	433	+8.0	3,726	5,292	+42.0	231	296	+28.1
Stolen property; buying, receiving, possessing	82,015	61,339	−25.2	23,964	12,400	−48.3	12,987	13,806	+6.3	3,113	2,202	−29.3
Vandalism	170,987	134,674	−21.2	85,417	54,957	−35.7	25,069	26,378	+5.2	9,835	8,766	−10.9
Weapons; carrying, possessing, etc.	138,622	88,251	−36.3	35,145	20,230	−42.4	11,848	7,812	−34.1	2,989	2,343	−21.6
Prostitution and commercialized vice	18,501	14,489	−21.7	305	232	−23.9	28,349	24,088	−15.0	303	565	+86.5
Sex offenses (except forcible rape and prostitution)	54,705	49,054	−10.3	9,945	9,916	−0.3	4,927	4,761	−3.4	820	1,034	+26.1
Drug abuse violations	621,938	745,452	+19.9	77,691	87,805	+13.0	128,421	173,091	+34.8	11,829	18,488	+56.3
Gambling	5,687	2,765	−51.4	731	306	−58.1	857	541	−36.9	47	14	−70.2
Offenses against the family and children	56,848	59,095	+4.0	2,076	2,330	+12.2	12,301	17,367	+41.2	1,096	1,438	+31.2
Driving under the influence	728,079	652,694	−10.4	7,366	9,200	+24.9	120,057	145,352	+21.1	1,251	2,295	+83.5
Liquor laws	242,837	263,033	+8.3	54,499	51,646	−5.2	63,581	92,479	+45.5	22,562	28,348	+25.6
Drunkenness	391,194	281,214	−28.1	9,600	7,841	−18.3	51,996	47,362	−8.9	1,877	2,335	+24.4
Disorderly conduct	308,177	260,122	−15.6	72,096	73,573	+2.0	86,291	89,948	+4.2	22,779	33,301	+46.2
Vagrancy	10,839	12,734	+17.5	2,218	1,044	−52.9	3,297	3,643	+10.5	557	353	−36.6
All other offenses (except traffic)	1,469,827	1,640,339	+11.6	174,408	160,150	−8.2	343,360	475,471	+38.5	52,112	60,983	+17.0
Suspicion	5,895	848	−85.6	1,104	241	−78.2	1,081	204	−81.1	251	77	−69.3
Curfew and loitering law violations	62,087	60,165	−3.1	62,087	60,165	−3.1	24,773	26,084	+5.3	24,773	26,084	+5.3
Runaways	55,194	30,724	−44.3	55,194	30,724	−44.3	73,488	43,949	−40.2	73,488	43,949	−40.2

[a]Does not include suspicion.
[b]Violent crimes are offenses of murder, forcible rape, robbery, and aggravated assault. Property crimes are offenses of burglary, larceny-theft, motor vehicle theft, and arson.

source: "Table 33. Ten-Year Arrest Trends, by Sex, 1994–2003," in *Crime in the United States: 2003*, U.S. Department of Justice, Federal Bureau of Investigation, October 27, 2004, http://www.fbi.gov/ucr/cius_03/pdf/03sec4.pdf (accessed June 20, 2005)

TABLE 10.3

Characteristics of Federal arrestees, October 1, 2001–September 30, 2002

| Arrestee characteristic | Number arrested | All offenses | Violent | Property | | Drug | Public-order | | Weapon | Immigration | Supervision | Material witness |
				Fraudulent	Other		Regulatory	Other				
All arrestees	124,074	100.0%	3.8%	11.4%	2.7%	27.4%	0.4%	6.7%	6.1%	20.6%	17.7%	3.2%
Male/female												
Male	106,726	86.0%	91.1%	70.7%	72.6%	85.2%	88.0%	85.7%	95.4%	93.5%	87.0%	81.9%
Female	17,340	14.0	8.9	29.3	27.4	14.8	12.0	14.3	4.6	6.5	13.0	18.1
Race												
White	86,419	70.2%	44.2%	63.9%	60.2%	67.6%	87.5%	71.2%	48.6%	96.0%	58.8%	92.6%
Black	32,397	26.3	42.3	31.8	33.1	30.4	6.3	23.5	49.4	2.6	36.6	3.4
Native American	2,081	1.7	11.8	0.8	3.3	0.6	2.3	2.5	1.0	0.1	3.6	0.2
Asian/Pacific Islander	2,180	1.8	1.7	3.5	3.4	1.4	3.9	2.8	1.0	1.2	0.9	3.7
Age												
Under 19 years	2,181	1.8%	5.2%	0.5%	3.4%	2.0%	0.8%	1.1%	1.3%	2.0%	0.7%	6.6%
19–20 years	6,766	5.5	8.8	3.1	6.9	6.4	5.7	5.0	5.9	6.1	2.8	11.7
21–30 years	49,641	40.0	39.6	28.2	30.8	44.2	16.3	29.3	46.0	46.9	35.8	50.5
31–40 years	36,995	29.8	25.3	30.7	29.4	28.8	28.7	26.9	26.2	31.4	34.0	21.4
Over 40 years	28,430	22.9	21.0	37.6	29.5	18.7	48.6	37.7	20.6	13.7	26.8	9.8
Citizenship												
U.S. citizen	71,889	62.7%	92.6%	82.1%	91.7%	70.2%	92.3%	91.7%	94.4%	5.7%	85.1%	4.3%
Not U.S. citizen	42,742	37.3	7.4	17.9	8.3	29.8	7.7	8.3	5.6	94.3	14.9	95.7

Note: Summing arrestees on a characteristic may not yield the total number of arrestees because some arrestees lack information on that characteristic.

SOURCE: "Table 1.3. Characteristics of Federal Arrestees Booked by USMS, October 1, 2001–September 30, 2002," in *Compendium of Federal Justice Statistics, 2002*, U.S. Department of Justice, Bureau of Justice Statistics, NCJ 205368, September 2004, http://www.ojp.usdoj.gov/bjs/pub/pdf/cfjs0201.pdf (accessed July 1, 2005)

PROPERTY CRIME ARRESTS. Arrests for property crimes (burglary, larceny-theft, motor vehicle theft, and arson) dropped among both males and females from 1994 to 2003, although less for females than for males (12.5% versus 27.4%). Property crime arrests dropped 21.1% for females younger than eighteen, compared with a drop of 43.7% for males younger than eighteen. Arrests for burglary, larceny, arson, and motor vehicle theft fell for females of all ages. (See Table 10.2.)

OTHER TYPES OF CRIMES. The numbers of female arrests for the majority of other offenses rose between 1994 and 2003, particularly for girls younger than age eighteen. Arrests for assault other than aggravated assault rose 32.1% for all females and 35.9% for girls under eighteen. Arrests for embezzlement rose 42% for all females and 28.1% for girls under eighteen. Arrests for drug abuse violations rose 34.8% for all females and 56.3% for girls under eighteen; in contrast, arrests for drug abuse violations rose 19.9% for all males and 13% for boys under eighteen. Arrests for driving under the influence rose 83.5% for females under eighteen, and 21.1% for all females. (See Table 10.2.)

Although males accounted for 77.3% of all arrests for offenses against family and children (including nonsupport, neglect, desertion, or abuse) in 2003, male arrests for such offenses rose only 4% from 1994, compared with a rise of 41.2% in female arrests. Arrests of females younger than age eighteen for such offenses rose 31.2%, compared with a 12.2% increase in arrests of males younger than eighteen. (See Table 10.2.)

Prostitution and commercialized vice and runaways were the only crimes for which more females than males were arrested in 2003. Runaways are limited to juveniles taken into protective custody under local statutes. From 1994 to 2003 prostitution and commercialized vice arrests of all females decreased 15% but increased 86.5% among females under age eighteen. (See Table 10.2.)

Federal Arrests

From October 1, 2001, to September 30, 2002, females accounted for 14% of all federal arrests. (See Table 10.3.) Women were arrested for 8.9% of federal arrests for violent crimes and 4.6% of all weapons charges. They accounted for 29.3% of arrests for fraudulent property crimes and 27.4% of arrests for other property crimes. Females accounted for 14.8% of drug arrests and 18.1% of arrests as material witnesses.

During the same time period Drug Enforcement Administration (DEA) agents arrested 5,452 women, 16.1% of all DEA arrests. (See Table 10.4.) Of these

TABLE 10.4

Characteristics of suspects arrested by Drug Enforcement Administration agents, by type of drug, October 1, 2001–September 30, 2002

Arrestee characteristic	Total arrested	Percent arrested	Drug type					
			Cocaine powder	Crack cocaine	Marijuana	Methamphetamine	Opiates	Other or non-drug
All arrestees	29,145	100%	7,261	4,400	5,402	6,406	2,387	3,289
Male/female								
Male	24,436	83.9%	6,239	3,794	4,620	5,158	1,991	2,634
Female	4,676	16.1	1.012	601	774	1,245	391	653
Race								
White	20,234	69.4	4,971	831	4,228	5,943	1,672	2,589
Black	7,839	26.9	2,108	3,516	958	134	644	479
Native American	139	0.5	39	7	42	39	5	7
Asian/Pacific Islander	534	1.8	42	20	86	199	20	167
Ethnicity								
Hispanic	11,304	38.8%	4,024	532	2,547	2,206	1,416	579
Non-Hispanic	16,786	57.6	2,989	3,683	2,668	3,998	882	2,566
Age								
Under 19 years	675	2.3%	122	125	161	143	47	77
19–20 years	1,805	6.2	352	342	409	347	113	242
21–30 years	12,778	44.0	3,243	2,296	2,252	2,495	924	1,568
31–40 years	8,314	28.7	2,224	1,042	1,420	2,050	751	827
Over 40 years	5,437	18.7	1,287	575	1,127	1,342	544	562
Citizenship								
U.S. citizen	21,456	73.6%	4,724	4,023	3,713	4,788	1,487	2,721
Not U.S. citizen	6,353	21.8	2,144	247	1,484	1,263	789	426

Note: Summing arrestees on a characteristic may not yield the total number of arrestees because some arrestees lack information on that characteristic.

SOURCE: "Table 1.4. Characteristics of Suspects Arrested by Drug Enforcement Administration Agents, By Type of Drug, October 1, 2001–September 30, 2002," in *Compendium of Federal Justice Statistics, 2002*, U.S. Department of Justice, Bureau of Justice Statistics, NCJ 205368, September 2004, http://www.ojp.usdoj.gov/bjs/pub/pdf/cfjs0201.pdf (accessed July 1, 2005)

female drug arrests, 26.6% involved methamphetamines, 21.6% involved cocaine powder, 16.6% were for marijuana, 12.9% were for crack cocaine, and 8.4% were for opiates. Only 2.5% of the arrested women were armed, compared with 5% of arrested males.

VIOLENT CRIMES COMMITTED BY WOMEN
Murder

According to the FBI, an estimated 16,043 murders were committed in 2003; of the known offenders, 9.9% were female. Women who committed murder were typically between the ages of seventeen and forty-four.

Among single-victim/single-offender murders in 2003, 499 women murdered males, and 185 murdered other women. There were 123 husbands killed by their wives and 160 boyfriends murdered by their girlfriends. The majority of these crimes occurred during the course of an argument.

Intimate Partner Crime

In the vast majority of intimate partner crime and violence, the victim is female and the perpetrator is male. According to the Bureau of Justice Statistics' BJS Bulletin *Intimate Partner Violence, 1993–2001*, in 2000, 1,247 females and 440 men were killed by intimate partners. In 2001 females were the victims of about 588,490 acts

(85%) of intimate partner violence. In contrast, men fell victim to about 103,220 acts of intimate crime in 2001. Intimate partner violence made up about 20% of all nonfatal violent crime experienced by women in 2001, as opposed to 3% of all nonfatal violent crime against men. The rate of intimate violence against women declined by 46.5% from 1993 to 2001, while the rate against men decreased by 36.6%.

WOMEN IN PRISON

The first female prison in the United States was Mount Pleasant Prison in New York, established in the 1830s. But before the end of the nineteenth century men were being imprisoned there to alleviate overcrowding at Sing Sing Prison. Until the 1930s, when more gender-segregated prisons were built, most female arrests were for prostitution, public drunkenness, vagrancy, and petty theft. But since then women have been committing a much greater range of crimes.

State and Federal Prisoners

According to the BJS Bulletin *Prisoners in 2003*, the number of females under state and federal jurisdiction increased by 3.6%, from 97,631 to 101,179, from 2002 to 2003. (See Table 10.5.) As of year-end 2003, there were 92,785 sentenced female inmates in state and federal prisons. (See Table 10.6.) (Although there appears to be

TABLE 10.5

Women under the jurisdiction of state or federal correctional authorities, year-end 1995, 2002, and 2003

Region and jurisdiction	Number of female inmates			Percent change		Incarceration rate, 2003[b]
	2003	2002	1995	2002 to 2003	Average, 1995 to 2003[a]	
U.S. total	101,179	97,631	68,468	3.6%	5.0%	62
Federal	11,635	11,234	7,398	3.6	5.8	6
State	89,544	86,397	61,070	3.6	4.9	56
Northeast	9,108	9,381	8,401	−2.9%	1.0%	28
Connecticut	1,548	1,694	975	−8.6	5.9	46
Maine	124	90	36	37.8	16.7	18
Massachusetts[c]	708	704	656	0.6	1.0	12
New Hampshire	117	144	109	−18.8	0.9	18
New Jersey	1,517	1,586	1,307	−4.4	1.9	34
New York	2,914	2,996	3,615	−2.7	−2.7	29
Pennsylvania	1,823	1,821	1,502	0.1	2.5	29
Rhode Island	222	214	157	3.7	4.4	10
Vermont	135	132	44	2.3	15.0	27
Midwest	15,682	15,306	10,864	2.5%	4.7%	47
Illinois	2,700	2,520	2,196	7.1	2.6	42
Indiana[c]	1,758	1,583	892	11.1	8.9	56
Iowa	716	703	425	1.8	6.7	48
Kansas	629	537	449	17.1	4.3	46
Michigan[c]	2,198	2,267	1,842	−3.0	2.2	43
Minnesota	435	455	217	−4.4	9.1	17
Missouri	2,239	2,274	1,174	−1.5	8.4	76
Nebraska	323	352	211	−8.2	5.5	35
North Dakota	113	103	29	9.7	18.5	34
Ohio	2,897	2,929	2,793	−1.1	0.5	49
South Dakota	269	227	134	18.5	9.1	69
Wisconsin	1,405	1,356	502	3.6	13.7	47
South	43,389	41,801	27,366	3.8%	5.9%	74
Alabama	2,003	1,697	1,295	18.0	5.6	82
Arkansas	887	854	523	3.9	6.8	63
Delaware	508	542	358	−6.3	4.5	53
Florida	5,068	4,595	3,660	10.3	4.2	58
Georgia	3,145	3,129	2,036	0.5	5.6	71
Kentucky	1,411	1,269	734	11.2	8.5	63
Louisiana	2,405	2,398	1,424	0.3	6.8	104
Maryland	1,248	1,264	1,079	−1.3	1.8	42
Mississippi	2,163	2,082	791	3.9	13.4	134
North Carolina[c]	2,256	2,173	1,752	3.8	3.2	37
Oklahoma	2,320	2,338	1,815	−0.8	3.1	127
South Carolina	1,576	1,671	1,045	−5.7	5.3	68
Tennessee[c]	1,826	1,735	637	5.2	14.1	61
Texas	13,487	13,051	7,935	3.3	6.9	98
Virginia	2,681	2,641	1,659	1.5	6.2	71
West Virginia	405	362	129	11.9	15.4	42
West	21,365	19,909	14,439	7.3%	5.0%	61
Alaska	392	349	243	12.3	6.2	55
Arizona	2,656	2,428	1,432	9.4	8.0	85
California[c]	10,656	9,987	9,082	6.7	2.0	57
Colorado	1,736	1,566	713	10.9	11.8	77
Hawaii	685	669	312	2.4	10.3	68
Idaho	592	592	212	0.0	13.7	86
Montana	419	345	112	21.4	17.9	91
Nevada	880	851	530	3.4	6.5	79
New Mexico	576	518	278	11.2	9.5	56
Oregon	883	812	465	8.7	8.3	49
Utah	427	371	161	15.1	13.0	35
Washington	1,288	1,254	793	2.7	6.3	41
Wyoming[c]	175	167	106	4.8	6.5	70

[a]The average annual percentage increase from 1995 to 2003.
[b]The number of female prisoners with sentences of more than 1 year per 100,000 female U.S. residents.
[c]Growth from 1995 to 2003 may be slightly overestimated due to a change in reporting from custody to jurisdiction counts.

SOURCE: "Table 6. Women Under the Jurisdiction of State or Federal Correctional Authorities, Yearend 1995, 2002, and 2003," in *Prisoners in 2003*, U.S. Department of Justice, Bureau of Justice Statistics, NCJ 205335, November 2004, http://www.ojp.usdoj.gov/bjs/pub/pdf/p03.pdf (accessed June 21, 2005)

some discrepancy between statistics, the larger numbers include all women who are incarcerated, whether or not they have been sentenced with a crime at the time of the gathering of information.) Of these sentenced prisoners, 42.1% were white women, 37.7% were African-American women, and 17.5% were Hispanic women. Black and Hispanic women were overrepresented in the prison population compared with their numbers in the larger

TABLE 10.6

Number of sentenced prisoners under state or federal jurisdiction, by gender, race, Hispanic origin, and age, 2003

	Number of sentenced prisoners							
	Males				Females			
	Total[a]	White[b]	Black[b]	Hispanic	Total[a]	White[b]	Black[b]	Hispanic
Total	1,316,495	454,300	586,300	251,900	92,785	39,100	35,000	16,200
18–19	25,200	7,100	12,600	4,900	1,100	400	500	200
20–24	208,300	59,400	99,900	46,200	11,100	4,400	4,200	2,300
25–29	231,400	63,100	111,400	54,700	13,900	5,600	5,300	2,600
30–34	221,000	70,300	100,000	47,900	17,200	7,200	6,500	3,100
35–39	209,400	75,400	91,900	37,800	18,800	7,800	7,300	3,200
40–44	182,300	71,700	78,100	27,900	15,600	6,800	5,800	2,500
45–54	178,400	74,800	73,900	24,800	12,400	5,400	4,700	1,800
55 or older	57,700	31,900	17,200	7,200	2,600	1,400	700	300

Note: Based on custody counts by race and Hispanic origin from National Prisoner Statistics and updated from jurisdiction counts by gender at yearend. Estimates by age were derived from the National Corrections Reporting Program, 2002. Estimates were rounded to the nearest 100.
[a]Includes American Indians, Alaska Natives, Asians, Native Hawaiians, and other Pacific Islanders.
[b]Excludes Hispanics.

SOURCE: "Table 11. Number of Sentenced Prisoners Under State or Federal Jurisdiction, by Gender, Race, Hispanic Origin, and Age, 2003," in *Prisoners in 2003*, U.S. Department of Justice, Bureau of Justice Statistics, NCJ 205335, November 2004, http://www.ojp.usdoj.gov/bjs/pub/pdf/p03.pdf (accessed June 21, 2005)

TABLE 10.7

Number of inmates under age 18 held in state prisons, by gender, June 30, 1990, 1995, and 1999–2004

	Inmates under age 18		
Year	Total	Male	Female
2004	2,477	2,369	108
2003	2,740	2,627	113
2002	3,038	2,927	111
2001	3,147	3,010	137
2000	3,896	3,721	175
1999	4,194	4,027	167
1995	5,309	—	—
1990	3,600	—	—

Note: Federal prisons held 39 inmates under age 18 in 1990, but none in 1995 and 1999 to 2004.
— Not available.

SOURCE: Paige M. Harrison and Allen J. Beck, "Table 5. Number of Inmates Under Age 18 Held in State Prisons, by Gender, June 30, 1990, 1995, and 1999–2004," in *Prison and Jail Inmates at Midyear 2004*, U.S. Department of Justice, Bureau of Justice Statistics, NCJ 208801, April 2005, http://www.ojp.usdoj.gov/bjs/pub/pdf/pjim04.pdf (accessed June 21, 2005)

---

population. African-American women (185 per one hundred thousand) were more than twice as likely as Hispanic women (eighty-four per one hundred thousand) and almost five times more likely than white women (thirty-eight per one hundred thousand) to be incarcerated in 2003. These differences were consistent across all age groups.

From 1995 to 2003 the number of female state and federal prisoners increased by an average of 5% annually, compared with an average annual increase of 3.3% for men. At the end of 2003 women accounted for 6.9% of all state and federal prisoners, up from 6.1% in 1995.

At year-end 2003 one in every 1,613 women in the United States was incarcerated in a state or federal prison. More than a third of the 101,179 women being held were in the three largest jurisdictions: Texas (13,487), the federal system (11,635), and California (10,656). States with the lowest female incarcerations were in the Northeast. (See Table 10.5.)

The numbers of both male and female prisoners who were younger than age eighteen declined from 1999 to 2004. In 1999 there were 167 female prisoners younger than eighteen, compared with 108 in midyear 2004. (See Table 10.7.)

HIV IN PRISON. According to the Bureau of Justice Statistics (BJS) publication *HIV in Prisons and Jails, 2002* (December 2004), the rate of confirmed HIV-infection among the nation's state prison population in 2002 was 2%, and the rate of HIV-positive inmates in federal prisons was 1.1%. The overall rate of confirmed AIDS in the prison population (0.48%) was more than three times higher than the rate in the general population.

At year-end 2002 there were 2,169 female inmates and 20,728 male inmates in state and federal prisons known to be HIV-positive. (See Table 10.8.) Although the actual number of HIV-positive females was far less than the number of HIV-positive males, the percentage of the inmate population was higher; 2.8% of all female inmates were HIV-positive compared with 1.9% of males. The rate of infection was higher in females in all regions and in most states, with New York (13.6%), Maryland (12.1%), and Rhode Island (9.3%) reporting the highest rates among females. Vermont, Minnesota, North Dakota, and Oregon reported no HIV-positive female inmates. AIDS-related deaths in state and federal prisons dropped

TABLE 10.8

Inmates in custody of state and federal prison authorities who are known to be positive for HIV, by gender, year-end 2002

Jurisdiction[a]	Male HIV cases		Female HIV cases	
	Number	Percent of population	Number	Percent of population
U.S. total				
Estimated[b]	21,704		2,280	
Reported	20,728	1.9%	2,169	2.8%
Federal	1,431	1.1%	116	1.2%
State	19,297	1.9	2,053	3.0
Northeast	6,920	4.4%	700	8.1%
Connecticut	563	3.3	103	7.2
Maine	—	—	—	—
Massachusetts	249	2.7	41	5.9
New Hampshire	15	0.6	1	0.6
New Jersey	691	3.1	65	5.1
New York	4,590	7.2	410	13.6
Pennsylvania	738	2.0	62	3.5
Rhode Island	68	2.1	18	9.3
Vermont	6	0.5	0	0
Midwest	1,841	1.0%	151	1.2%
Illinois	520	1.3	50	2.0
Indiana	—	—	—	—
Iowa	29	0.4	4	0.6
Kansas	41	0.5	7	1.2
Michigan	544	1.1	47	2.1
Minnesota	37	0.6	0	0
Missouri	250	0.9	12	0.5
Nebraska	23	0.6	1	0.3
North Dakota	4	0.4	0	0
Ohio	388	1.0	29	1.0
South Dakota	5	0.2	1	0.4
Wisconsin	—	—	—	—
South	8,786	2.2%	1,044	3.5%
Alabama	252	1.1	24	1.5
Arkansas	89	0.8	11	1.4
Delaware	116	1.9	12	2.3
Florida	2,508	3.6	340	7.4
Georgia	1,023	2.3	100	3.2
Kentucky	—	—	—	—
Louisiana	472	2.5	31	3.0
Maryland	815	3.6	152	12.1
Mississippi	—	—	—	—
North Carolina	—	—	—	—
Oklahoma	138	1.0	8	0.5
South Carolina	502	2.4	42	2.6
Tennessee	194	1.5	24	2.1
Texas	2,261	1.8	267	2.7
Virginia	394	1.4	31	1.5
West Virginia	22	0.7	2	0.8

TABLE 10.8

Inmates in custody of state and federal prison authorities who are known to be positive for HIV, by gender, year-end 2002 [CONTINUED]

Jurisdiction[a]	Male HIV cases		Female HIV cases	
	Number	Percent of population	Number	Percent of population
West	1,750	0.7%	158	0.9%
Alaska	14	0.5	2	0.8
Arizona	117	0.4	13	0.5
California	1,107	0.7	74	0.8
Colorado	156	1.1	26	1.7
Hawaii	21	0.6	1	0.2
Idaho	17	0.5	1	0.2
Montana	7	0.4	1	0.5
Nevada	98	1.1	15	4.2
New Mexico	27	0.5	3	0.6
Oregon	42	0.4	0	0
Utah	48	1.2	10	3.4
Washington	91	0.6	10	0.8
Wyoming	5	0.5	2	2.2

— Not reported.

[a]At yearend 2001 responsibility for housing District of Columbia sentenced felons was transferred to the Federal Bureau of Prisons.

[b]Includes estimate of the number of inmates with HIV/AIDS by gender for Maine, Wisconsin, Kentucky, Mississippi, and North Carolina. Estimates were based on the most recent data available by gender.

SOURCE: Laura M. Maruschak, "Table 2. Inmates in Custody of State and Federal Prison Authorities Known to be Positive for the Human Immunodeficiency Virus, by Gender, Yearend 2002," in *HIV in Prisons and Jails, 2002,* U.S. Department of Justice, Bureau of Justice Statistics, NCJ 205333, December 2004, http://www.ojp.usdoj.gov/bjs/pub/pdf/hivpj02.pdf (accessed June 21, 2005)

from one hundred per one hundred thousand inmates in 1995 to twenty-two per one hundred thousand in 2002.

STATE PRISONERS. According to the BJS, the number of female inmates under state jurisdiction increased by 18,100 women between 1995 and 2001. In comparison, the number of male inmates increased by 189,300. Violent offenders accounted for 48.6% of the increase in female inmates and 63.9% of the increase in male inmates. Drug offenses accounted for 12.8% of the increase in female inmates and 15.2% of the increase in male inmates. Property crimes accounted for 22.3% of the increase in female inmates but dropped by an estimated two hundred offenders among the male population. The remainder of the increase was the result of public-order offenses.

Women in Jails

Jails differ from prisons in that they hold inmates for shorter sentences (less than one year). Jails also house inmates for federal, state, and other authorities because of overcrowding of those facilities. Persons awaiting trial, sentencing, and conviction are housed in jails, as are mentally ill individuals pending movement to an appropriate health-care facility. Juveniles are temporarily detained in jail until they can be transferred to juvenile authorities, and individuals in the military are housed in jail for protective custody or while awaiting appearance as court witnesses. According to the 1999 BJS report *Census of Jails* (August 2001), 2,980 jails housed men and women separately, 383 housed men only, and thirteen housed women only.

LOCAL JAILS. According to the BJS, the number of female jail inmates consistently rose about 7% annually from 1994 to 2004, while the male jail population grew 4.2% annually. On June 30, 2004, 12.3% of the local jail inmate population was female. The number of female jail inmates rose 6.6% over the previous twelve months; the number of male inmates increased 2.8% during that time.

Mothers in Prison

According to BJS publication *Incarcerated Parents and Their Children* (August 2000), in 1999, 2.1% of all minor children in America had a parent in prison. An estimated 336,300 households with children were missing a parent because of incarceration in 1999. An estimated 35,400 households with minor children had mothers incarcerated in 1999, with 53,600 women who were mothers incarcerated in state or federal prisons. This meant that at year-end 1999 an estimated 126,100 children had a mother in prison, nearly doubling the number (up 98%) from 1991. In federal prisons in 1999, 59% of women had children younger than age eighteen. Among state prisoners, 65% of female prisoners had minor children.

Of the households in which a mother was incarcerated in state prison, 53% reported a child was being raised by grandparents; 28% reported children with their father; 25.7% were reported with another relative; and 20% stated that their children were in foster care or with a friend (some prisoners had children in different homes). Although 60% of mothers in state prisons reported some type of weekly contact (visits, phone calls, or letters), a majority of these mothers (54%) never had visits from their children.

In a presentation given at a conference for the National Center on Fathers and Families on November 15, 2001, Christopher J. Mumola of the BJS gave updated 2000 estimates for *Incarcerated Parents and Their Children*. The estimated number of households with children missing a parent because of incarceration in 2000 had grown to 344,100. From 1991 to 2000 the number of incarcerated mothers of minor-aged children grew 87%. The total mean time a mother was expected to serve was about four years and one month. About 65% of mothers in prison had used drugs in the month before their crime was committed, and 43% had been using drugs when the crime occurred.

The Center for Children of Incarcerated Parents, in "How Many Children of Incarcerated Parents Are There?" (http://www.e-ccip.org/publication.html), estimated that on June 30, 2004, 70% of the 190,309 women incarcerated in the United States were parents—a total of 133,216 mothers. Mothers in prison averaged 2.4 children; the Center estimated that 319,718 children in the United States had a mother in prison.

Some states have mother–infant programs within their prison systems to help prisoners care for their infants. The federal system has the Mothers and Infants Together (MINT) program to help pregnant women and mothers with infants. But most mothers in prison rely on relatives to care for their children. Additionally, many children of women prisoners are in foster care.

Probation and Parole

According to the BJS, women accounted for about 23% of all adult probationers at the end of 2003, a statistic virtually unchanged from 2000 (22%) and slightly up from 1995 (21%). Women accounted for 13% of all parolees at the end of 2003, up from 12% in 2000 and 10% in 1995.

SENTENCES OF DEATH
Women on Death Row

According to the BJS Bulletin *Capital Punishment 2003* (November 2004), at the end of 2003, 3,374 prisoners were under sentence of death in thirty-seven states and the federal prison system. For the fifth year in a row, death row admissions dropped: there were 304 in 1998; 282 in 1999; 232 in 2000; 163 in 2001; 159 in 2002; and 144 in 2003. During 2003, 267 inmates were removed from death row, the largest number since the Supreme Court reinstated the death penalty in 1976.

Of the 144 prisoners sentenced to death in 2003, two were female. From the time the death penalty was reinstated in 1976 until year-end 2003, 146 death sentences were imposed upon female offenders; ten were executed. The number of women on death row decreased from fifty-one in 2002 to forty-seven in 2003. This number was still higher than the thirty-six women on death row in 1992. These women were under sentence of death in seventeen states and represented 1.4% of all death row inmates. The women included twenty-nine whites, fifteen African-Americans, and three of other races. Two-thirds of the women on death row were being held in four states: California (14), Texas (8), Pennsylvania (5), and North Carolina (4). Women spent an average of seven years and eight months in prison after their sentencing, compared with nine years and seven months for men.

Executions

In 2003 sixty-five people were executed by eleven states and the federal government, the lowest number since 1996. According to advance figures released in *Capital Punishment 2003*, fifty-nine people were executed in twelve states in 2004.

No women were executed during 2003 or 2004. A total of ten women had been executed since the reinstatement of the death penalty in 1976. The first was Velma Barfield, put to death by the state of North Carolina in 1984. She had been convicted of poisoning her boyfriend with arsenic. During her trial it came out that she had also poisoned her mother and two other people who were in her care. While in prison she also admitted to causing the deaths of her first and second husbands.

Two women were executed in 1998. Karla Faye Tucker was executed in Texas for murdering two people with a pickax while on drugs. Judias Beunoano was the first female to be executed in Florida in 150 years. Known as the "Black Widow," she had poisoned her husband with arsenic, drowned her paralyzed son, and tried to blow up her fiancé.

In February 2000 Betty Lou Beets was put to death in Texas after being found guilty of murdering her fifth husband. On May 2, 2000, a mentally ill woman, Christina Riggs, was executed in Arkansas by lethal injection.

On January 11, 2001, Wanda Jean Allen was executed by lethal injection in Oklahoma. She was the first African-American female to be executed in the United States since 1954. She had been convicted of murdering a childhood friend and later killing her lesbian lover. It has been suggested that she was mentally retarded. On May 1, 2001, Marilyn Plantz was executed by lethal injection in Oklahoma for the 1988 murder of her husband. Lois Nadean Smith was executed by lethal injection on December 4, 2001, for killing her son's ex-girlfriend.

On May 10, 2002, Lynda Lyon Block was electrocuted in Alabama for murdering a police officer. Later that year, on October 9, Aileen Wournos was executed by lethal injection in Florida for murdering six men.

The death penalty has always been controversial in terms of ethics and effectiveness as a deterrent to crime. In January 2003 Illinois Governor George Ryan revoked the death sentence on all 171 inmates in his state because he had grave concerns about the dependability of a legal system he found seriously flawed. This included four women on death row. As a result, the state legislature enacted several death penalty reforms. Illinois accounted for 60% of the reduction in death row inmates from 2002 to 2003.

According to a May 2005 Gallup Poll, support for the death penalty was higher (75%) than it had been in several years. In 2005 more Americans said they supported the death penalty for convicted murderers, more preferred it to life imprisonment, and more believe that the death penalty is administered fairly. More than half of Americans believed the death penalty should be imposed more often.

CHAPTER 11
WOMEN'S HEALTH

In 2002 the life expectancy at birth was 79.9 years for American females and 74.5 years for males. Both African-American and white women had a longer life expectancy than men within each racial and ethnic group. White women had a life expectancy of 80.3 years; white males had a life expectancy of 75.1 years. African-American women had a life expectancy of 75.6 years; African-American men had a life expectancy of 68.8 years. By the year 2100 the U.S. Census Bureau projects that female life expectancy at birth will be between 89.3 and 95.2 years.

Women are generally healthier than men. Women tend to take better care of themselves and smoke and drink less than men. Women in America are no longer as likely to die from complications of childbirth as they were in the past. However, because more women than men survive into old age, they are more likely to suffer from chronic illnesses. Furthermore, because more women than men live in poverty, they may have less access to preventative medicine and advanced medical treatments.

In 2004 the National Health Interview Survey (NHIS), conducted by the National Center for Health Statistics (NCHS) of the Centers for Disease Control and Prevention (CDC), found that the number of males who assessed their health and that of family members living in the same household as "excellent" was somewhat higher than the number of females. (See Figure 11.1.) Among women between the ages of eighteen and sixty-four, 65.1% rated their health as excellent or very good, compared with only 37.7% of women age sixty-five and older. A greater portion of non-Hispanic whites (69.9%) and Hispanics (58.8%) rated their overall health as very good or better compared with African-Americans (58.2%).

The health-care needs and the medical problems of women are often very different from those of men. After the onset of menarche (the first menstrual period, usually between the ages of about nine and thirteen), for the rest of their lives women's health issues may be focused on their reproductive systems. They may experience menstrual irregularities, amenorrhea (lack of menstruation), cramping and other side effects of menstruation, premenstrual syndrome (PMS), or other difficulties associated with their menstrual cycles. Women must deal with contraception, fertility, abortion, pregnancy, and childbearing, as well as the possibility of postpartum depression and other complications of pregnancy. In their forties or fifties women enter menopause, experiencing multiple symptoms and making decisions about possible treatments such as estrogen supplementation. Many women are affected by diseases or abnormalities of the reproductive system, and hundreds of thousands of women have hysterectomies (removal of the uterus) every year.

WOMEN'S ACCESS TO HEALTH CARE
Sources of Health Care

According to the NCHS compendium *Health, United States, 2004*, in 2001–02, among adults ages eighteen to sixty-four, 11.4% of women had no usual source of health care, compared with 21.3% of men. Women also made far more health-care visits than men. Only 11.4% of women made no visits in 2002, compared with 20.6% of men. Many more women than men made ten or more visits to health care providers in 2002 (16.1% and 10.7%, respectively). Women visited the emergency room more often than men; 20.5% had visited the emergency room at least once in the past year (compared with 18.9% of men), and 7.9% had made two or more visits (compared with 6.2% of men).

Between 1995 and 2002 the rate of office visits to physicians increased from 271 per one hundred population to 316 per one hundred population. The increase was smaller for people between eighteen and forty-four than for other age groups. The age-adjusted rate of office visits for females in 2002 was 359 per one hundred; for males it

FIGURE 11.1

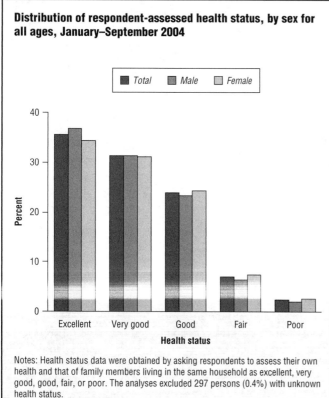

Distribution of respondent-assessed health status, by sex for all ages, January–September 2004

Notes: Health status data were obtained by asking respondents to assess their own health and that of family members living in the same household as excellent, very good, good, fair, or poor. The analyses excluded 297 persons (0.4%) with unknown health status.

SOURCE: "Figure 11.2. Percent Distribution of Respondent-Assessed Health Status, by Sex for all Ages: United States, January–September 2004," in *Early Release of Selected Estimates Based on Data from the January–September 2004 National Health Interview Survey*, Centers for Disease Control and Prevention, National Center for Health Statistics, March 23, 2005, http://www.cdc.gov/nchs/data/nhis/earlyrelease/200503_11.pdf (accessed June 21, 2005)

was only 270. Among female adults, older women had a higher rate of office visits than did younger women. (Age-adjusted means that the rate is determined for a population with a standard age distribution, so that the rates for different years can be compared, even though the age distribution of the population may have changed.)

In 2002 women were as likely as men to have activity limitations because of a chronic condition (12.3% of both groups). In 1999, the latest year for which data were available, 1,091,700 women age sixty-five and over were nursing-home residents, up from 695,800 in 1973–74, for an age-adjusted rate of 49.8 per one thousand population. This compared with 377,800 males over sixty-five who were nursing-home residents, for an age-adjusted rate of 30.6 per one thousand. Furthermore, in 2000, 64.8% of all home health-care patients were female, as were 57.4% of all people in hospice care.

Health Insurance

In 2002, 15.1% of all females under age sixty-five had no health insurance, compared with 18.2% of males. (See Table 11.1.) People between the ages of eighteen and forty-four were most likely to be without insurance; 28.2% of those between eighteen and twenty-four, 23.8% of those between twenty-five and thirty-four, and 17.8% of those between thirty-five and forty-four were without health insurance. Due largely to Medicare, almost all adults age sixty-five and older had health insurance. The percentage of people with private health insurance declined between 1989 and 2002. In 1989, 77.4% of men and 75.4% of women had private health insurance; by 2002, only 62% of men and 59.6% of women had private health insurance.

According to the Census Bureau report *Income, Poverty, and Health Insurance Coverage in the United States, 2003*, in 2003 an estimated forty-five million people in America were uninsured, about 15.5% of the population (including those over age sixty-five, not included in the *Health, United States, 2004* data). This was a slight increase from 15.2% in 2002.

Among the population ages eighteen to sixty-four, workers were more likely (82%) than nonworkers (74.3%) to have health insurance in 2002. But among those in the same age category who lived in poverty, workers were less likely (52.6%) than nonworkers (61.9%) to be covered in 2002. In 2003 health insurance coverage rates did not change from the previous year for those with household incomes of more than $75,000, but rates fell for those in each lower category of income. People under the poverty level had an overall high rate of lack of health insurance coverage (31.4%); however, the rates decreased with deepening poverty, as households became eligible for government-sponsored health insurance. (See Table 11.1.)

The total number of people with employer-based health insurance dropped from 61.3% to 60.4% of the population from 2002 to 2003. The percentage of people with Medicare increased slightly from 13.4% in 2002 to 13.7% in 2003; the percentage of people with Medicaid increased from 11.6% in 2002 to 12.4% in 2003. *Health, United States 2004* found that in 2002 about 31.8% of women had private insurance through an employer, compared with 38.9% of men. In that year Medicaid covered 5.7% of men and 9.7% of women.

In addition to poverty and the decrease in employer-based coverage, another barrier to having health insurance was nativity. The foreign-born population was almost three times as likely as the native-born population to lack health insurance in 2003 (34.5% and 13%, respectively).

Early release statistics from the 2004 NHIS found that women between the ages of eighteen and forty-four were more likely to be insured than men, although women and men between forty-five and sixty-four were equally likely to be insured. (See Figure 11.2.) Hispanics

TABLE 11.1

Persons under age 65 with no health insurance coverage, according to selected characteristics, selected years 1984–2002

[Data are based on household interviews of a sample of the civilian noninstitutionalized population]

Characteristic	1984	1989	1995	1997[a]	1998	1999	2000	2001	2002
					Number in millions				
Total[b]	29.8	33.4	37.1	41.0	39.2	38.5	40.5	39.2	40.6
					Percent of population				
Total, age adjusted[b,c]	14.3	15.3	15.9	17.4	16.5	16.1	16.8	16.2	16.6
Total, crude[b]	14.5	15.6	16.1	17.5	16.6	16.1	16.8	16.1	16.5
Age									
Under 18 years	13.9	14.7	13.4	14.0	12.7	11.9	12.4	11.0	10.7
Under 6 years	14.9	15.1	11.8	12.5	11.5	11.0	11.7	9.7	9.1
6–17 years	13.4	14.5	14.3	14.7	13.3	12.3	12.8	11.7	11.5
18–44 years	17.1	18.4	20.4	22.4	21.4	21.0	22.0	21.7	22.5
18–24 years	25.0	27.1	28.0	30.1	29.0	27.4	29.7	29.3	28.2
25–34 years	16.2	18.3	21.1	23.8	22.2	22.1	22.7	22.3	23.8
35–44 years	11.2	12.3	15.1	16.7	16.4	16.3	16.8	16.7	17.8
45–64 years	9.6	10.5	10.9	12.4	12.2	12.2	12.7	12.3	13.1
45–54 years	10.5	11.0	11.6	12.8	12.6	12.8	12.8	13.0	14.1
55–64 years	8.7	10.0	9.9	11.8	11.4	11.4	12.5	11.0	11.6
Sex[c]									
Male	15.0	16.4	17.2	18.5	17.5	17.2	17.8	17.2	18.2
Female	13.6	14.3	14.6	16.2	15.5	15.0	15.8	15.1	15.1
Race[c,d]									
White only	13.4	14.2	15.3	16.3	15.2	14.6	15.2	14.7	15.3
Black or African American only	20.0	21.4	18.2	20.2	20.7	19.5	20.0	19.3	19.3
American Indian and Alaska Native only				38.2	39.0	38.3	38.2	33.4	38.7
Asian only	18.0	18.5	18.2	19.3	18.1	16.4	17.3	17.1	17.2
Native Hawaiian and other Pacific Islander only	—	—	—	—	—	*	*	*	*
2 or more races	—	—	—	—	—	16.8	18.4	18.6	19.2
Hispanic origin and race[c,d]									
Hispanic or Latino	29.1	32.4	31.5	34.3	34.0	33.9	35.4	34.8	33.8
Mexican	33.2	38.8	36.2	39.2	40.0	38.0	39.9	39.0	37.0
Puerto Rican	18.1	23.3	18.3	19.4	19.4	19.8	16.4	16.0	19.5
Cuban	21.6	20.9	22.1	20.5	18.4	19.7	25.2	19.2	20.5
Other Hispanic or Latino	27.5	25.2	29.7	32.9	31.1	30.8	32.7	33.1	32.9
Not Hispanic or Latino	13.0	13.5	14.0	15.1	14.1	13.5	14.1	13.4	14.0
White only	11.8	11.9	12.9	13.7	12.5	12.1	12.5	11.9	12.6
Black or African American only	19.7	21.3	18.1	20.1	20.7	19.4	20.0	19.2	19.2
Age and percent of poverty level[e]									
All ages:[c]									
Below 100 percent	34.7	35.8	31.7	35.2	35.7	35.6	35.2	34.0	31.4
100–149 percent	27.0	31.3	31.7	35.4	35.6	34.7	35.2	32.0	32.8
150–199 percent	17.4	21.8	24.0	26.3	26.3	27.2	27.2	26.5	25.6
200 percent or more	5.8	6.8	8.6	10.0	9.2	9.1	10.0	9.9	10.9
Under 18 years:									
Below 100 percent	28.9	31.6	20.0	23.2	22.7	22.3	21.8	20.6	16.9
100–149 percent	22.8	26.1	24.8	26.5	27.4	24.2	25.1	19.4	19.2
150–199 percent	12.7	15.8	18.0	19.9	17.5	19.1	17.6	17.3	14.2
200 percent or more	4.2	4.4	6.4	7.1	6.0	5.4	6.5	5.8	6.7

were more likely (32.3%) than non-Hispanic whites (10.4%) and African-Americans (15.9%) to lack health insurance coverage.

Barriers to Obtaining Health Care

According to the early release analysis of the 2004 NHIS, in the first nine months of 2004, 5.4% of the total population was unable to obtain medical care over the previous twelve months because of financial barriers. From 1998 through June 2004 the percentage of people who experienced a lack of access to medical care due to costs increased. The percentage was virtually the same

for male and female children under age eighteen, but significantly more adult women than men failed to obtain needed medical care in the first nine months of 2004. (See Figure 11.3.) African-Americans (6.5%) and Hispanics (6.2%) were more likely than non-Hispanic whites (5.1%) to have been unable to obtain medical care because of cost.

LEADING CAUSES OF DEATH AMONG WOMEN

According to *Health, United States, 2003,* the age-adjusted death rate for females in 2002 was 715.2 per one

TABLE 11.1

Persons under age 65 with no health insurance coverage, according to selected characteristics, selected years 1984–2002 [CONTINUED]

[Data are based on household interviews of a sample of the civilian noninstitutionalized population]

Characteristic	1984	1989	1995	1997[a]	1998	1999	2000	2001	2002
Geographic region[c]				Percent of population					
Northeast	10.1	10.7	13.1	13.4	12.3	12.2	12.1	11.6	12.7
Midwest	11.1	10.5	12.1	13.1	11.9	11.5	12.3	11.7	12.4
South	17.4	19.4	19.2	20.7	20.0	19.8	20.4	20.0	20.2
West	17.8	18.4	17.7	20.4	19.9	18.6	20.2	18.6	18.8
Location of residence[c]									
Within MSA[f]	13.3	14.9	15.2	16.7	15.8	15.3	16.3	15.6	16.1
Outside MSA[f]	16.4	16.9	18.7	19.9	19.2	18.9	18.8	18.5	18.9

*Estimates are considered unreliable.
—Data not available.
[a]In 1997 the National Health Interview Survey (NHIS) was redesigned, including changes to the questions on health insurance coverage.
[b]Includes all other races not shown separately and, in 1984 and 1989, unknown poverty level.
[c]Estimates are for persons under 65 years of age and are age adjusted to the year 2000 standard using three age groups: under 18 years, 18–44 years, and 45–64 years. Age-adjusted estimates in this table may differ from other age-adjusted estimates based on the same data and presented elsewhere if different age groups are used in the adjustment procedure.
[d]The race groups, white, black, American Indian and Alaska Native (AI/AN), Asian, Native Hawaiian and other Pacific Islander, and 2 or more races, include persons of Hispanic and non-Hispanic origin. Persons of Hispanic origin may be of any race. Starting with data year 1999 race-specific estimates are tabulated according to 1997 Standards for Federal data on Race and Ethnicity and are not strictly comparable with estimates for earlier years. The five single race categories plus multiple race categories shown in the table conform to 1997 Standards. The 1999 and later race-specific estimates are for persons who reported only one racial group: the category "2 or more races" includes persons who reported more than one racial group. Prior to data year 1999, data were tabulated according to 1977 Standards with four racial groups and the category "Asian only" included Native Hawaiian and other Pacific Islander. Estimates for single race categories prior to 1999 included persons who reported one race or, if they reported more than one race, identified one race as best representing their race. The effect of the 1997 Standard on the 1999 estimates can be seen by comparing 1999 data tabulated according to the two standards. Age-adjusted estimates based on the 1977 Standards of the percent with no health insurance coverage are: 0.1 percentage points higher for the white group; identical for the black group; 0.1 percentage points lower for the Asian and Pacific Islander group; and 1.5 percentage points higher for the AI/AN group than estimates based on the 1997 standards.
[e]Poverty status was unknown for 10–11 percent of persons under 65 years of age in 1984 and 1989. Missing family income data were imputed for 15–16 percent of persons under 65 years of age in 1994–96. Missing family income data were imputed for 24 percent of persons under 65 years of age in 1997 and 28–31 percent in 1998 to 2002.
[f]MSA is metropolitan statistical area.
Notes: Persons not covered by private insurance, Medicaid, State Children's Health Insurance Program (SCHIP), public assistance (through 1996), state-sponsored or other government-sponsored health plans (starting in 1997), Medicare, or military plans are considered to have no health insurance coverage and are included in this table.

SOURCE: "Table 131. No Health Insurance Coverage among Persons Under 65 Years of Age, according to Selected Characteristics: United States, Selected Years 1984–2002," in *Health, United States, 2004*, Centers for Disease Control and Prevention, National Center for Health Statistics, September 2004, http://www.cdc.gov/nchs/data/hus/hus04trend.pdf (accessed June 9, 2005)

hundred thousand people, compared with a male death rate of 1,013.7. In 1950 the female age-adjusted death rate from all causes was 1,236 per one hundred thousand. In 2002 the leading causes of death among women were heart disease, malignancies, cerebrovascular diseases, chronic lower respiratory diseases, Alzheimer's disease, diabetes mellitus, unintentional injuries, influenza/pneumonia, nephritis/nephrosis, and septicemia. (See Table 11.2.)

Cardiovascular Disease

Cardiovascular disease (CVD) is the leading cause of death among American males and females of all races/ethnicities, causing 36.7% of female deaths and 33.7% of male deaths in 2002. CVD includes both diseases of the heart and cerebrovascular diseases such as stroke and high blood pressure. According to a publication from the American Heart Association (AHA), *Heart Disease and Stroke Statistics—2005 Update*, from 1979 to 2002 CVD mortality declined among men and rose among women, and more women than men have died of CVD since 1984. (See Figure 11.4.) According to *Health, United States, 2004*, 456,064 women and 402,555 men died of some form of CVD in 2002. Women represented 53.1% of all CVD deaths in 2002.

CVD accounted for 36.8% of white female deaths, 36% of African-American female deaths, 32.2% of Hispanic female deaths, 35.8% of Asian-American/Pacific Islander female deaths, and 24.5% of Native American female deaths in 2002.

Until recently, CVD was believed to be more prevalent and more serious in men than in women. The first Framingham Study, one of the most comprehensive and influential medical studies ever carried out, did not include older women. Since premenopausal women's production of estrogen appears to help protect them from CVD, the Framingham Study led researchers to believe that CVD was primarily a male problem. Since then, the follow-ups to the original study have shown that women first experience cardiovascular events about ten years later than men; but this gender gap decreases with age as women's estrogen levels drop at menopause. Despite the similar percentages of men and women with CVD, men were much more likely than women to have cardiovascular operations requiring hospitalizations in 2002; nearly four million men had vascular and cardiac surgery but only 2.8 million women did. (See Table 11.3.)

The AHA states that one in four American women have CVD and that smoking, a diet high in fats, and lack

FIGURE 11.2

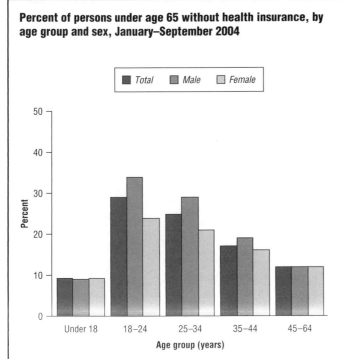

Percent of persons under age 65 without health insurance, by age group and sex, January–September 2004

Notes: A person was defined as uninsured if he or she did not have any private health insurance, Medicare, Medicaid, State Children's Health Insurance Program (SCHIP), state-sponsored or other government-sponsored health plan, or military plan at the time of the interview. A person was also defined as uninsured if he or she had only Indian Health Service coverage or had only a private plan that paid for one type of service such as accidents or dental care. The analyses excluded 621 persons (1.0%) with unknown health insurance status. The data on health insurance status were edited using an automated system based on logic checks and keyword searches. The resulting estimates of persons not having health insurance coverage are generally 0.1–0.2 percentage points lower than those based on the editing procedures used for the final data files.

SOURCE: "Figure 1.2. Percent of Persons Under Age 65 Years without Health Insurance Coverage, by Age Group and Sex: United States, January–September 2004," in *Early Release of Selected Estimates Based on Data from the January–September 2004 National Health Interview Survey*, Centers for Disease Control and Prevention, National Center for Health Statistics, March 23, 2005, http://www.cdc.gov/nchs/data/nhis/earlyrelease/200503_01.pdf (accessed June 21, 2005)

FIGURE 11.3

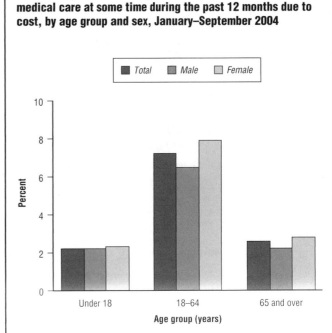

Percent of persons of all ages who failed to obtain needed medical care at some time during the past 12 months due to cost, by age group and sex, January–September 2004

Note: The analyses excluded 259 persons (0.4%) with unknown success in obtaining needed medical care.

SOURCE: "Figure 3.2. Percent of Persons of All Ages Who Failed to Obtain Needed Medical Care Due to Cost at Some Time during the Past 12 Months, by Age Group and Sex: United States, January–September 2004," in *Early Release of Selected Estimates Based on Data from the January–September 2004 National Health Interview Survey*, Centers for Disease Control and Prevention, National Center for Health Statistics, March 23, 2005, http://www.cdc.gov/nchs/data/nhis/earlyrelease/200503_03.pdf (accessed June 21, 2005)

of exercise are all risk factors for developing CVD. The use of oral contraceptives, especially if combined with smoking, also increases the risk factor for women.

DISEASES OF THE HEART. Heart disease, which includes all diseases of the heart such as coronary heart disease and angina, was the leading cause of death among American men and women in 2002, killing 356,014 women, 28.6% of all female deaths. (See Table 11.2.) Diseases of the heart were the leading cause of death among women of all races and ethnicities except Native American/Alaska Native and Asian-American/Pacific Islander females, among whom it was the second-leading cause of death. Diseases of the heart were also the leading cause of death among women in 1980, accounting for 38.9% of all female deaths that year.

According to the AHA, coronary heart disease (CHD) accounts for more than half of all CVD events

in men and women under age seventy-five. CHD is the most common form of heart disease and often results in heart attacks, 41% of which are fatal. One in twenty white females (5.4%) and 7.5% of African-American females have CHD. About 64% of women who die suddenly of CHD (compared with 50% of men) have no warning symptoms. CHD is the result of clogged arteries that are no longer able to carry fresh nutrients and oxygen to the heart. The lifetime risk of developing CHD after age forty is 32% for women and 49% for men. Postmenopausal women are two to three times more likely than premenopausal women to have CHD.

According to the AHA, because women experience heart attacks at older ages than men, they are more likely to die within a few weeks. For women, the average age for a first heart attack is 70.4, compared with 65.8 for men. Within one year of their first recognized heart attack, about 38% of women and 25% of men die. Within six years of their first heart attack, 35% of women and 18% of men will have a second heart attack. Women are more than twice as likely as men to be disabled by heart failure.

TABLE 11.2

Leading causes of death and numbers of deaths among women, 1980 and 2002

[Data are based on death certificates]

Sex, race, Hispanic origin, and rank order	1980		2002	
	Cause of death	Deaths	Cause of death	Deaths
Female				
...	All causes	914,763	All causes	1,244,123
1	Diseases of heart	355,424	Diseases of heart	356,014
2	Malignant neoplasms	190,561	Malignant neoplasms	268,503
3	Cerebrovascular diseases	100,252	Cerebrovascular diseases	100,050
4	Unintentional injuries	31,538	Chronic lower respiratory diseases	64,103
5	Pneumonia and influenza	27,045	Alzheimer's disease	41,877
6	Diabetes mellitus	20,526	Diabetes mellitus	38,948
7	Atherosclerosis	17,848	Unintentional injuries	37,485
8	Chronic obstructive pulmonary diseases	17,425	Influenza and pneumonia	36,763
9	Chronic liver disease and cirrhosis	10,815	Nephritis, nephrotic syndrome and nephrosis	21,279
10	Certain conditions originating in the perinatal period	9,815	Septicemia	18,918
White female				
...	All causes	804,729	All causes	1,077,393
1	Diseases of heart	318,668	Diseases of heart	309,972
2	Malignant neoplasms	169,974	Malignant neoplasms	232,614
3	Cerebrovascular diseases	88,639	Cerebrovascular diseases	86,760
4	Unintentional injuries	27,159	Chronic lower respiratory diseases	59,986
5	Pneumonia and influenza	24,559	Alzheimer's disease	39,184
6	Diabetes mellitus	16,743	Influenza and pneumonia	32,965
7	Atherosclerosis	16,526	Unintentional injuries	32,399
8	Chronic obstructive pulmonary diseases	16,398	Diabetes mellitus	30,349
9	Chronic liver disease and cirrhosis	8,833	Nephritis, nephrotic syndrome and nephrosis	16,765
10	Certain conditions originating in the perinatal period	6,512	Septicemia	15,191
Black or African American female				
...	All causes	102,997	All causes	143,216
1	Diseases of heart	35,079	Diseases of heart	40,527
2	Malignant neoplasms	19,176	Malignant neoplasms	29,990
3	Cerebrovascular diseases	10,941	Cerebrovascular diseases	11,028
4	Unintentional injuries	3,779	Diabetes mellitus	7,480
5	Diabetes mellitus	3,534	Nephritis, nephrotic syndrome and nephrosis	4,061
6	Certain conditions originating in the perinatal period	3,092	Unintentional injuries	3,901
7	Pneumonia and influenza	2,262	Chronic lower respiratory diseases	3,490
8	Homicide	1,898	Septicemia	3,434
9	Chronic liver disease and cirrhosis	1,770	Influenza and pneumonia	3,103
10	Nephritis, nephrotic syndrome, and nephrosis	1,722	Human immunodeficiency virus (HIV) disease	2,534
American Indian or Alaska Native female				
...	All causes	2,730	All causes	5,665
1	Diseases of heart	577	Malignant neoplasms	1,094
2	Malignant neoplasms	362	Diseases of heart	1,055
3	Unintentional injuries	344	Unintentional injuries	485
4	Chronic liver disease and cirrhosis	171	Diabetes mellitus	408
5	Cerebrovascular diseases	159	Cerebrovascular diseases	331
6	Diabetes mellitus	124	Chronic lower respiratory diseases	232
7	Pneumonia and influenza	109	Chronic liver disease and cirrhosis	228
8	Certain conditions originating in the perinatal period	92	Influenza and pneumonia	160
9	Nephritis, nephrotic syndrome, and nephrosis	56	Nephritis, nephrotic syndrome and nephrosis	124
10	Homicide	55	Septicemia	100

CEREBROVASCULAR DISEASES. In 2001 cerebrovascular diseases, including stroke, atherosclerosis, and high blood pressure (hypertension), were the third-, fourth-, or fifth-leading cause of death among females of all races/ethnicities. (See Table 11.2.) They accounted for 8% of all female deaths in 2002, compared with 11% in 1980. According to the AHA, about forty thousand more women than men die from stroke.

In 2002 almost one-third of all women age twenty and over (32.8%) have high blood pressure. Mexican-American women have a lower prevalence of high blood pressure (28.7%) than non-Hispanic white women (31%) or African-American women (45.4%). According to the AHA, up to age fifty-five high blood pressure is more prevalent among men, but over age fifty-five it is more prevalent among women. High blood pressure is two to three times more

TABLE 11.2

Leading causes of death and numbers of deaths among women, 1980 and 2002 [CONTINUED]

[Data are based on death certificates]

Sex, race, Hispanic origin, and rank order	1980		2002	
	Cause of death	Deaths	Cause of death	Deaths
Asian or Pacific Islander female				
...	All causes	4,262	All causes	17,849
1	Diseases of heart	1,091	Malignant neoplasms	4,805
2	Malignant neoplasms	1,037	Diseases of heart	4,460
3	Cerebrovascular diseases	507	Cerebrovascular diseases	1,931
4	Unintentional injuries	254	Diabetes mellitus	711
5	Diabetes mellitus	124	Unintentional injuries	700
6	Certain conditions originating in the perinatal period	118	Influenza and pneumonia	535
7	Pneumonia and influenza	115	Chronic lower respiratory diseases	395
8	Congenital anomalies	104	Nephritis, nephrotic syndrome and nephrosis	329
9	Suicide	90	Alzheimer's disease	231
10	Homicide	60	Essential (primary) hypertension and hypertensive renal disease	221
Hispanic or Latino female				
...	—	—	All causes	51,432
1	—	—	Diseases of heart	13,089
2	—	—	Malignant neoplasms	10,906
3	—	—	Cerebrovascular diseases	3,448
4	—	—	Diabetes mellitus	3,133
5	—	—	Unintentional injuries	2,408
6	—	—	Chronic lower respiratory diseases	1,433
7	—	—	Influenza and pneumonia	1,426
8	—	—	Certain conditions originating in the perinatal period	1,050
9	—	—	Alzheimer's disease	1,010
10	—	—	Chronic liver disease and cirrhosis	972

... Category not applicable.
— Data not available.

SOURCE: Adapted from "Table 31. Leading Causes of Death and Numbers of Deaths, according to Sex, Race, and Hispanic Origin: United States, 1980 and 2002," in *Health, United States, 2004*, Centers for Disease Control and Prevention, National Center for Health Statistics, September 2004, http://www.cdc.gov/nchs/data/hus/hus04trend.pdf (accessed June 9, 2005)

FIGURE 11.4

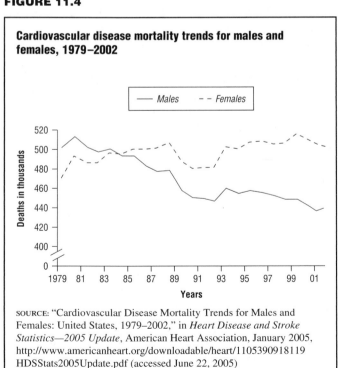

Cardiovascular disease mortality trends for males and females, 1979–2002

SOURCE: "Cardiovascular Disease Mortality Trends for Males and Females: United States, 1979–2002," in *Heart Disease and Stroke Statistics—2005 Update*, American Heart Association, January 2005, http://www.americanheart.org/downloadable/heart/1105390918119 HDSStats2005Update.pdf (accessed June 22, 2005)

prevalent among women taking oral contraceptives, particularly among older and obese women.

Cancer

Malignant neoplasms (cancers) were the first- or second-leading cause of death in 2002 among women of all races/ethnicities. (See Table 11.2.) Cancer caused 21.6% of all female deaths in 2002. The age-adjusted death rates from cancer were 163.1 per one hundred thousand females and 238.9 males per one hundred thousand males in 2002, compared with 182.3 females and 208.1 males per one hundred thousand in 1950.

The American Cancer Society (ACS) estimated that 662,870 new cases of cancer would be diagnosed in women in 2005, compared with 710,040 newly diagnosed cases in men (*Cancer Facts & Figures, 2005*, 2005). The ACS estimated that 275,000 women would die of cancer in 2005, an increase from the 268,503 women who died of cancer in 2002.

Breast cancer is the most common type of cancer in females, and prostate cancer is the most common form in males. Cancer of the lung and bronchus are the second

TABLE 11.3

Estimated inpatient cardiovascular operations, procedures, and patient data, by sex, age, and region, 2002

[In thousands]

Operations/procedures/patients		Total	Sex Male	Female	<15	15–44	Age 45–64	65+	Northeast	Region[g] Midwest	South	West
Angioplasty	Procedures	1,204	802	402	—	76	517	608	211	323	416	254
PTCA[a]	Procedures	657	434	223	—	37	283	331	110	182	223	130
	Patients	640	423	217	—	41	278	321	112	175	221	132
Stenting	Procedures	537	363	174	—	34	228	273	95	138	186	118
Cardiac revascularization (bypass)[b]												
	Procedures	515	373	142	—	19	217	279	104	117	204	90
	Patients	306	219	88	—	12	128	166	60	68	125	54
Diagnostic cardiac catheterizations[a]												
	Procedures	1,463	884	579	10	123	597	732	281	342	585	255
Endarterectomy	Procedures	134	79	56	—	—	33	101	33	29	55	17
Implantable defibrillators	Procedures	63	45	11	—	—	21	36	13	14	20	9
Open-heart surgery[c]	Procedures	709	476	233	30	41	261	368	160	150	258	127
Pacemakers[d]	Procedures	199	101	99	—	—	21	172	50	36	78	36
Valves[e]	Procedures	93	49	44	—	9	19	56	25	15	25	18
Total vascular and cardiac surgery and procedures[f]		6,813	3,967	2,845	210	681	2,384	3,538	1,370	1,463	2,601	1,378

Note: (—) = data not available.

[a]Does not include procedures in the outpatient or other non-hospitalized setting; thus, excludes some cardiac catheterizations and PTCAs (percutaneous transluminal coronary angioplasty).

[b]Because one or more procedure codes are required to describe the specific bypass procedure performed, it's impossible from this (mixed) data to determine the average number of grafts per patient.

[c]Includes valves, bypass and 101,000 "other" open-heart procedures.

[d]There are additional insertions, revisions and replacements of pacemaker leads, including those associated with temporary (external) pacemakers.

[e]Open heart valvuloplasty without replacement; replacement of heart valve; other operations on heart valves.

[f]Totals include procedures not shown here.

[g]Regions: Northeast—Connecticut, Maine, Massachusetts, New Hampshire, New Jersey, New York, Pennsylvania, Rhode Island, Vermont
Midwest—Illinois, Indiana, Iowa, Kansas, Michigan, Minnesota, Missouri, Nebraska, North Dakota, Ohio, South Dakota, Wisconsin
South—Alabama, Arkansas, Delaware, District of Columbia, Florida, Georgia, Kentucky, Louisiana, Maryland, Mississippi, North Carolina, Oklahoma, South Carolina, Tennessee, Texas, Virginia, West Virginia
West—Alaska, Arizona, California, Colorado, Hawaii, Idaho, Montana, Nevada, New Mexico, Oregon, Utah, Washington, Wyoming

SOURCE: "Estimated Inpatient Cardiovascular Operations, Procedures and Patient Data by Sex, Age and Region, United States: 2002," in *Heart Disease and Stroke Statistics—2005 Update*, American Heart Association, January 2005, http://www.americanheart.org/downloadable/heart/1105390918119HDSStats2005 Update.pdf (accessed June 22, 2005)

most common cancers among both men and women, followed by cancer of the colon and rectum.

BREAST CANCER. The ACS estimated that 211,240 new cases of invasive breast cancer would be diagnosed in American women in 2005, 32% of all newly diagnosed female cancers. Women account for 99.2% of newly diagnosed breast cancers. The ACS also estimates that another 58,490 cases of in situ breast cancer (cancerous tissue that has not yet become invasive) will be diagnosed in 2004. The increase in the diagnosis rate of this type of cancer in the last quarter of the twentieth century is attributed to the increase in the use of mammography screening, which can detect breast cancer before it can be felt.

Risk factors for breast cancer include a family history of the disease, early menarche and/or late menopause, childlessness or having a first child after age thirty, use of oral contraceptives, lack of exercise, smoking, obesity, and alcohol consumption. Worldwide, the incidence of breast cancer appears to correlate with dietary fat intake.

The ACS estimated in *Cancer Facts & Figures 2004* that as of 1998–2000 about one in seven American

women will develop breast cancer at some point in their lives. Between the ages of birth and thirty-nine, a woman's chance of being diagnosed with breast cancer is about 1 in 229. Between forty and fifty-nine it is one in twenty-four, and by the time she reaches sixty to seventy-nine, a woman has a one in thirteen chance of being diagnosed with breast cancer. The rate of incidence from 1996 to 2000 (the latest data available from the ACS) was lowest for Native American and Alaska Natives (fifty-eight per one hundred thousand) and highest for white women (140.8 per one hundred thousand); African-American (121.7 per one hundred thousand), Asian-American and Pacific Islander (97.2 per one hundred thousand), and Hispanic women (89.8 per one hundred thousand) fell between.

The ACS estimated that breast cancer would kill 40,870 American women in 2005, representing 15% of all female cancer deaths. The mortality from breast cancer declined 2.3% between 1990 and 2001, with larger decreases in younger women due to increased awareness, earlier detection, and improved treatment. Although the incidence of breast cancer for white women was higher

(141.7 per one hundred thousand) than for African-American women (119.9 per one hundred thousand) between 1997 and 2001, the age-adjusted death rate from breast cancer was highest for African-American women, at 35.4 per one hundred thousand; white women had the next highest mortality rate, at 26.4 per one hundred thousand. This difference is probably due to the fact that African-American women are more likely than white women to be poor and lack health insurance coverage, and therefore not have access to early detection and high-quality treatment.

According to the ACS, in 2005 the five-year survival rate for breast cancer that had not yet spread was approximately 98%, compared with a rate of 72% in the 1940s. If the cancer had spread locally, the survival rate dropped to about 80%. If the cancer had metastasized (spread to other parts of the body), the survival rate was about 26%. The rate of survival is directly linked to a woman's income as well as level of health insurance. Women of lower incomes and without health coverage tend to be diagnosed at later stages and so have poorer survival rates.

The percentage of women having mammograms, a low-dose X-ray examination that can detect very small cancers, increased steadily from 1987 to 2000, across all age groups over age forty, all race/ethnicities, poverty levels, and levels of educational attainment. (See Table 11.4.) In 1987 only 29% of women age forty and over had had a mammogram in the previous two years, compared with 70.3% in 2000. Among women ages fifty to sixty-four, 78.6% had had a mammogram in 2000, compared with only 31.7% of women in that age group in 1987. In 2000 white women in all age groups were more likely than African-American or Hispanic women to have had a mammogram, as were women who lived at or above the poverty level, compared with those below the poverty threshold. The likelihood of a woman having had a mammogram also correlated with her educational attainment.

In December 2003 researchers at Duke University developed a new breast scanner designed to detect subtle changes in breast cells before a lump can be felt by hand or seen with X-ray mammography. In addition, researchers at Johns Hopkins University announced the results of a 2003 study involving a new imaging technique designed to help identify breast cancer. The results were published in the December–January 2004 issue of the *Journal of Magnetic Resonance Imaging*. For the first time, researchers are able to take pictures of choline, a product of membrane synthesis that becomes elevated when cancer is present.

In January 2004 President George W. Bush signed into law the Consolidated Appropriations Act of 2004, which included several provisions related to breast cancer:

- Funding for research programs

- $209.7 million for the National Breast and Cervical Cancer Early Detection Program, which has screened more than two million women nationwide and diagnosed more than fourteen thousand cases of breast cancer in uninsured and underinsured women

- Reauthorization of the Breast Cancer Research stamp for another two years, the proceeds of which go directly back into research; the stamp has thus far generated more than $34.5 million for research

- Funding to study the results of the Mammography Quality Standards Act

In September 2005 results from a study conducted by the American College of Radiology Imaging Network and funded by the National Cancer Institute showed that new mammograms using digital imaging instead of standard X-ray techniques allowed doctors to better detect cancer for younger women and those with dense breasts.

LUNG CANCER. Lung cancer was estimated to be the leading cause of cancer deaths in women and men in 2005 (27% of all female cancer deaths, compared with 31% of male cancer deaths). The ACS estimated that 73,020 women would die of cancers of the lung and bronchus in 2005, 91.8% of the 79,560 estimated new cases in that year.

According to the NCHS, the age-adjusted death rates for cancers of the trachea, bronchus, and lung were 41.6 per one hundred thousand females and 73.2 per one hundred thousand males in 2002, compared with 5.8 females and 24.6 males per one hundred thousand in 1950. Since 1987, more women have died each year from lung cancer than from breast cancer, which had been the leading cause of cancer deaths among women since the 1960s. The increase in lung cancers among women is primarily due to increased cigarette smoking among women in the second half of the twentieth century. Smoking is the major cause of lung cancer, and the ACS estimates that half of all smokers who continue the habit will die from lung cancers related to their addiction. According to the ACS, smoking was responsible for 440,000 premature deaths in the United States each year from 1995 to 1999, accounting for 30% of all cancer deaths and 87% of all lung cancer deaths. Other causes include exposure to industrial materials such as arsenic; some organic chemicals such as radon and asbestos, particularly among smokers; radiation; air pollution; tuberculosis; and environmental tobacco smoke (secondhand smoke). The one-year survival rate for lung cancer is 42%; the five-year survival rate is only 15%.

Other Leading Causes of Death in Women

Chronic lower respiratory diseases (including bronchitis, asthma, emphysema, and other obstructive lung diseases) caused the deaths of 64,103 women in 2002 and 60,713 male deaths in 2002. (See Table 11.2.) These

TABLE 11.4

Use of mammography for women 40 years of age and over according to selected characteristics, selected years 1987–2000

Characteristic	1987	1990	1991	1993	1994	1998	1999	2000
	Percent of women having a mammogram with in the past 2 years[a]							
40 years and over, age adjusted[b,c]	29.0	51.7	54.7	59.7	61.0	67.0	70.3	70.3
40 years and over, crude[b]	28.7	51.4	54.6	59.7	60.9	66.9	70.3	70.3
Age								
40–49 years	31.9	55.1	55.6	59.9	61.3	63.4	67.2	64.2
50–64 years	31.7	56.0	60.3	65.1	66.5	73.7	76.5	78.6
65 years and over	22.8	43.4	48.1	54.2	55.0	63.8	66.8	68.0
65–74 years	26.6	48.7	55.7	64.2	63.0	69.4	73.9	74.0
75 years and over	17.3	35.8	37.8	41.0	44.6	57.2	58.9	61.3
Race[d]								
40 years and over, crude:								
White only	29.6	52.2	55.6	60.0	60.6	67.4	70.6	71.4
Black or African American only	24.0	46.4	48.0	59.1	64.3	66.0	71.0	67.8
American Indian and Alaska Native only	*	43.2	54.5	49.8	65.8	45.2	63.0	47.3
Asian only	*	46.0	45.9	55.1	55.8	60.2	58.3	53.3
Native Hawaiian and other Pacific Islander only	—	—	—	—	—	—	*	*
2 or more races	—	—	—	—	—	—	70.2	69.2
Hispanic origin and race[d]								
40 years and over, crude:								
Hispanic or Latino	18.3	45.2	49.2	50.9	51.9	60.2	65.7	61.4
Not Hispanic or Latino	29.4	51.8	54.9	60.3	61.5	67.5	70.7	71.0
White only	30.3	52.7	56.0	60.6	61.3	68.0	71.1	72.1
Black or African American only	23.8	46.0	47.7	59.2	64.4	66.0	71.0	67.9
Age, Hispanic origin, and race[d]								
40–49 years:								
Hispanic or Latino	*15.3	45.1	44.0	52.6	47.5	55.2	61.6	54.2
Not Hispanic or Latino:								
White only	34.3	57.0	58.1	61.6	62.0	64.4	68.3	67.1
Black or African American only	27.8	48.4	48.0	55.6	67.2	65.0	69.2	60.9
50–64 years:								
Hispanic or Latino	23.0	47.5	61.7	59.2	60.1	67.2	69.7	66.4
Not Hispanic or Latino:								
White only	33.6	58.1	61.5	66.2	67.5	75.3	77.9	80.5
Black or African American only	26.4	48.4	52.4	65.5	63.6	71.2	75.0	77.7
65 years and over:								
Hispanic or Latino	*	41.1	40.9	*35.7	48.0	59.0	67.2	68.2
Not Hispanic or Latino:								
White only	24.0	43.8	49.1	54.7	54.9	64.3	66.8	68.3
Black or African American only	14.1	39.7	41.6	56.3	61.0	60.6	68.1	65.5
Age and poverty status[e]								
40 years and over, crude:								
Poor	16.4	30.8	35.2	41.1	44.2	50.5	56.9	55.2
Near poor or nonpoor	31.3	54.1	57.5	61.8	63.4	69.3	71.5	72.2
40–49 years:								
Poor	23.0	32.2	33.0	36.1	43.0	44.9	52.5	47.2
Near poor or nonpoor	33.4	57.0	58.1	62.1	63.4	65.0	68.7	65.9
50–64 years:								
Poor	15.1	29.9	37.3	47.3	46.2	53.5	61.1	62.7
Near poor or nonpoor	34.3	58.5	63.0	66.8	68.8	76.7	77.4	80.6
65 years and over:								
Poor	13.6	30.8	35.2	40.4	43.9	52.3	57.3	55.4
Near poor or nonpoor	25.5	46.2	51.1	56.4	57.7	66.2	67.8	70.0

diseases were the fourth-leading cause of death among females that year. The death rates from chronic lower respiratory diseases were 37.4 per one hundred thousand females and 53.5 per one hundred thousand males in 2002, compared with 14.9 females and 49.9 males per one hundred thousand in 1980.

Diabetes mellitus resulted in the deaths of 38,948 women and 34,301 men in 2002. (See Table 11.2.) The age-adjusted death rate from diabetes was twenty-three females and 28.6 males per one hundred thousand in 2002, compared with twenty-seven females and 18.8 males per one hundred thousand in 1950. Alzheimer's disease killed 41,877 women in 2002, accounting for 3.4% of deaths among women; the disease was not among the top ten causes of deaths of males in that year. (See Table 11.2.) Nephritis, nephrotic syndrome, and nephrosis (kidney disease), influenza and pneumonia, unintentional injuries, and septicemia were all among

TABLE 11.4

Use of mammography for women 40 years of age and over according to selected characteristics, selected years 1987–2000 [CONTINUED]

Characteristic	1987	1990	1991	1993	1994	1998	1999	2000
Age and education[f]								
40 years and over, crude:								
No high school diploma or GED	17.8	36.4	40.0	46.4	48.2	54.5	56.7	57.7
High school diploma or GED	31.3	52.7	55.8	59.0	61.0	66.7	69.2	69.6
Some college or more	37.7	62.8	65.2	69.5	69.7	72.8	77.3	76.1
40–49 years of age:								
No high school diploma or GED	15.1	38.5	40.8	43.6	50.4	47.3	48.8	46.9
High school diploma or GED	32.6	53.1	52.0	56.6	55.8	59.1	60.8	59.0
Some college or more	39.2	62.3	63.7	66.1	68.7	68.3	74.4	70.5
50–64 years of age:								
No high school diploma or GED	21.2	41.0	43.6	51.4	51.6	58.8	62.3	66.3
High school diploma or GED	33.8	56.5	60.8	62.4	67.8	73.3	77.2	76.6
Some college or more	40.5	68.0	72.7	78.5	74.7	79.8	81.2	84.1
65 years of age and over:								
No high school diploma or GED	16.5	33.0	37.7	44.2	45.6	54.7	56.6	57.5
High school diploma or GED	25.9	47.5	54.0	57.4	59.1	66.8	68.4	72.0
Some college or more	32.3	56.7	57.9	64.8	64.3	71.3	77.1	74.1

*Estimates are considered unreliable.
—Data not available.
[a]Questions concerning use of mammography differed slightly on the National Health Interview Survey across the years for which data are shown.
[b]Includes all other races not shown separately, unknown poverty status, and unknown education.
[c]Estimates are age adjusted to the year 2000 standard using four age groups: 40–49 years, 50–64 years, 65–74 years, and 75 years and over.
[d]The race groups, white, black, American Indian and Alaska Native (AI/AN), Asian, Native Hawaiian and other Pacific Islander, and 2 or more races, include persons of Hispanic and non-Hispanic origin. Persons of Hispanic origin may be of any race.
[e]Poor persons are defined as below the poverty threshold. Near poor persons have incomes of 100 percent to less than 200 percent of the poverty threshold. Nonpoor persons have incomes of 200 percent or greater than the poverty threshold. Missing family income data were imputed for 13–16 percent of adults in the sample in 1990–94. Poverty status was unknown for 25 percent of persons in the sample in 1998, 28 percent in 1999, and 27 percent in 2000.
[f]Education categories shown are for 1998 and subsequent years. GED stands for General Educational Development high school equivalency diploma. In years prior to 1998 the following categories based on number of years of school completed were used: less than 12 years, 12 years, 13 years or more.

SOURCE: "Table 81. Use of Mammography for Women 40 Years of Age and Over according to Selected Characteristics: United States, Selected Years 1987–2000," in *Health, United States, 2004*, Centers for Disease Control and Prevention, National Center for Health Statistics, September 2004, http://www.cdc.gov/nchs/data/hus/hus04trend.pdf (accessed June 9, 2005)

the top ten causes of death among all women in 2002. Chronic liver disease and cirrhosis were among the top ten causes of death among Native American and Hispanic women in 2002. Human immunodeficiency virus (HIV) was the tenth-leading cause of death for African-American women in 2002.

Childbearing

For centuries childbearing was a major cause of death among women. According to the CDC, the risk of death from complications of pregnancy in the United States decreased substantially during the twentieth century, from 850 maternal deaths per one hundred thousand live births in 1900 to 7.5 in 1982. This number remained between about six and nine deaths per one hundred thousand births from 1982 to 2002. The age-adjusted maternal death rate per one hundred thousand live births was 7.6 in 2002, compared with 73.7 in 1950. (See Table 11.5.) Among women age twenty and older, the maternal death rate rose with age up to 18.4 per one hundred thousand live births for women thirty-five and over in 2002. This compared with 222 maternal deaths per one hundred thousand births among women older than thirty-four in 1950. African-American women (22.9 per one hundred thousand) were significantly more likely than either Hispanic women (six per one hundred thousand) or white

women (4.8 per one hundred thousand) to suffer maternal mortality in 2001.

HIV/AIDS

Women Who Get AIDS

AIDS (acquired immune deficiency syndrome), caused by the human immunodeficiency virus (HIV), was the tenth-leading cause of death among African-American women in 2002. (See Table 11.2.) According to the *HIV/AIDS Surveillance Report, 2003*, the cumulative total of all American women older than age thirteen who died from AIDS from the beginning of the epidemic to 2002 was 81,864. (See Table 11.6.) In 2003, 18,017 people died of AIDS, up from 17,557 in 2002. In 2003, 4,736 females died of AIDS—26.4% of the total. Among those who died of AIDS in 2003, 26.6% were white, 50.6% were African-American, 21.9% were Hispanic, and less than 1% were Asian-American/Pacific Islander or Native American/Alaska Native.

The percentage of AIDS cases among females over age thirteen increased steadily from 7% in 1985 to 27% in 2003. (See Figure 11.5.) The number of cases increased from 1985 to 1993 and then held steady until 1996 at about thirteen thousand cases each year. After 1996 the incidence of AIDS among females began to decline with the success of new

TABLE 11.5

Maternal mortality for complications of pregnancy, childbirth, and the puerperium, according to race, Hispanic origin, and age, selected years 1950–2002

[Data are based on death certificates]

Race, Hispanic origin, and age	1950[a]	1960[a]	1970	1980	1990	1995	1999[b]	2000	2001	2002
					Number of deaths					
All persons	**2,960**	**1,579**	**803**	**334**	**343**	**277**	**391**	**396**	**399**	**357**
White	1,873	936	445	193	177	129	214	240	228	190
Black or African American	1,041	624	342	127	153	133	154	137	150	148
American Indian or Alaska Native	—	—	—	3	4	1	5	6	5	0
Asian or Pacific Islander	—	—	—	11	9	14	18	13	16	19
Hispanic or Latino[c]	—	—	—	—	47	43	67	81	81	62
White, not Hispanic or Latino[c]	—	—	—	—	125	84	149	160	151	128
All persons					Deaths per 100,000 live births					
All ages, age adjusted[d]	73.7	32.1	21.5	9.4	7.6	6.3	8.3	8.2	8.8	7.6
All ages, crude	83.3	37.1	21.5	9.2	8.2	7.1	9.9	9.8	9.9	8.9
Under 20 years	70.7	22.7	18.9	7.6	7.5	3.9	6.6	*	8.8	6.7
20–24 years	47.6	20.7	13.0	5.8	6.1	5.7	6.2	7.4	6.9	5.8
25–29 years	63.5	29.8	17.0	7.7	6.0	6.0	8.2	7.9	8.5	7.5
30–34 years	107.7	50.3	31.6	13.6	9.5	7.3	10.1	10.0	10.1	9.3
35 years and over[e]	222.0	104.3	81.9	36.3	20.7	15.9	23.0	22.7	18.9	18.4
White										
All ages, age adjusted[d]	53.1	22.4	14.4	6.7	5.1	3.6	5.5	6.2	6.5	4.8
All ages, crude	61.1	26.0	14.3	6.6	5.4	4.2	6.8	7.5	7.2	6.0
Under 20 years	44.9	14.8	13.8	5.8	*	*	*	*	7.4	*
20–24 years	35.7	15.3	8.4	4.2	3.9	3.5	4.0	5.6	5.3	3.4
25–29 years	45.0	20.3	11.1	5.4	4.8	4.0	5.4	5.9	5.8	4.6
30–34 years	75.9	34.3	18.7	9.3	5.0	4.0	7.0	7.1	8.1	6.7
35 years and over[e]	174.1	73.9	59.3	25.5	12.6	9.1	16.6	18.0	11.4	13.3
Black or African American										
All ages, age adjusted[d]	—	92.0	65.5	24.9	21.7	20.9	23.3	20.1	22.4	22.9
All ages, crude	—	103.6	60.9	22.4	22.4	22.1	25.4	22.0	24.7	24.9
Under 20 years	—	54.8	32.3	13.1	*	*	*	*	*	*
20–24 years	—	56.9	41.9	13.9	14.7	15.3	14.0	15.3	14.6	14.9
25–29 years	—	92.8	65.2	22.4	14.9	21.0	26.6	21.8	24.7	27.1
30–34 years	—	150.6	117.8	44.0	44.2	31.2	36.1	34.8	30.6	28.4
35 years and over[e]	—	299.5	207.5	100.6	79.7	61.4	69.9	62.8	71.0	62.9
Hispanic or Latino[c,f]										
All ages, age adjusted[d]	—	—	—	—	7.4	5.4	7.9	9.0	8.8	6.0
All ages, crude	—	—	—	—	7.9	6.3	8.8	9.9	9.5	7.1
White, not Hispanic or Latino[c]										
All ages, age adjusted[d]	—	—	—	—	4.4	3.3	4.9	5.5	5.8	4.4
All ages, crude	—	—	—	—	4.8	3.5	6.4	6.8	6.5	5.6

—Data not available.
–Quantity zero.
*Rates based on fewer than 20 deaths are considered unreliable and are not shown.
[a]Includes deaths of persons who were not residents of the 50 states and the District of Columbia.
[b]Starting with 1999 data, changes were made in the classification and coding of maternal deaths. The large increase in the number of maternal deaths between 1998 and 1999 is due to these changes.
[c]Prior to 1997, excludes data from states lacking an Hispanic-origin item on the death certificate.
[d]Rates are age adjusted to the 1970 distribution of live births by mother's age in the United States.
[e]Rates computed by relating deaths of women 35 years and over to live births to women 35–49 years.
[f]Age-specific maternal mortality rates are not calculated because rates based on fewer than 20 deaths are considered unreliable.

SOURCE: "Table 43. Maternal Mortality for Complications of Pregnancy, Childbirth, and the Puerperium, according to Race, Hispanic Origin, and Age: United States, Selected Years 1950–2002," in *Health, United States, 2004*, Centers for Disease Control and Prevention, National Center for Health Statistics, September 2004, http://www.cdc.gov/nchs/data/hus/hus04trend.pdf (accessed June 9, 2005)

---

drug therapies. From 2000 to 2002 the incidence of AIDS in women was approximately 10,500 cases per year, rising to more than eleven thousand cases in 2003. (See Table 11.7.)

From 1999 through 2003 the number of AIDS diagnoses increased 14.9% among females and only 1.5% among males. The CDC gave the number of cumulative reported cases of AIDS for females since the beginning of the epidemic to 2003 as 170,679, compared with 749,887 males. The CDC estimated rates of AIDS diagnoses at 9.2 per one hundred thousand women and 26.5 per one hundred thousand men in 2003. (See Table 11.7.)

African-American women accounted for 67.4% of estimated female AIDS cases in 2003; non-Hispanic

TABLE 11.6

Estimated numbers of deaths of persons with AIDS, by year of death and selected characteristics, 1999–2003

	Year of death					Cumulative through 2003[a]
	1999	2000	2001	2002	2003	
Age at death (years)						
<13	97	51	48	35	29	5,103
13–14	18	8	4	11	8	252
15–24	232	216	270	199	229	9,789
25–34	3,258	2,823	2,512	2,143	1,928	142,761
35–44	7,706	7,138	7,525	6,896	6,970	216,093
45–54	4,994	5,203	5,548	5,737	5,964	104,064
55–64	1,556	1,631	1,873	1,840	2,146	33,717
≥65	630	670	743	696	741	12,282
Race/ethnicity						
White, not Hispanic	5,834	5,559	5,524	5,128	4,767	230,289
Black, not Hispanic	9,106	8,832	9,345	8,923	9,048	195,891
Hispanic	3,341	3,162	3,435	3,274	3,915	92,370
Asian/Pacific Islander	113	103	108	94	85	3,340
American Indian/Alaska Native	79	67	83	79	78	1,529
	Transmission category					
Male adult or adolescent						
Male-to-male sexual contact	6,703	6,316	6,479	6,012	6,015	257,898
Injection drug use	4,425	4,182	4,298	4,126	4,166	107,797
Male-to-male sexual contact and injection drug use	1,335	1,334	1,396	1,285	1,233	38,083
Heterosexual contact	1,403	1,417	1,585	1,526	1,644	23,080
Other[b]	194	204	174	166	140	9,846
Subtotal	14,061	13,454	13,932	13,116	13,198	436,704
Female adult or adolescent						
Injection drug use	2,051	1,925	1,985	1,956	2,056	39,848
Heterosexual contact	2,157	2,192	2,444	2,335	2,584	37,901
Other[b]	97	92	92	89	95	4,115
Subtotal	4,305	4,209	4,521	4,379	4,736	81,864
Child (<13 yrs at diagnosis)						
Perinatal	117	72	67	58	78	4,961
Other[c]	8	5	4	4	5	531
Subtotal	124	78	71	62	83	5,492
Region of residence						
Northeast	5,698	5,294	5,344	5,015	6,140	168,213
Midwest	1,712	1,685	1,839	1,550	1,343	50,258
South	7,406	7,352	7,624	7,526	7,068	178,447
West	2,952	2,681	2,817	2,520	2,588	107,767
U.S. dependencies, possessions, and associated nations	723	729	900	947	877	19,375
Total[d]	**18,491**	**17,741**	**18,524**	**17,557**	**18,017**	**524,060**

Note: These numbers do not represent reported case counts. Rather, these numbers are point estimates, which result from adjustments of reported case counts. The reported case counts are adjusted for reporting delays and for redistribution of cases in persons initially reported without an identified risk factor. The estimates do not include adjustment for incomplete reporting.
[a]Includes persons who died with AIDS, from the beginning of the epidemic through 2003.
[b]Includes hemophilia, blood transfusion, perinatal, and risk factor not reported or not identified.
[c]Includes hemophilia, blood transfusion, and risk factor not reported or not identified.
[d]Includes persons of unknown race or multiple races and persons of unknown sex. Cumulative total includes 640 persons of unknown race or multiple races. Because column totals were calculated independently of the values for the subpopulations, the values in each column may not sum to the column total.

SOURCE: "Table 7. Estimated Numbers of Deaths of Persons with AIDS, by Year of Death and Selected Characteristics, 1999–2003—United States," in *HIV/AIDS Surveillance Report: Cases of HIV Infection and AIDS in the United States, 2003*, vol. 15, Centers for Disease Control and Prevention, 2004, http://www.cdc.gov/hiv/stats/2003surveillancereport.pdf (accessed June 22, 2005).

white women accounted for 15.4% of cases and Hispanic women 15.6%. (See Table 11.7.) The rate of estimated diagnosis for African-American females was 50.2 per one hundred thousand, compared with 12.4 for Hispanic females, 4.8 for Native American/Alaska Native females, two for non-Hispanic white females, and 1.6 for Asian-American/Pacific Islanders.

How Women Are Infected

Of the newly diagnosed cases of AIDS in 2003, 70.7% of women over the age of thirteen were infected through heterosexual intercourse with an infected person. (See Table 11.8.) Another 26.9% contracted AIDS through intravenous (IV) drug use. A much smaller percentage of women with AIDS (2.4%) contracted the

FIGURE 11.5

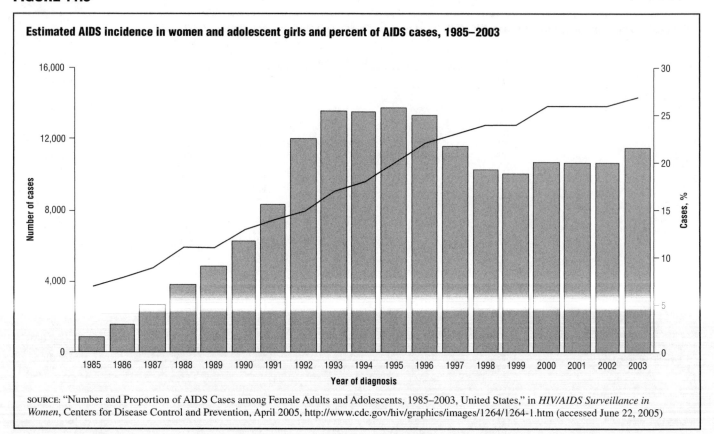

Estimated AIDS incidence in women and adolescent girls and percent of AIDS cases, 1985–2003

SOURCE: "Number and Proportion of AIDS Cases among Female Adults and Adolescents, 1985–2003, United States," in *HIV/AIDS Surveillance in Women*, Centers for Disease Control and Prevention, April 2005, http://www.cdc.gov/hiv/graphics/images/1264/1264-1.htm (accessed June 22, 2005)

TABLE 11.7

Estimated numbers of cases and rates (per 100,000 population) of AIDS, by race/ethnicity, age category, and sex, 2003

| | Adults or adolescents | | | | | | Children (<13 yrs) | | Total | |
| | Males | | Females | | Total | | | | | |
Race/ethnicity	No.	Rate	No.	Rate	No.	Rate	No.	Rate	No.	Rate
White, not Hispanic	10,450	12.8	1,725	2.0	12,175	7.2	9	0.0	12,184	6.1
Black, not Hispanic	13,624	103.8	7,551	50.2	21,174	75.2	40	0.5	21,214	58.2
Hispanic	6,087	40.3	1,744	12.4	7,831	26.8	7	0.1	7,839	20.0
Asian/Pacific Islander	408	8.3	86	1.6	494	4.8	0	0	494	4.0
American Indian/Alaska Native	150	16.2	46	4.8	196	10.4	0	0	196	8.1
Total*	30,851	26.6	11,211	9.2	42,062	17.7	58	0.1	42,120	14.5

Note: These numbers do not represent reported case counts. Rather, these numbers are point estimates, which result from adjustments of reported case counts. The reported case counts are adjusted for reporting delays. The estimates do not include adjustment for incomplete reporting.
Data exclude cases from the U.S. dependencies, possessions, and associated nations, as well as cases in persons whose state or area of residence is unknown, because of the lack of census information by race and age categories for these areas.
*Includes persons of unknown race or multiple races. Total includes 193 persons of unknown race or multiple races. Because column totals were calculated independently of the values for the subpopulations, the values in each column may not sum to the column total.

SOURCE: "Table 5. Estimated Numbers of Cases and Rates (per 100,000 population) of AIDS, by Race/Ethnicity, Age Category, and Sex, 2003," in *HIV/AIDS Surveillance Report: Cases of HIV Infection and AIDS in the United States, 2003*, vol. 15, Centers for Disease Control and Prevention, 2004, http://www.cdc.gov/hiv/stats/2003surveillancereport.pdf (accessed June 22, 2005)

disease as a result of hemophilia, blood transfusion, transmission from their mother, and other sources.

Thus, high-risk women (such as IV drug users) who have sex with high-risk men double their chances of contracting HIV. Furthermore, women may transmit

HIV to their newborns during childbirth. The CDC estimates that 92.9% (8,749) of the cumulative total (9,419) of all children under age thirteen who had been diagnosed with AIDS by 2003 were infected via mothers with, or at risk for, HIV infection. However, planned cesarean deliveries combined with antiviral drug therapy throughout

TABLE 11.8

Estimated numbers of AIDS cases, by year of diagnosis and selected characteristics of persons, 1999–2003

	Year of diagnosis					Cumulative through 2003[a]
	1999	2000	2001	2002	2003	
Age at diagnosis (years)						
<13	187	117	119	105	59	9,419
13–14	57	56	76	68	59	891
15–24	1,541	1,642	1,625	1,810	1,991	37,599
25–34	11,349	10,385	9,947	9,504	9,605	311,137
35–44	17,165	17,295	16,890	17,008	17,633	365,432
45–54	8,099	8,566	8,929	9,310	10,051	148,347
55–64	2,218	2,422	2,468	2,724	2,888	43,451
≥65	739	783	779	759	886	13,711
Race/ethnicity						
White, not Hispanic	12,626	12,047	11,620	11,960	12,222	376,834
Black, not Hispanic	19,960	20,312	20,291	20,476	21,304	368,169
Hispanic	8,141	8,233	8,204	8,021	8,757	172,993
Asian/Pacific Islander	369	373	409	452	497	7,166
American Indian/Alaska Native	162	186	179	196	196	3,026
Transmission category						
Male adult or adolescent						
Male-to-male sexual contact	16,556	16,272	16,383	16,971	17,969	440,887
Injection drug use	7,710	7,425	6,772	6,406	6,353	175,988
Male-to-male sexual contact and injection drug use	2,323	2,071	2,026	1,942	1,877	62,418
Heterosexual contact	4,243	4,299	4,578	4,890	5,133	56,403
Other[b]	328	319	315	308	281	14,191
Subtotal	31,159	30,387	30,074	30,517	31,614	749,887
Female adult or adolescent						
Injection drug use	3,448	3,498	3,269	3,024	3,096	70,558
Heterosexual contact	6,350	7,011	7,119	7,380	8,127	93,586
Other[b]	212	254	251	261	276	6,535
Subtotal	10,010	10,763	10,639	10,666	11,498	170,679
Child (<13 yrs at diagnosis)						
Perinatal	185	115	116	103	58	8,749
Other[c]	3	2	3	3	1	670
Subtotal	187	117	119	105	59	9,419
Region of residence						
Northeast	11,885	12,516	11,350	10,551	11,461	285,040
Midwest	4,069	4,139	4,094	4,337	4,498	91,926
South	17,224	16,757	17,693	18,482	19,609	337,409
West	6,892	6,661	6,468	6,843	6,667	186,100
U.S. dependencies, possessions, and associated nations	1,286	1,194	1,228	1,075	935	29,511
Total[d]	**41,356**	**41,267**	**40,833**	**41,289**	**43,171**	**929,985**

Note: These numbers do not represent reported case counts. Rather, these numbers are point estimates, which result from adjustments of reported case counts. The reported case counts are adjusted for reporting delays and for redistribution of cases in persons initially reported without an identified risk factor. The estimates do not include adjustment for incomplete reporting.

[a]Includes persons with a diagnosis of AIDS from the beginning of the epidemic through 2003.
[b]Includes hemophilia, blood transfusion, perinatal, and risk factor not reported or not identified.
[c]Includes hemophilia, blood transfusion, and risk factor not reported or not identified.
[d]Includes persons of unknown race or multiple races and persons of unknown sex. Cumulative total includes 1,796 persons of unknown race or multiple races and 1 person of unknown sex. Because column totals were calculated independently of the values for the subpopulations, the values in each column may not sum to the column total.

SOURCE: "Table 3. Estimated Numbers of AIDS Cases, by Year of Diagnosis and Selected Characteristics of Persons, 1999–2003," in *HIV/AIDS Surveillance Report: Cases of HIV Infection and AIDS in the United States, 2003*, vol. 15, Centers for Disease Control and Prevention, 2004, http://www.cdc.gov/hiv/stats/2003surveillancereport.pdf (accessed June 22, 2005)

pregnancy lower the chances of an HIV-positive mother delivering an HIV-positive baby.

OTHER SEXUALLY TRANSMITTED DISEASES

In addition to AIDS, a number of other sexually transmitted diseases (STDs) are of particular concern to women. According to the American Social Health Asso-ciation, although women account for about half of all STD infections, they are more vulnerable to STDs than men. Genital infections, including HIV, are more easily passed from men to women than from women to men. Women may have less control than men over whether to have sex and whether to use a condom. Women are less likely than men to have noticeable symptoms of STD, and they are more likely than men to have long-term

TABLE 11.9

Reported cases of sexually transmitted diseases, by sex and reporting source, 2003

Disease	Non-STD clinic			STD clinic			Total[a]		
	Male	Female	Total	Male	Female	Total	Male	Female	Total
Chlamydia	114,814	555,957	672,073	66,354	88,444	154,944	190,244	685,017	877,478
Gonorrhea	82,627	131,780	214,819	69,335	30,766	100,173	160,106	174,230	335,104
Primary syphilis	1,081	122	1,205	751	99	851	1,863	229	2,095
Early latent syphilis	3,692	1,695	5,393	1,892	962	2,854	5,664	2,691	8,361
Late and late latent syphilis[b]	7,016	5,071	12,124	3,357	2,369	5,739	10,666	7,601	18,319
Neurosyphilis	387	117	504	25	3	28	420	121	541
Chancroid	8	7	15	17	18	35	25	29	54

[a]Total include unknown sex and reporting source.
[b]Late and late latent syphilis incudes cases of unknown duration, late syphilis with clinical manifestations, and neurosyphilis.

SOURCE: "Table A2. Reported Cases of Sexually Transmitted Disease by Sex and Reporting Source: United States, 2003," in *Sexually Transmitted Disease Surveillance, 2003*, Centers for Disease Control and Prevention, September 2004, http://www.cdc.gov/std/stats/03pdf/BySexandSource.pdf (accessed June 22, 2005)

consequences, including infertility, tubal pregnancy, and cervical cancer. Essentially every STD can be passed from a woman to her fetus or newborn, sometimes with tragic consequences.

Chlamydia, Gonorrhea, and Syphilis

In 2003 women accounted for 78.1% of all reported cases of *Chlamydia trachomatis*, a vaginal bacterial infection. (See Table 11.9.) This STD was diagnosed in 685,017 women in 2003. Reported cases of chlamydial infection among women have increased steadily since the late 1980s, when public programs were instituted for detecting and treating the infection in women. The number of reported cases among males has also increased with better screening. For females the rate of reported infection increased from 78.5 cases per one hundred thousand population in 1987 to 466.9 cases per one hundred thousand population in 2003 (*Sexually Transmitted Disease Surveillance 2003 Supplement, Chlamydia Prevalence Monitoring Project*, Centers for Disease Control and Prevention, October 2004).

Women accounted for slightly more than half (52%) of all reported cases of gonorrhea in 2003. (See Table 11.9.) The rate of gonorrheal infection decreased steadily from 1975 to 2003, to a rate of 116.2 cases per one hundred thousand population in 2003, the lowest rate ever. In 2003 the gonorrhea rate among women was 118.8 per one hundred thousand and the rate among men was 113 per one hundred thousand. In 2003 the highest gonorrhea rate among females was among fifteen- to nineteen-year-olds and twenty- to twenty-four-year-olds (634.7 and 595.2, respectively). The highest rates of gonorrhea were among fifteen- to nineteen-year-old African-American women (2,947.8 per one hundred thousand) and twenty- to twenty-four-year-old African-American women (2,715.5 per one hundred thousand).

Most women with chlamydia (about 70%) and about 50% of women with gonorrhea have no symptoms, so screening for infection is essential. If not adequately treated, 20 to 40% of women infected with chlamydia and 10 to 40% of women infected with gonorrhea develop pelvic inflammatory disease (PID), which can lead to infertility and other reproductive complications. According to Planned Parenthood, one in five women with PID becomes infertile. PID also is a major cause of ectopic or tubal pregnancy. The rate of ectopic pregnancy increased fivefold in the last two decades of the twentieth century. Ectopic pregnancies account for about 9% of all pregnancy-related deaths in the United States. Chlamydial and gonorrheal infections during pregnancy can result in blindness and pneumonia in the newborn infants.

The rate of primary and secondary syphilis declined by 89.7% between 1990 and 2000, leading the Surgeon General to announce the CDC's National Plan to Eliminate Syphilis in 1999; but primary and secondary syphilis rates remained unchanged during the following two years and increased during 2002 and 2003. The rate of primary and secondary syphilis is particularly high among African-Americans who live in the South.

Women accounted for 33.9% of new syphilis cases in 2003. (See Table 11.9.) The rate increased 13.5% among men from 2002 to 2003, but decreased by 27.3% among women during that period. The incidence of syphilis was highest among women ages twenty to twenty-four (2.4 cases per one hundred thousand population). Syphilis may be transmitted to a fetus in utero, resulting in death or disabilities, although most cases of congenital syphilis may be preventable with early diagnosis and treatment. It is estimated that undetected syphilis in the mother causes perinatal death in 40% of cases, a figure that increases to 70% if the mother has gone undiagnosed for the four years prior to the pregnancy.

In addition to the complications that chlamydia, gonorrhea, and syphilis cause to the infected woman and possibly her children, infection with gonorrhea, chlamydia, and syphilis make women two to five times more vulnerable to HIV infection. According to the Alan Guttmacher Institute, at all ages women are more likely than men to contract genital herpes, chlamydia, or gonorrhea. For people who choose to be sexually active, consistent and careful use of condoms is the best protection against HIV and other STDs.

OSTEOPOROSIS

Osteoporosis and arthritis are chronic diseases that affect large numbers of older women and can restrict their mobility. Osteoporosis, the loss of bone mass and deterioration of bone tissue, puts women at risk for debilitating bone fractures. According to the National Osteoporosis Foundation, as of July 2005, about ten million Americans had this disease and thirty-four million more had low bone mass, placing them at risk for osteoporosis; 80% of these people were female. Five percent of African-American women, 10% of Hispanic women, and 20% of non-Hispanic white and Asian-American women over age fifty are estimated to have osteoporosis. About half of all women older than fifty will have a bone fracture related to osteoporosis in the remainder of their lifetimes.

Osteoporosis is associated with the drop in estrogen production at menopause; women can lose up to 20% of their bone mass in the five to seven years following menopause. Thin, small-boned women of northern European descent are at the highest risk for the disease. Menstruation at an early age, smoking, alcohol consumption, and certain medications can increase the risk of osteoporosis. Weight-bearing exercise, such as running, and consumption of adequate levels of calcium, vitamin D, and magnesium reduce the risk of osteoporosis.

MENTAL HEALTH

According to the National Institute of Mental Health (NIMH), about twice as many women as men suffer from depression. About 12% of women, compared with only about 6.6% of men, will experience a depressive disorder within a one-year period. Anxiety disorders affect two to three times more women than men. Women also are much more at risk for developing post-traumatic stress disorder (13% of women versus 6% of men).

Depression

Hormonal factors including menstrual cycle changes, pregnancy, miscarriage, the postpartum period, premenopause, and menopause can bring about depression in women. Furthermore, women may experience more emotional stress than men from balancing home, family, and

TABLE 11.10

Symptoms of depression and mania

Depression
- Persistent sad, anxious, or "empty" mood
- Feelings of hopelessness, pessimism
- Feelings of guilt, worthlessness, helplessness
- Loss of interest or pleasure in hobbies and activities that were once enjoyed, including sex
- Decreased energy, fatigue, being "slowed down"
- Difficulty concentrating, remembering, making decisions
- Insomnia, early-morning awakening, or oversleeping
- Appetite and/or weight loss or overeating and weight gain
- Thoughts of death or suicide; suicide attempts
- Restlessness, irritability
- Persistent physical symptoms that do not respond to treatment, such as headaches, digestive disorders, and chronic pain

Mania
- Abnormal or excessive elation
- Unusual irritability
- Decreased need for sleep
- Grandiose notions
- Increased talking
- Racing thoughts
- Increased sexual desire
- Markedly increased energy
- Poor judgment
- Inappropriate social behavior

SOURCE: Margaret Strock, "Symptoms of Depression and Mania," in *Depression*, National Institutes of Mental Health, September 2000, http://www.nimh.nih.gov/publicat/nimhdepression.pdf (accessed June 22, 2005)

work responsibilities. Reproductive hormones and stress hormones have been linked to depression in women.

Some types of depression include:

- Major depression

- Dysthymia, a long-term chronic but less severe depression

- Seasonal affective disorder (SAD)

- Bipolar disorder (manic-depressive illness), which is characterized by extreme highs and extreme lows

Symptoms of depression and mania (the high periods of bipolar disorder) are listed in Table 11.10. Major depression occurs in episodes, which may affect someone once in a lifetime or become recurrent. Women seem to be especially susceptible to SAD, a depression that usually occurs in the fall and winter and subsides in the spring. Men and women are equally at risk for bipolar disorder.

Causes of depression include:

- Heredity, particularly for bipolar disorder

- Upbringing

- Brain biochemistry

- Hormone production

- Emotional stress, such as loss of a loved one, relationship difficulties, or financial problems

- Physical illness

About one-third of people with any type of depressive disorder also exhibit some form of substance abuse.

Treatments for depression include:

- A wide variety of medications, including antidepressants
- Psychotherapy
- Counseling

Eating Disorders

The most common eating disorders are anorexia nervosa and bulimia nervosa. Anorexia is severe weight loss to at least 15% below normal body weight. Anorexics see themselves as overweight even when they are dangerously thin. Bulimics may binge-eat (eat large amounts of food in a short period of time) and then force themselves to vomit and/or abuse laxatives. Eating disorders are frequently experienced by those with other psychiatric disorders, such as depression, anxiety disorders, and/ or substance abuse.

According to a 2001 report on eating disorders ("Eating Disorders: Facts about Eating Disorders and the Search for Solutions," National Institute of Mental Health, 2005), 85 to 95% of those with anorexia or bulimia are women, as are about 65% of those with binge-eating disorder. It is estimated that 0.5 to 3.7% of females suffer from anorexia and 1.1% to 4.2% of females suffer from bulimia at some point in their lives. According to Anorexia Nervosa and Related Eating Disorders, Inc. (ANRED), research suggests that about 1% of adolescent females have anorexia and about 4% of college-age women have bulimia. According to the National Association for Anorexia Nervosa and Associated Disorders (ANAD), eating disorders affect about seven million American women. About 86% of eating disorders first appear before the age of twenty.

The mortality rate for people with anorexia has been estimated at 0.56% annually, or twelve times higher than the annual death rate from all other causes for females ages fifteen to twenty-four in the general population. The most common causes of death are cardiac arrest, electrolyte imbalance, and suicide. Less severe consequences of anorexia may include a cessation in menstruation, lowered pulse and blood pressure, heart irregularities, anemia (low red blood cell count), swollen joints, hair loss, osteoporosis, and depression.

In 2003 a Canadian study revealed that anorexia reduces the amount of lung tissue, which can lead to emphysema. Until further study is done, it is unclear whether or not the structural damage is permanent. If it is, researchers say it is important that anorexia

patients get treatment early on to prevent the onset of emphysema.

PREVENTION

Many diseases and deaths and some mental disorders may be caused by unhealthy lifestyle choices. This makes prevention of these choices and their negative outcomes of utmost importance in keeping women physically and mentally healthy.

Smoking

During the first half of the twentieth century, most cigarette smokers were men. By 1955 more than 50% of men smoked and more and more women had taken up smoking. By the time the U.S. Surgeon General's first report on the health hazards of smoking was released in 1964, smoking rates among men had already begun to decline, but smoking among women was on the increase.

The rise in smoking among women has led to large increases in the death rates from smoking-related illnesses. In 1987 lung cancer passed breast cancer as the leading cause of cancer mortality among women. The American Cancer Society reported in 2005 that smoking causes 30% of all cancers and 87% of lung cancers each year. Smoking is associated with an increased risk for at least fifteen different types of cancer; in addition to lung cancers, smoking increases the risks of pancreatic, oral, esophageal, laryngeal, urinary, and cervical cancers. Smoking can cause chronic lung disease and increases a woman's risk of lower respiratory infections, CVD, osteoporosis, and other debilitating diseases.

According to the CDC report *Health, United States, 2004*, in 2002, 20.1% of all females over age eighteen smoked (age-adjusted figure), compared with 24.8% of men. This was down dramatically from 1965, when 33.7% of women smoked. In 2002, 24.6% of all women ages eighteen to twenty-four smoked, the highest of any age category, compared with 32.4% of men in that age group. Among white females in that age category, 26.9% smoked in 2002; 17.1% of African-American women in that age bracket smoked, up sharply from only 10% the year before. Across all age groups twenty-five and over, the percentage of smokers decreased as the level of educational attainment increased.

In 2002 the NHIS found that a higher percentage of women than men had never smoked. A higher percentage of men than women were current smokers (23.3% versus 18.3%) or former smokers. (See Figure 11.6.)

According to the AHA, about 80% of all people using tobacco begin before they are age eighteen, and the usual first-time use is between fourteen and fifteen years old. In 2003, 9.7% of female students in grades nine through twelve reported current cigarette use, down

FIGURE 11.6

Percent distribution of smoking status among adults aged 18 years and over, by sex, January–September, 2004

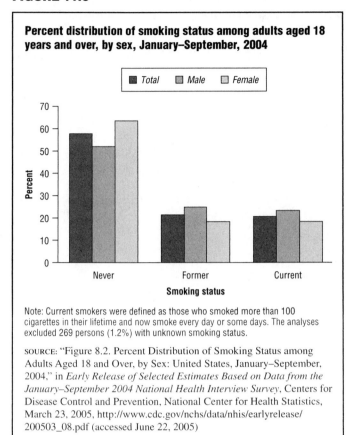

Note: Current smokers were defined as those who smoked more than 100 cigarettes in their lifetime and now smoke every day or some days. The analyses excluded 269 persons (1.2%) with unknown smoking status.

SOURCE: "Figure 8.2. Percent Distribution of Smoking Status among Adults Aged 18 and Over, by Sex: United States, January–September, 2004," in *Early Release of Selected Estimates Based on Data from the January–September 2004 National Health Interview Survey*, Centers for Disease Control and Prevention, National Center for Health Statistics, March 23, 2005, http://www.cdc.gov/nchs/data/nhis/earlyrelease/200503_08.pdf (accessed June 22, 2005)

from 29.5% in 2001; 2.4% reported they smoked more than ten cigarettes daily.

According to the American Cancer Society, smoking-related deaths are the most preventable forms of death. Half of all current smokers will die as a result of their addiction, and lung cancer mortality rates are 12% higher for female smokers than for never-smokers. Moreover, secondhand smoke, also known as environmental tobacco smoke (ETS), has become recognized as a major risk factor in health. The American Heart Association reported in its 2004 update that the risk of CHD increases by 30% for those exposed to ETS at home or work and 35,000 die each year from CHD caused by ETS. The ACS states that each year 3,000 people die of lung cancer caused by ETS. In addition, ETS causes 150,000 to 180,000 cases of pneumonia and bronchitis in infants and children younger than eighteen months. These infections result in 7,500 to 15,000 hospitalizations annually. ETS increases the number and severity of asthma attacks in about 200,000 to one million children each year.

As a result of the knowledge we now have regarding tobacco use and ETS, smoking in public has become somewhat of a stigma, as it once was for women in the late nineteenth and early twentieth centuries. The price for a pack of cigarettes has risen drastically in the early 2000s, and public smoking has been banned in many

TABLE 11.11

Alcohol consumption by women 18 years of age and over, 1997–2002

[Data are based on household interviews of a sample of the civilian noninstitutionalized population]

Characteristic	1997	1999	2002
Drinking status[a]	Percent distribution		
18 years and over, age adjusted[b]			
All	100.0	100.0	100.0
Lifetime abstainer	27.6	29.3	28.7
Former drinker	15.3	14.4	14.8
Infrequent	10.1	9.2	9.3
Regular	5.2	5.2	5.5
Current drinker[c]	57.0	56.3	56.5
Infrequent	18.1	17.4	16.5
Regular	38.9	38.9	39.1
18 years and over, crude			
All	100.0	100.0	100.0
Lifetime abstainer	27.7	29.4	28.8
Former drinker	15.4	14.5	14.9
Infrequent	10.1	9.3	9.4
Regular	5.2	5.2	5.6
Current drinker[c]	57.0	56.1	56.2
Infrequent	18.1	17.3	16.5
Regular	38.8	38.8	38.9
	Percent current drinkers among all persons		
Age			
All persons:			
18–44 years	64.2	63.6	62.8
18–24 years	57.7	57.1	57.6
25–44 years	66.1	65.6	64.5
45–64 years	56.2	56.1	58.2
45–54 years	60.7	61.7	61.3
55–64 years	49.4	47.6	53.6
65 years and over	36.6	34.2	33.5
65–74 years	42.0	38.9	36.6
75 years and over	30.2	29.0	30.4
Race[b,d]			
White only	60.7	60.1	60.2
Black or African American only	40.9	40.6	40.3
American Indian and Alaska Native only	45.2	43.5	46.8
Asian only	31.6	31.3	35.3
Native Hawaiian and other Pacific Islander only	—	*	*
2 or more races	—	56.0	62.1
Hispanic origin and race[b,d]			
Hispanic or Latino	42.1	39.8	38.1
Mexican	38.9	34.3	37.0
Not Hispanic or Latino	58.7	39.8	38.1
White only	62.9	62.4	62.9
Black or African American only	40.7	40.4	40.3
Geographic region[b]			
Northeast	63.8	63.4	65.3
Midwest	61.1	62.3	60.8
South	49.2	47.7	49.0
West	58.9	57.2	56.4
Location of residence[b]			
Within MSA[e]	59.1	58.1	58.1
Outside MSA[e]	49.5	49.7	50.5

cities across the nation. All fifty states have clean indoor air provisions that restrict smoking in certain places.

Alcohol

In 2002, 56.5% of women eighteen years of age and over drank alcohol, 39.1% regularly. (See Table 11.11.)

TABLE 11.11

Alcohol consumption by women 18 years of age and over, 1997–2002 [CONTINUED]

[Data are based on household interviews of a sample of the civilian noninstitutionalized population]

Characteristic	Female 1997	Female 1999	Female 2002
Level of alcohol consumption in past year for current drinkers[f]	Percent distribution of current drinkers[g]		
18 years and over, age adjusted[b]			
All drinking levels	100.0	100.0	100.0
Light	81.0	80.4	79.6
Moderate	12.0	12.7	12.8
Heavier	7.0	6.9	7.6
18 years and over, crude			
All drinking levels	100.0	100.0	100.0
Light	81.4	80.7	79.9
Moderate	11.7	12.5	12.5
Heavier	6.9	6.7	7.5
Number of days in the past year with 5 or more drinks	Percent distribution of current drinkers		
18 years and over, crude			
All current drinkers	100.0	100.0	100.0
No days	78.6	78.9	79.2
At least 1 day	21.4	21.1	20.8
1–11 days	14.6	13.6	13.4
12 or more days	6.8	7.5	7.3
Hispanic origin, race, and age[d]	Percent of persons with 5 or more drinks on at least one day among current drinkers		
All persons:			
18 years and over, age adjusted[b]	20.2	19.7	19.9
18 years and over, crude	21.4	21.1	20.8
18–44 years	28.7	28.5	29.0
18–24 years	40.2	42.0	41.3
25–44 years	25.7	24.8	25.4
45–64 years	12.9	12.5	12.0
45–54 years	15.3	15.1	14.2
55–64 years	8.3	7.3	8.2
65 years and over	4.4	3.5	3.6
65–74 years	5.5	4.5	5.4
75 years and over	*2.5	*	*
Race[b,d]			
White only	20.9	20.5	20.7
Black or African American only	14.9	13.8	15.1
American Indian and Alaska Native only	38.4	39.7	38.6
Asian only	16.6	12.2	*9.5
Native Hawaiian and other Pacific Islander only	—	*	*

TABLE 11.11

Alcohol consumption by women 18 years of age and over, 1997–2002 [CONTINUED]

[Data are based on household interviews of a sample of the civilian noninstitutionalized population]

Characteristic	Female 1997	Female 1999	Female 2002
Hispanic origin and race[b,d]			
Hispanic or Latino	22.3	16.5	17.4
Mexican	20.3	17.3	19.5
Not Hispanic or Latino	20.0	16.5	17.4
White only	21.0	20.9	21.0
Black or African American only	14.4	13.9	15.2
Geographic region	Percent of persons with 5 or more drinks on at least one day among current drinkers		
Northeast	18.9	20.1	18.7
Midwest	21.6	22.2	22.7
South	19.2	16.4	17.8
West	20.8	21.4	19.9
Location of residence[b]			
Within MSA[e]	19.8	19.4	19.7
Outside MSA	21.2	21.1	19.8

*Estimates are considered unreliable.
— Data not available.
[a]Drinking status categories are based on self-reported responses to questions about alcohol consumption. Lifetime abstainers had fewer than 12 drinks in their lifetime. Former drinkers had at least 12 drinks in their lifetime and none in the past year. Former infrequent drinkers are former drinkers who had fewer than 12 drinks in any one year. Former regular drinkers are former drinkers who had at least 12 drinks in any one year. Current drinkers had 12 drinks in their lifetime and at least one drink in the past year. Current infrequent drinkers are current drinkers who had fewer than 12 drinks in the past year. Current regular drinkers are current drinkers who had at least 12 drinks in the past year.
[b]Estimates are age adjusted to the year 2000 standard population using four age groups: 18–24 years, 25–44 years, 45–64 years, and 65 years and over.
[c]Current drinkers include about 1 percent of persons who did not provide information on frequency or amount of current drinking.
[d]The race groups, white, black, American Indian and Alaska Native (AI/AN), Asian, Native Hawaiian and other Pacific Islander, and 2 or more races, include persons of Hispanic and non-Hispanic origin. Persons of Hispanic origin may be of any race. Starting with data year 1999 race-specific estimates are tabulated according to 1997 Standards for Federal data on Race and Ethnicity and are not strictly comparable with estimates for earlier years. The five single race categories plus multiple race categories shown in the table conform to 1997 Standards. The 1999 race-specific estimates are for persons who reported only one racial group; the category "2 or more races" includes persons who reported more than one racial group. Prior to data year 1999, data were tabulated according to 1977 Standards with four racial groups and the category "Asian only" included Native Hawaiian and Other Pacific Islander. Estimates for single race categories prior to 1999 included persons who reported one race or, if they reported more than one race, identified one race as best representing their race.
[e]MSA is metropolitan statistical area.
[f]Level of alcohol consumption categories are based on self-reported responses to questions about average alcohol consumption and defined as follows: light drinkers: 3 drinks or fewer per week; moderate drinkers: more than 3 drinks and up to 7 drinks per week; heavier drinkers: more than 7 drinks per week.
[g]Percent based on current drinkers with known frequency and amount of drinking.

SOURCE: Adapted from "Table 66. Alcohol Consumption by Persons 18 Years of Age and Over, according to Selected Characteristics: United States, Selected Years 1997–2002," in *Health, United States, 2004*, Centers for Disease Control and Prevention, National Center for Health Statistics, September 2004, http://www.cdc.gov/nchs/data/hus/hus04trend.pdf (accessed June 9, 2005)

In addition, 14.8% of women were former drinkers. About one in four (28.7%) were lifelong abstainers from alcohol; about 14.7% of men were lifelong abstainers in 2002. The highest percentages of drinkers were between the ages of twenty-five and forty-four (64.5% of women and 77.7% of men). Among all age groups, higher percentages of non-Hispanic white women were current drinkers (62.9%), compared with African-American women (40.3%) and Hispanic women (38.1%).

Among current drinkers, 79.6% of women and 58.8% of men were light drinkers; only 7.6% of women were heavy drinkers. (See Table 11.11.) According to the 2004 NHIS, far more men (27.1%) than women (10.8%) in every age group drank excessively (defined as five or more drinks on at least twelve occasions in the past twelve months.) Younger women and men were more likely than older adults to drink excessively, and 8.9% of all adults drank excessively, according to 2004 statistics. The highest percentages of heavy drinkers among female adults was in the eighteen to twenty-four age group (21.2%).

According to the *Youth Risk Behavior Surveillance*, in 2003, 45.8% of female high school students and 43.8% of male high school students had used alcohol in the past thirty days. A little more than a quarter of female students (27.5%) had had at least five drinks on at least one occasion in the past month, compared with 29% of male students.

Women are at greater risk for developing chronic alcohol-related diseases than men because of their greater sensitivity to alcohol and their smaller body size. As a result, women are more subject to the side effects of heavy drinking, such as vomiting, slurred speech, hangovers, and depression. Women are at risk for developing cirrhosis of the liver with lower levels of alcohol consumption and at earlier ages than men. According to the ACS, alcohol can cause cancers of the oral cavity, esophagus, and larynx, particularly in combination with smoking. Alcohol consumption also increases the risk of breast cancer.

Other Substance Abuse

According to the Substance Abuse and Mental Health Services Administration (SAMHSA) report *National Survey on Drug Use and Health 2003*, in 2003, 6.5% of females age twelve and older had used an illicit drug within the past month, compared with 10% of males. Among women ages eighteen to twenty-five, 16.5% had used an illicit drug in the past month and 57.4% had used an illicit drug in their lifetime.

According to *Youth Risk Behavior Surveillance*, in 2003, 19.3% of female high school students had used marijuana in the last month; 37.6% had tried it in their lifetimes. Male students were more likely to have used marijuana in the past month (25.1%) or in their lifetimes (42.7%). Fewer students had tried cocaine (7.7% of females, 9.5% of males) or illegal intravenous drugs (2.5% of females and 3.8% of males). Female students were also less likely than male students to use heroine (2% and 4.3%, respectively), methamphetamines (6.8% and 8.3%, respectively), or Ecstasy (10.4% and 11.6%, respectively).

Obesity

After smoking, obesity is the second-leading cause of preventable death in the United States, according to the ACS. Obesity is estimated to cause about 300,000 premature deaths each year and is associated with increased mortality rates for most causes of death, particularly CVD. According to the ACS, obesity in women is correlated with cancers of the breast, uterus and cervix, ovaries, and gallbladder. The risk of breast cancer is 50% higher for postmenopausal women who are obese.

The percentage of obese men and women (with a body mass index of thirty or more or about thirty pounds overweight for a 5' 4" person) in the United States has increased steadily through the decades. (See Table 11.12.) According to *Health, United States, 2004*, in 2002, 61.7% of females ages twenty to seventy-four were overweight, and 34% were obese—more than double the 15.7% of women who were obese in 1962. Almost half of African-American females between the ages of twenty and seventy-four were obese (49.6%); 38.9% of Mexican-American females and 31.3% of non-Hispanic white females were obese. Women between the ages of fifty-five and sixty-four had the highest percentage of obesity of any age group (42.1%).

According to *Health, United States, 2004*, among school children ages six to eleven, 14.7% of girls were overweight, compared with 3.6% in the years from 1971 to 1974. (See Table 11.13.) Among female children from twelve to nineteen years of age, 15.4% were overweight. Ethnicity played a role in which children were overweight in both age groups. For girls ages six to eleven, 13.1% of non-Hispanic whites were overweight, compared with 22.8% of African-Americans and 17.1% of Mexican-American girls. Among girls ages twelve to seventeen, 12.7% of whites, 19.6% of Mexican-Americans, and 23.6% of African-Americans were overweight.

Fat Intake

Nutritionists generally recommend that diets should contain less than 30% of total calories from fat. Diets high in saturated fats (animal fats present in meat and dairy products) contribute to cardiovascular diseases. Excess saturated fats can raise blood cholesterol and fat levels, clogging arteries and leading to heart disease. But polyunsaturated and monounsaturated fats can be beneficial, and some of these fats are essential to the diet. Vegetable oils, as well as green vegetables, nuts, many types of seeds, and cold-water fish, are high in these types of fats.

According to the ACS, fruits and vegetables, especially green and dark yellow vegetables, legumes, soy, and vegetables in the cabbage family, help protect against a variety of cancers. These foods are rich in substances, including weak estrogens, that protect against cancer in general and particularly cancers, such as breast cancer, that are affected by hormones. Furthermore, vegetables that are high in antioxidants can help protect against biochemical events that can lead to cancer.

Exercise

Only a minority of Americans, and fewer females than males, participate in even light to moderate leisure-time physical activity (defined as at least thirty minutes of physical activity at least five times per week). (See

TABLE 11.12

Healthy weight, overweight, and obesity among persons 20 years of age and over, according to sex, age, race, and Hispanic origin, 1960–62, 1971–74, 1976–80, 1988–94, and 1999–2002

[Data are based on measured height and weight of a sample of the civilian noninstitutionalized population]

Sex, age, race, and Hispanic origin[a]	Overweight[b]				
	1960–62	1971–74	1976–80[e]	1988–94	1999–2002
20–74 years, age adjusted[d]			Percent of population		
Both sexes[e,f]	44.8	47.7	47.4	56.0	65.2
Male	49.5	54.7	52.9	61.0	68.8
Female[e]	40.2	41.1	42.0	51.2	61.7
Not Hispanic or Latino:					
White only, male	—	—	53.8	61.6	69.5
White only, female[e]	—	—	38.7	47.2	57.0
Black or African American only, male	—	—	51.3	58.2	62.0
Black or African American only, female[e]	—	—	62.6	68.5	77.5
Mexican male	—	—	61.6	69.4	74.1
Mexican female[e]	—	—	61.7	69.6	71.4
20 years and over, age adjusted[d]					
Both sexes[e,f]	—	—	—	56.0	65.1
Male	—	—	—	60.9	68.8
Female[e]	—	—	—	51.4	61.6
Not Hispanic or Latino:					
White only, male	—	—	—	61.6	69.4
White only, female[e]	—	—	—	47.5	57.2
Black or African American only, male	—	—	—	57.8	62.6
Black or African American only, female[e]	—	—	—	68.2	77.1
Mexican male	—	—	—	68.9	73.2
Mexican female[e]	—	—	—	68.9	71.2
20 years and over, crude					
Both sexes[e,f]	—	—	—	54.9	65.2
Male	—	—	—	59.4	68.6
Female[e]	—	—	—	50.7	62.0
Not Hispanic or Latino:					
White only, male	—	—	—	60.6	69.9
White only, female[e]	—	—	—	47.4	58.2
Black or African American only, male	—	—	—	56.7	61.7
Black or African American only, female[e]	—	—	—	66.0	76.8
Mexican male	—	—	—	63.9	70.1
Mexican female[e]	—	—	—	65.9	69.3
Male					
20–34 years	42.7	42.8	41.2	47.5	57.4
35–44 years	53.5	63.2	57.2	65.5	70.5
45–54 years	53.9	59.7	60.2	66.1	75.7
55–64 years	52.2	58.5	60.2	70.5	75.4
65–74 years	47.8	54.6	54.2	68.5	76.2
75 years and over	—	—	—	56.5	67.4
Female[e]					
20–34 years	21.2	25.8	27.9	37.0	52.8
35–44 years	37.2	40.5	40.7	49.6	60.6
45–54 years	49.3	49.0	48.7	60.3	65.1
55–64 years	59.9	54.5	53.7	66.3	72.2
65–74 years	60.9	55.9	59.5	60.3	70.9
75 years and over	—	—	—	52.3	59.9

Figure 11.7.) Only 33.1% of women ages eighteen to twenty-four and 31.7% of women ages twenty-five to sixty-four participated in physical activity from January to September of 2004. Among women ages sixty-five to seventy-four, 25% engaged in physical exercise, but among women ages seventy-five or older, the percentage dropped to 13.2%.

According to the American Obesity Association (AOA), low-income women in minority populations tend to be overweight and obese more than their wealthier counterparts. The AOA also points out that middle-aged women are at a particular risk for obesity (ages thirty-five to sixty-four). Since 1960 the prevalence for obesity in this age group has increased two points every year.

TABLE 11.12

Healthy weight, overweight, and obesity among persons 20 years of age and over, according to sex, age, race, and Hispanic origin, 1960–62, 1971–74, 1976–80, 1988–94, and 1999–2002 [CONTINUED]

[Data are based on measured height and weight of a sample of the civilian noninstitutionalized population]

Sex, age, race, and Hispanic origin[a]	Obesity[g]				
	1960–62	1971–74	1976–80[c]	1988–94	1999–2002
20–74 years, age adjusted[d]	Percent of population				
Both sexes[e,f]	13.3	14.6	15.1	23.3	31.1
Male	10.7	12.2	12.8	20.6	28.1
Female[e]	15.7	16.8	17.1	26.0	34.0
Not Hispanic or Latino:					
White only, male	—	—	12.4	20.7	28.7
White only, female[e]	—	—	15.4	23.3	31.3
Black or African American only, male	—	—	16.5	21.3	27.9
Black or African American only, female[e]	—	—	31.0	39.1	49.6
Mexican male	—	—	15.7	24.4	29.0
Mexican female[e]	—	—	26.6	36.1	38.9
20 years and over, age adjusted[d]					
Both sexes[e,f]	—	—	—	22.9	30.4
Male	—	—	—	20.2	27.5
Female[e]	—	—	—	25.5	33.2
Not Hispanic or Latino:					
White only, male	—	—	—	20.3	28.0
White only, female[e]	—	—	—	22.9	30.7
Black or African American only, male	—	—	—	20.9	27.8
Black or African American only, female[e]	—	—	—	38.3	48.8
Mexican male	—	—	—	23.8	27.8
Mexican female[e]	—	—	—	35.2	38.0
20 years and over, crude					
Both sexes[e,f]	—	—	—	22.3	30.5
Male	—	—	—	19.5	27.5
Female[e]	—	—	—	25.0	33.4
Not Hispanic or Latino:					
White only, male	—	—	—	19.9	28.4
White only, female[e]	—	—	—	22.7	31.3
Black or African American only, male	—	—	—	20.7	27.5
Black or African American only, female[e]	—	—	—	36.7	48.8
Mexican male	—	—	—	20.6	26.0
Mexican female[e]	—	—	—	33.3	37.0
Male					
20–34 years	9.2	9.7	8.9	14.1	21.7
35–44 years	12.1	13.5	13.5	21.5	28.5
45–54 years	12.5	13.7	16.7	23.2	30.6
55–64 years	9.2	14.1	14.1	27.2	35.5
65–74 years	10.4	10.9	13.2	24.1	31.9
75 years and over	—	—	—	13.2	18.0
Female[e]					
20–34 years	7.2	9.7	11.0	18.5	28.4
35–44 years	14.7	17.7	17.8	25.5	32.1
45–54 years	20.3	18.9	19.6	32.4	36.9
55–64 years	24.4	24.1	22.9	33.7	42.1
65–74 years	23.2	22.0	21.5	26.9	39.3
75 years and over	—	—	—	19.2	23.6

TABLE 11.12

Healthy weight, overweight, and obesity among persons 20 years of age and over, according to sex, age, race, and Hispanic origin, 1960–62, 1971–74, 1976–80, 1988–94, and 1999–2002 [CONTINUED]

[Data are based on measured height and weight of a sample of the civilian noninstitutionalized population]

| Sex, age, race, and Hispanic origin[a] | Healthy weight[b] | | | | |
	1960–62	1971–74	1976–80[c]	1988–94	1999–2002
20–74 years, age adjusted[d]			Percent of population		
Both sexes[e,f]	51.2	48.8	49.6	41.7	32.9
Male	48.3	43.0	45.4	37.9	30.2
Female[e]	54.1	54.3	53.7	45.3	35.6
Not Hispanic or Latino:					
White only, male	—	—	45.3	37.4	29.5
White only, female[e]			56.7	49.2	39.7
Black or African American only, male	—	—	46.6	40.0	35.5
Black or African American only, female[e]			35.0	28.9	21.3
Mexican male	—	—	37.1	29.8	25.6
Mexican female[e]			36.4	29.0	27.5
20 years and over, age adjusted[d]					
Both sexes[e,f]	—	—	—	41.6	33.0
Male	—	—	—	37.9	30.2
Female[e]	—	—	—	45.0	35.7
Not Hispanic or Latino:					
White only, male	—	—	—	37.3	29.6
White only, female[e]				48.7	39.5
Black or African American only, male	—	—	—	40.1	34.7
Black or African American only, female[e]				29.2	21.7
Mexican male	—	—	—	30.2	26.5
Mexican female[e]				29.7	27.5
20 years and over, crude					
Both sexes[e,f]	—	—	—	42.6	32.9
Male	—	—	—	39.4	30.4
Female[e]	—	—	—	45.7	35.4
Not Hispanic or Latino:					
White only, male	—	—	—	38.2	29.2
White only, female[e]				48.8	38.7
Black or African American only, male	—	—	—	41.5	35.9
Black or African American only, female[e]				31.2	21.9
Mexican male	—	—	—	35.2	29.4
Mexican female[e]				32.4	29.4
Male					
20–34 years	55.3	54.7	57.1	51.1	40.3
35–44 years	45.2	35.2	41.3	33.4	29.0
45–54 years	44.8	38.5	38.7	33.6	24.0
55–64 years	44.9	38.3	38.7	28.6	23.8
65–74 years	46.2	42.1	42.3	30.1	22.8
75 years and over	—	—	—	40.9	32.0

TABLE 11.12

Healthy weight, overweight, and obesity among persons 20 years of age and over, according to sex, age, race, and Hispanic origin, 1960–62, 1971–74, 1976–80, 1988–94, and 1999–2002 [CONTINUED]

[Data are based on measured height and weight of a sample of the civilian noninstitutionalized population]

Sex, age, race, and Hispanic origin[a]	Healthy weight[h]				
	1960–62	1971–74	1976–80[c]	1988–94	1999–2002
Female[e]					
20–34 years	67.6	65.8	65.0	57.9	42.6
35–44 years	58.4	56.7	55.6	47.1	37.1
45–54 years	47.6	49.3	48.7	37.2	33.1
55–64 years	38.1	41.1	43.5	31.5	27.6
65–74 years	36.4	40.6	37.8	37.0	26.4
75 years and over	—	—	—	43.0	36.9

— Data not available.

[a]Persons of Mexican origin may be of any race. Starting with data year 1999 race-specific estimates are tabulated according to 1997 Standards for Federal Data on Race and Ethnicity and are not strictly comparable with estimates for earlier years. The two non-Hispanic race categories shown in the table conform to 1997 standards. The 1999–2002 race-specific estimates are for persons who reported only one racial group. Prior to data year 1999, data were tabulated according to 1977 standards. Estimates for single race categories prior to 1999 included persons who reported one race or, if they reported more than one race, identified one race as best representing their race. The effect of the 1997 standard on the 1999–2002 estimates can be seen by comparing 1999–2002 data tabulated according to the two standards: Estimates based on the 1977 standards of the percent of the population 20–74 years, age adjusted, who were overweight are: 0.2 percentage points higher for white males; 0.1 percentage points higher for white females; unchanged for black males; and 0.2 percentage points higher for black females than estimates based on the 1997 standards.
[b]Body mass index (BMI) greater than or equal to 25.
[c]Data for Mexicans are for 1982–84.
[d]Age adjusted to the 2000 standard population using five age groups. Age-adjusted estimates in this table may differ from other age-adjusted estimates based on the same data and presented elsewhere if different age groups are used in the adjustment procedure.
[e]Excludes pregnant women.
[f]Includes persons of all races and Hispanic origins, not just those shown separately.
[g]Body mass index (BMI) greater than or equal to 30.
[h]BMI of 18.5 to less than 25 kilograms/meter^2.
Notes: Percents do not sum to 100 because the percent of persons with BMI less than 18.5 is not shown and the percent of persons with obesity is a subset of the percent with overweight. Height was measured without shoes; two pounds were deducted from data for 1960–62 to allow for weight of clothing.

SOURCE: "Table 69. Overweight, Obesity, and Healthy Weight among Persons 20 Years of Age and Over, according to Sex, Age, Race, and Hispanic Origin: United States, 1960–62, 1971–74, 1976–80, 1988–94, and 1999–2002," in *Health, United States, 2004*, Centers for Disease Control and Prevention, National Center for Health Statistics, September 2004, http://www.cdc.gov/nchs/data/hus/hus04trend.pdf (accessed June 9, 2005)

TABLE 11.13

Overweight children and adolescents 6–19 years of age, according to sex, age, race, and Hispanic origin, selected years, 1963–2002

[Data are based on physical examinations of a sample of the civilian noninstitutionalized population]

Age, sex, race, and Hispanic origin[a]	1963–65 1966–70[b]	1971–74	1976–80[c]	1988–94	1999–2002
6–11 years of age			Percent of population		
Both sexes[d]	4.2	4.0	6.5	11.3	15.8
Boys	4.0	4.3	6.6	11.6	16.9
Not Hispanic or Latino:					
White only	—	—	6.1	10.7	14.0
Black or African American only	—	—	6.8	12.3	17.0
Mexican	—	—	13.3	17.5	26.5
Girls[e]	4.5	3.6	6.4	11.0	14.7
Not Hispanic or Latino:					
White only	—	—	5.2	*9.8	13.1
Black or African American only	—	—	11.2	17.0	22.8
Mexican	—	—	9.8	15.3	17.1
12–19 years of age					
Both sexes[d]	4.6	6.1	5.0	10.5	16.1
Boys	4.5	6.1	4.8	11.3	16.7
Not Hispanic or Latino:					
White only	—	—	3.8	11.6	14.6
Black or African American only	—	—	6.1	10.7	18.7
Mexican	—	—	7.7	14.1	24.7
Girls[e]	4.7	6.2	5.3	9.7	15.4
Not Hispanic or Latino:					
White only	—	—	4.6	8.9	12.7
Black or African American only	—	—	10.7	16.3	23.6
Mexican	—	—	8.8	*13.4	19.6

*Estimates are considered unreliable.

— Data not available.

[a]Persons of Mexican origin may be of any race. Starting with data year 1999 race-specific estimates are tabulated according to 1997 Standards for Federal Data on Race and Ethnicity and are not strictly comparable with estimates for earlier years. The two non-Hispanic race categories shown in the table conform to 1997 standards. The 1999–2002 race-specific estimates are for persons who reported only one racial group. Prior to data year 1999, data were tabulated according to 1977 standards. Estimates for single race categories prior to 1999 included persons who reported one race or, if they reported more than one race, identified one race as best representing their race. The effect of the 1997 standard on the 1999–2002 estimates can be seen by comparing 1999–2002 data tabulated according to the two standards: Estimates based on the 1977 standards of the percent of the children 6–11 years who were overweight are: 0.1 percentage points lower for white males; 0.1 percentage points lower for black males; 0.3 percentage points lower for white females; and 0.1 percentage points higher for black females than estimates based on the 1997 standards. Estimates based on the 1977 standards of the percent of adolescents 12–19 years of age who were overweight are: 0.2 percentage points lower for white males; unchanged for black males and white females; and 0.3 percentage points higher for black females than estimates based on the 1997 standards.

[b]Data for 1963–65 are for children 6–11 years of age; data for 1966–70 are for adolescents 12–17 years of age, not 12–19 years.

[c]Data for Mexicans are for 1982–84.

[d]Includes persons of all races and Hispanic origins, not just those shown separately.

[e]Excludes pregnant women starting with 1971–74. Pregnancy status not available for 1963–65 and 1966–70.

Notes: Overweight is defined as body mass index (BMI) at or above the sex- and age-specific 95th percentile BMI cutoffpoints from the 2000 CDC Growth Charts: United States. Age is at time of examination at mobile examination center. Crude rates, not age-adjusted rates, are shown.

SOURCE: "Table 70. Overweight Children and Adolescents 6–19 Years of Age, According to Sex, Age, Race, and Hispanic Origin: United States, Selected Years 1963–65 through 1999–2002," in *Health, United States, 2004*, Centers for Disease Control and Prevention, National Center for Health Statistics, September 2004, http://www.cdc.gov/nchs/data/hus/hus04trend.pdf (accessed June 9, 2005)

FIGURE 11.7

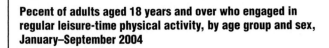

Pecent of adults aged 18 years and over who engaged in regular leisure-time physical activity, by age group and sex, January–September 2004

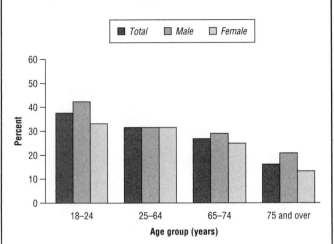

Notes: This measure reflects the definition used for the physical activity Leading Health Indicator (Healthy People 2010). Regular leisure-time physical activity is defined as engaging in light-moderate leisure-time physical activity for greater than or equal to 30 minutes at a frequency greater than or equal to five times per week or engaging in vigorous leisure-time physical activity for greater than or equal to 20 minutes at a frequency greater than or equal to three times per week. The analyses excluded 681 persons (3.0%) with unknown physical activity participation.

SOURCE: "Figure 7.2 Percent of Adults Aged 18 Years and Over Who Engaged in Regular Leisure-Time Physical Activity, by Age Group and Sex: United States, January–September 2004," in *Early Release of Selected Estimates Based on Data from the January–September 2004 National Health Interview Survey*, Centers for Disease Control and Prevention, National Center for Health Statistics, March 23, 2005, http://www.cdc.gov/nchs/data/nhis/earlyrelease/200503_07.pdf (accessed June 22, 2005)

IMPORTANT NAMES AND ADDRESSES

AARP (formerly American Association of Retired Persons)
601 E St. NW
Washington, DC 20049
1-888-687-2277
E-mail: member@aarp.org
URL: http://www.aarp.org

The Alan Guttmacher Institute
120 Wall St.,
21st Floor
New York, NY 10005
(212) 248-1111
FAX: (212) 248-1951
E-mail: info@guttmacher.org
URL: http://www.agi-usa.org

American Association of University Women
1111 16th St. NW
Washington, DC 20036
1-800-326-AAUW
FAX: (202) 872-1425
E-mail: info@aauw.org
URL: http://www.aauw.org

American Cancer Society
1599 Clifton Rd. NE
Atlanta, GA 30329-4251
1-800-ACS-2345
(404) 320-3333
FAX: (404) 329-7530
URL: http://www.cancer.org

American Heart Association
7272 Greenville Ave.
Dallas, TX 75231
1-800-242-8721
URL: http://www.americanheart.org

Amnesty International USA
5 Penn Plaza,
14th Floor
New York, NY 10001
(212) 807-8400
FAX: (212) 627-1451

E-mail: aimember@aiusa.org
URL: http://www.amnesty-usa.org

Association for Women in Science
1200 New York Ave. NW,
Suite 650
Washington, DC 20005
(202) 326-8940
E-mail: awis@awis.org
URL: http://www.awis.org

Catalyst
120 Wall St.,
5th Floor
New York, NY 10005
(212) 514-7600
FAX: (212) 514-8470
E-mail: info@catalystwomen.org
URL: http://www.catalystwomen.org

Center for American Women and Politics Eagleton Institute of Politics Rutgers, The State University of New Jersey
191 Ryders Lane
New Brunswick, NJ 08901-8557
(732) 932-9384
FAX: (732) 932-0014
URL: http://www.cawp.rutgers.edu

Center for Women's Business Research
1411 K Street NW,
Suite 1350
Washington, DC 20005-3407
(202) 638-3060
FAX: (202) 638-3064
E-mail: info@womensbusinessresearch.org
URL: http://www.nfwbo.org

Center on Budget and Policy Priorities
820 First St. NE,
Suite 510
Washington, DC 20002
(202) 408-1080
FAX: (202) 408-1056

E-mail: center@cbpp.org
URL: http://www.cbpp.org

EMILY's List
1120 Connecticut Ave. NW,
Suite 1100
Washington, DC 20036
(202) 326-1400
FAX: (202) 326-1415
E-mail: information@emilyslist.org
URL: http://www.emilyslist.org

Families and Work Institute
267 5th Ave.,
Floor 2
New York, NY 10016
(212) 465-2044
FAX: (212) 465-8637
URL: http://www.familiesandwork.org

Feminist Majority Foundation
1600 Wilson Blvd.,
Suite 801
Arlington, WV 22209
(703) 522-2214
FAX: (703) 522-2219
URL: http://www.feminist.org

Institute for Women's Policy Research
1707 L St. NW,
Suite 750
Washington, DC 20036
(202) 785-5100
FAX: (202) 833-4362
E-mail: iwpr@iwpr.org
URL: http://www.iwpr.org

International Center for Research on Women
1717 Massachusetts Ave. NW,
Suite 302
Washington, DC 20036
(202) 797-0007
FAX: (202) 797-0020
E-mail: info@ircw.org
URL: http://www.icrw.org

National Abortion Federation
1755 Massachusetts Ave. NW,
Suite 600
Washington, DC 20036
(202) 667-5881
Hotline: 1-800-772-9100
FAX: (202) 667-5890
E-mail: naf@prochoice.org
URL: http://www.prochoice.org

National Association of Anorexia Nervosa and Associated Disorders (ANAD)
P.O. Box 7
Highland Park, IL 60035
(847) 831-3438
FAX: (847) 433-4632
E-mail: info@anad.org
URL: http://www.anad.org

National Coalition against Domestic Violence
1201 East Colfax Ave.,
Suite 385
P.O. Box 18749
Denver, CO 80218-0749
(303) 839-1852
Hotline: 1-800-799-7233
FAX: (303) 831-9251
E-mail: mainoffice@ncadv.org
URL: http://www.ncadv.org

National Coalition for the Homeless
2201 P St. NW,
Suite 600
Washington, DC 20037
(202) 462-4822
FAX: (202) 462-4823
E-mail: info@nationalhomeless.org
URL: http://nationalhomeless.org

National Coalition of Girls' Schools
57 Main St.
Concord, MA 01742
(978) 287-4485
FAX: (978) 287-6014
URL: http://www.ncgs.org

National Gay and Lesbian Task Force
1325 Massachusetts Ave. NW,
Suite 600
Washington, DC 20005
(202) 393-5177
FAX: (202) 393-2241
E-mail: thetaskforce@thetaskforce.org
URL: http://www.thetaskforce.org

National Older Women's League (OWL)
1750 New York Ave. NW,
Suite 350
Washington, DC 20006
1-800-825-3695
(202) 783-6686
FAX: (202) 628-0458
E-mail: owlinfo@owl-national.org
URL: http://www.owl-national.org

National Organization for Women (NOW)
1100 H Street NW,
3rd Floor
Washington, DC 20005
(202) 628-8669
FAX: (202) 785-8576
E-mail: now@now.org
URL: http://www.now.org

National Osteoporosis Foundation
1232 22nd St. NW
Washington, DC 20037-1292
(202) 223-2226
URL: http://www.nof.org

Planned Parenthood Federation of America
434 W. 33rd St.
New York, NY 10001
1-800-230-PLAN
(212) 541-7800
FAX: (212) 245-1845
E-mail: communications@ppfa.org
URL: http://www.plannedparenthood.org

The Urban Institute
2100 M St. NW
Washington, DC 20037
(202) 833-7200
E-mail: paffairs@ui.urban.org
URL: http://www.urban.org

U.S. Department of Commerce U.S. Census Bureau
4700 Silver Hill Rd.
Washington, DC 20233
(301) 763-INFO
URL: http://www.census.gov

U.S. Department of Health and Human Services Centers for Disease Control and Prevention National Center for Health Statistics Division of Data Services
Hyattsville, MD 20782-2003
(301) 458-4000
URL: http://www.cdc.gov/nchs

U.S. Department of Labor U.S. Bureau of Labor Statistics
Postal Square Building
2 Massachusetts Ave. NE
Washington, DC 20212-0001
(202) 691-5200
FAX: (202) 691-6325
URL: http://www.bls.gov

U.S. Government Accountability Office
441 G St. NW
Washington, DC 20548
(202) 512-4800
FAX: (202) 512-3000
URL: http://www.gao.gov

Women's Research and Education Institute
1750 New York Ave. NW,
Suite 350
Washington, DC 20006
(202) 628-0444
FAX: (202) 628-0458
E-mail: wrei@wrei.org
URL: http://www.wrei.org

RESOURCES

The U.S. Census Bureau (Washington, DC) publishes the findings of its annual surveys in a variety of publications. *Current Population Reports* used in the preparation of this publication include *The Foreign-Born Population in the United States: 2003* (August 2004); *America's Families and Living Arrangements: 2003* (November 2004); *Women and Men in the United States: March 2002* (March 2003); *Income, Poverty and Health Insurance Coverage in the United States: 2003* (August 2004); *Fertility of American Women: June 2002* (October 2003); *Children's Living Arrangements and Characteristics: March 2002* (June 2003); *Voting and Registration in the Election of November 2002* (July 2004); and *School Enrollment: Social and Economic Characteristics of Students: October 2003* (May 2005). *Statistical Abstract of the United States: 2004–2005* (2005), published by the Census Bureau, is an important source of statistics on all facets of American life.

The National Center for Education Statistics of the U.S. Department of Education (Washington, DC) provides detailed information in the 2003 edition of its annual *Digest of Education Statistics* (December 2004) and in *The Condition of Education 2004* (June 2004). Also helpful in the preparation of this publication was *Projections of Education Statistics to 2013* (October 2003), *Trends in Educational Equity of Girls & Women: 2004* (November 2004), and *Distance Education at Degree-Granting Postsecondary Institutions, 2000–2001* (July 2003). For more detailed national statistics on the subjects of reading, science, and mathematics, and how well American children fare, consult *The Nation's Report Card* on the various subjects, which is updated annually.

The Bureau of Labor Statistics (BLS; Washington, DC) of the U.S. Department of Labor (DOL) is the major source of statistical information on the nation's labor force. The monthly publication *Employment and Earnings* provides complete statistics on employment, unemployment, earnings, and occupations. The *BLS News* is an important

source for the most recent labor force statistics. The *Monthly Labor Review* is also an important source for labor force statistics. Other BLS publications used in the preparation of this work include *Women in the Labor Force: A Databook* (May 2005); *Average Annual Tables* (2004); *Highlights of Women's Earnings in 2003* (September 2004); *Earnings by Educational Attainment and Sex, 1979 and 2002* (October 2003); and *National Compensation Survey: Employee Benefits in Private Industry in the United States, March 2004* (November 2004).

The National Science Foundation (Arlington, VA) published *Women, Minorities, and Persons with Disabilities in Science and Engineering: 2004* (2004).

The U.S. Department of Agriculture (USDA) publishes economic information in its *FoodReview*. Other pertinent information is published and updated regularly in the *Food Assistance and Nutrition Research* reports. Particularly useful was *Household Food Security in the United States, 2003* (October 2004).

The Office on Women's Health of the U.S. Department of Health and Human Services (HHS) published *HHS Blueprint for Action on Breastfeeding* (Washington, DC, Fall 2000). The National Adoption Information Clearinghouse (NAIC), a service of the Children's Bureau of the HHS, and the Child Care Bureau of the HHS provided useful information. Information on Early Head Start came from the Administration of Children, Youth, and Families of the HHS.

The Substance Abuse and Mental Health Services Administration (SAMHSA) publishes a helpful annual report, *National Survey on Drug Use and Health*.

The Federal Interagency Forum on Child and Family Statistics publishes an annual report, the most recent edition of which is *America's Children in Brief: Key National Indicators of Well-Being, 2004* (July 2004). This is a collaborative effort of twenty federal agencies.

Within the U.S. Department of Justice, the Bureau of Justice Statistics (BJS; Washington, DC) conducts an annual National Crime Victimization Survey (NCVS) and publishes numerous statistics about victims and crimes. Its publications include *Criminal Victimization, 2003* (September 2004); *Family Violence Statistics* (June 2005); *National Crime Victimization Survey* (September 2004); *Intimate Partner Violence, 1993–2001* (February 2003); *Compendium of Federal Justice Statistics, 2002* (September 2004); *Prisoners in 2003* (November 2004); *Prison and Jail Inmates at Midyear 2004* (April 2005); *HIV in Prisons and Jails, 2002* (December 2004); *Capital Punishment, 2003* (November 2004); *Census of State and Federal Correctional Facilities, 2000* (rev. October 2003); *Criminal Victimization 2002* (August 2003); and *Women Offenders* (rev. 2000).

The BJS and the National Institute of Justice (NIJ) published *The Sexual Victimization of College Women* (December 2000). The Federal Bureau of Investigation (FBI) published *Crime in the United States 2002* (Washington, DC, October 27, 2003) and *Hate Crime Statistics, 2002*. In July 2000 the NIJ and the Centers for Disease Control and Prevention (CDC) published *Extent, Nature, and Consequences of Intimate Partner Violence*.

The National Center for Health Statistics (NCHS) of the CDC publishes the *National Vital Statistics Reports* and the annual overview of the health of the nation, *Health, United States, 2003* (2003). The NCHS's 2002 National Health Interview Survey, and preliminary results of the 2003 survey, provided data on women and health. The CDC also published *Sexually Transmitted Disease Surveillance 2002, Mean Age of Mother, 1970–2000* (December 2002), and *HIV/AIDS Surveillance in Women*.

The Center for Women's Business Research is a definitive source for information on the role of women in business, with a focus on women-owned businesses. Particularly helpful for the revision of this book was the April 2003 publication, *Completing the Picture: Equally-Owned Firms in 2002*.

The National Institute of Mental Health (Bethesda, MD) publishes information about women's mental health, including *The Numbers Count: Mental Disorders in America* (rev. May 2003) and *Facts about Eating Disorders and the Search for Solutions* (2001).

The Human Rights Campaign published *Gay and Lesbian Families in the United States: Same-Sex Unmarried Partner Households: A Preliminary Analysis of 2000 United States Census Data* (Washington, DC, August 22, 2001). The U.S. Conference of Mayors provided important information in *A Status Report on Hunger and Homelessness in America's Cities: 2002* (Washington, DC, December 2002).

The American Association of University Women (AAUW) Education Foundation and the National Coalition of Girls' Schools provided information on single-sex education. The College Board (Princeton, NJ) provided information on college-bound high school seniors and the SATs.

The American Association for the Advancement of Science published its *Survey of Life Scientists* in 2001. Catalyst, a nonprofit research and advocacy organization concerned with women in business, published *Women in Financial Services: The Word on the Street* (2001), *Women in Law: Making the Case* (2001), and the *2000 Catalyst Census of Women Corporate Officers and Top Earners of the Fortune 500*. The National Foundation for Women Business Owners provided research summaries that included *Women of All Races Share Entrepreneurial Spirit, Access to Credit Continues to Improve for Women Business Owners, Women-Owned Businesses Top 9 Million in 1999*, and *Women-Owned Businesses Thrive in the Nation's Top 50 Metropolitan Areas*. The Women's Research and Education Institute (Washington, DC) published *The American Woman 2001–2002: Getting to the Top* (2001) and *Women in the Military: Where They Stand* (3rd ed., 2000). It also published *Midlife Women: Insurance Coverage and Access*.

The AFL-CIO publishes information on working women. With the Institute for Women's Policy Research (IWPR), it published *Equal Pay for Working Families: National and State Data on the Pay Gap and Its Costs* (Washington, DC, 1999). The IWPR also published *How Much Can Child Support Provide? Welfare, Family Income, and Child Support* (1999) and *The Gender Gap in Pension Coverage: What Does the Future Hold?* (May 2001). The Center on Budget and Policy Priorities (Washington, DC) publishes information on low-income women, including *Poverty Trends for Families Headed by Working Single Mothers: 1993 to 1999* (August 2001) and *The Initial Impacts of Welfare Reform on the Incomes of Single-Mother Families* (1999).

The Alan Guttmacher Institute (New York and Washington, DC) publishes a wide variety of materials on human sexuality and reproduction, including *The Guttmacher Report on Public Policy* and *Facts in Brief*.

AARP (formerly the American Association of Retired Persons) published a study in July 2001 on the child- and elder-care responsibilities of the "sandwich generation." The Center for Law and Social Policy published *Child Care after Leaving Welfare: Early Evidence from State Studies* (October 1999). Useful publications from the Families and Work Institute include the *1998 Business Work-Life Study: A Sourcebook* (New York, 1998). The Foundation for Child Development published a working paper entitled *Child Care Employment: Implications for Women's Self-Sufficiency and for Child*

Development (January 1999). The National Center for Children in Poverty published *Better Strategies for Babies: Strengthening the Caregivers and Families of Infants and Toddlers* (2000). OWL (National Older Women's League) is a good source for information on older women. The Urban Institute (Washington, DC), a nonpartisan economic and social policy research organization, publishes a wealth of research on a variety of subjects. Among the publications used in the preparation of this work were *Who's Caring for Our Youngest Children? Child Care Patterns of Infants and Toddlers* (Occasional Paper Number 42, January 2001) and *Parental Care at Midlife: Balancing Work and Family Responsibilities Near Retirement* (March 2000).

Child Trends is a nonprofit, nonpartisan, Washington, D.C.-based research organization that conducts studies on children, youth, and families and publishes an annual statistical study of teen childbearing.

The Center for American Women and Politics is an excellent source of online information on women and American politics. EMILY's List conducted the survey *The Women's Vote and the 2000 Elections* (December 14, 2000), among others. The Feminist Majority Foundation published a report on the 2000 presidential election entitled *How the Gender Gap Shaped Election 2000* (January 24, 2001). This organization publishes valuable data on the role of women in politics.

The American Medical Association and the National Coalition Against Domestic Violence (NCADV) publish information on domestic violence. Amnesty International USA publishes information about prisoners and the death penalty in the United States. It published the 1999 report *"Not Part of My Sentence": Violations of the Human Rights of Women in Custody* and a follow-up 2001 study, *Abuse of Women in Custody: Sexual Misconduct and Shackling of Pregnant Women*.

The American Cancer Society's *Cancer Facts and Figures 2003* (Atlanta, GA, 2003) was an important source on women and cancer, while the American Heart Association's *Heart and Stroke Statistics—2003 Update* (Dallas, TX, 2002) played a similar role for information on cardiovascular and other diseases. The American Social Health Association publishes information about women's health and sexually transmitted diseases.

INDEX

Page references in italics refer to photographs. References with the letter t *following them indicate the presence of a table. The letter* f *indicates a figure. If more than one table or figure appears on a particular page, the exact item number for the table or figure being referenced is provided.*

A

AARP, 127–128
Abortion, 107–109, 108t
Academia, 63t, 64
Adoption, 109–111
Advanced placement tests, 20–21
After-school care, 121–122, 121t
Age
　birth rates, 93, 99–102
　labor force participation, 34
　maternal age, 93
　population, 1
Air Force Academy, 160, 160f
Alcohol consumption, 104, 191–193, 191t–192t
Alternative work arrangements, 38–39, 42, 43t
American Association for the Advancement of Science survey, 64
Anorexia, 190
Armed Forces 2002 Sexual Harassment Survey, 158–159
Arrests, 163, 164t–165t, 166–167, 166t, 167t
Associate degrees, 22
Athletics, 28, 30, 31t

B

Bachelor's degrees, 22, 25t
Backup child care, 125–126
Birth rates
　foreign-born women, 97
　history, 93
　mothers' age, 93
　race/ethnicity, 93, 94t–95t, 96t, 97, 97t
　teenage childbearing, 97, 99, 99f, 99t
　unmarried women, 101t, 102f
Breast cancer, 179–181
Breast-feeding, 106–107
Business
　child-care policies, 124–126, 125t
　corporate employment, 60–61
　elder care assistance programs, 128–129
　women-owned businesses, 65–66, 66f

C

Cabinet members, 141–142
Cancer, 179–181
Capital punishment, 171–172
Cardiovascular disease, 176–177, 179f, 180t
Caregiving. *See* Child care; Elderly
Cerebrovascular diseases, 178–179
Cesarean births, 104–105
Child-care
　after-school care, 121t
　arrangements, 117–122
　assistance programs, 123–127
　breakdowns in, 122–123
　child care centers, 120–122
　children in, percentage of, 120f
　costs, 123
　employer assistance, 124–126, 125t
　government assistance programs, 126–127
　home-based, 120
　parental care, 119–120
　preschools, 122, 123f
　by relatives, 120, 122t
Child Care and Development Fund, 126–127
Child support, 84, 88–89
Childbirth. *See* Pregnancy and childbirth
Childlessness, 109, 110t
Children, 198t
　See also Child care
Chlamydia, 188–189
Citadel, 28

Cohabitation, 7
College. *See* Higher education
Comparable worth, 74–75
Congress, U.S., 136–139, 137(t 8.6), 138t
Construction industry, 57–58
Contraception, 103(t 6.8), 107–109
Corporate employment, 60–61
Costs, child-care, 123
Crime
　arrests, 163, 164t–165t, 166–167, 167t
　"date rape" drugs, 148
　domestic violence, 151–157, 153t, 154f, 167
　hate crimes, 161
　homicide, 149–150, 150t, 151t, 152t, 167
　National Violence Against Women Survey, 151–154, 156–157
　rape and sexual assault, 145t, 146–149, 148f, 152–154
　rates of, 143
　reporting, 146, 147t, 149, 156
　sexual harassment, 157–161, 159f, 160f
　victim/offender relationship, 145–146, 145t, 147t
　violent crime committed by women, 167
　violent crime victimization involving strangers, 146t
　violent crime victimization rates, 143–146, 144f, 144t
　See also Prisons and prisoners

D

"Date rape" drugs, 148
Death row, 171
Democratic Party, 137(t 8.5)
Department of Defense, U.S., 158–161
Depression, 189–190, 189t
Diet and nutrition, 193
Discouraged workers, 46–47
Discrimination
　athletics, 28–29
　corporate employment, 60–61

military schools, 26–27
  Wall Street, 59–60
  women soldiers, 65
Disease transmission, 185–187
Distance education, 30*f*
Doctorate degrees, 22–23, 28*t*, 62, 63*t*
Domestic violence, 150–157, 153*t*,
  154*f*, 167
Drugs, illegal, 167*t*, 193
D&X (Intact Dilation and Extraction), 109

E

Earnings. *See* Wages and earnings
Eating disorders, 190
Education
  academia, 63*t*, 64
  athletics, 28, 30, 31*t*
  attainment levels, 15, 16*t*, 19
  birth rates by, 99–100
  college enrollment, 21–22, 23*t*
  degrees conferred, 22–24, 24*f*, 25*t*, 26*f*,
    27*t*, 28*t*, 29*t*
  distance education, 24, 30*f*
  dropout rates, 19*t*
  earnings by, 70, 80*f*, 81*f*, 83*t*
  employment and, 47–48, 52*t*, 53*t*
  fertility indicators by, 98*t*
  military schools, 26, 28
  preschool and kindergarten, 122,
    123*f*, 124*f*
  school enrollment by age, sex, and
    race/ethnicity, 17*t*–18*t*
  science, engineering, and technology,
    61–62
  single-sex education, 24, 26
  test scores, 19–21, 20*f*, 21*f*
Elderly
  elder care, 127–129
  poverty, 89–91
Elections
  reported voting and registration by sex
    and age, 136(*t* 8.3)
  voter turnout in presidential elections,
    136(*t* 8.4)
  voting and voter turnout, 131–135, 132*t*
  voting rates by race/ethnicity, 135*f*
  women elected officials, 135–140,
    137(*t* 8.6), 138*t*
EMILY's List, 140
Employment
  academia, 63*t*, 64
  alternative work arrangements, 38–39,
    42, 43*t*
  birth rates by, 100
  child-care friendly company policies,
    124–126, 125*t*
  corporate, 60–61
  education and, 47–48, 52*t*, 53*t*
  elder care assistance programs, 128–129
  entrepreneurs, 65–66, 66*f*, 67*f*

in families, 36*t*
  fertility indicators by employment
    status, 98*t*
  financial management, 59–60
  future, 66–68
  history, 33
  job tenure, 37–38
  labor force participation, 33–38,
    113*f*, 115*t*
  military, 64–65, 65*t*
  multiple jobholders, 42–43
  by occupation, 41*t*, 57*t*
  projections, 48–49
  in science, engineering, and technology,
    61–62, 63*t*, 64
  sectors, 36–37, 40*t*
  sexual harassment, 157–158
  status, 37*t*–38*t*
  status by age, sex, and race, 45*t*–50*t*
  status by marital status and presence
    of children, 118*t*–119*t*
  status of civilian noninstitutional
    population, 34*t*–35*t*
  unemployment by reason and
    duration, 51*t*
  voting and voter registration by
    employment status, 133*t*–134*t*
  working mothers, 112, 114*t*, 115*t*, 117,
    118*t*–119*t*
  working parents, 36, 37*t*–38*t*,
    39*t*, 70, 82*t*
  working poor, 81, 84*t*
  See also Child care; Wages and earnings
Engineering, 61–62, 64
Entrepreneurs, 65–66, 66*f*
Equal pay laws, 72–75
Executions, 171–172
Exercise, 28, 30, 31*t*, 193–194, 199*f*

F

Families
  child care by relatives, 120, 122*t*
  employment in, 36*t*
  households, 10–11, 13*f*
  median income, 75
  size, 100
Family and Medical Leave Act, 123–124
Family Violence Statistics, 156
Fat intake, 193
Federal arrests, 166–167, 166*t*
Federal prisons, 167–170, 168*t*–169*t*
Fertility indicators, 98*t*
Fertility rates, 93, 94*t*–95*t*, 97, 99–100
Fields of study
  bachelor's degrees, 22, 25*t*
  doctorate recipients by, 28*t*
  employed doctoral scientists and
    engineers in academia by, 63*t*
  master's degrees conferred by race/
    ethnicity and field of study, 27*t*

professional degrees conferred, 29*t*
  science, engineering, and technology,
    61–62, 64
Financial managers, 59–60
Financing of women-owned businesses, 66
Flextime, 38–39, 42*t*
Food programs, 83–84, 88*f*, 88*t*, 89*t*
Foreign-born population, 2–3, 7*f*, 97, 98*t*
Fortune 500 companies, 60–61
Foster care adoptions, 110–111
Funding
  child care programs, 127
  political campaign finance, 140

G

Gays and/or lesbians
  adoption by, 111
  population estimates, 7–9
Gender
  population by sex and age groups, 2*t*
  population ratios, 1, 5(*f*1.1), 5(*f*1.2)
Gender disparities
  earnings, 69–72, 72*t*–73*t*
  education, 24–25
  pensions, 90–91
  political opinion gap, 132–134
  test scores, 19–21
  voting gap, 134–135
"Glass ceiling," 60–61
Gonorrhea, 188–189
*Good for Business: Making Full Use of the
  Nation's Human Capital,* 61
Government assistance programs
  child care, 126–127
  child support and, 84, 88–89
  elder care, 129
  food programs, 83–84, 88*f*, 88*t*
  Personal Responsibility and Work
    Opportunity Reconciliation Act,
    81–84
  poverty assistance, 88*f*
  Social Security, 89–90
  teenage mothers, 104
  Women, Infants and Children
    program participants, 89*t*
Governors, 139
Graduate education, 22, 26*f*, 27*t*

H

Harvard University, 62
Hate crime victims, 161
Health care access, 173–175, 177(*f*11.3)
Health insurance, 174–175, 175*t*–176*t*,
  177(*f*11.2)
Health issues
  alcohol consumption, 104, 191–193,
    191*t*–192*t*
  cancer, 179–181
  cardiovascular disease, 176–177,
    179*f*, 180*t*

cerebrovascular diseases, 178–179

exercise, 28, 30, 31*t*, 193–194, 199*f*

fat intake, 193

health care access, 173–175, 177(*f*11.3)

HIV/AIDS, 169–170, 183–187, 185*t*, 186*f*, 186*t*, 187*t*

insurance, 174–175, 175*t*–176*t*, 177(*f*11.2)

pregnancy and childbirth, 104–107, 105*t*, 106*t*, 183, 184*t*

self-reported health status, 174*f*

sexually transmitted diseases, 187–189, 188*t*

smoking, 190–191, 191*f*

substance abuse, 193

weight issues, 193, 194*t*–197*t*

Heart disease, 177

High school students

exercise, 31*t*

sexual activity, 103*t*

testing, 19–21

Higher education

academia, 63*t*, 64

college enrollment, 21–22, 23*t*

degrees conferred, 22–24, 24*t*, 25*t*, 26*f*, 27*t*, 28*t*, 29*t*

distance education, 24, 30*f*

sexual victimization on campuses, 148–149

History

birth rates, 93

education, 15

labor force participation, 33

occupations, 55

suffrage, 131

HIV/AIDS, 169–170, 170*t*, 183–187, 185*t*, 186*f*, 186*t*, 187*t*

Home-based businesses, 66

Home-based child care, 120

Homelessness, 91, 92*t*

Homicide, 149–150, 150*t*, 151*t*, 152*t*

Hourly wages, 71–72

Households, 9–11, 11*f*, 12*t*, 13*f*, 75, 85*t*–86*t*

Hunger prevalence, 90*t*, 92*t*

I

Illegal aliens, 2–3

Illegal drugs, 104, 167*t*, 193

Immigrants. *See* Foreign-born population

In the Middle: A Report on Multicultural Boomers Coping with Family and Aging Issues (AARP), 127–128

Income. *See* Wages and earnings

Infants, 105–107

Insurance, health, 174–175, 175*t*–176*t*, 177(*f*11.2)

Intact Dilation and Extraction (D&X), 109

International adoption, 111

Intimate partner violence. *See* Domestic violence

J

Jails, 170

See also Crime; Prisons and prisoners

K

Kindergarten, 122, 124*f*

L

Labor force participation. *See* Employment

Labor unions, 72

Land of Plenty: Diversity as America's Competitive Edge in Science, Engineering, and Technology, 62, 64

Laws

equal pay, 72–75

Family and Medical Leave Act, 123–124

Personal Responsibility and Work Opportunity Reconciliation Act, 81–82, 84, 88–89, 104, 126

same-sex couples, 7–8, 9

sexual harassment, 157–158

Title IX, 28, 30

Lawsuits, 26, 28, 59–60

Lawyers, 58–59

Leadership, political, 138–139, 140

Leading causes of death, 175–183, 178*t*–179*t*

Life expectancy, 1–2, 6*t*

Living arrangements, 9–11

Low birth weight, 105–106

M

Mammography, 181, 182*t*–183*t*

Management, corporate, 60–61

Mania, 189*t*

Marital rape, 152–154

Marital status

birth rates by, 100

children by presence of married parents in household, 111*f*

earnings by, 70, 82*t*, 83*t*

employment by, 37*t*–38*t*, 114*t*, 118*t*–119*t*

fertility indicators by, 98*t*

labor force participation, 35–36

by sex and age, 8*t*

voting and voter registration, 133*t*–134*t*

Marriage

age at first marriage, 9*f*

characteristics of married spouses, 10*t*

Master's degrees, 22, 27*t*

Mathematics test scores, 21(*f*2.2)

Mayors, 140

Mental health, 189–190

Merrill Lynch, 59–60

Mifepristone, 109

Military

child care, 126

employment and occupations, 64–65, 65*t*

sexual harassment, 158–161, 159*f*, 160*f*

Military schools, 26, 28

Moonlighting, 42–43

"Morning after pill," 109

Mortality

leading causes of death, 175–183, 178*t*–179*t*

pregnancy and childbirth, 184*t*

Mothers

labor force participation, 112, 114*t*, 115*t*, 117, 118*t*–119*t*

maternal age, 93

poverty, 81

prisoners, 170–171

unemployment, 44

Multiple births, 100

Multiple jobholders, 42–43

Municipal offices, 140

Murder, 149–150, 150*t*, 151*t*, 152*t*, 167

N

National Family Caregiver Support Program (NFCSP), 129

National Science Foundation, 61–62

National Violence Against Women Survey, 151–154, 156–157

Never-married women, 7

New jobs, 34

NFCSP (National Family Caregiver Support Program), 129

Nontraditional occupations, 56–60

Nontraditional work arrangements, 39

Nursery schools. *See* Preschools

O

Obesity, 193, 194*t*–197*t*

Occupations

academia, 64

doctoral scientists and engineers, 63*t*

earnings by, 70, 74*t*–80*t*

employed persons by, 57*t*, 58*t*–59*t*

employment by, 41*t*

future, 66–68

history, 55

leading occupations of employed women, 56*t*

military, 64–65, 65*t*

nontraditional, 56–60

traditional, 55–56

One-person households, 11

Opinion gap, 132–134

P

Parole, 171
Part-time work, 38, 70, 84*t*
Partial-birth abortion. *See* Intact Dilation and Extraction (D&X)
Pay equity, 74–75
Pension gap, 90–91
Perpetrators of domestic violence, 155
Personal Responsibility and Work Opportunity Reconciliation Act (PRWORA), 81–82, 84, 88–89, 104, 126
Physical fitness activities, 28, 30, 31*t*, 193–194, 199*f*
Politics
    cabinet members, 141–142
    states, 138(*t* 8.6), 139–140
    voting and voter turnout, 131–135, 132*t*, 135*f*, 136(*t* 8.3), 136(*t* 8.4)
    women elected officials, 136–140, 137(*t* 8.6), 138*t*
Population
    foreign-born persons, 2–3, 7*f*
    gays and/or lesbians, 7–9
    by gender, 1, 2*t*
    life-expectancy, 1–2
    by marital status, 8*t*
    race/ethnicity, 3*t*–5*t*
    sex ratios, 5(*f* 1.1), 5(*f* 1.2)
Postgraduate education, 22–24, 28*t*, 29*t*, 62
Poverty
    elderly women, 89–91
    by family size and number of children, 87(*t* 5.8)
    government assistance programs, 81–84, 88–89, 88*f*, 88*t*, 89*t*
    homelessness, 91, 92*t*
    hunger, 90*t*, 92*t*
    measures of, 75–76, 79
    by sex, 87(*t* 5.9)
    working poor, 81
Pregnancy and childbirth, 104–107, 105*t*, 106*t*, 183, 184*t*
Prenatal care, 104, 106*t*
Preschools, 122, 123*f*
Presidential elections, 132, 135, 136(*t* 8.4), 140–141
Preterm births, 104–105
Prevention, disease, 190–194
Prisons and prisoners, 161, 167–172, 168*t*, 169*t*, 170*t*
    See also Crime
Probation, 171
Professional degrees, 23–24, 26*f*, 29*t*
Property crimes, 143
Protection orders, 157
PRWORA (Personal Responsibility and Work Opportunity Reconciliation Act), 81–82, 84, 88–89, 104, 126
Psychological issues, 155–156

Public opinion
    political opinion gap, 132–134
    political parties, 137(*t* 8.5)

R

Race/ethnicity
    abortion, 108*t*
    alcohol consumption, 191*t*–192*t*
    alternative work arrangements, 43*t*
    bachelor's degrees conferred, 25*t*
    birth rates, 93, 96*t*, 97, 97*t*
    breast-feeding, 106–107
    in Congress, 137–138
    domestic violence, 154–155
    earnings, 70*t*, 71, 83*t*
    elder care, 128
    employed persons by occupation, 58*t*–59*t*
    employment status by, 45*t*–50*t*
    entrepreneurs, 66, 67*f*
    homicide victims, 150*t*
    labor force participation, 35
    life expectancy, 6*t*
    mammography, 181, 182*t*–183*t*
    master's degrees conferred, 27*t*
    population, 1, 3*t*–5*t*
    prenatal care, 106*t*
    prisoners, 169*t*
    professional degrees conferred, 29*t*
    school dropout rates, 19*t*
    school enrollment, 17*t*–18*t*
    single mothers, 101*t*
    smoking and pregnancy, 105*t*
    state executive offices, 139–140
    state legislators, 140
    teenage sexual activity, 103(*t* 6.7)
    violent crime victimization rates, 144*t*
    voting, 132, 133*t*–134*t*, 135*f*
    weight issues, 194*t*–197*t*
    workers paid hourly rates below minimum wage, 84*t*
Rape and sexual assault, 145*t*, 146–149, 148*f*, 152–154
Reading test scores, 20*f*
Registration, voter, 131–132, 133*t*–134*t*, 136(*t* 8.3)
Reporting, crime, 146, 147*t*, 149, 156
Reproductive rights, 109
Republican Party, 137(*t* 8.5)
Rohypnol, 148
RU-486, 109

S

"Sandwich generation," 127–128
SAT scores, 19–20
School dropout rates, 19*t*
Science, 21(*f* 2.3), 61–62, 64
Senate, U.S., 136–137, 139
Senior citizens, 89–91, 127–129

September 11th attacks, 150, 152*t*
Sexual activity of teenagers, 102, 103*t*
Sexual assault. *See* Rape and sexual assault
Sexual harassment, 157–161, 159*f*, 160*f*
The Sexual Victimization of College Women, 148–149
Sexually transmitted diseases, 187–189, 188*t*
Single mothers
    adoption by, 111
    birth rates, 101*t*, 102*f*
    never-married mothers, 102
    poverty, 81
    race/ethnicity, 100–102
    work and, 111–112
Single parents, 112*f*
Single-sex education, 24, 26
Smith Barney Inc., 60
Smoking, 104, 105*t*, 190–191, 191*f*
Social issues, 103–104
Social Security, 89–90
A Solid Investment: Making Full Use of the Nation's Capital, 61
Sports. *See* Athletics; Exercise
States
    prisons, 167–170, 168*t*, 169*t*
    women elected officials, 137(*t* 8.6), 139–140
Statistical information
    after-school care, 121*t*
    alcohol consumption, 191*t*–192*t*
    alternative and traditional work arrangements, 43*t*
    arrests, 164*t*–165*t*, 166*t*, 167*t*
    bachelor's degrees conferred, 25*t*
    birth rates for unmarried women, 101*t*, 102*f*
    births and birth/fertility rates, 94*t*–95*t*
    births and birth rates by race/ethnicity, 96*t*
    businesses, women-owned, 66*f*
    cardiovascular disease, 179*f*, 180*t*
    child care, children in, 120*f*
    child care by relatives, 122*t*
    college enrollment, 23*t*
    degrees conferred, 24*f*, 25*t*, 26*f*, 27*t*, 28*t*, 29*t*
    distance education enrollment, 30*f*
    doctorate recipients by field of study, 28*t*
    domestic violence, 153*t*, 154*f*
    earnings by age, race/ethnicity, marital status, and educational attainment, 83*t*
    earnings by educational attainment, 80*f*, 81*f*
    earnings by full-time workers, 71*f*
    earnings by marital status and presence of children, 82*t*
    earnings by occupation, 74*t*–80*t*

earnings by sex, age, and race/ethnicity, 70t

earnings gap, 72t–73t

education and employment, 52t, 53t

educational attainment levels, 16t

educational test scores, 20f, 21f

employed persons by occupation, 57t

employed persons by occupation and race/ethnicity, 58t–59t

employment by occupation, 41t

employment by sector, 40t

employment in families, 36t

employment in science, engineering, and technology, 63t

employment status by age, sex, and race, 45t–50t

employment status by marital status and presence of children, 37t–38t, 118t–119t

employment status of civilian noninstitutional population, 34t–35t

employment status of mothers, 114t

employment status of parents, 39t

exercise, 199f

fertility indicators, 98t

flextime employment, 42t

food programs, 88f, 88t

food security, food insecurity, and hunger prevalence, 90t

foreign-born population by age and sex, 7f

graduate and professional degrees conferred by age, 26f

health care access, 177(f11.3)

health status, self-reported, 174f

HIV/AIDS, 185t, 186f, 186t, 187t

homicide circumstances, 151t

homicide victims, 150t

household income, 85t–86t

households by type, 11f, 12t

hunger and homelessness, 92t

inmates with HIV, 170t

kindergarten enrollment, 124f

labor force participation of mothers, 115t

labor force participation of parents, 113f

leading causes of death, 178t–179t

life expectancy, 6t

mammography, 182t–183t

marriage, age at first, 9f

master's degrees conferred, 27t

maternal mortality, 184t

military service, 65t

minority women-owned firms, 67f

occupations, leading, 56t

physical fitness activities and education by race/ethnicity, 31(t2.9)

population by marital status, 8t

population estimates by sex and age groups, 2t

population estimates by sex and race/ethnicity, 3t–5t

poverty, 88t

poverty by sex, 87(t5.9)

poverty thresholds by family size and number of children, 87(t5.8)

prenatal care, 106t

preschool enrollment, 123f

prisoners, 168t, 169t

professional degrees conferred, 29t

school dropout rates, 19t

school enrollment by age, sex, and race/ethnicity, 17t–18t

September 11th attacks victims, 152t

sex ratios, 5(f1.1), 5(f1.2)

sexual harassment, 159f, 160f

sexually transmitted diseases, 188t

single parents, 112f

smoking, 191f

smoking and pregnancy, 105t

teenage birth rates, 99f, 99t

teenage sexual activity, 103t

Temporary Assistance for Needy Families (TANF) program, 88f

unemployment by reason and duration, 51t

uninsured persons, 175t–176t, 177(f11.2)

unmarried partners and married spouses, characteristics of, 10t

victim/offender relationship, 145t

violent crime reporting, 147t

violent crime victimization involving strangers, 146t

violent crime victimization rates, 144f, 144t

voter turnout, 132t

voter turnout in presidential elections, 136(t8.4)

voting and registration by sex and age, 136(t8.3)

voting and voter registration, 132t, 133t–134t

voting rates by race/ethnicity, 135f

weight and obesity, 194t–197t

Women, Infants and Children (WIC) program participants, 89t

women elected officials, 137(t8.6), 138t

workers paid hourly rates below minimum wage by sex, age, race/ethnicity, 84t

Studies

American Association for the Advancement of Science survey, 64

Armed Forces 2002 Sexual Harassment Survey, 158–159

Family Violence Statistics, 156

Good for Business: Making Full Use of the Nation's Human Capital, 61

Land of Plenty: Diversity as America's Competitive Edge in Science, Engineering, and Technology, 62, 64

In the Middle: A Report on Multicultural Boomers Coping with Family and Aging Issues (AARP), 127–128

National Violence Against Women Survey, 151–154, 156–157

The Sexual Victimization of College Women, 148–149

single-sex education, 24, 26

A Solid Investment: Making Full Use of the Nation's Capital, 61

Women, Minorities, and Persons with Disabilities in Science and Engineering: 2002, 61–62

Substance abuse, 193

Suffrage rights, 131

Summers, Lawrence H., 62

Syphilis, 188–189

T

TANF (Temporary Assistance for Needy Families), 82, 88f, 104, 127

Technology, 61–62, 64

Teenagers
child care, 126
childbearing, 97, 99, 99f, 99t, 101–104

Telecommuting, 39, 42

Temporary Assistance for Needy Families (TANF), 82, 88f, 104, 127

Terrorism, 150

Test scores, educational, 19–21, 20f, 21f

Title IX, 28, 30

Trafficking in persons, 2–3

U

Undocumented foreign-born women, 2–3

Unemployment, 43–47, 45t–50t, 51t

Uninsured persons, 174–175, 175t–176t, 177(f11.2)

Unmarried partners, 10t

U.S. Air Force Academy, 160, 160f

V

Vice-presidential candidates, 141

Victim/offender relationship, 145–146, 145t, 147t

Victims of crime
"date rape" drugs, 148
domestic violence, 153t, 154f
hate crimes, 161
homicide, 149–150, 150t, 151t
National Violence Against Women Survey, 151–154, 156–157
prisoner sexual harassment victims, 161
rape and sexual assault, 146–149, 148f
reporting crimes, 146, 147t, 149

September 11th attacks, 152*t*

sexual harassment, 157–161, 159*f*

victim/offender relationship, 145–146, 145*t*

violent crime victimization involving strangers, 146*t*

violent crime victims, 143–146, 144*f*, 144*t*

Violent crime

arrests of women, 163

homicide, 149–150, 150*t*

homicide circumstances, 151*t*

National Violence Against Women Survey, 151–154, 156–157

rates of, 143

reporting, 147*t*, 149

victim/offender relationship, 145–146, 145*t*, 147*t*

victimizations involving strangers, 146*t*

victims of, 143–146, 144*f*, 144*t*

women perpetrators, 167

Virginia Military Institute, 28

Voting. *See* Elections

W

Wages and earnings

by educational attainment, 80*f*, 81*f*

equal pay laws, 72–75

gender gap, 69–72, 72*t*–73*t*

hourly earnings by age, race/ethnicity, marital status, and educational attainment, 83*t*

hourly wages, 71–72

household income, 85*t*–86*t*

by marital status and presence of children, 82*t*

median earnings by full-time workers, 71*f*

median weekly earnings by sex, age, and race/ethnicity, 70*t*

by occupation, 74*t*–80*t*

workers paid hourly rates below minimum wage by sex, age, race/ethnicity, 84*t*

See also Poverty

Wall Street, 59–60

War, 65

Weight issues, 193, 194*t*–197*t*

Welfare, 81–84, 88–89, 88*f*, 88*t*, 89*t*, 104

Women, Infants and Children (WIC) program, 83, 89*t*

Women, Minorities, and Persons with Disabilities in Science and Engineering: 2002, 61–62

Working Mother magazine, 60

Working mothers, 112, 114*t*, 115*t*, 117, 118*t*–119*t*

See also Child care

Working parents, 36, 37*t*–38*t*, 39*t*, 70, 82*t*

Working poor, 81, 84*t*

Workplace sexual harassment, 157–161

Y

Youth

sexual victimization on campuses, 148–149

teenage childbearing, 97, 99, 99*f*, 99*t*, 101–104